A JOURNEY THROUGH THE BOOK OF JOB (2ND EDITION)

EVEN THE MONSTERS

LIVING WITH GRIEF, LOSS, AND DEPRESSION

FROM THE AUTHOR OF *KEZIAH'S SONG* AND *BLIND MAN'S LABYRINTH*

DARYL POTTER

PAPER STONE
PRESS

Paper Stone Press
Oakville, ON, Canada
www.paperstonepress.com
First Edition Published: October 3, 2015
Second Edition (Paper Stone Press Edition) Published: February 10, 2022
Copyright © 2021 by Daryl Potter

All rights reserved. Without limiting rights reserved under the copyright above, no part of this publication may be reproduced, stored in or introduced into a retrieval system, or transmitted in any form or by any means (electronic, mechanical, photocopying, recording, or otherwise) without the prior, written permission of the copyright owner.

Oakville, ON, Canada

Paperback ISBN: 9781777557867
Hardcover ISBN: 9781777557874
Large Print ISBN: 9781777557881

eBook (ePub) ISBN: 9781777557898
Audiobook ISBN: 9781990388002

Biblical quotations are organized, with their associated copyright notices, as follows:

Unless otherwise noted, all biblical quotations in chapters 1–48 of this book (which cover chapters 1–31 of the book of Job) are from the ESV translation of the Bible and are subject to the following copyright notice:
Scripture quotations are from *The Holy Bible, English Standard Version*® (ESV®), copyright © 2001 by Crossway, a publishing ministry of Good News Publishers. Used by permission. All rights reserved.

Unless otherwise noted, all biblical quotations from chapters 49 onward (which equates to the examination of chapters 32–42 of the book of Job) are from the NIV translation of the Bible and are subject to the following copyright notice:
Scripture taken from *The Holy Bible, New International Version*®, copyright © 1973, 1978, 1984, 2011 Biblica.
Used by permission of Zondervan. All rights reserved.

Please see the appendix at the end of this book for more information regarding this division of biblical quotations.

Edited by Amelia Wiens of Amelia Wiens Editing
Proofread by S. Robin Larin of Robin Editorial
Cover design and typeset by Damonza

*For my wife, Carolyn,
my Cinnamon Girl and
my life's companion
on this and every journey.*

A PERSONAL INTRODUCTION

In the rugged and beautiful land of British Columbia, in the year 2000, I began a journey through the book of Job. It is a journey that has lasted for over two decades now. I did not sign up for it. Not explicitly. I volunteered for a simple, short assignment. That was all. I did not intend to change the rest of my life.

A minister friend of mine, Jamie Robbins, gave me the following opportunity and challenge: to prepare and deliver a three-part sermon series on a book in the Bible. I was not a preacher—I was the manager of a securities brokerage office. The challenge, however, appealed to my intellectual curiosity and pride. I accepted the challenge and signed up to prepare and deliver an engaging trio of sermons. Jamie gave me the freedom to choose whatever book I wished. I chose Job.

I did not volunteer to study Job for twenty years and counting.

I did not sign up to have my life turned upside down and my comfortable happiness torn apart.

I was not expecting what happened—and neither was my wife who accompanied me on this journey.

I thought I was choosing to study Job for a short three-part sermon series. Instead, God was choosing me. The book of Job is one of the many texts God has given as his Word to us, but God also works through life events in the present day, in real time. In my case, God walked me to his book about Job and then, once I was oriented, introduced life circumstances that shattered my shallow understanding of his poem and hollowed out my childhood faith and hope. It has been the most painful and heartbreaking experience of my life.

I would like to share this journey, here, with you, not because my story must be told—we all have stories, and your story is no less important than mine. But I would like to share this journey with you because too often I find that, when it comes to books about the Bible and personal spiritual growth, the scholarly and the practical are separated by an unacceptable divide. The depth in the academic literature is obtuse and inaccessible to the nonacademic. Accessibility in the more personal accounts often sacrifices accuracy, richness, and lasting meaning by mainly focusing on emotional and subjective material. The scholarly cannot be easily digested, and the popular supplies inadequate nutrition. My initial three-part sermon series would have fallen into the category of accessible junk food had it ever been presented—as quickly forgotten by its preacher as its audience.

*

Our journey starts in Job chapter one, but you should know a few things about my wife and me before we begin. A brief content warning: the next three paragraphs will cover some personal material covering two sexual assaults. This is background material to help you understand the lens through which I approach the book of Job and these life experiences. You can skip the next three paragraphs if this sort of material is too difficult for you. It won't come up again in the rest of this book.

My wife, Carolyn, grew up with an alcoholic father who modeled marriage and parenting with his fists and an acidic tongue. He had a lasting effect on her perception of fathers, the institution of marriage, and men in general. Following her childhood, the sinful and damaging relationship abuses that are all too common in what the world calls romance came next. A sexual assault left additional emotional wounds. This history of abuse almost seemed to be a coordinated effort to permanently harden my future bride's heart and soul. If that was indeed the plan, it backfired. A neighbor invited Carolyn to church. She studied the Bible and became a Christian. At twenty-five years old, my wife-to-be was done with the world.

In stark contrast to the world's pattern of behavior, the first time I ever kissed my wife was on a stage in front of several hundred witnesses, seconds after the minister said, "You may kiss your bride." It was lightning. Our honeymoon was everything a honeymoon should be. But as the intimacy and joy that we found in each other increased, so did my wife's sense of risk and fear. She had a strong and abiding knowledge of relationship abuse and knew much more about how relationships could go wrong than how they might go right. Post-honeymoon, those tensions within her exploded across our relationship. Our marriage was a catalyst that drove long-buried wounds to the surface.

My background was more straightforward. I had a preacher for a father and a homemaker mother. I never saw my father raise a hand or a voice in anger. I did, however, experience a sexual assault when I was in my early teens. We lived in the country, and one day, wandering the shores of the Sacramento River in Northern California, I was discovered by a pedophile who didn't see an innocent, skinny preacher's kid on his own; he saw prey. In some respects, the police statements, the suspect lineup, and the courtroom drama that followed left a stronger mark than the actual assault. The assault was short-lived, sudden, and aborted. I was big enough to escape before suffering the worst of my attacker's intentions. But the small-town sheriff's department, the witness statement, and the legal hearing held social dangers for a teen boy that dwarfed all else. The anticipation, humiliation, stage fright, shame, public discovery, and aftermath were more vivid than anything I had ever experienced before. I lost innocence in several categories. I lost all my friends but one—the one not lost lived nearly two thousand miles away. Perhaps I drove the others away. Time plays tricks on memory, and I'm inclined to be more charitable as I get older.

I was in my twenties before I made another friend—before I accepted friendship again. Trust, or lack thereof, is not always a rational process. One evil man did not represent the world of people, but my juvenile response suggested otherwise. The only resource I had to help me through was my own meager psychological toolbox, that of a lonely adolescent in a small farming community in Northern California. Living ten miles from the nearest town and choosing to finish high school from home compounded with my poor coping skills. All that isolation left its mark. I'd been brutally bucked from the social horse. Rather than reintegrate socially, rather than get back in the saddle, I sold the saddle, turned the horse into glue, and burned down the barn.

In addition to leaving my social life behind, as soon as I was old enough, I left both religion and my parent's geography behind as well. I moved away from that small town where my dad was the preacher. I left the state. I left the country. Two weeks after turning nineteen, I emigrated back to Canada, the country of my birth. I went to university to study science and make a good atheist of myself and give myself the freedom to indulge in the chemical, social, and sexual sins that I felt I had been robbed of in my teen years. I gradually discovered that I knew better. My sin only succeeded in making me disgusting even to myself.

I began shopping for a church. Six months later, my eventual church home found me. A stranger invited me. Through the course of my studies, I discovered I had never been a Christian at all. Understanding the Bible and being able to apply it to my own life and character had escaped me. I became a Christian finally at twenty-one.

So I, too, walked into marriage not perfectly equipped. To be frank, I was socially inept. My social development was measurably and obviously seven years behind my peers. When I married at twenty-seven, I had the clear-eyed vision of the inexperienced and the skill set of the clueless to complement my wife's sudden eruption of what I pejoratively thought of as her "issues." There were fireworks. The intimate aspects were beautiful—our relationship maturity, however, was not good.

Every marriage has its stuff, its history, and often the participants bring an inadequate supply of wisdom and useful experience to the relationship. Proverbs says that love covers a multitude of sins, and this is remarkably evident in any successful marriage. But covering sin is not always about love. Sometimes it is about cowardice, and I was a social coward with a volatile wife. I was in a marriage that terrified me. I had turned the social horse into glue and burned its barn when I was still just a boy. Married, I was back in the saddle—glued to the saddle. She was with me for life. I loved her, and I was afraid.

Like many newlyweds, we were communication misfits, but we loved each other, and so we were determined to learn and grow together. And we succeeded.

※

By the time this journey through the book of Job started, we had been married for three and a half years, our marriage was stronger than it had ever been, and Carolyn was pregnant with our first child.

When my preacher friend Jamie suggested that I study a book of the Bible to preach a three-week series in the coming months, I tackled the new challenge with enthusiasm. I spent a few months studying Job. In digging up materials to supplement my understanding, I encountered a volume entitled A Handbook on the Book of Job. It was a translator's handbook by the United Bible Society. It was heavy, overly thick, and very dry. After thumbing through a few off-putting pages, I put it back on the bookstore shelf.

I also had in my library a book my parents had given me years before: Conflict and Triumph: The Argument of the Book of Job Unfolded by William Henry Green, first published in 1873. Green had been the chair of Biblical and Oriental Literature at Princeton Theological Seminary for nearly fifty years. His book was a scholarly work, but wading through the text would have taken far more effort than I cared to devote to this simple speaking assignment. I don't think I even took it out of its storage box.

Without these tools, I pulled together the outline for a short series on the book of Job. I strung together some witty observations, a few practical applications, and a snap judgment or two. I tied this bundle together with a nice oratory bow, ready for delivery at the appointed time. The church calendar shifted, and the congregation no longer had a preaching gap for this series, so we canceled it. The change in direction did not bother me as I had not put a lot of effort into the series, and we had a baby on the way. Plenty of other exciting life developments laid claim to my attention.

I set my notes on Job aside as the year 2001 dawned. Carolyn and I were a month shy of our fourth wedding anniversary and in perfect health, had two incomes, a healthy baby on the way, and were living in one of the most beautiful cities in the world. Life was perfect.

And then, three and a half weeks early, in early February, our daughter, Mackenzie Emily Potter was born.

We went to bed tired and happy on a Friday night, and Carolyn woke that Saturday morning already in the early stages of labor. Our baby was early, but not alarmingly so, and we leisurely gathered our things together. I have a picture of Carolyn from that morning before we left the house. She was unutterably, breathtakingly beautiful. Most brides can only dream of looking as beautiful as my wife looked that morning getting ready to deliver a baby—and I've got the picture to prove it.

We arrived at the hospital midmorning. The delivery was natural and drug free other than a gas mask to ease the hardest contractions. If there were a script for the perfect delivery, I would imagine that our daughter Mackenzie's delivery would fit the bill.

I used to talk to my baby girl in the womb. I would put my head near my wife's growing belly and tell my girl stories of fatherly love and fantastic adventures to come. When she was born, I cut the cord, and she cried up a terrible storm as the staff washed and inspected and delivered her to Carolyn's arms. I finally spoke to her as she lay crying, skin to skin on my wife's breast. And she stopped. At the sound of my voice, she stopped crying. Her wobbly newborn head pivoted, unfocused eyes staring around. She knew me. She knew my voice—and she stopped crying at the sound of it. "She knows her daddy's voice," the delivery nurse said.

I gave Mackenzie her first bath that night, changed her first micro-diaper, and my wife and I took turns holding her.

She was born on a Saturday evening. We went home on Monday. The following Friday, a nurse came by to visit. Mackenzie had dropped several more ounces. She was below the minimum healthy range the medical textbooks described, and this caused some concern. The nurse booked a follow-up for the next Monday. When we measured her that Monday, Mackenzie's weight had dropped further, and so the nurse arranged for us to visit the breastfeeding clinic at the Vancouver General Hospital.

Mackenzie was the most beautiful baby girl I had ever seen. Six pounds, nine ounces of innocence. I had two weeks of vacation time set aside for this baby honeymoon. Friends brought us home-cooked meals. We slept when she slept, and we talked about dreams and plans for the future. One of my happiest memories from that first week is feeling Mackenzie while she was tucked into the warmth against my ribs, her little lips puckered, her little chest rising and falling rhythmically, breathing in mommy and daddy's warm scent and affection as she slept. I would have fought lions barehanded for this little six-pound girl, but all I was tasked to do was breathe quietly and keep her safe and warm as she slept, and I was happy. I remember looking at my wife as our daughter slept between us, thinking it could not get any better. We enjoyed our cozy baby honeymoon immensely, and I had no fears about the upcoming appointment.

During that period, my wife asked me to share the Job lessons that I'd written with her. I no longer have the notes, but I recall that the material for a trio of lessons amounted to half a dozen handwritten pages, which I cheerfully shared and then forgot.

I was near the end of my second week of two weeks' vacation when we set off for that Vancouver General Hospital appointment. We brought a picnic lunch with us. The appointment would take an hour, and then we would head over to Stanley Park for a nice afternoon in the mild late February sunshine beside the ocean. Vancouver's beautiful weather dashes the international stereotype of Canada as a universally frozen Arctic region. The myth within Canada that Vancouver is a permanently rainy depression bowl is propaganda meant to keep Torontonians and Quebeckers on their side of the Rockies. It was a beautiful, sunny day.

The appointment at Vancouver General Hospital did not go well. The simple checkup developed into a series of consultations and a general buzz that we were slow to understand. It was a medical vibe that, over the following years, we developed the radar to recognize at its first triggering—but the buzz escaped us this first time. We noticed it but did not understand it. The commotion culminated in a recommendation that hurriedly sent us from Vancouver General Hospital's breastfeeding clinic, not to Stanley Park and a picnic, but to the emergency room at BC Children's Hospital.

We arrived at the Children's Hospital in a flurry of activity, still not entirely clear what the fuss was about. I was instructed to hold Mackenzie down while the staff inserted an IV line in her wrist. The vein burst. Another wrist. Another burst vein. Another attempt. Failure. My ten-day-old daughter wailed and fixed her father with desperate eyes as the nurses tried veins in both wrists and both ankles until they finally found a vein strong enough to hold the tiniest available needle.

Throughout the rest of that day, Mackenzie alternated between crying and sleeping. She lay on her comically oversized gurney, wedged into the safe center with rolls of blankets and towels. Doctors came through and asked questions. Interns came by and asked the same questions. Then the lab specialists. Then the pediatrician. Then the medical students. Then the next shift came on, and we reenacted the same routine with a new wave of doctors, interns, lab specialists, a pediatrician, and a fresh crop of students. Over and over again, we answered the same questions. By the end of that day, we knew that she was dehydrated, and yes, she was still losing weight, and no, what this meant was not clear.

As the sun set that evening, we were sent to our third hospital that day. We drove ourselves and our baby from Vancouver across Burnaby to New Westminster. A bed was available in the pediatric unit there. We arrived, traumatized, still unsure of what was going on. We searched for a long time, trying to find the entrance to this hospital on a hill. Once inside, we wandered the strange, dimly lit halls, trying to identify the pediatric unit. Once we had discovered it, we explained our situation over and over again to various administrative staff and medical professionals until, after much questioning and searching, we discovered someone who was expecting us. We then reexplained Mackenzie's first ten days of life and just over eight months of pregnancy. No, my wife did not smoke or drink or fall down any stairs. Yes, the delivery had been relatively uneventful—more eventful than any Saturday either of us had ever experienced before, but from a medical point of view, a complete yawner. And then we explained it all again to another person in a long coat. And then another. And then a fourth. This was our third hospital admission that day, and the questions were endless. In the years to come, my wife would prepare a printout that we carried around with us everywhere listing medications, symptoms, and the like to hand to medical staff—each got a personal copy. It was practical. On this night, though, we weren't there yet. This night, we were unprepared and afraid of what was happening.

Mackenzie's bed that night was in a room with perhaps a dozen other beds. The children in that large ward faced all manner of illness and injury. It was a long, dark room of beds without even the privacy of curtains. I had never seen a room like it before, nor have I seen one since. It was like something from the 1940s—something from a war movie, perhaps. The lights were kept dim in the mid-evening hours, and the atmosphere made the room feel like a place people are sentenced to endure rather than volunteer to stay.

Stanley Park was supposed to take the spotlight in the day's original script. Instead, we found ourselves sidetracked into this alternate reality. Our baby honeymoon was over. Picnic plans seemed like another life ago.

So much of what happened now seems like another lifetime altogether.

You might say that when I first started studying Job and prepared that forgettable sermon series to accompany it, I was just buying a ticket for a journey. I did not recognize that that's what I was doing, but it was a start. On this day, as we checked unexpectedly into three different hospitals, the journey began in earnest. This was not a one-day hospital visit. Though I did not know it at the time, it was not just my daughter who was in trouble. This day, the train left the station, and there was no turning back. I had no idea what was coming around the bend or around the one after that.

❧

One last word before we begin: my personal journey, and a thorough study of Job, are woven together throughout this book. We will leave no stone unturned as we work through God's ancient poem, and as we go, I'll share with you how my journey progressed. If this qualifies as a commentary on the book of Job, then it is a very personal one. I no longer see how Job can be understood in any way except through a personal lens. There will be times in our study where it appears that the personal story has been forgotten. In these places, God's ancient poem demands our undivided attention, so my story would only distract from the truths that need our focus. By contrast, there will also be places where it appears that I've forgotten the book of Job altogether as I share my personal journey with you. The twin themes of textual study and personal experience are woven together deliberately. One, by the grace of God, will illuminate the other. More specifically, the personal parts will help the modern reader connect with some of the passages that would not be as meaningful with only a purely literary analysis. The book of Job requires emotional connection, not just academic understanding. Emotion is a key component of its message. We'll explore what that means as we get into the text itself.

But enough preamble. The book of Job starts in chapter one. So let's go there.

1
BLAMELESS AND UPRIGHT

Here is how the book of Job starts.

> *¹There was a man in the land of Uz whose name was Job, and that man was blameless and upright, one who feared God and turned away from evil. ²There were born to him seven sons and three daughters. ³He possessed 7,000 sheep, 3,000 camels, 500 yoke of oxen, and 500 female donkeys, and very many servants, so that this man was the greatest of all the people of the east.*
>
> Job 1:1–3[1]

Beyond the conspicuous lack of details about the land of Uz, the first thing that stands out about Job is that he was "blameless and upright."

The phrase "blameless and upright" in English sounds repetitive. But the two original words in Hebrew convey two distinct ideas: that Job was both morally good (blameless) and spiritually good (upright).[2]

Job's moral goodness meant that he was the kind of man you'd like to

---

[1] English Standard Version. See "Appendix: Explanation Regarding Biblical Quotations and Copyright Rules" for an explanation of which English translations are used in various sections of this book.

[2] See Reyburn, William D.1992. *A Handbook on the Book of Job*. 30-31. New York. United Bible Societies as well as Janzen, Gerald J 1932. *Interpretation: A Bible Commentary for Teaching and Preaching*. 34-37. Atlanta. John Knox Press.

have as a neighbor. A good citizen. Fair. Honest. What we might call, generally, a good man.

The second concept, upright, speaks to Job's spiritual standing before God. He was a person in a right relationship with God.

This distinction between Job's two kinds of goodness is important. You can have one without the other. More precisely, you can have moral goodness (blamelessness) without spiritual goodness (uprightness). This distinction will be important later in Job as these concepts blur and then are pulled apart in discussions between Job and his friends.

It is not just the narrator that makes this distinction. In Job 1:8, God himself refers to Job as "a blameless and upright man, who fears God and turns away from evil."

In Job 2:8, God again uses the phrase "blameless and upright, a man who fears God and turns away from evil" to describe Job.

In his speech in chapters twenty-nine and thirty, Job looks back on his early life before the troubles came, and he describes himself as having been both morally good (referencing his community standing and community service) and spiritually good (describing a life in which God's friendship blessed his house).

This distinction between moral and spiritual goodness carries on throughout the book of Job. We will come back to this topic again later in our study. For now, let's move on.

SUPER RICH

The second thing in this passage that strikes me is how rich Job was. Here was a person who had both earned God's praise for being morally and spiritually good and had acquired a great deal of wealth.

For the modern reader, particularly one without a rural or farming background or an academic appreciation for ancient economics, a livestock census may not be a clear or compelling marker of Job's status in his society. It is worth taking a moment to evaluate how truly wealthy Job was to better understand my later arguments.

First of all, what do farmers do with sheep? Job had seven thousand of them. Having that many sheep suggests that Job likely owned two separate operations for producing meat and wool. Of course, you need to kill sheep to sell their meat, so a subsidiary breeding operation would have been a significant component of this sort of enterprise. If half of Job's sheep were female and only 10 percent were of the appropriate age and health to breed successfully, each spring would have seen three hundred and fifty births. Clearly, this is a grossly conservative number. How many flocks would a population of seven thousand sheep be divided into? How many shepherds would be hired to tend and protect those sheep throughout the year? How many shearers? How many would package the wool for transport and sale? Was Job a grower and wholesaler only? Or did he have a textile operation as well? How many workers were engaged in monitoring the breeding operations? How many engaged in culling animals for the market, dealing with diseased or injured animals, and properly disposing of the bodies of the inevitable casualties of a harsh environment to avoid attracting predators? As the verse states, Job had "a large number of servants." The sheep side of Job's operation alone would have had hundreds of workers. Let's call it fifty workers just to be super conservative.

Five hundred yoke of oxen is the next animal listed. What does a farm use oxen for? Certainly, oxen can be raised for their meat, but the verse explicitly describes them as "five hundred yoke of oxen." A yoke is a large brace that straddles the neck and shoulders of laboring animals and can then be attached to a plow, wagon, or some other piece of equipment. Oxen, in other words, were the farm tractors of Job's day. If Job had five hundred yoke of oxen, how many actual animals was this? These may have been single-yoke animals—one ox per yoke. Often two were attached to a yoke, pulling in tandem. Attaching three, four, or even more oxen to a single yoke was not unheard of either. The more oxen on a yoke, the bigger the tractor engine handling the plowing burden. Multiple oxen on one yoke could do more work but still only needed one driver. So how many actual oxen did Job have? Five hundred? One thousand? Fifteen hundred? It would have been some multiple of the original five hundred (you can't put half an ox on a yoke!), but the primary point for our purposes is that Job had five hundred yoke. Put into modern terms, that meant Job had five hundred tractors. What does a farmer do with tractors? He pulls loads, plows ground, drags seeders, turns grinders, and powers irrigation equipment. In Job 1:14, we learn that plowing had been on the agenda for these animals at the very minimum. In other words,

Job had an agricultural operation to complement his wool, meat, and breed stock operations and had five hundred tractors to do the work.

How many workers were required to operate five hundred yoke of oxen? If all the animals were working, then five hundred drivers. The likelihood of every yoke ever being out in the fields all at once is unlikely. Animals can be injured, too young, or otherwise incapable of working. Oxen breed, and a wise farmer would not risk a miscarried calf by using a pregnant ox for heavy plowing. Even if Job's maximum productivity was to have 50 percent of his animals in service (and there is a strong motivation to maximize productivity as these animals would cost him sheep pasture, water, predator protection, and other expenses), that would have required at least two hundred and fifty drivers.

So we're looking at a worker population of at least three hundred workers between the sheep business and the oxen. This assumes that the oxen drivers were also the grain harvesters and bailers—a multitasking assumption that is very conservative.

Now, what about these camels? They could have been raised for meat and milk; however, transport seems a more likely purpose. There were no transport trucks available to show up at the farm at regular intervals. There was no local train station. Sheep shearing would have been a spring activity, and perhaps the harvest would have started in late summer and continued through the fall. Depending on the climate, they may even have grown winter crops. In any live animal sales, they would have made the animals walk themselves to market, but Job's apparent crop and textile (or at least wool production) operations would have required extensive market hauling. Grain and wool don't walk themselves to market. Camels seem like a good solution. How many camels did Job have? Three thousand. Imagine a farm with three thousand trucks! Granted, some of these camels would not have been suitable for transportation duties. In particular, pregnant or juvenile animals might have been spared long-haul duties. Still, these considerations and complications expand the scope of Job's operations rather than diminish them, adding camel breeding to the existing sheep- and ox-breeding components of the farm.

To camels, let's add donkeys: five hundred female donkeys. Presumably, male donkeys were present as well. Donkeys are not as strong as oxen. Job 1:14 describes how the oxen were plowing while the donkeys were grazing, suggesting that plowing duties, at least for that crop or season, were off the agenda for the donkeys. But donkeys are useful load haulers as well, particularly if the loads are stacked in packs or loaded on wagons.

At the risk of oversimplifying, to add some valuable modern context, we might describe Job's farm this way: if the oxen were the tractors and the camels were the big long-haul rigs, then the donkeys were the pickup trucks. They were mixed-use machines. They were less efficient than the oxen at plowing and the camels at carrying, but that lack of specialization also meant that they were more flexible and could work where needed to enhance productivity across the farm. And, in a culture different from my own, perhaps donkeys could have also been a source of meat and milk. If we think of the donkey as Job's version of the utilitarian Western plow horse, we start to get a clearer picture of what Job's farm was like. How many cowboys to round up and manage five hundred donkeys?

The text says that Job also had a large number of other servants. Hundreds of servants. Shepherds and shearers. Harvesters. Drivers. Market sellers who negotiated prices, collected payment, and managed the farm's accounts. Plowmen. General laborers to handle irrigation, prune crops, build fences, protect livestock, repair equipment. If there was not just a wholesale wool operation but also a textile business, then there must also have been washers and carders and spinners and weavers.

The text itself reminds us that "this man was the greatest of all the people of the east" (Job 1:3b). Job wasn't just a farmer. He was a very rich man who had an extensive agriculture and livestock operation, possibly a value-added textile operation, and definitely his own transportation division. The people he employed were not just general laborers. Such a large operation would have required foremen to oversee the laborers and additional supervisors to oversee the foremen and specific divisions of Job's business, filling roles that today we might define as operations managers or general managers.

And he had ten kids, including seven sons who would undoubtedly have been closely involved with Job's various businesses, learning the ropes for the operation that would one day become their collective inheritance.

CURSING MISUNDERSTOOD

As we've already discussed, Job was not only a very wealthy person; the text also repeatedly describes him as a man who was "blameless and upright," one who "feared God and turned away from evil." Not your stereotypical positioning of the rich in scripture! These next two verses in Job 1:4–5, however, seem at odds with that image:

> ⁴*His sons used to go and hold a feast in the house of each one on his day, and they would send and invite their three sisters to eat and drink with them.* ⁵*And when the days of the feast had run their course, Job would send and consecrate them, and he would rise early in the morning and offer burnt offerings according to the number of them all. For Job said, "It may be that my children have sinned, and cursed God in their hearts." Thus Job did continually.*
>
> Job 1:4–5

What kind of father was Job if he let his children party all night long and curse God in their hearts, attempting to paper it over with a next-day sacrifice? Where was the fatherly instruction? Where was the concern for godliness in the next generation?

Was Job a good person but an incompetent father?

The fault here lies not with Job's character but rather with the unfortunate translation of the word curse, which is the favored word in most English translations. The term curse in the original Hebrew does not mean what we in English understand curse to mean. The same Hebrew word is translated as bless in other passages. For example:

> *Early in the morning Laban arose and kissed his grandchildren and his daughters and blessed them. Then Laban departed and returned home.*
>
> Genesis 31:55

The word "blessed" here is the exact same Hebrew word translated as "cursed" in Job 1:4.

Here's another example:

So Joshua blessed them and sent them away, and they went to their tents.

JOSHUA 22:6

The context in Joshua is the completion of the conquest of Canaan and the eastern tribes of Israel being released from their commitment to help their western brothers finish conquering and settling their side of the Jordan River. It was a happy time. Joshua didn't curse the eastern tribes for their assistance; he blessed them. Their work was done. But the word "blessed" here is again the same word translated in Job 1:5 as "cursed."

So was Job concerned that his children had "blessed God in their hearts"? This alternative translation doesn't make sense either. The truth is not that mysterious.

TRANSLATION COMPLEXITY

The original Hebrew word does not mean to bless or curse. One of the challenges of translation work is finding a way to communicate the meaning of a word when that word just doesn't exist in the other language. There is not always a clear one-to-one relationship between words across different languages.

We will talk about the difficulty of translating ancient Hebrew into modern English in more detail later. For now, perhaps it's easiest to think of the original Hebrew word as meaning "bid adieu" or "say goodbye." You can say goodbye to someone positively or negatively. In the case of Laban and Joshua, the intention of the passage is positive. Instead of translating that these men "said goodbye in a positive manner," the translators of Genesis and Joshua used the word blessed. This, unfortunately, carries with it the image of a priestly or popish-style blessing which was not what Laban or Joshua were doing. They were simply saying goodbye in a manner like the modern Arabic greeting of as-salamu alaykum (peace be with you) used by Arabic-speaking Muslims and Christians. [3]

---

[3] Per Green, William Henry. 1999. Conflict and Triumph: The Argument of the

Likewise, Job was concerned that, while partying it up with their brothers and sisters, his children might have "said goodbye to God in their hearts." This wasn't a fear that they had hostilely rejected God by cursing him. This was a concern that they had taken their leave of him in their hearts. In their focus on a good time, perhaps their hearts had drifted. Maybe they used some inappropriate language. Maybe they made some coarse jokes. Maybe they walked up to the line in the alcohol department—not drunk, but perhaps not one hundred percent on the money as far as righteousness was concerned. Maybe they said or thought a few things that they would regret in the light of day. Kids will be kids. Even kids old enough to have their own houses and host parties will sometimes act like kids and not always act wisely.

Job's kids were sinners; Job knew that. He was not under any illusions that they were perfect, but he also knew that they were not evil kids; they were not kids who cursed God in the English sense of the word cursed. The translation colors them false. The most they were likely guilty of was a careless joy that ran the risk of crossing wisdom's line. And the cause of their carelessness was a celebration with siblings. How many parents would like to have Job's problems here? Ten children who loved each other enough to have a blast together regularly, hosting each other in homes that, in all likelihood, they had helped each other build.

JOB ON FATHERHOOD

We have addressed a common misinterpretation of Job 1:4–5, but what can we positively learn from this discussion?

Job is not a book about fatherhood. But God commended Job highly, without qualification, and since we do get a glimpse of his style of fatherhood, we can probably learn a thing or two from his example.

The first thing that stands out is that he must have been doing a pretty good job of it so far: his family was close-knit and loving. Job 1:4 says that each son took turns holding feasts "each on his day." This phrase is a little ambiguous. It can simply mean that they took turns. Or it can mean that each hosted their personal birthday celebration—"his day" being his special day, his birthday.

Book of Job Unfolded. 11-12. Edinburgh. The Banner of Truth Trust.

Verse five talks about how the feasts would run their course before Job engaged with his children, which suggests that these might have been multi-day affairs, further supporting an interpretation that these parties were irregular events for special occasions. Regardless, we can learn that Job must have been the kind of father that helped nurture bonds among his children that lasted into adulthood.

In particular, it is worth noting that Job would not crash these parties and attempt to micromanage his children's celebrations. He would let the feasts run their course. Then he would send for them the next day, not after a long delay but definitely after everything had wrapped up. And he would make a sacrifice for each of them. What did he sacrifice? A lamb? An ox? Whatever the case, he had ten children and he sacrificed for each of them. Job spent money on their purification. He spent material goods and significant time ensuring that his children remained spiritually pure. How many parents meet with their adult children ten times a year for a time of focused spiritual renewal for the good of their children? How many parents invest not just time but attention and material goods into their adult children's spiritual welfare? This wasn't a case of Thanksgiving or Easter, mom in the kitchen with the turkey, dad on the couch with a game on the TV. This was an engaged dad, off the couch, in his adult children's lives, still providing care, attention, and guidance that was not about a lecture but rather about his own personal financial sacrifice and a time of collective prayer to God.

Job was a good person. This was Job's regular custom. He did this continually. Job ran a huge operation, but being a busy career guy did not stop him from being a dad. He had good fatherly habits. He was a good soul.

And now the trouble comes.

2
KNOW YOUR ENEMY

WHAT HAPPENS NEXT in the book of Job is what my fiction editor likes to call "the inciting incident." This is the scene that kicks into gear everything else that follows.

> *⁶Now there was a day when the sons of God came to present themselves before the Lord, and Satan also came among them. ⁷The Lord said to Satan, "From where have you come?" Satan answered the Lord and said, "From going to and fro on the earth, and from walking up and down on it." ⁸And the Lord said to Satan, "Have you considered my servant Job, that there is none like him on the earth, a blameless and upright man, who fears God and turns away from evil?" ⁹Then Satan answered the Lord and said, "Does Job fear God for no reason? ¹⁰Have you not put a hedge around him and his house and all that he has, on every side? You have blessed the work of his hands, and his possessions have increased in the land. ¹¹But stretch out your hand and touch all that he has, and he will curse you to your face." ¹²And the Lord said to Satan, "Behold, all that he has is in your hand. Only against him do not stretch out your hand." So Satan went out from the presence of the Lord.*
>
> JOB 1:6–12

There's one thing we need to note right away about these verses. The word satan in Hebrew means "enemy" or "accuser," and in fact, the original Hebrew doesn't just say "an enemy" or "an accuser." It says "the enemy." "The accuser."

Often, in the Psalms, when David talks about "my enemies," the Hebrew reads "my satans." The word satan is just the normal word in Hebrew for an enemy or accuser.

Given that the book of Job is set in a pre-Moses era,[4] we might infer from this word choice that, from the earliest times, humanity's most terrible opponent, embodied in a snake in Genesis, was known simply as "the enemy." Over time, this title was condensed to just "enemy." In English translation, this Hebrew word, satan, was transliterated instead of translated. Instead of interpreting the Hebrew word satan in English as enemy, translators have instead phonetically spelled out the Hebrew word in English letters. When we say "Satan," we're speaking ancient Hebrew. In addition to transliterating the Hebrew word, translators also capitalized the word in English. So now the casual English reader infers that "Satan" is a bad guy's proper name, rather than what it originally was: a bad guy's description.

On the day the sons of God, or as other translations put it, the angels, came to present themselves before the Lord, the enemy also came with them. The accuser also came with them.

And immediately, the Lord speaks to the enemy. Throughout this entire passage, this is the language that the original Hebrew uses. Let's read it again, in English, with this direct translation instead of the transliteration:

> *⁶Now there was a day when the sons of God came to present themselves before the Lord, and [the enemy] also came among them. ⁷The Lord said to [the enemy], "From where have you come?" [The enemy] answered the Lord and said, "From going to and fro on the earth, and from walking up and down on it." ⁸And the Lord said to [the enemy], "Have you considered my*

---

4 We skipped over an important detail in Job 1:5 that helps establish the dating for the story's events. The Mosaic law forbids anyone but the priests from offering sacrifices, whereas previously heads of households would often offer sacrifices without any restriction. Thus, we can confidently date the events in Job to an era before the Mosaic law was revealed.

> *servant Job, that there is none like him on the earth, a blameless and upright man, who fears God and turns away from evil?" ⁹Then [the enemy] answered the Lord and said, "Does Job fear God for no reason? ¹⁰Have you not put a hedge around him and his house and all that he has, on every side? You have blessed the work of his hands, and his possessions have increased in the land. ¹¹But stretch out your hand and touch all that he has, and he will curse you to your face." ¹²And the Lord said to [the enemy], "Behold, all that he has is in your hand. Only against him do not stretch out your hand." So [the enemy] went out from the presence of the Lord.*
>
> JOB 1:6–12

This business of repeating the reference to "the enemy" over and over again is important. Bad stuff is going to happen to Job, and Job's community is going to be confused about who is responsible for causing this bad stuff. There is going to be a knee-jerk tendency for Job's friends to blame Job, and Job will question whether God has become his opponent. However, the opening chapter of the book of Job is making it exceedingly clear that it is not Job or God or even just bad luck that is the author of Job's troubles. Job is innocent of wrongdoing. God was involved in the bad stuff, but he was not the bad stuff's author (we'll address this later).

The author of the evil in Job's life was a creature not given the dignity of a name. This creature is given a label instead—a description. This is the enemy. Get this detail straight early on. The enemy does this stuff to Job.

The point is so important that seven times in seven verses, Job's opponent is identified as "the enemy." From a stylistic perspective (and we're going to discover that style is significant in Job; nothing in the book's language is accidental or arbitrary), it would be smoother at some of these points to substitute "him" for "the enemy." For example, in verse eight, it would be very appropriate to state, "Then the Lord said..." and get on with what the Lord said. But the text doesn't do that. Instead, it states, "Then the Lord said to the enemy..." By now, it is very obvious who God is talking to, but the text makes a point of using the phrase "the enemy" at every possible opportunity.[5]

---

5 This pattern of using repetition for emphasis is present throughout scripture. The

Satan is the enemy. Not God. Not Job. Not even Job's wife or Job's friends who are going to say and do some very foolish and even damaging things in the chapters to come. These people are not the enemy. Satan is the enemy.

Seven times in seven verses it says "the enemy."

PRACTICAL APPLICATION: KNOW YOUR ENEMY

The practical application here practically shouts at the reader.

What stress invades your life? What relationship is plagued with friction—that with a spouse, a parent, a child, a troublesome sibling, roommate, neighbor, friend, boss, or coworker? It is easy in the course of life to get a form of relationship tunnel vision. This restricted vision focuses our emotions on the person in front of us rather than on the enemy. The true enemy will use miscommunication, hormones, lack of sleep, health challenges, financial stress, time stress, any stress, anything at all, even actual sin, to pry relationships apart and hurt individuals.

To focus our frustration on the person before us is to get drawn into Satan's game. To be the perpetual critic, the hurtful accuser, the perennial negative force that belittles or torments is to go beyond playing Satan's game and instead to play Satan's role. Often the most fiercely acid-tongued among us are those who are, or have been in the past, the most hurt. This is yet another example of Satan's web: Satan's victim becomes a hurt heart perfectly disguised as a foe who takes on Satan's role as the enemy in the lives of others and thus creates a new victim who can become part of the ongoing negative cycle.

How do you view the difficult people in your life? Do you view them as worldly people do, as uncomplex adversaries only worthy of your opposition or anger? Or do you view them as pawns of the enemy?

When you are the unnecessarily difficult person in a social situation, do

---

repeated use of the Hebrew word hebel in Ecclesiastes (translated as "meaningless" in the New International Version and "vanity" in the King James Version) is an example of emphasis through repetition. The word-for-word repeat of select verses in Proverbs is another illustration of this idea. The four different detailed accounts of the crucifixion in the gospels is an event-level example of this method. Repetition in scripture is the literary equivalent of highlighting and underlining key concepts for emphasis.

you view yourself as just a bit antisocial or stubborn by nature? Or do you recognize that you may be playing an evil role?

THE ENEMY'S WORK ETHIC

Satan is the enemy—in the book of Job and in life. So what kind of enemy is this Satan? We get some insight from the text itself.

> *⁸And the Lord said to Satan, "Have you considered my servant Job, that there is none like him on the earth, a blameless and upright man, who fears God and turns away from evil?" ⁹Then Satan answered the Lord and said, "Does Job fear God for no reason? ¹⁰Have you not put a hedge around him and his house and all that he has, on every side? You have blessed the work of his hands, and his possessions have increased in the land. ¹¹But stretch out your hand and touch all that he has, and he will curse you to your face."*
>
> JOB 1:8–11

When God asked Satan that question, Satan did not need to scratch his head and think for a while. Out of all the possible people on earth, Satan knew exactly who Job was. He knew him by name and by character and had a strategy for dealing with Job already plotted out. He knew all this right off the top of his head. Satan did not have to go out and research who Job was.

So what kind of enemy was this Satan?

We can learn two very sobering things from these few verses. The first thing is that our common enemy is hurtfully diligent. He does his job of being the enemy very, very well. At the beginning of Job's story, his homework was complete. His survey of potential victims had been thorough and thoughtful. He had been "going to and fro on the earth" and "walking up and down on it" (1:7). He hadn't been aimlessly wandering. He had been surveying. He had gathered names, characters, and details and had made plans. When God asked about Job, Satan had his database complete, his analysis up to date, and an action plan ready. Satan had a position on interpreting Job's righteousness and had an angle on how he wanted to undermine that righteousness. Satan had a logical thread he wanted to pull, and it was one he believed would unravel Job's reputation and spiritual standing. Satan had given Job some thought and was ready for this window of opportunity to attack him. It's what enemies do.

Satan's actions were not a unique literary device that Job's author made up. We see this deliberate strategic work from Satan throughout both the Old Testament and the New Testament.[6] First Peter 5:8 states this truth in the bluntest manner possible: "Your adversary the devil prowls around like a roaring lion, seeking someone to devour."[7]

Satan had been prowling—the enemy had been prowling. Going to and fro on the earth, he had not just been wandering but also cataloging people. His territory was the whole earth, and he sought a new victim—someone else to devour.[8] That's a grim picture of the kind of enemy we're dealing with here.

One final detail here is worth highlighting. God asked Satan a closed-ended question: "Have you considered...?" (1:8). Closed-ended questions are designed to yield a "yes" or "no" answer. But Satan saw an opening and had so much more to say than simply "yes." Satan wanted a piece of Job, and so he shot through the opening God had provided with a complete argument for how Job's righteousness was an artificial and easily dismantled construct. Like an evil Boy Scout, Satan was prepared, and he answered a closed-ended question with an open-ended response.

THE ENEMY'S REAL OBJECTIVE

The second sobering truth to be found in this exchange is Satan's end goal. Ultimately, Satan's objective was not to hurt Job. It's easy to lose sight of that point when we consider Job's trouble in subsequent verses. Satan's objective was to get Job to curse God to his face.

Recall Job 1:5 and our discussion on the meaning of the Hebrew word curse. Satan's goal was not for Job to literally curse God, as in to swear at

---

[6] Satan tempting Jesus in the desert is a classic example from the Gospels. In another place, Jesus tells Peter that "Satan demanded to have you, that he might sift you like wheat" (Luke 22:31).

[7] Here "adversary" is a very effective translation of the Hebrew word *satan*. It is a nice blending of *enemy* and *accuser* in one word.

[8] For a speculative fiction treatment of this theme that does an outstanding job of making this concept tangible, see C.S. Lewis's classic *The Screwtape Letters*.

God or to try to put some sort of hex on the Almighty. Satan wanted Job to "say goodbye" to God. To say goodbye "to his face." Right to his face. Satan wanted God and Job separated.

If health and happiness could have achieved his goal of separating Job from God, then that is what Satan would have tried to attack Job with. If boredom could have driven Job to leave God, then boredom would have been Satan's ammunition. To cause pain is never Satan's objective. Nor to cause success. Separating people from God, for eternity, is the enemy's objective. Fear, greed, wealth, poverty, success, failure, happiness, contentment, insecurity, pain—these are all just tools in the toolbox to fix you good. And you're fixed, from Satan's perspective, when you're separated from God.

SATAN'S CAPE AND GOD'S APPROVAL

Satan is the enemy. When dealing with a powerful, attentive, dangerous enemy, it helps to know what he is trying to accomplish. When a bull focuses on the matador's red cape, it completely overlooks the sword. Joy and pain, success and failure are Satan's cape. The sword behind the cape has one objective in mind: to separate you from God.

Notice as this scene continues how Satan tries to separate Job and God.

> ^{11}"But stretch out your hand and touch all that he has, and he will curse you to your face." ^{12}And the Lord said to Satan, "Behold, all that he has is in your hand. Only against him do not stretch out your hand." So Satan went out from the presence of the Lord.
>
> JOB 1:11–12

In 1:6, the angels presented themselves to God, and Satan came with them.

In 1:7, God began asking Satan questions, and Satan answered.

In 1:9–11, Satan laid out a scenario that he believed would make Job quit on God. Satan believed that Job's loyalty to God was dependent on his material success. Take away the material success, and Job would leave God.

And in 1:12, God permitted Satan to carry out his test.

Why?

Why in heaven or on earth would God agree to such a plan?

Why would God turn such a dangerous, evil enemy loose on one of his most loyal subjects, one declared to be "blameless and upright"? Why? What kind of God is this?

That is a question for the ages, but not just for the ages. It is a question relevant to our lives as well, and it is the question that haunts this book. That question is what we're going to explore in our journey through the book of Job. That question is where I went when I started this study, and I look forward to showing you the path I have found.

The answer is in the book of Job.

But it is not to be found in chapter one.

So we'll ask the question "why?" and then, as we pass from chapter to chapter, we'll watch for the answer to reveal itself in the pages of Job's life and in his interactions with friends and with God. Suffice to say, the book in no way tries to hide God's role in the troubles that came Job's way. It clearly states that God approved the trial. God set the boundaries for the trial, and Job's body was off-limits in the first stage. As we'll see toward the end of the book, when God speaks directly to Job, he never ducks his role in the trouble. But—and this is important—even as 1:12 clearly articulates God's role, the entire chapter reminds us over and over again that, while 1:12 exists and is true—God was involved—Satan is the enemy. The enemy is Satan. Even in 1:12 it states, "the Lord said to the enemy."

Satan is not granted the dignity of a proper name but is given a description instead: the enemy. God was involved, but God was not and is not the enemy.

3
WHAT DO YOU SAY?

WHAT DO YOU tell a father who has worked hard, loved much, and seen the joy of his spiritual life, his friendships, his marriage, and his career blossom; who planned well for the birth of his first child; who dreamed during the pregnancy that he was having a daughter; who talked to her in the womb and fell deeply in love with her from the day of her birth—what do you tell that father when he then sees the bottom suddenly drop out?

What do you tell a father who checks his child into three different hospitals in one day? What do you tell a father who doesn't just witness the horror of veins bursting in his ten-day-old daughter's tiny arms and legs but also has to participate in that terrible event and who wishes that his little girl understood language and that he could explain that he wasn't trying to be cruel, that his heart was suddenly breaking, that this was all happening too fast?

What do you tell a father who sleeps beside his wife in a ward packed with dozens of beds full of sick children, beside his own infant daughter who is suddenly, mysteriously not well, who is now just one of hundreds in this building with little plastic identification tags on tiny wrists and ankles? His daughter had been well this morning. Nothing seems different now. But the scales say she's rapidly losing weight, and the medical literature spots dramatic weight loss as the first sign of trouble.

Two decades later, there is only one thing I can think of that I would tell that man: it's okay to cry.

FROM PREACHER'S KID TO ATHEIST

I was born into a nonreligious family. When I was seven years old, some neighborly people from a local church knocked on our door and invited my parents to a home Bible study. One thing led to another, and my parents eventually were baptized in a Mennonite Brethren church. Newly converted in his mid-thirties, my dad quit his job and went back to school. After graduating from Bible school, our family moved from southern to northern British Columbia, where my dad took a position as an associate minister in a Mennonite Brethren church in Fort St. John. After a few years in the north country, another move led to his first lead minister role in an American Baptist church in California. Later, my dad's conversion from Baptist theology to Reformed (Calvinistic) theology led him to start a new Reformed church in a neighboring town in California. To say that I grew up religious (from seven years old onward) is an understatement. As one of nearly a million home-schooled Californian kids at the time, I studied New Testament Greek as my high school foreign language course for two years.

I immigrated back to Canada on my own at nineteen and embarked on a brief atheistic phase. I tried to use atheism to shake my preacher's kid issues, and frankly, I wanted to indulge in the sin I thought I'd been denied living in my father's household. An international border between myself and my family and a science degree from the University of British Columbia (UBC) seemed to be just the ticket to a happy and distraction-free sinfulness.

By twenty-one, after only a few years in the wild, I figured out that the promises of the world were a sham—all glitter and perfume to mask the ugliness and foul odor of sin's true character.

I started praying again. I studied a variety of world religions to discover for myself what the right path was. Studies in other religions led me back to Christianity, so I studied the evidence for Christianity and the Bible's history. If I was going to take the religious plunge again, I would do it this time with my eyes wide open rather than just inheriting my family's faith. C.S. Lewis's Mere Christianity was an early help in this regard, as were many other books I studied over the following years.

I shopped around for a church family. I explored Reformed churches, a Plymouth Brethren group near UBC, a Pentecostal congregation, Catholic mass—and then, instead of finding a spiritual home, a spiritual home found me. A timid Japanese student invited me out to a Bible talk on campus. The rest, as they say, is history.

So I had the religious thing down cold.

A TRIPLE HANDICAP

During my atheistic phase, my time in the wild taught me to look skeptically at faith and what I had previously believed. While I was still lost in the woods but not feeling lost, a Christian friend commented that "a true Christian should never be sad," which led to a fierce debate among the Christians present. I observed the discussion with some amusement but did not participate. As the sole atheist-in-training, I found the discussion irrelevant. But I did pay attention, and even as an atheist, I silently sided with most of the Christians present who opposed the plastic viewpoint of continual happiness. It seemed to me that despite heavenly assurances and divine comforts, Christians had just as hard a time as anyone else dealing with the stresses of life. It seemed to me that Christians have a harder time coping with life's challenges and hurts—they have three handicaps.

The first handicap I observed was that most coping mechanisms for emotional pain were disallowed for Christians. Christians couldn't deal with a bad day or a bad week by turning to a few good, stiff drinks. Abusing prescription drugs was out. It was sinful to even toy with the idea of illegal drugs. The whole chemical-escape path was out. This sin-avoidance handicap extended beyond simply closing the door on chemical-escape routes. Swearing like a sailor when things reached a snapping point was a sin to be confessed and changed. Being rude to friends and family as a form of stress leakage was something to apologize for and not do again. Fistfights, name-calling, and shouting were not valid responses to stress spikes. Hatreds hidden or revealed were forbidden. The religion even banned impure releases from the pressure of sexual temptations and related biological demands. It seemed that every natural response to life's stressors was prohibited. The minimum acceptable-behavior standard for Christians was an unrealistically high bar. The task was difficult in good times and surely impossible in a crisis.

The second handicap I saw was that Christians were supposed to always do good in addition to not sinning. It was not enough to not sin when under stress. The standard called for more: offer kindness in response to hurt, rejoice in all circumstances, love your enemies, and so on. The whole Christian life was entirely unrealistic.

Then came the third handicap: the examples of Job, Jesus, Paul, and so many others in scripture. These examples were perhaps supposed to inspire believers, but it seemed to me that they only set the Christian performance bar unreasonably high. These examples of successful saints erased all excuses for failure.

Or so I thought.

Job does something after his first trial that too many of us misunderstand.

But before we look at his response, we need to understand Job's first trial at a deep level. There is more going on here than meets the eye.

4

A FIRST LOOK AT JOB'S FIRST TRIAL

Not only is Job's response to his trials frequently misunderstood, but the trial itself is often read too quickly. To understand Job's actual response, it helps to identify more deeply with what actually happened to him. Let's take a moment and study this passage.

> [13]*Now there was a day when his sons and daughters were eating and drinking wine in their oldest brother's house,* [14]*and there came a messenger to Job and said, "The oxen were plowing and the donkeys feeding beside them,* [15]*and the Sabeans fell upon them and took them and struck down the servants with the edge of the sword, and I alone have escaped to tell you."* [16]*While he was yet speaking, there came another and said, "The fire of God fell from heaven and burned up the sheep and the servants and consumed them, and I alone have escaped to tell you."* [17]*While he was yet speaking, there came another and said, "The Chaldeans formed three groups and made a raid on the camels and took them and struck down the servants with the edge of the sword, and I alone have escaped to tell you."* [18]*While he was yet speaking, there came another and said, "Your sons and daughters were eating and drinking wine in their oldest brother's house,* [19]*and behold, a great wind came across the wilderness and struck the four corners of the house, and it fell*

> *upon the young people, and they are dead, and I alone have escaped to tell you."*
>
> Job 1:13–19

The text makes a point of noting the location of Job's children in verse thirteen. As we discussed in the last chapter, perhaps it was the oldest son's birthday, or it was just his turn to host. Why were Job's kids eating and drinking while so much of the rest of the farm was working? The text doesn't say. Perhaps each child's day to host was special enough that it called for a holiday. Perhaps there was a lull in the workload at the farm. The oxen were plowing, but the donkeys were just grazing. And if the camels were Job's long-haul transportation force, they appear to have been idle as well since they were all on the farm rather than on the road to the markets.

If we take our modern understanding of farming and make a few reasonable assumptions about Job's work calendar, then he would have had two plowing seasons: one in spring to prepare for seeding and one in late fall to bury the post-harvest refuse back under the earth in preparation for next year's planting. The agricultural part of the farm then had been either gearing up for a new planting season or winding down for the fallow winter months. Job's sheep would have been sheared in the spring once the weather had warmed. If he had been running a wholesale wool operation, then the camels would have been on hand to begin transporting wool once shearing was complete.

So this catastrophe struck Job in a season when all his children, his workers, and his livestock would have been concentrated on the farm instead of, for example, being off to market. If it was early spring, then it would have been a critical time in Job's economic calendar when crops needed to go in the ground and when wool was at its thickest and ready for shearing. It would have been planting season for crops and harvest season for wool.

If the time instead was late fall, then the harvest would have just come in, the field hands would have still been plowing the stalks and stubble under, and the camels and donkeys would have been on hand to begin their market journeys. Whether it was spring or fall, trouble came at the worst possible time: in modern terms, this was the time when Job met payroll.

If this tragedy happened in spring, then the first assault on the donkeys and oxen would have wiped out Job's imminent planting season. In modern terms, 500 heavy tractors and 500 pickups were stolen. If it happened instead in fall, then the assault sabotaged his ability to get his harvest to market by eliminating his short-haul transportation team.

The effect of this assault was not just economic, of course. Five hundred yoke of oxen called for up to 500 drivers. In the last chapter, I conservatively estimated that this part of the farm employed 250 drivers. The text, however, suggests that all the teams had been engaged, so 250 might be too conservative, but for a working number, it will do. Two hundred and fifty men dead, in addition to the animals. And how many had been tending the donkeys? We don't know. Let's call the total number of men impacted by this first disaster an even 250 and be done with it. Odds were that most of these men were married, but again, we'll be conservative and say only 50 percent were married. And we'll pick another likely understated number and say that those 125 married men had an average of 2 children—a very conservative estimate in an era before birth control!

So 1,000 animals stolen, 250 men dead, and 125 widows with 250 children left behind.

Do you grasp the scale of what Job would have absorbed by just this first assault?

Can you imagine Job, staggered by the loss, thinking, "Where are my kids? I need them here now to help me handle this."

But Job did not have time to ask for his children. The first grim messenger had still been speaking when a second showed up and started talking over the first messenger (1:16). If you are a people manager, have you ever had the aggravation of staff talking over each other in their rush to get information out?

Seven thousand sheep were now dead by some freak fire that had fallen from the sky. The original Hebrew uses an idiom that usually means lightning, although it could mean actual fire given the following detail: the sheep and shepherds were burned up. Fire or lightning suddenly attacking and consuming 7,000 animals plus shepherds makes this more than just a freak weather event. This is an unprecedented lightning storm. If this happened in the spring, then it would have destroyed the wool harvest with the sheep. If this occurred in the fall, then the wool wouldn't have been ready yet, but many animals would have been pregnant as lambing season approached. How many shepherds were killed? In a previous chapter, we conservatively said there were 50 shepherds, so we'll stick with that. Fifty shepherds, which means 25 wives widowed and 50 children left fatherless. To be conservative.

"Where are my kids? Somebody get my kids." But there was no time to verbalize this request because a third servant showed up, out of breath, talking over the other two because, not knowing what else has already occurred, the third servant believed that his news was unlike anything else and was the most important.

The news was that the Chaldeans had come and stolen 3,000 camels—3,000 long-haul trucks. The last of Job's transportation network was gone. If it was fall, the harvest would rot in the fields and not get to market. If it was spring, then this loss would add insult to injury as there would no longer be a way to get the destroyed wool to market anyway. Contracts would go unfulfilled. Job was not going to meet payroll, which sounds superfluous given that the camel drivers are all dead as well, but their widows and orphans still need to eat. How many camel drivers were murdered? We didn't calculate this before. For the sake of a guess, let's call it 1 driver for 30 camels. That's 100 drivers dead, 50 widows, 100 additional children left fatherless.

"Where are my kids? I need my sons and daughters here to help me deal with these disasters."

Conservatively, we're at 400 dead farmworkers. Many had likely worked for Job for years—some perhaps for decades. There would have been men who were junior laborers right up to foremen of teams and managers of divisions. These are men who would have joked with Job over a fire at night; rejoiced over the successful delivery of a particular lamb, foal, or calf; bartered at the market as Job's representative; risked their lives driving carnivores away from grazing herds; and put in long hours during the key planting and harvest seasons. These disasters called for 400 burials. If they buried 3 a day, every day, it would have taken more than 4 months to get every body into the ground. And who was supposed to gather the bodies and dig the graves?

There were at least 200 widows suddenly in mourning and 400 fatherless children. Everyone, Job included, was wiped out economically. How do you feed 600 women and children when you yourself have just lost everything?

All of the above assumes a male-only workforce with stay-at-home mothers. While some mothers may indeed have been at home (for example, those in late stages of pregnancy), the reality for the era was likely that many of the women worked in the fields as well. With this in mind we could play around with our assumptions and come up with a higher count of women among the victims. This only adds to the horror. Women field hands introduces the specter of sexual assaults amidst the pillage, and children not in the fields may have lost both fathers and mothers.

Do you grasp the enormity of what had just taken place?

But the horror was not yet finished.

"Where are my children?"

It turned out that death had come for all ten of Job's children that day as well. It had been a time of celebration, and perhaps Job had already been planning his usual post-party spiritual refocus and purification time with each of his children. Now they were all dead, killed at once, on the heels of three other disasters whose messengers were all standing around spilling out the details of their stories even as they grasped that their story was not the only headline that day. There was no disaster recovery plan for a crisis on this scale. The shocked grief and first wails of mourning would have already started before the announcement of the next tragedy. If we take our conservative estimates as pinpoint accurate, then the deaths of Job's children merely supplemented the day's other headlines, bringing the day's total number of deaths to 410.

But there was another layer to this first trial that many casual readers completely overlook.

5
A SECOND LOOK AT THE FIRST TRIAL: THE PATTERN

These proclamations in Job 1:13–19 have a layer of complexity that goes beyond just the intensity of accumulating disasters. There was a pattern to the news flow and something particular about the language the messengers used.

First, the pattern:

- Disaster from an earthly source: the Sabeans attack.
- Disaster from a heavenly source: fire from the sky.
- Disaster from an earthly source: the Chaldeans attack.
- Disaster from a heavenly source: a mighty wind from the wilderness.

First, earthly warrior bands attacked, then fire came down from the sky. Next, more earthly warrior bands attacked, then wind came, another threat from the air.

Psychologically, Job was surrounded. The threats were what modern insurance language would describe as "acts of God" and "acts of war." The rare and uncontrollable had burst out against Job all at once.

Both heaven (sky, air) and earth (human opponents) were against Job and his people.

A THIRD LOOK AT THE FIRST TRIAL: THE LANGUAGE

The language of the original Hebrew passage contains many meaningful nuances as it describes these events.

Job 1:4–5 establishes the groundwork for understanding the feasts of Job's children. Regardless of whether these were birthday parties or other celebrations, the text makes it clear that the children enjoyed regular feasts with one another.

As the first trial kicks off in verse 13, Job's children are at another one of these feasts, eating and drinking.

In verse 15, the Sabeans attacked, but the report's language is odd. The men here were not killed "by the sword," as most modern translations put it. Instead, a direct translation of the original Hebrew would say that they were killed by "the mouth of the sword."[9]

The next disaster is fire, and in verse 16, the messenger, in the original Hebrew, states that the fire "ate the sheep and the servants."[10] Not that it burned them up, as would be more natural, but that it ate them.

And in verse 17, death comes to another area of the farm, again, "by the mouth of the sword."

So while Job's kids were eating together, death came to dine on the farm in three courses: twice by the mouth of a sword and once by a fire that eats its victims. Then in the final stroke, Job's kids were killed as they were enjoying a meal. They were all dead at their table, along with almost everyone who was with them.

Did Job have grandkids in that house? Is it likely that Job's kids were old enough to have their own homes and host dinners, but none of them were married? Probably not. At least some must have had spouses. Did the married ones have children born or on the way? Before birth control—probably. Were children present? We don't know. Whoever was there, they all died. Job either lost grandchildren, or he had orphaned grandchildren added to his pain. Just one servant escaped to tell Job. Perhaps he had been a kitchen helper who went out back to dump some refuse, was knocked down by the wind, and witnessed the building's collapse and the deaths of its inhabitants.

---

9 See Reyburn, William D.1992. *A Handbook on the Book of Job*. 48-49. New York. United Bible Societies

10 Reyburn, 50.

A FOURTH LOOK AT THE FIRST TRIAL: ITS TIMING

Do you remember our discussion on "the enemy"? Do you remember that he was a very dangerous, deliberate, systematic, and intense enemy—a focused enemy? When God called him to consider Job, he needed no time to ponder his case. He was ready. When God gave him the green light, he did not just persecute Job randomly but put together a program.

He orchestrated the first trial's events for maximum impact. Blow after blow after blow—first earth-sent, then heaven-sent, then earth-sent again, and then another heavenly assault.

The Sabeans did not teleport onto Job's farm. They rode a great distance to get there. They planned the attack ahead of time and then traveled perhaps for days or weeks.

The Sabeans then attacked at the same time as the Chaldeans. Had the two groups conferred with one another to coordinate their assaults? Perhaps. Or perhaps the enemy had merely lured the two groups to attack separately at the same time. Regardless, the attacks happened simultaneously, coinciding not just with each other but also with the feast, and not just any feast but the oldest brother's feast. The attacks did not come a week later or a week earlier. They arrived at the same time.

The enemy coordinated the timing of these tragedies not just to the date but also to the hour. You don't raise thousands of sheep on an acre. You don't need five hundred yokes of oxen to plow a small field. You don't graze five hundred donkeys and three thousand camels on the back lawn. The NIV version of verse 19 mentions a nearby desert, which has significant agricultural implications for the farm. To have enough land for both grazing and planting, the farm must have spanned miles. It may have taken a day or more to travel from one end to the other. Some of these attacks may have occurred a long journey away. Still, the enemy timed them so that Job would get the news not only all at once but also in a specific order—an order that had economic as well as emotional and spiritual significance. The enemy designed the events and announcements to inflict increasing shock waves of trauma and grief until the volume of pain approached the unbearable, culminating in the enemy's coup de grâce: the announcement of the death of Job's children.

All this tragedy, however, was not enough. Satan had a plan that went beyond simply ruining Job's life.

6
GRIEF MISUNDERSTOOD

THE NEXT STEP in Satan's plan was for Job to curse God.

This is where many readers of Job's book start to go wrong and misread the message of the following passage:

> [20] Then Job arose and tore his robe and shaved his head and fell on the ground and worshiped. [21] And he said, "Naked I came from my mother's womb, and naked shall I return. The Lord gave, and the Lord has taken away; blessed be the name of the Lord." [22] In all this Job did not sin or charge God with wrong.
>
> JOB 1:20–22

The Lord gave, and the Lord has taken away; blessed be the name of the Lord.

What well of strength does a person need to have to respond to such deep tragedy like this?

How many of us would have responded differently?

Some of us might have immediately lashed out at God: "How could you let this happen?" Some might have lashed out at the messengers: "Why didn't you do something?" Or some may have cried out to God for relief: "Make it go away! Save me from this crisis!" Some of us might not have even thought of God at all. Instead, we might have turned to friends—looking for a shoulder to cry on—or to escapes: drinking, smoking, comfort foods.

Some of us might have retreated, closed the door on the world, and begun a slow slide into an immobile depression.

How we initially react to trouble says a lot about our personalities and our spiritual health. Anyone can look the part of a mature Christian in good times. When life goes suddenly wrong, however, it is much harder to wear a pious mask. Much gets revealed when our stress levels climb and our problems become unmanageable.

I'm sure we'd all like to be like Job in times of trouble—capable of responding to trouble, even during the initial shock, with a calm, memorable spirituality. Except that this standard of calmness, responding to adversity with "naked I came… naked shall I return" seems to be a high bar that only those unengaged or in denial are able to reach. Job here almost sounds like an eastern mystic, a Zen Buddhist. Is Job's dispassionate calm the Christian standard, the model to aspire to?

The question falsely assumes that Job's response is as calm as the text sounds. "Naked I came from my mother's womb, and naked shall I return. The Lord gave, and the Lord has taken away; blessed be the name of the Lord." Job did say that. The English translation is true to the original Hebrew, with the slight exception that Job is not implying a literal return to his mother's womb. Instead, the original Hebrew phrase is expressing a departure from this life, a detail that most English translations make clear. Otherwise, there is no ambiguity here.

But this is where Christians often go wrong: the poetic line in verse 21 is impressive, it is meaningful, and it is memorable. It is recited at funerals worldwide, even by people who know little about Job or the Bible. Verse 21 stands out. But verse 21 doesn't immediately follow the crescendo of tragedies in verses 14–19. Between the last announcement in verse 19 and Job's poetic line in verse 21 stands verse 20.

People remember the poetic line. Very few pay attention to the prose line before it:

> [20] *Then Job arose and tore his robe and shaved his head and fell on the ground and worshiped.*
>
> Job 1:20

Ask most Christians how Job responded to the first wave of crises, and the most common response is, "Naked I came from my mother's womb, and naked shall I return. The LORD gave, and the LORD has taken away; blessed be the name of the LORD."

Very few will remember that he tore his robe and shaved his head.

In the last chapter I noted that the events in Job occurred sometime prior to Moses's ministry, meaning that Job may have lived in Abraham's time or even earlier. That puts Job in 2,000 BCE or earlier. Over four thousand years ago.

Four thousand years ago, you could say that Job "tore his robe and shaved his head" and tell a whole story in those few words. To a modern Western audience, it sounds like some strange cultural ritual, has very little emotional resonance, and perhaps even reads as pointless textile damage and personal grooming. We might shave our heads for style or to address a lice problem. We might vaguely grasp the idea that Job is communicating something different with these actions, but they have no emotional meaning for the average modern reader.

WHAT IT MEANT THEN

Those few words are full of deep meaning. As modern readers, we need to plumb those depths, understand them, and translate them into our cultural context. In this process, it's helpful to seriously consider for a moment the fact that there is no universal, genetically programmed method for working out deep grief. The way people express grief is as much a cultural construct as it is a personal expression.

Even in modern times, the differences between cultures are profound. In some cultures, the process of grieving is loud and public. In others, it is stoic and comparatively private. The expressive may view the stoics as in denial and unable to connect with their deepest pain. The stoics may view the loud as cheapening and disrespecting the profound intensity of personal grief. One culture's value is that grief should be shared. Another culture's value is that widely distributing grief would dilute the validity of the suffering. Some cultures expect the mourning period to be brief and emphasize the importance of "moving on." Other cultures have a calendar of traditional mourning stages that may take months or years to pass. Even within a culture or within a family, there can be differences.[11] The challenge for the modern reader is not to critique the ancient method of expressing grief but rather to measure its depth and understand the practice's intensity, just as we understand the practices of our own time and culture. If Romeo had gone for ice cream after finding Juliet dead, we would know he did not care. Instead, he killed himself, and so we can grasp the depth of grief that Shakespeare was attempting to convey to his contemporaries. We need to arrive at a similar familiarity with what Job was doing in verse 20.

So what do we make of Job damaging his clothing and shaving his head? What did it mean back then?

In Genesis 37, Joseph's brothers plotted to kill him. Reuben was the only one who protested this plot, and he worked out a compromise with his homicidal siblings. Instead of outright killing him, they temporarily put Joseph in a cistern for safekeeping. For reasons the story does not make clear, Reuben then wandered off. While he was gone, his brothers reworked their evil plans, pulled Joseph from the cistern, and sold him as a slave to passing Midianite merchants. In Genesis 37:29, Reuben returned and found the cistern empty. He then either assumed that Joseph had been killed or else learned right away that he had lost his younger brother to slavery. Regardless of what exactly he knew, Reuben was distraught. He had thought he had saved Joseph, but instead, death—or a fate worse than death—had befallen his brother. Reuben's grief was the grief of rescuing and then losing his brother, perhaps the grief of realizing that his absence contributed to the loss, the grief that his remaining siblings turned out to be unspeakably cruel beings, and the fear of explaining this to his father.

How did a person in Reuben's day express these conflicted and out-

---

11 David's story in 2 Samuel provides an interesting study in grief. He mourned in ways that his contemporaries did not expect. For example, when David mourned both his first son with Bathsheba in 2 Samuel 12:15–23 and Absalom in 2 Samuel 19:1–8, David's contemporaries questioned his mourning pattern. David's wives had approached mourning differently as well: Bathsheba committed to a formal period of mourning in 2 Samuel 11 for her first husband, whereas Abigail does not appear to have lingered between husbands in 1 Samuel 25. Though these women may have mourned differently because of the nature of their relationships to their previous husbands, their stories nevertheless illustrate how there were different expressions of grief even within the Jewish culture.

rageous emotions that come from such unjust tragedies? Reuben tore his clothes (Gen. 37:29).

Joseph was Jacob's favorite son. How did Jacob respond when his remaining sons concocted an animal-attack story and presented Joseph's clothing dipped in blood as evidence of the boy's death, leaving it to the father to deduce that a "fierce animal has devoured" Joseph and "torn [him] to pieces" (Gen. 37:33)? He tore his clothes.

If your brother was kidnapped and threatened with death, and if you had succeeded in temporarily rescuing him, and if his captors then returned and sold him into slavery—if you lost your brother in such a way, how would you respond? You probably would not tear your clothes. It's just not part of our culture today. Or what would you do if your child was attacked by wild animals and eaten alive? How would you respond to the horror of holding in your hands the bloody clothes that remained? Again, you most likely would not tear your own clothes. So what would you do? Stop eating? Overeat? Start drinking? Shout and cry uncontrollably? Bottle it up and eat yourself from the inside out with sealed pain and grief? How would you respond? How would you respond to such horror?

These were personal tragedies of the highest order, and the act of tearing one's clothes was, in Job's day, personal grief expressed at the deepest and most intense level.

But what about this business of Job shaving his head?

Leviticus 21:5–6 warns priests not to shave their heads as it would be considered a profane act. This verse does not directly explain Job's actions because the law found in Leviticus came long after Job's day. Still, it hints at the fact that head shaving had culturally significant implications. Written over a thousand years later, Ezekiel 44:20 repeats the rule, suggesting that the cultural significance of this act had some serious longevity.

But Ezekiel 5 says that God came to Ezekiel, a priest,[12] and told him to shave his head and beard. Why? God himself said that priests should not do this. The full explanation requires an extensive study of the book of Ezekiel, the history surrounding the book, and the message of this priest-prophet. Still, for our purposes, the primary point of interest is that Ezekiel's head shaving was an exception to the law in Leviticus, an exception that would

---

12 See Ezekiel 1:3.

have graphically and intensely horrified the book's original audience. Ezekiel's audience was a stubborn and obstinate one (Ezek. 2). The head shaving was a communication tool—a shock technique designed to drive a message home. The message was a warning of intense horror to come: the Babylonians would soon sack Jerusalem. With the Babylonian siege would come a famine so extreme that families would resort to cannibalism (Ezek. 4:16–17; Ezek. 5:10). Four fates awaited the population: plague, famine, death by sword or captivity, and slavery in Babylon (Ezek. 5:12). Each person to their destiny. The mode of expressing and illustrating this anticipated horror was the shaving of Ezekiel's head and beard.

Another reference to head shaving occurs in Jeremiah 48:37 involving the people of Moab. The text describes these people as being in a state of intense public grief as their nation is destroyed (Jer. 48:42), a land where "there is nothing but lamentation," for God has "broken Moab like a vessel for which no one cares" (Jer. 48:38). In response to the overwhelming destruction of their civilization, "every head is shaved and every beard cut off" (Jer. 48:37).

Ezekiel was trying to communicate the horror of an entire city about to be under siege—a horror that would lead to plague, famine, cannibalism, and either death or slavery. Jeremiah spoke of the entire Moabite nation being erased from existence—we have Egyptians and Israelites and other descendants of ancient peoples today, but we don't have Moabites. The Babylonians eliminated them as a nation.

How would you deal with your city being invaded, abused, and then destroyed before your eyes? How would you express that grief? In the days of Ezekiel, head and beard shaving was part of one of the highest expressions of otherwise inexpressible pain.

How would you respond to your entire nation being destroyed, to all future progress of its civilization and culture being wiped out? Jeremiah describes such a people as having shaved heads and beards.

Notice something here: head shaving was associated with public tragedies, the tearing of clothes with personal tragedies. Both were among the deepest expressions of pain and grief within the culture. They were level eight or nine on the emotional Richter scale. Try to find a place in the Bible where both of these expressions come together in one place: clothes tearing and head shaving. The personal and the public, both at the most extreme level.

There is only one place:

> [20] *Then Job arose and tore his robe and shaved his head and fell on the ground and worshiped.*
>
> JOB 1:20

THE PEAK OF PAIN

It is very appropriate that Job used the most intense expressions available in his culture for personal pain and public horror because both had occurred in his situation—his children were gone, and so were hundreds of people that worked for him. Job's wife was now childless. Hundreds of women on the farm were now widows and hundreds of children were fatherless. Job's finances were destroyed, and so were the incomes of hundreds of suddenly widowed women and fatherless children. The tragedy was on an awful scale. In verse 20, Job expresses this by both tearing his clothes and shaving his head—level ten on the emotional Richter scale.

Consider as well that this progression of mourning took some time. This was not the impulsive result of a flash of emotion. Job probably did not have a razor in the pocket of his robe. He had to find a knife. Not a safety razor, but a knife. And in Job's culture, men did not shave. He probably didn't have the best tools for the task and he probably wasn't very good at it, which would have made the process take even longer. With an operation of Job's size, it had probably been a while since he'd had to get down on his knees to shear a sheep himself. And when his own shearing was done, he probably looked a fright with cuts all over his freshly scraped scalp.

SEEING BIBLICAL GRIEF MORE CLEARLY

I said earlier that this is where Christians often go wrong. Christians sometimes truncate grief as though it is an unfaithful act. Readers of the book of Job too often jump from the announcement of tragedy to Job's faithful prayer, overlooking the fact that verse 20 might have taken several hours or a day or more. While he was on his way to find a knife good enough for shaving, people probably kept talking to him. He probably asked questions of his own. Widows and fatherless children must have poured in as they heard the news. Those around Job would have gone through their own expressions of shock and grief, further upsetting Job as he tried to deal with this onslaught of horror. Things got messy, and not just from the cuts on Job's head.

Job is not the only biblical figure to express intense grief. Jesus wept at Lazarus's tomb. Why? He had come to raise Lazarus from the dead. What was there to grieve about?

Death is a tragedy, even if it will be overcome shortly. Some Christians can feel conflicted about mourning the death of another Christian, as though a mature knowledge of heaven should make us immune to grief due to the comfort of knowing we will see our loved one again one day. It can seem as if grieving as a Christian is a sign of weak faith.

Jesus knew about heaven. Not only that, Jesus knew that in a couple of minutes, Lazarus would be alive again in this life, never mind waiting for heaven. But Jesus still wept.[13]

Hebrews 5:7 says that "In the days of his flesh, Jesus offered up prayers and supplications, with loud cries and tears…" What were the tears for? Why was Christ crying in prayer? Did he not trust God the Father? Was he faithless? Did Jesus not understand the path he was on, and did he not already know how it would all turn out? Of course, Jesus wasn't faithless or in the dark about the plan or lacking trust. But emotions are emotions. He felt stuff. He was a man, tempted just as we are,[14] feeling things just like we do, and so sometimes, when he prayed, there were loud cries. There were tears.

If Jesus could cry, so can we.

Job is held up as an example: God commends him at both the beginning and the end of the book. And before Job prayed—pay attention here, this is critical—before Job prayed, he tore his robe and shaved his head. Before he prayed, he went to level ten on the emotional Richter scale.

Christians who dodge all emotional reactions to serious tragedies in their lives are not super spiritual; they are super unhealthy. Placidity is not a higher spiritual state that Christians should try to attain to measure their maturity. That logic is like some of the Greek Stoic philosophies Paul battled against in the New Testament.

Job went straight from bad news to his culture's deepest expressions of grief. But how can we translate this action of tearing clothing and shaving

---

13 The full story can be found in John 11.

14 See Hebrews 4:15.

hair into a modern context that we can emotionally connect to? Perhaps we could say something like this:

Job began to make a horrible, wordless sound that came from deep inside, slowly building up until it burst out in a roar. He threw himself to the ground, stood up again, paced, didn't see the people or the things around him. He crashed into them, blind with tears, smashing anything breakable that he encountered, all while making that horrible, wordless cry.

For a more buttoned-up audience, we might say something like:

Job turned pale and cold. He locked himself in his room and fell into a nearly catatonic state. He wouldn't see or speak to anyone. He did not eat and lost twenty pounds in the first ten days.

Smashing things or yelling or going pale or not eating or locking yourself in your room were not meaningful acts in Job's culture. Tearing your clothes and shaving your head were meaningful.

It was only after all this drama that Job prayed.

In whatever way we try to relate to Job's actions, the bottom line is that Job did not go straight from bad news to worship—he went straight from bad news to a deep shock and very public grief.[15]

It's okay to cry.

---

[15] For additional examples of expressions of grief in scripture, see the book of Psalms. Psalms that have made a particular impression on me in this regard are Psalms 73, 74, 77, and 79 by Asaph; Psalms 3, 4, 5, 12, and 13 (among many others) by David; and finally Psalm 102, whose author identifies himself only as "an afflicted man." Ezekiel 3:12–15 is another interesting example: the shock and unhappiness that Ezekiel expresses is actually his own reaction to his personal call to be a prophet. This calling did not suit Ezekiel's plans for his own life, and his first reaction to the call was to spend seven days dealing with his own emotions. God did not change the assignment in response to Ezekiel's reaction. But God did give Ezekiel the space (and the grace) to work through his unhappiness with it.

7
AFTER GRIEF, PRAYER

It might be helpful here if we acknowledge that Job's initial deep grief reaction was just his first response. His second act was, in fact, worship. His third action was a return to grief, which we'll start to study in Job chapter three. Later come anger and bitterness and other things—we are going to study the whole book of Job and see that working through strong emotions and the spiritual impacts of those emotions takes time and sometimes involves repeating stages.

But for now, his initial response is shock, grief, and then prayer. Like a man drowning in the sea, Job saw no need to pretend that he was feeling fine as he sank beneath the waves. Crying out is not a lack of faith but the natural response of a drowning person overwhelmed by the water. But like a soul drowning, he also saw the value of not just crying out but reaching out for an available life buoy. With his whole body in the sea, Job put one firm hand on the buoy that is God.

Let's observe how Job does this in the next few verses.

CONTRADICTORY EMOTIONS

[20] Then Job arose and tore his robe and shaved his head and fell on the ground and worshiped. [21] And he said, "Naked I came from my mother's womb, and naked shall I return. The Lord

gave, and the Lord has taken away; blessed be the name of the Lord." [22] In all this Job did not sin or charge God with wrong.

JOB 1:20–22

Three things stand out to me about Job's expression of faith amid pain:

1. Job had a clear-sighted and objective view of reality. He came to the world as an infant with nothing, and he would depart with nothing. He came without children, wealth, or workers, and he would leave without them as well. Job was rich, but he was not a materialist. His self-worth was not bound up in his stuff.
2. Job never forgot where his stuff came from. His children, his wealth, the people who worked for him—they were all gifts from God. They were all on loan from God. God could take them back at any time—and now he had. They were his. Job still felt pain at this loss, and he was allowed to feel it. But the pain did not take away the fact that, underneath his emotions, the things taken from Job were never his to begin with—they were God's all along. You can know the facts and still grieve. Let me repeat: you can know the facts and still grieve. Jesus knew that Lazarus was coming back, but he still wept. It is contradictory, but it is okay. Life is not neat, and emotions are not logical.
3. Last, Job gave thanks to God in all circumstances. Ephesians 5:20 and 1 Thessalonians 5:18 also speak of this idea of unconditional gratitude. Christians sometimes read those New Testament passages in isolation, and it traps them in an "I have to be thankful no matter what" paradigm that lacks the context of the rest of scripture. Job praised God. He was thankful for the gifts he'd had. This fulfills the demands of Ephesians and Thessalonians. But he still grieved. He still hurt. It is contradictory, but it is okay. Life is not neat.

You can be unhappy about going to the dentist and still be grateful for dentistry and for healthy teeth and gums. It is contradictory, this unhappiness mixed with gratitude, but you can see in this dentistry example how it still makes sense. Likewise, you can be grateful to God for what he has given you, understand that it is his to take away, be faithful through this in praise, and still grieve, mourn, and even wail at the deepest possible level for your loss and hurt. But amid that loss and hurt, it is crucial that you also throw a hand over that life buoy that is God—just like Job did.

Remember your enemy. Satan is the enemy, even in pain. Especially in pain. If he can use the waves to make you turn against God—perfect. His goal was not to hurt you to begin with. His goal was to hurt your relationship with God. If making you drown in a sea of emotion is what will separate you from God, he will kick up a storm. If giving you calm water and a yacht will make you walk away, then here come the sunshine and gently rocking mahogany-paneled masterpiece. Neither the storm nor the sunshine is the point. Separating you from God is the point.

KEEPING ONE THING STRAIGHT

In chapter one, it states:

> *²²In all this Job did not sin or charge God with wrong.*
>
> JOB 1:22

The verse in Hebrew does not say that Job committed no sin. It says that Job did not sin by charging God with wrong. We are all sinners—Job too. But the sin that Satan said Job would commit was the sin of turning on God during stress. The claim was that Job would "curse [God] to [his] face" (Job 1:11). But Job did not do that. He did not charge God with wrong.

The better wording found in the New International Version (NIV) translation—"Job did not sin by charging God with wrongdoing" still means something slightly different than the original Hebrew. The word wrongdoing is better translated as unreason, unsteadiness, or foolishness.[16] Job did not sin by calling God a fool. Job did not lash out at God and accuse him of not knowing what he was doing or of making a mistake or of being crazy. He might have sinned over the course of his initial grief reaction—perhaps the writers omitted any such misstep from the text in an act of silent grace, or perhaps Job really did not sin at all in his initial response—but in the Hebrew,

---

16 Reyburn, 55.

verse 22 tells us very specifically that, whether or not he sinned at all, he most definitely did not sin by turning on God in response to these tragedies. He turned to God; he did not turn on God. He did not charge God with wrongdoing, with unreasonableness, with unsteadiness, or with foolishness.

That is an important detail. Job felt stuff. He did not go straight from tragedy to prayer—he went from tragedy to pain and to his culture's deepest expression of that pain. But he did not let that pain swallow him and turn him against God. Very quickly, even amid his deepest pain, without denying or rejecting the pain and anguish he felt, he still reached out to God.

It would make no sense for a drowning soul to curse and turn away from the nearby life buoy. Instead, even amid pain and panic, the drowning person had better reach out and grab that life buoy.

Job hurt, and he turned to the only one who could help.

FEARING EMOTIONAL HONESTY

The words I've written here were ones that I needed to hear in the first few months after Mackenzie's birth, but tragically I did not. I did not turn against God. But I did sin. My most damaging sin during the initial few months was forcing myself into a deeply unhealthy religiousness, one that I tried to force on my wife as well. I thought that any kind of honest emotional reaction to my daughter's crisis was a sign of a lack of faith that would cause God to not save her. The book of James says that a person petitioning God must "ask in faith, with no doubting, for the one who doubts is like a wave of the sea that is driven and tossed by the wind" (James 1:6). I repeatedly prayed for my daughter with a desperate, rigid kind of faith that admitted to no doubt for fear that any admission of doubt or pain or weakness would signal my unworthiness and result in unanswered prayer. I failed to note the context of James: the passage is about asking for wisdom. I took a passage on gaining wisdom and applied it to every kind of prayer to God, an overgeneralization that the text does not call for. It was an unwise application of a passage on wisdom. I only noted the irony years later.

So I misused James and strapped a heavier burden to myself than was called for or was healthy. And I overlooked the vast amount of scripture that shows that the righteous cry: Jesus in tears, Paul in distress, Jeremiah, Ezekiel, David, Moses—so many exemplary figures in scripture who cried and petitioned God with tears and admissions of pain and sometimes, particularly in many of the prophets' cases (although not in Jesus's), even doubt and fear.

I had already done a cursory study of Job before Mackenzie's birth. But I had learned the wrong things: Job did not sin (so I thought), and Job went straight from tragedy to worship (so I thought). And this false-Job standard was one I applied not only to myself but also to my wife. Pressuring her to "be more faithful" and to "pray harder" during this time was a passionate distraction, driven by a misguided belief that her behavior was crucial to God healing our daughter. Our daughter failing to thrive would be a sign that somebody, somewhere, was not faithful enough, and I was determined that neither I nor my wife would fail to have faith. It might have been a well-meaning position, but it was ultimately an evil one. It was unbiblical, and it nearly destroyed my marriage.

A GUY LIKE ME

When I went through the book of Job after Mackenzie's birth, I discovered a fellow believer in my false theology: a guy named Eliphaz. He was a friend who did Job a lot of damage by trying to foist his false beliefs on his suffering friend, and Eliphaz got into a lot of trouble with God for it. I completely missed the point of Eliphaz when I studied the book the first time.

My wife and I were both Jobs in the sense that we both suffered. But my wife had the additional burden of having an Eliphaz in her life—someone close to her that made the suffering worse.

We will figure out Eliphaz's role in Job's story when we get to his first appearance in Job chapter two. We'll get to Bildad and Zophar as well. These three men are all very different from each other, each having their own characteristic sins and methods of communicating. Whereas I was Eliphaz in my trial, perhaps you will find a kindred soul in Bildad or Zophar's personalities. Maybe not. But there is much to learn in Job, not just from Job himself but also from the friends. Things to do. Things not to do. Things to believe. And things to not believe. Ways to be, and ways to be wary of.

But I did not understand these things then. I was still religious. Religious, but not wise.

I did ask "why?" a lot during the first few months after my daughter's birth, during that first day spent at three hospitals—Vancouver General, BC

Children's, and New Westminster General—during that picnic day turned sour that did not end when the sun went down. It took ten days before we could bring Mackenzie home. Only one parent was allowed to stay in the hospital, and since my wife was still nursing, she had the task. For the first few days, I was there all day into the evening, but then I had to go back to work and could only come in the evenings. It was February 2001, my work's crunch time as the annual RRSP deadline approached,[17] the year following the dotcom collapse, and not a good time to be in the brokerage business.

I would go to the hospital each night, worn out emotionally and physically from work and excessive commuting. There, I would face my even more distraught young wife, who was still recovering from delivering her first baby, left alone to deal with doctors, needles, tubes, and theories all day long. The night offered no relief with its noisy, machine-beeping, staff-talking, interrupted sleep. Around midnight, I would leave the hospital for home. The following morning I would get up at six for the hour-plus commute to the office and do it all over again.

I asked "why?" a lot.

One night I came home from the hospital to find the main floor of our house flooded. Our water heater had burst.

One night I left the hospital around eleven at night and found a thief in my car. He had smashed a passenger window and strewn the glove box's contents across the driver's seat. I caught him still sitting in the passenger's seat. He attacked me with a screwdriver. After a brief tussle, he was gone, sprinting down the street.

I looked up then at the hospital on the hill in the dark, looming above me, where my six-pound daughter was struggling for life, where my wife was probably crying with stress, grief, and exhaustion. I looked back at my vandalized car and the now-empty street, wondered how and when to get the window fixed and how to not fall apart, how to drive home without driving into something to put a stop to the stress, how to function as a manager and professional in a brokerage office set in the middle of the postal code

---

17 For readers unfamiliar with the RRSP season, the acronym stands for the Registered Retirement Savings Program. The RRSP season refers to the annual March 1 deadline for contributions to these plans to qualify for Canadian tax deductions. The main point here is that the month of February is rush hour in the investment business in Canada.

area with the highest per capita registered savings in Canada and the sort of high-demand, high-expectation clients that came with that demographic, how to manage that pressure in the middle of the dotcom meltdown, how to function tomorrow, how to function now, how to drive home with no window, how to still the hurricane swirling in my heart and mind.

But I did not cry. Jesus wept, but I did not.

I would tell that man, now, to cry. Son, you had better cry. You'd better start getting it out now. It is only going to get worse, and nobody has what it takes to bottle it forever.

You better learn how to cry.

8

A REMINDER OF WHO THE ENEMY IS

Job chapter two starts a new day and a new scene. We could think of this as the inciting incident extended.

> *¹Again there was a day when the sons of God came to present themselves before the Lord, and Satan also came among them to present himself before the Lord. ²And the Lord said to Satan, "From where have you come?" Satan answered the Lord and said, "From going to and fro on the earth, and from walking up and down on it." ³And the Lord said to Satan, "Have you considered my servant Job, that there is none like him on the earth, a blameless and upright man, who fears God and turns away from evil? He still holds fast his integrity, although you incited me against him to destroy him without reason." ⁴Then Satan answered the Lord and said, "Skin for skin! All that a man has he will give for his life. ⁵But stretch out your hand and touch his bone and his flesh, and he will curse you to your face." ⁶And the Lord said to Satan, "Behold, he is in your hand; only spare his life." ⁷So Satan went out from the presence of the Lord and struck Job with loathsome sores from the sole of his foot to the crown of his head.*
>
> Job 2:1–7

Once again, in chapter two, we see the word "Satan," whereas, in Hebrew, it simply reads "the enemy." And once again, seven times in seven verses, we read "the enemy." The enemy still does not get a proper name but is just denoted as "the enemy." The repetition tells the reader to pay attention: this is the enemy in the book of Job—not Job, not God, not Job's friends, not even the Chaldean or Sabean raiders—Satan is the enemy.

This passage references "the enemy" seven times. In addition to using repetition for emphasis, the Old Testament writers also used specific numbers for symbolism as well. We will see more symbolic numbers in later chapters. A group of seven is called a heptad. In biblical texts, a heptad denotes a complete total. The number three serves a similar role in English literature, so this literary technique is really not as strange and mysterious as it may sound at first. If you're not a literature major and don't immediately grasp the significance of the number three in English literature, think instead of the number ten. A "top ten list" sounds like a complete list. A "top eight list" is just odd—it doesn't sound complete. We will talk about this more later when we get to another biblical literary device called a double heptad.

The critical point here is that the text repeatedly uses the phrase "the enemy," reminding us again who the real enemy is—both Job's true enemy and our true enemy. Our enemy is not our spouse, our co-worker, or a problematic neighbor or distant relative. Our enemy is the same as Job's. To focus on people as our opponents, to succumb to grudges or hatreds or even plots of revenge against people who have offended or injured us, is to fall into Satan's trap. He is the enemy. He will use others, but they are just his puppets. The puppet master is Satan. And he will gladly have you focus on his puppets rather than on the true enemy.

The beginning of chapter two also indicates that this next series of events began "on another day," as the original Hebrew puts it. Two days later? A week later? Months later? We don't know. The fact that Job's friends arrive later in the chapter suggests that this time period was relatively short, but we don't know for sure.

What we do learn from his answer to God's question is that Satan had not been focused on watching the drama of Job's post-disaster life unfold. Job, personally, wasn't that interesting to Satan. Instead, he had been "going to and fro on the earth, and walking up and down on it" (Job 2:2). He had had other things to do. But when asked specifically about Job in verse 2:3, Satan did know how Job was doing. He had been roaming the earth, but he had kept tabs on Job as well. Job had been just one of many objects Satan had handled in his efforts to oppose God. His attack on Job had not been personal for Satan. It had just been business, and Satan knew his business.

A NEW TEST

In chapter one, Satan's theory had been that Job's righteousness was purely environmental: God had made it easy for Job to be righteous. Satan's first test had been to tear down the environmental structures that were supposedly the source of Job's goodness. Satan's theory that Job's righteousness was wholly materialistic turned out to be false: Job did not curse God after his initial round of tragedies. Job mourned, Job wept, and Job turned to God in his pain, not against God.

Confronted with the failure of his test and proof that his theory was wrong, Satan did not even spend a moment reflecting on or acknowledging Job's goodness and righteousness. There was not even a whisper of "I was wrong." This was Satan, after all. Instead, Satan came up with a new theory: Job's righteousness was still entirely selfish—specifically, he would give up his external skin (his family, possessions, and friends) in exchange for his internal skin (his health and life).

The new theory looks a lot like the old theory. The scope of environmental factors influencing Job's righteousness has simply shrunk—the theory now goes that Job was more motivated by health than money or relationships. The idea that someone loves God because they love God does not compute in Satan's world. Job's righteousness must be selfish, and Satan is keen to uncover the one weakness that will unravel what he believes is merely an appearance of godliness.

WAIT A MINUTE—WHAT IS GOD DOING HERE?

This question naturally arises: why would God allow these trials at all? Satan had a theory. God let him test it. Satan was wrong. Now Satan had another theory and wanted to test the new one out. Satan wanted to ruin Job's life even more. He was convinced that then Job would curse God to his face. Then Job would walk away from God. And so God said okay. Why? Why would God allow such a thing? Why would God even bring Job's name up the first time, and then why bring it up the second time? And why, both times after mentioning his name, would God allow Satan to execute his plan against Job?

It is almost as if God had been setting Satan up to propose Job's trials.

Satan is the enemy. But reflecting on my initial study of Job, I could not shake the conviction that Satan was the enemy, but God was also responsible. God did not cause the evil to happen to Job—but he allowed it. He even raised the topic. God opened the door—then agreed to the trouble that entered. Satan might be the enemy, but it seemed to me that there was no shaking God's responsibility.

THE BOOK OF JOB PROVED USELESS

Around six months after my daughter's birth, I reviewed my notes on the book of Job again. I read through them carefully. I found them to be completely useless. My notes were useless, and the book of Job, it seemed, was useless.

My life and my family's life did not just go through a bad ten days shortly after my daughter's birth. She continued to deteriorate, and we were in and out of hospitals for months. The doctors diagnosed her with cystic fibrosis and put her on a special enzyme diet while doing more tests to verify the diagnosis. We were warned to expect a difficult life for our little girl and that she would finally die of the disease in her teens or twenties. That was the first diagnosis.

But no, it wasn't cystic fibrosis. It was a brain tumor impacting key areas close to her brain stem. No, it wasn't that either. It was Williams syndrome. It was Angelman syndrome, a rare genetic error, a hormone production problem, several known biochemical deficiencies, a neurological, genetic, or endocrine problem. It was none of those things. It was a nightmare, and she continued to lose weight. What became clear was that she was a medical mystery.

She was born in early February, plump and healthy. By May, she had burned off all her body fat and lived on lean tissue, including her heart. Her body was starting to consume her own heart to survive. She was a skeleton. You could see where her skull plates joined. Every tube and needle and even every dirty diaper was torture for her emaciated frame. She had big, quiet, scared eyes that were fearful of everyone in the world that was not mommy or daddy or nana. The people in white coats were the most terrifying. She would burst into tears as soon as she saw anyone in white—the vampires who came to draw blood, insert fluid lines, and find other ways to torture her shrinking body.

Oh, I asked "why?" a lot during those first few months. I was still religious and unbroken on the outside, but I was becoming angry on the inside. Only on the inside. I dared not vent at God for fear he would not answer my prayers for healing.

As though God could not read my heart.

I began to study Job again. If God's scriptures contained a book about suffering that proved useless when it really mattered, what did that say about God? What did that say about the rest of the Bible that he claimed to be author of?

I started studying Job again, but this time I was not preparing a sermon. This time I was preparing a case. A case for faith. Or against it.

I decided early on not to accept platitudes or a whitewash. I went back to that bookstore and bought that immensely dry translator's handbook, the one I had avoided the first time. I dug out Green's nineteenth-century text, and I started buying a heavier class of commentaries. I wanted the truth.

9
FINDING THE TRUTH

IN MY SECOND study through Job, I discovered something I had missed the first time, something that did not require a handbook or commentary to learn. It just needed a reader who was paying attention. Let's read this next bit carefully.

> ³*And the Lord said to Satan, "Have you considered my servant Job, that there is none like him on the earth, a blameless and upright man, who fears God and turns away from evil? He still holds fast his integrity, although you incited me against him to destroy him without reason."*
>
> JOB 2:3

From God's own mouth came an acceptance of responsibility. And then again, at the end of Job, there comes a similar statement from the narrator:

> *[Job's friends and family] showed him sympathy and comforted him for all the evil that the Lord had brought upon him.*
>
> JOB 42:11B

Satan is the enemy, but at no point did God shirk responsibility. The Bible itself says that God was "incited... to destroy [Job] without reason" and that it was God who had brought "all the evil" upon him. I did not need to challenge God on this point. He had already acknowledged his role. Satan was the enemy, but God had allowed the events to happen as they did, and God never tried to hide his role.

Why? Why would God allow such terrible things to happen in the life of a very good person?

This is the central question the book of Job asks. The answer is not in chapter two, so we will have to move on in our study to learn more.

SATAN TURNS OUT TO BE A FRINGE CHARACTER

Another detail stood out to me as I studied through Job a second time: this is the last mention of Satan in the book of Job. The enemy vanishes seven verses into the second chapter, and the following forty-and-a-half chapters have nothing to do with him. Satan does not even appear at the end to be defeated or have his second theory pointedly dashed. Satan is gone. He does not matter. There are forty-two chapters in this book, and barely into the second chapter, he drops out of the text.

The book is not about the enemy. He was a catalyst to start something that God allowed, but the enemy never even gets a proper name, just a description, and then he exits the book just as the story barely gets going. If the book of Job were a movie, Satan's character would be gone right when the opening credits roll. By the end, you would have forgotten that he had even been involved at all.

Satan dug his own grave a bit deeper in his second assault on Job, and the puppet master turned out to have been a pawn in a larger plan. The enemy was a fringe character.

This is all very interesting, but it does not answer the question "why?" So let's keep going in our study.

THE SECOND TRIAL BEGINS

> *⁷So Satan went out from the presence of the Lord and struck Job with loathsome sores from the sole of his foot to the crown of his head. ⁸And he took a piece of broken pottery with which to scrape himself while he sat in the ashes.*

> ⁹Then his wife said to him, "Do you still hold fast your integrity? Curse God and die." ¹⁰But he said to her, "You speak as one of the foolish women would speak. Shall we receive good from God, and shall we not receive evil?" In all this Job did not sin with his lips.
>
> JOB 2:7–10

Job was now entirely in Satan's hands except for his actual life. Verse 2:7 describes how Satan took advantage of this free rein, and his chosen torment was "loathsome sores," which the Hebrew describes as "painful sores," head to toe. It is just one verse, and like the tragedies that unfold in chapter one, it's easy to miss the significance of this affliction. Since Satan had free rein regarding Job's health, we might guess that verse seven is not doing justice to the depth of Job's torment. However, the text does not provide a specific medical description, so how do we bring verse seven to life and try to understand it closely?

The book itself provides clues as Job later relates the extent of his affliction:

> "My flesh is clothed with worms and dirt;
> my skin hardens, then breaks out afresh."
>
> JOB 7:5

> "… I would choose strangling
> and death rather than my bones."
>
> JOB 7:15

> ²⁷"My inward parts are in turmoil and never still;
> days of affliction come to meet me.
> ²⁸I go about darkened, but not by the sun;
> I stand up in the assembly and cry for help.
> ²⁹I am a brother of jackals
> and a companion of ostriches.
> ³⁰My skin turns black and falls from me,
> and my bones burn with heat."
>
> JOB 30:27–30

In 19:17–20, Job describes himself as someone whose breath has become loathsome, who is detested by and revolting to friends, family, and even the community's (fatherless) children. He says that he has become nothing but, as the Hebrew describes it, "skin and bones" (Job 19:20).[18]

> [7] *"My eye has grown dim from vexation,*
> *and all my members are like a shadow."*
>
> JOB 17:7

The death of Job's children, the murder of his staff, and the theft or destruction of his property had been severe trials. This second trial involved physical torment, which took his ordeal one terrible step further. The burden Job carried was something that very few of us have ever experienced. Certainly, his pain was beyond my own limited experiences.

It is important to remember that Job had no modern medications to blunt the impact of each of these blows; there were no physicians with salves or drugs to ease his physical pain, no psychiatrists available to prescribe a narcotic or antidepressant.

Job went on to describe what he was experiencing further:

> [4]*"When I lie down I say, 'When shall I arise?'*
> *But the night is long,*
> *and I am full of tossing till the dawn.*
> [5]*My flesh is clothed with worms and dirt;*
> *my skin hardens, then breaks out afresh."*
>
> JOB 7:4–5

Job's body was covered with worms and dirt, or as the NIV more accurately translates it, "worms and scabs." His skin was broken and festering, blackened with disease, peeling and feverish. We can add insomnia to Job's list of torments. He was not even granted the once-a-night comfort and relief of sleep to help ease the passage of time.

How did Job possibly endure all this?

---

18 NIV translation.

EMOTIONAL ENDURANCE VERSUS INTEGRITY

Job's wife questioned his endurance as well.

> *⁹Then his wife said to him, "Do you still hold fast your integrity? Curse God and die."*
>
> JOB 2:9

First, let's unpack the implications of what she said. People do not simply decide to die. You cannot "curse God and die" in the same way you can curse God and then fall asleep.

Job's wife also did not tell her husband to prepare to die because it was evident that he would linger and suffer for a long time. His death would not happen on its own.

This is where the first sentence about Job holding on to his integrity comes in. The only way for Job to die was for him to let go of his integrity—and kill himself. His suffering was so severe, the compounding of emotional and physical pain so intense, that Job's wife counseled him to end it all. She did not explicitly say suicide, but that would have been Job's only way to follow her advice.

But to choose suicide would require Job to turn his back on his core convictions, to surrender his integrity and defy God—effectively, to curse God, to say goodbye to God. This is the result that Satan had been aiming for all along: not Job's death but Job's separation from God.

That is the practical, factual view of what Job's wife said, but there was also a deeply emotional component to her statement. Job's wife had friends among those hundreds of widows. She knew children among those hundreds who were now fatherless. Perhaps she had attended their births. Some of the younger men killed in the fields may have been second-generation servants and may have once been her children's playmates. Her ten children had been killed and perhaps her grandchildren as well. She carried, gave birth to, nursed, and raised every one of those ten children and had likely been involved in the birth of grandchildren as well. She appears to have kept herself together through all this, and only when her husband was afflicted did she finally crack. Only then did she talk "like a foolish woman" (2:10) by counseling her husband to say goodbye to God and die.

Job's wife did not know about the heavenly conversation between Satan and God. All she knew was that her husband was consumed with unrelieved torment, and she wanted it to end—even if that meant his death.

Her statements were wrong, and they played into Satan's hands, but can we withhold judgment on a mother, grandmother, and wife who was enduring agony and spoke emotionally in a crisis? I think we can. God did: Job's friends get in trouble at the end of the book, but Job's wife does not.

COUNTERING VOLATILE EMOTION

Here is how Job responded to his wife:

> *[10]But he said to her, "You speak as one of the foolish women would speak. Shall we receive good from God, and shall we not receive evil?"*
>
> *In all this Job did not sin with his lips.*
>
> JOB 2:10

Job's response was rooted in his convictions and was a blend of perspective and correction: "Shall we receive good from God, and shall we not receive evil?" In other words, should we only accept from God the things we like?

Job's integrity was not conditional as Satan had charged. Circumstances put that integrity under stress, but they did not redefine it. As God himself had said, Job was "blameless and upright," he "feared God and turned away from evil" (Job 1:8). This was not a cover or a social posture he adopted for the public. This was who he was.

TRUTH EXPOSED THROUGH CRISIS

A crisis is, among other things, an opportunity to test what is true. We can have all sorts of opinions about ourselves, our character, or our relationships, but a crisis is an opportunity to test the truth of those beliefs.

In the New Testament, we get this advice:

> *²Count it all joy, my brothers, when you meet trials of various kinds, ³for you know that the testing of your faith produces steadfastness. ⁴And let steadfastness have its full effect, that you may be perfect and complete, lacking in nothing.*
>
> JAMES 1:2–4

Hebrews 12:4–13 is another instructive passage on the positive side of difficulty.

So what did Job go through early in life to shape his character and help him develop such perseverance that he could withstand these assaults on his family, community, finances, and even his own body and still hold on to his integrity?

The Bible is silent on Job's journey to steadfast faith before chapter one, but it is safe to say that Job was not born with this strength. Stuff happened. David learned to be a warrior by shepherding sheep and fighting off wild animals as a boy. He learned to be a king by leading a band of rogues through the wilderness for a decade.

Even Jesus, the Son of God, the Messiah himself, learned through suffering.[19]

The odds are that Job learned the same way everyone else learns. He will learn even more through these forty-two chapters of Job, but he passed the test for now.

> *In all this Job did not sin with his lips.*
>
> JOB 2:10B

It does not say that he did not sin at all. It just says that Job did not sin in what he said. He did not sin by saying what Satan expected him to, by cursing God as his wife had counseled him to. He did not say goodbye to God.

---
19 See Hebrews 5:7–10.

10

THE FIRST SIX MONTHS

MACKENZIE WAS BORN in early February. By the end of February, we had checked into a total of four hospitals (the three described above, plus Burnaby Hospital where Mackenzie was born). We spent more days and nights living out of the parents' fridges outside the various nurses' stations than we did in our own home.

From that first night in the very public ward of New Westminster's pediatric unit, things seemed to slide from bad to worse. We transferred to a private room, but not for good reasons. Our daughter was rated too fragile to risk exposure to the bugs that might be circulating in the more open ward. Surgical-style cap-and-gown outerwear became mandatory. Enteric isolation protocols were put in place. So started what became our daughter's first year of learning to relate to people: mommy and daddy and nana wore caps and gowns but were otherwise normal; everyone else also wore caps and gowns but came bearing tubes and stethoscopes and needles. Other visitors were not permitted. She learned to fear everyone except mommy and daddy and nana.

There were needles, tests, X-rays, head ultrasound, and all manner of pokes, prods, and questions in New Westminster. My vacation time ran out and I returned to work. We stayed in the hospital in New Westminster for just over a week, but it felt like a month.

Through March and April, Mackenzie continued to lose weight and was in and out of the hospital. For three months after she was born, the weight loss continued despite IV lines and tube feeds until we could count all of her ribs and vertebrae.

In May of 2001, fearing that she would not live until the end of the year, we were readmitted to BC Children's Hospital and commenced new tests: MRI, CT scan, several spinal taps, barium swallow X-rays, biochemical studies. My wife stayed weekdays at the hospital around the clock, sleeping in a cot in Mackenzie's room. On the weekends, I stayed at the hospital so my wife could go home and sleep. We started becoming strangers to one another. Like our daughter's body, our marriage ate through its fat until we, too, were living off of lean tissue. We traded shifts and survived. I dare say that we got to the point where we did not even like each other that much. We were each other's necessary support in the mission to care for our child, but we were also each other's stress-inducing source of the daily shift-change update and a reminder of the shared life and shared dreams that were unraveling in front of us.

We were in Vancouver, on Canada's west coast. Carolyn's family lived in Ontario, over halfway across the country. My family was in Pennsylvania. Both of our families visited, and friends came and went. One thing, however, became clear: no one could release us from the tunnel-like trap we were in. This was our road to walk. Others were occasional walking companions, but for us, this was not a visit. This was now our life.

THREE THINGS ABOUT THREE FRIENDS

Job had walking companions as well: three friends. Actually, he had four, the last only revealing himself toward the end of the book, but the book's initial focus is on just the first three friends: Eliphaz, Bildad, and Zophar.

> [11]*Now when Job's three friends heard of all this evil that had come upon him, they came each from his own place, Eliphaz the Temanite, Bildad the Shuhite, and Zophar the Naamathite. They made an appointment together to come to show him sympathy and comfort him.* [12]*And when they saw him from a distance, they did not recognize him. And they raised their voices and wept, and they tore their robes and sprinkled dust on their heads toward heaven.* [13]*And they sat with him on the*

ground seven days and seven nights, and no one spoke a word to him, for they saw that his suffering was very great.

JOB 2:11–13

These three friends get rough treatment in most commentaries and for good reasons. They also get lumped together as though their thoughts and ideas were identical. That is a mistake. We will get to know each of these men through our study, but it is sufficient to understand a couple of main points for now.

First, these men heard about Job's troubles, and they made a plan together. They were Job's friends. Whatever critiques we might give these men for their words in the coming chapters, they were Job's friends, and they came together with good intentions.

Second, they came to sympathize with Job. The Hebrew word here literally means to "rock back and forth" or "shake."[20] They didn't just come to give Job a shoulder to cry on. They came to cry with Job. They came not just to witness his pain but to feel it with him. They were his friends.

Third, they came to comfort him. The word that the text translates as "comfort" is a word that could be better translated as "repent" or "change his mind."[21] They came to help Job repent or turn away from his pain and grief. In plain English, we might say that "they came to fix it." Many men (and likely many women, too) have difficulty letting trouble be trouble and giving hard emotions space to work themselves out. When faced with trouble, there is something in guys that wants to fix it—in fact, seemingly must try to fix it—or he's not a man. That's how it often feels anyway.

Job's friends came to feel his pain, and they came to make it go away as well. That was the mission they mutually agreed to. So far, they seem like pretty good guys, and on a regular day, with no particular drama to address, they were probably excellent friends.

A crisis, however, touches more than just the person who is at the center of the crisis. It has a ripple effect on other relationships as well. Learning how to handle that ripple effect is one of the many lessons that the book of Job offers and is one we will continue to explore as we work our way through his story.

---

20 Reyburn, 63-64 with Janzen, 56.

21 Janzen, 57.

FRIENDS ALSO HURT

Before we move on, let's consider the torn clothes in verse twelve. Like Job's torn clothes, his friends tearing their clothes was a deep expression of pain and grief. They came to sympathize with him, to "rock back and forth." To "shake." When they saw him, they hardly recognized him, they felt his pain, and they expressed it with the same torn clothes, their culturally relevant expression of deep pain and grief. They did not shave their heads, but they did sprinkle dust over themselves. This is similar to Job sitting among the ashes in verse eight.

They were also silent for seven days. They came to fix things for Job, but they were either speechless for the first week in the face of Job's tragedy and deep sorrow, or they were very patient men who were waiting until Job appeared capable of engaging in a conversation.

During the weeks checking in and out of various hospitals from February to April in 2001, finally moving into BC Children's Hospital for May, we had friends that were with us nearly every day. They brought food; they watched at the bedside while my wife went out for a walk to cry and clear her head in fresh air; they even did our laundry—anything to serve.

We also had other close friends that we did not see for six months; perhaps they did not know what to do and hid. Others expressed a candid paranoia of hospitals and would not come around. Various behaviors manifested. Some friends' responses were predictable. Others surprised us as their deeper characters—some wonderful, some questionable—were revealed.

Yet another lesson in Job is how to help (and how not to help) someone in a crisis. We can learn from Job. But we can also learn from his three friends and from his fourth friend, who later offers a wise and better example to emulate. And, of course, the book wraps up with God himself addressing Job. But without thoroughly understanding the context of the conversations that lead up to God's speeches, it's easy to misunderstand those final divine words.

So we will be patient for now. We will look at Job's extended speech in chapter three, then Eliphaz's response in chapter four, and so on, making our way carefully through the book as it unveils what it has to offer.

11

A LITERARY DETOUR

BEFORE MOVING FURTHER into the book of Job or into my own story, we need to take a brief detour and talk about something unusual. I'll need you to bear with me for a bit while we explore literary elements of Job that will become critical to our understanding of this ancient book.

Here's a point that should be obvious: Job was not originally written in English but rather in ancient Hebrew.

If you have ever read through the entire book, here is another point that should also be very obvious: chapters one, two, and forty-two are prose; the rest of the book, except for a sentence here or there, is poetry.

So the book was originally written in ancient Hebrew, it begins and ends in prose, and the thirty-nine chapters in the middle are poetry. So far, so good.

Here is what might not be so obvious: ancient Hebrew poetry is not modern English poetry. By that, I mean that the way their poetry works is different.

We have already talked about how culture shapes what methods of grieving seem natural to an individual. Culture shapes other subjective tastes as well, including food preferences, clothing styles, and even the form of that culture's poetry.

There are, however, universals even within cultural differences. While different cultures have different grieving practices, the end purpose is the same: to deal with pain and loss. Likewise, one culture may include a great deal of spice in their recipes, and another culture may tilt toward simpler fare, but the purpose remains to satisfy hunger, sustain oneself, and perhaps socialize around a shared meal.

Poetry also has a fantastic variety of forms and styles, but it likewise has universal components. Universally, poetry is a form of communication that uses elevated language to evoke emotion. Prose—the literary term for ordinary writing—can evoke emotion too, but it tends to use more common language, and its primary purpose is usually to communicate ideas rather than evoke emotion.

If you have ever read Job cover to cover and felt like it was dry, that is why—you missed the poem's emotional impact. If you don't pick up on the poem's emotional resonance, you're missing an incredibly important part of the book of Job. It is mostly poetry. It is mostly about eliciting an emotional response. Emotion is not a side component of poetry; it is the point of poetry.

TRANSLATION COMPLICATIONS

Now that we've briefly discussed the difference between poetry and prose, let's quickly look at the unique challenges in translating poetry.

You might already be familiar with the challenges of translating prose: do you translate for each word's literal meaning or each phrase's practical meaning?

Let's use an easy example that comes up frequently in scripture. Where is the seat of emotions? In English, we think of the heart as the symbolic seat of emotions. Hearts get broken. They ache. They overflow, or they burst. They melt. When we're anxious or excited or scared, our heart beats faster.

For the ancient Hebrews, the stomach was the seat of emotion. There is a sensual logic to this: when you're nervous, you get "butterflies in your stomach." When you're really anxious, you might even get nauseous. A full stomach makes you feel good. An empty stomach might make you feel bad or impatient or even angry. When psyching ourselves up for a challenge, we might unconsciously suck in our stomach. In ancient Hebrew culture, the stomach represented the seat of emotion.

So when the Hebrew Bible talks about the stomach being deceitful, do we translate it literally? If we do, we might mislead modern readers into thinking that the passage is about literal hunger or illness. But when we understand that the stomach was the seat of emotion to the original audience, we know what the Bible is saying. "The stomach is being deceitful" means that our feelings are deceiving us. Having deceptive feelings, rather than a deceptive stomach, is an entirely different idea to a modern audience. So how do we translate it? A literal, word-for-word translation is guaranteed to mislead the reader. So do we translate the meaning only and say "emotions are deceitful"? Or do we keep the imagery and translate it as "the heart is deceitful"? The latter is the most common choice in English Bibles.

Either way, the translators have chosen to aim not for a word-for-word translation but for an idea-for-idea translation. But in some cases, a word-for-word translation is critical for maintaining an idea's essential nuance. For example, some passages are deliberately ambiguous and layered with multiple potential meanings. If the translator takes the idea-for-idea route, then they need to decide which potential meaning to translate and which idea to leave behind. An English reader would then never realize that the verse could have multiple meanings.

Those are the challenges with translating prose.

Translating poetry has yet another layer of difficulty. Not only is there tension between word-for-word and idea-for-idea meaning, but the translation also needs to capture the poem's emotion. And adding a footnote stage direction that says "this next paragraph should make you feel happy" or "the next one will make you feel sad" won't cut it. That's because poetry communicates emotion not through plain statements but through specific poetic techniques, through things like meaning, sound, and rhythm. As a result, poetry translators also need to contend with translating poetic-effect-for-poetic-effect. The best translation for poetic effect might be at odds with both the exact words and the exact meaning.

So poetry translators have to balance the competing demands of word-for-word, idea-for-idea, and poetic-effect-for-poetic-effect translation. And the odds are that the translator is never going to satisfy all three concerns with one translation.

Translating ancient poetry is an impossible task to do perfectly.

So we have some barriers to grasping the poetry in Job. It is never going to ring the same way in English as it does in ancient Hebrew. Poetry is universal, but poetic styles are not.

ANCIENT HEBREW POETRY

English poetry often uses rhyme, rhythm, biblical, and other literary allusions, the visual arrangement of the words on the page, punctuation, and sometimes even capitalization, boldface, or italics to help create an emotional effect. Ancient Hebrew operates differently.

So how does ancient Hebrew poetry work?

The first thing that stands out is that, while it does rely on rhymes, it does not rhyme words. Rather, it rhymes ideas. Scholars call this parallelism. The poem says one thing. Then it repeats the same thing in a different way. There is usually a subtle shift in the second phrase. The idea's scope becomes bigger or smaller, the meaning sharper or broader. There is repetition—the ideas rhyme—but there is also direction. The ideas rhyme and they point in a direction. Most of the verses in the book of Proverbs are ancient Hebrew couplets, which are two lines of poetry bound by some parallel structure. Whereas English poetic couplets usually rhyme sounds, Hebrew poetic couplets rhyme ideas.

Ancient Hebrew poetry also uses other devices. Acrostics, heptads, double heptads, chiastic structures, even puns. Don't worry if you don't know what these words mean. As required, I'll explain how they work later as we get to them in the text. The most important thing to remember as we start reading the poetry in Job is that ancient Hebrew poetry rhymes ideas. This is not about boring repetition—it is an emotional technique. We are going to learn to feel it as we go.

This will take a little bit of work, but it will be worth it! This is not just another sonnet or haiku. This is a poem God wrote.

Let's go.

12

CURSING A BIRTH

Job chapter three opens with some tough material.

> ^{1}*After this Job opened his mouth and cursed the day of his birth.*
> ^{2}*And Job said:*[22]
> ^{3}*"Let the day perish on which I was born,*
>   *and the night that said,*
>   *'A man is conceived.'*
> ^{4}*Let that day be darkness!*
>   *May God above not seek it,*
>   *nor light shine upon it.*
> ^{5}*Let gloom and deep darkness claim it.*
>   *Let clouds dwell upon it;*
>   *let the blackness of the day terrify it.*
> ^{6}*That night—let thick darkness seize it!*
>   *Let it not rejoice among the days of the year;*
>   *let it not come into the number of the months.*
> ^{7}*Behold, let that night be barren;*
>   *let no joyful cry enter it.*
> ^{8}*Let those curse it who curse the day,*
>   *who are ready to rouse up Leviathan.*[23]

---

22 In the original Hebrew, this is the shortest verse in the Bible. Pure trivia.

23 The phrase "those . . . who are ready to rouse up Leviathan" means "those who are

> ^{9}Let the stars of its dawn be dark;
>> let it hope for light, but have none,
>> nor see the eyelids of the morning,
> ^{10}because it did not shut the doors of my mother's womb,
>> nor hide trouble from my eyes."
>
> JOB 3:1–10

Did you notice that word "cursed" in 3:1 again? This is a different word than the one we defined previously as "bid adieu" or "say goodbye." The Hebrew word found here in chapter three means exactly what it says in English: cursed. Job is so angry with his very existence that he wishes he had never been born.

CURSING A PARTICULAR NIGHT OF SEX

The very first thing Job does is curse the day of his birth. Then in the following parallel line, he curses the night that his parents had sex and conceived him. Some modern English translators seem to get squeamish when discussing sex and obscure the reference to conception that opens this chapter. They instead translate the verse as though Job only refers to his birth throughout the chapter. But Job does discuss his conception, and he makes a distinction between conception and birth. The phrase "the day" in this chapter refers to his birth, and the phrase "the night" refers to his conception. Let's see how this parallel imagery unfolds by reading those verses again.

> ^{4}"Let that day be darkness!
>> May God above not seek it,
>> nor light shine upon it.
> ^{5}Let gloom and deep darkness claim it.
>> Let clouds dwell upon it;
>> let the blackness of the day terrify it."
>
> JOB 3:4–5

---

ready to call up a monster." In this verse, Job is calling people who have the will to summon monsters to curse the day of his birth. The emotion Job is communicating here is a no-holds-barred intensity in the service of his pain-fueled curse.

As we have discussed, Hebrew poetry rhymes ideas, not sounds. Job's thoughts progress from darkness to God not caring, from no light to darkness again—then come shadow, clouds, and finally blackness. These two verses present one idea: the image of a progressively gloomy, oppressive, deepening, darkening deadness that Job wishes on the day of his birth. It is emotional language.

If this were a movie, we would hear a progressively gloomier soundtrack in the background. Layers of darkness accumulate in this cursed picture. Job did not sit on the ground with his friends, silent, for seven days and seven nights, static. His grief grew.

Job said:

> *⁶"That night—let thick darkness seize it!*
> *Let it not rejoice among the days of the year;*
> *let it not come into the number of the months"*

JOB 3:6

Job wanted the date his parents had sex and conceived him identified and then stricken from the calendar. There is a specificity and intensity here that is startling.

He went on:

> *⁷"Behold, let that night be barren;*
> *let no joyful cry enter it."*

JOB 3:7

What joyful cry? The joyful cry when he was born? No. Job is talking about the night of his conception. What had happened that night? His parents had made love and conceived him. "No more!" Job shouts. Not just his parents, but no one. Remove that night from the calendar. Let there never again be shouts of joyful consummation on that night.

Many of our modern translations are very modest. The Bible, in its original language, is not always so subtle. In the Bible, sex is described as potentially joyously loud! But Job wants an end to that—not because of sudden new modesty but because his life has become too painful. He is striking back at every good thing associated with his conception and birth, and he is incredibly specific as he does so.

Just listen to his phrasing here:

> ^{8}*"Let those curse it who curse the day,*
> *who are ready to rouse up Leviathan.*
> ^{9}*Let the stars of its dawn be dark;*
> *let it hope for light, but have none,*
> *nor see the eyelids of the morning,*
> ^{10}*because it did not shut the doors of my mother's womb,*[24]
> *nor hide trouble from my eyes."*
>
> JOB 3:8–10

WISHING FOR NON-EXISTENCE

We talked previously about the artificial pressure Christians can place on themselves to maintain a happy exterior in the face of true tragedies. We talked about this when we explored Job 1:20 and the meaning behind Job's torn clothes and shaved head. We looked to David and Ezekiel and even Jesus to see that an artificial calm is not a scriptural expectation. People in the Bible experienced life in all its ups and downs and felt deeply about those things. Even Jesus's experiences deeply affected him. It is okay to admit to your emotions and even express them openly in response to intense life events.

Job experienced far more tragedy than most of us ever will, and he did not maintain an artificial calm but rather openly expressed his feelings with a deep emotional intensity.

He uses this kind of language:

> ^{11}*"Why did I not die at birth,*
> *come out from the womb and expire?*

---

[24] The reference here is not to a closed womb that would have prevented Job's birth–that would have been a curse upon Job's mother! The phraseology is also found in Genesis 29:31–32, 1 Samuel 1:6, and elsewhere and is a reference to conception. Job is cursing the day of his birth for not having, retroactively, prevented his conception to begin with.

> *¹²Why did the knees receive me?*
>   *Or why the breasts, that I should nurse?*
> *¹³For then I would have lain down and been quiet;*
>   *I would have slept; then I would have been at rest,*
> *¹⁴with kings and counselors of the earth*
>   *who rebuilt ruins for themselves,*
> *¹⁵or with princes who had gold,*
>   *who filled their houses with silver."*
>
> JOB 3:11–15

Suicide rarely comes up in the Bible as an issue for theological debate. In 2:9, Job's wife had counseled him to die, implying that suicide was an option, and Job had shut down that line of thought very quickly. But his underlying desire for an absolute escape was real. Job was beyond looking for happiness to replace his pain. With his emotions and body pushed to extremes, Job only found comfort in the idea of nonexistence. He desired not good things but the cessation of bad things.

THOUGHTS OF SUICIDE

I had many days and nights where I drove from our house to work in the morning, to hospital in the evening, and then back to the house at night, where I felt the pressure relentlessly build. The usual new-parent insecurities, the work and commute stress, and the pain of a good marriage starting to unravel all added to the swelling panic of a parent slowly losing their child. I was not equipped to bear these things.

When Mackenzie was just a few months old, during a brief leave from hospitals when we had her at home, while she was still losing weight but not yet checked into BC Children's Hospital for our first extended stay, the three of us visited our friends Ray and Stephanie. It was after church. Carolyn was still nursing. The women went to a side room so Carolyn could nurse, and the guys hung out in the living room. These brief times of friendship and normality were precious.

Partway through nursing, Carolyn suddenly stopped, took Mackenzie, and handed her to Stephanie. Stephanie later reported that "I don't feel well" were my wife's last words before she began to convulse. Carolyn slipped straight into a full grand mal seizure.[25] The house filled with shouting, Stephanie called for help, somebody got an ambulance on its way, and we took turns holding my wife as still as possible to protect her head and keep her from hurting herself. Waves of confusion and panic swept everyone present.

Eventually, Carolyn calmed down and stopped seizing. She tried to talk, but then another wave of seizures overran her. She seized three times before the paramedics came. When they arrived, they got her under control, onto a gurney, down the stairs, and into the ambulance.

In the ambulance, Carolyn began to seize and black out again. In the emergency room, the full-body seizures eased, but over the next twelve hours, she kept suddenly blacking out mid-sentence, mid-breath, remaining unconscious for a minute or five or ten before coming around again as though nothing had happened. It was like someone was constantly blowing a circuit breaker or toggling a light switch. She would talk, scared, not knowing what was going on, and then suddenly, mid-sentence, drop in the bed, limp, lights out, no warning. It would have been funny if it hadn't been so deadly serious. She blacked out thirty or forty times throughout the rest of the day and into the night. We slept fitfully in the emergency room that night. There were no beds available in the regular ward. As a result, Carolyn spent the night on her gurney. I sat in a white plastic chair beside the bed with Mackenzie strapped into a car seat in front of me. It was a long night. Eighteen inches away, on the other side of a curtain, an elderly man had a prolonged heart attack. On the other side of us, a younger man with a drug overdose was pumped and resuscitated. Hundreds of deadly dramas intersect in an emergency room every day and every night, and that night it seemed that they all swirled around my wife's bed and our weakening, skeletal baby.

Late that night, with Carolyn sleeping in her bed, curtain drawn for privacy, the bed's bars up and padded waist strap in place for her protection, Mackenzie on the floor buckled into her car seat, also sleeping, I went looking for the ER doctor for answers. They had done a variety of tests and scans already. The final diagnosis was still pending, but the symptoms read as either a brain tumor or a series of multiple escalating strokes. My wife was thirty-one years old. My daughter was less than three months old. My world

---

25 We later learned that grand mal is outdated terminology. Tonic-clonic is the modern language for this type of seizure.

was already on a downhill slide, and this day felt like a fatality at a funeral. How could this be added to what we were already dealing with?

The next day, Carolyn was checked into a room with Mackenzie as her roommate. Over the next few days, I was told to brace myself. There was a good chance I was going to lose both my wife and my child, but the reasons for the approaching losses were still unclear. Neither my wife nor my daughter could be explained, but they were both leaving me.

My vacation time had been long used up. I called Human Resources the next day to talk about a Leave of Absence. At the time, Personal Leaves of Absence were unpaid. Stress Leaves were, however, covered by the Disability Plan. Personal Leaves were rare and impractical (who could afford them?), and Stress Leaves were a career death sentence. Times have changed, but they had not yet changed then. I could not afford an unpaid Personal Leave, and though any doctor in the country would have written me a prescription for a Medical Stress Leave, I didn't dare take that option. I was starting to look like the only breadwinner for our family for years to come, and I could not afford to lose the paycheck. I asked HR for options with tears in my eyes and was informed over the phone that if my wife died, I would get three days of Bereavement Leave. If my daughter died as well, I could get another three days for a total of six. I was wished well. It was unclear whether "well" meant my family's survival and the extension of my endurance test, or if "well" meant their deaths and the resulting six extra days off. She wished me well, and I silently wished her—not well. I hung up the phone in my brokerage office with my door closed, clients outside demanding better service, and my hands shaking.

Suicide was not an option. But I thought about it.

There is a stretch of Highway 99 approaching Vancouver from the south that I took every day on the way from my office to the hospital. There are a couple of overpasses supported by thick concrete columns that at the time were unshielded by impact absorption barriers. A slight turn of the wheel and a driver could hit that thick concrete at a speed of their choosing. Our old car didn't have airbags. It would have been over very quickly. I thought about it every time I passed those concrete solutions. I kept the steering wheel straight, but I thought about it.

JOB'S ALTERNATIVE TO SUICIDE

Suicide was a genuine temptation but not an option.

Job knew that. But he thought about alternatives that would have achieved the same result. If suicide was out, regretting that he had not been a stillborn baby was in. He describes how, in contrast to his current miserable state, he would be "at rest with kings and counselors of the earth."

> *^{16}"Or why was I not as a hidden stillborn child,*
> *as infants who never see the light?*
> *^{17}There the wicked cease from troubling,*
> *and there the weary are at rest.*
> *^{18}There the prisoners are at ease together;*
> *they hear not the voice of the taskmaster.*
> *^{19}The small and the great are there,*
> *and the slave is free from his master."*
>
> JOB 3:16–19

When life becomes intolerable, a natural death can start to look like peace. There is peace beyond the grave for a Christian, but the theology of Job's day did not provide insight into either heaven or eternity. The Christian's peace is not the peace that Job was talking about. Death in Job's day was the cessation of life with nothing to come after it. It was eternal sleep, and in this respect, the rich and poor, the wicked, the slave, the small and the great were all equally at rest in the grave.

This first speech foreshadows an important theme of the book of Job. The issue of eternity is going to come up again later. This discussion on eternity will shape one of the two major turning points in Job's understanding of God and theology. Still, in the current context, Job's outburst is one of simple pain and frank acknowledgment that his grief and torment have gone beyond looking for a cure—now, he only wants the simple escape afforded to the dead. The extension of life to those in misery gnaws at Job. It seems to Job that even the wicked have peace in the grave.

JOB'S COMPLAINT ABOUT LIGHT (AND LIFE)

So why is life prolonged for those who are good, who are suffering, and who understand that it is not an option to take matters into their own hands and end their own lives?

That is the question Job asked next.

> [20] *"Why is light given to him who is in misery,*
> *and life to the bitter in soul,*[26]
> [21] *who long for death, but it comes not,*
> *and dig for it more than for hidden treasures,*
> [22] *who rejoice exceedingly*
> *and are glad when they find the grave?*
> [23] *Why is light given to a man whose way is hidden,*
> *whom God has hedged in?*
> [24] *For my sighing comes instead of my bread,*
> *and my groanings are poured out like water.*
> [25] *For the thing that I fear comes upon me,*
> *and what I dread befalls me.*
> [26] *I am not at ease, nor am I quiet;*
> *I have no rest, but trouble comes."*
>
> JOB 3:20–26

I would like to say that I clung to Job's words and that his honesty was my heart during those early tormented months. Why did I have to live with this unrelenting fear and pressure, this nonstop mix of hospital procedures, commuting, a mugging, false diagnoses, work stresses in a declining eco-

---

[26] This is one of those poetic phrases that forces a translator to make choices that rob the passage of some of its full poetic feeling. The word here translated as "soul" can, in the original Hebrew, also mean throat, breath, appetite, desire, or life. Clearly the translator had to choose one of the meanings, and the choice of soul is a reasonable solution. The original, however, would have captured these alternate meanings so that the reader would not only understand the emotional intent of the phrase—the bitterness of a soul unhappy with life—but also recognize the visceral taste embedded in the phrase as Job described the bitterness as something he can even taste—life given to those who are bitter in throat, bitter in desire, bitter in appetite. Life had left him with an emotional hurt so intense he could taste its bitterness.

nomic cycle, my daughter's deterioration, a burst water heater, car troubles, bills piling up, taxes due, my wife's collapse and hospitalization, normal life events like the flu, another round of medical procedures while I lost track of whether it was my daughter or my wife that was the needle recipient, the test subject, the subject of the bad news discussion? Why was life prolonged, like smelling salts applied to a torture victim to keep them alert for the next procedure? Why was there suddenly no peace, no quietness, no rest, only trouble and the expectation that what was coming was yet more trouble?

Job's words were perhaps in my wordless heart, but I had not yet learned to acknowledge and own them. I did not vocalize them. I bottled them like acid. From February through August, I bottled the emotion, following, it turns out, the false theology of Eliphaz, the first friend to respond to Job's outburst. But we will get to Eliphaz in the next chapter. In the meantime, there are a couple of additional details hiding in Job's speech that are worth considering.

In 3:20, Job asked, "Why is light given to him who is in misery?" It is a legitimate question, but its phrasing in most modern translations comes across as somewhat impersonal. It sounds like a philosophical question. Why is light, as a concept of physics, made available? Actually, it is a very personal question with an embedded theological challenge. The Hebrew does not read "why is light given," hiding who the giver is with a passive voice construction. Instead, the Hebrew reads, "Why does he give light to those in misery?" Why does God give light to those in misery? Job is not talking about generic physics. Job is talking about God. His speech is what English majors would call a soliloquy. It is a speech addressed to no audience in particular. But it is a speech that specifically addresses God's role in the world. Why does God give light to those in misery?

Genesis 1:3 reads that "God said, 'Let there be light,' and there was light." In Job 3:1, Job cursed his birth and conception. We find the details of that curse a few verses later:

> ⁴*"Let that day be darkness!*
> *May God above not seek it,*
> *nor light shine upon it.*
> ⁵*Let gloom and deep darkness claim it.*

> *Let clouds dwell upon it;*
> *let the blackness of the day terrify it.*
> *⁶That night—let thick darkness seize it..."*
>
> Job 3:4–6a

Job's outburst here went beyond just expressing his pain, and it even went beyond just vocalizing the desire for a suicidal alternative. Job called for the undoing of God's first act of creation, if not on a global scale, then at the very least in Job's personal piece of that creation.

This, however, was only a wish, and one he knew God would not respond to, which is why he asked his question: Why did God create light and give it to those who God knows will only suffer within that light? Why did God create life itself only to give it to those who would taste bitterness and long for death? Why give something so amazing to someone whose life God himself would then hedge in?

These are good questions. They are legitimate questions. People get in trouble in the book of Job, but Job will not get in trouble for expressing real hurt and asking hard questions. The answers to these questions, however, are not found in this chapter either. So we must move on.

13

WHERE THINGS START TO GO WRONG

Have you ever argued and wondered later how the argument got started? In chapters four and five of the book of Job, we encounter the first speech from one of Job's friends, and in it, we find encapsulated the seeds for the argument that subsequently grows throughout the rest of the book.

Here is how it starts:

> *¹Then Eliphaz the Temanite[27] answered and said:*
> *²"If one ventures a word with you, will you be impatient?*

---

[27] Genesis 36:10–11 mentions an Eliphaz who had a son named Teman. They were the son and grandson of Esau, Jacob's brother. It is unlikely that the Eliphaz in Job is the same as in Genesis 36, in part because the text would probably not reference a man (Eliphaz) as belonging to a people named after his son (Teman). What is more likely is that Teman from Genesis 36 went on to found the settlement that was named after him and was located in the land of Edom, south of the Dead Sea. The subsequent residents of Teman would have been called Temanites. The Eliphaz we meet in the book of Job was one such Temanite who had been given the name of one of his early ancestors. A later passage in Genesis 36 mentions that Uz was another one of Esau's descendants, and Job is also from the land of Uz. We noted earlier that the book of Job is set before Moses's time, as Job was able to offer his own sacrifices. The place names in Job combined with Genesis 36 suggest that Job's story took place shortly after Esau's descendants had founded settlements and begun to multiply. In our attempt to date Job's story, that still leaves around a four-hundred-year window, roughly 1800 BC to 1400 BC, when the events in the book of Job could have taken place.

Even the Monsters

Yet who can keep from speaking?"

JOB 4:1–2

Eliphaz's initial statements appear very tentative. Job's lament was raw and volatile, and Eliphaz's hesitation is perfectly understandable. In Hebrew, his hesitation is even more apparent.

The ESV translation reads "If one ventures a word with you, will you be impatient?" Yet a more word-for-word translation of the Hebrew would read "If someone tries on a word with you, will you be able to bear it?"[28]

The idea of "trying on a word with you" is like someone trying on clothes to see if they fit. The same Hebrew phrase can be found in 1 Samuel 17:39 when David "tried on" Saul's armor. In that example, the garment David tried on most definitely did not fit. Eliphaz does not know whether his words will fit Job. Job's situation is intense, and his lament's candor makes his pain very clear, which in turn makes Eliphaz that much more uncertain.

At the beginning of his speech, Eliphaz was concerned that his words might not fit. He was also concerned that even if they do fit, Job may not bear what Eliphaz had to say. The truth hurts, and Eliphaz wondered if the truth might hurt too much. Eliphaz seems to have started on sound footing. He had come to sympathize with Job and comfort him in chapter two, and he spent a week in shocked silence upon seeing the depth of Job's trouble. Eliphaz's opening words expressed his uncertainty about how to proceed and whether Job was even capable of absorbing what he might say.

Have you ever had a friend dealing with a terrible loss or some other severe difficulty and been at a loss on how to help? There is much to learn in Job. There are deep theological mines to plumb in search of answers to some of the most intense questions in life, such as why good people suffer. What is God's role in suffering? How are we to endure in the face of events that make it appear that God has abandoned the innocent? There are also very practical, mundane things to learn in Job as well. There are important lessons on communication, on good and bad ways to help someone in trouble, on godly and ungodly ways of working through disagreements. This book offers many practical lessons.

From Eliphaz, we will learn a lot about how not to help someone going

---

28 Reyburn, 90=91.

through trouble. We will learn a lot about a common but false religiousness that colors many people's interpretations of hardship. Before we get into that, it will help if we do not pin Eliphaz up against the wall as the poster boy for "bad friend." Eliphaz did not want to be a bad friend. He had come to help. He had traveled far and spent more than a week in silent empathy, and his initial foray into trying to help poignantly expresses his insecurity about getting his words right.

Eliphaz continues his speech as follows:

> *³"Behold, you have instructed many,*
>   *and you have strengthened the weak hands.*
> *⁴Your words have upheld him who was stumbling,*
>   *and you have made firm the feeble knees."*
>
> Job 4:3–4

Listen carefully. You can hear Eliphaz feeling his way forward. He chose to start where the ground was solid: Job was a good guy. Job had been a strength and support to many people, a solid rock in the community. Eliphaz was not just blowing smoke here. God himself spoke highly of Job, and in chapter twenty-nine, we will hear in Job's own words how he served and supported those in need around him. He was the sort of person that commanded respect not by force but by kindness, by the life he lived and the positive impact he had on his community.

Eliphaz started his speech on solid ground, but then he added this next bit:

> *⁵"But now it [trouble] has come to you, and you are impatient;*
>   *it touches you, and you are dismayed.*
> *⁶Is not your fear of God your confidence,*
>   *and the integrity of your ways your hope?*
> *⁷Remember: who that was innocent ever perished?*
>   *Or where were the upright cut off?"*
>
> Job 4:5–7

If we had to pick a point where Eliphaz started to tilt in a direction that leads to trouble, this is it. Job was a pillar, a moral rock, and a beacon in his community. Do you know people like that? The person who is always reliable, who always gives, who always serves? Do you know someone whose marriage is fine, whose kids turn out okay, who serves on a school or church committee, who can be counted on to deliver meals to a sick friend or to support shelters for the homeless, or who otherwise makes doing good their life's work? Some people work hard to overcome selfishness and give to others. Others are naturally gifted at service or have worked hard to make it an area of strength. They are people without whom communities would be so much poorer.

Do you know people like that? And have you seen them fall into hard times or trouble, and suddenly the community they served is left at a loss? So-and-so always coordinated the efforts to meet the community's needs—and now so-and-so is down and the community does not have its leader and it throws the community off-balance. Many community servants have suffered double when trouble strikes them because the community they served fails to serve them back in their time of need. The reversed relationship forces social circles to realign, and sometimes that realignment is slow or inadequate.

Job was down, and not only was he down, but he was candid in his pain. The community pillar longed for death, lamented that he was ever born, and questioned why God gives life as a vehicle for suffering. He packed his speech with unsettling stuff, which is all the more unsettling coming from Job, the one who strengthened and supported others.

INTRODUCING THE STANDARD VIEW

Job's candid expression of pain unsettled Eliphaz. His unease over Job-the-rock being shaken caused him to encourage Job to look for confidence and hope despite the facts. "Who that was innocent ever perished?" Eliphaz asked, and the easy answer is Abel. And countless after him.

Eliphaz's statement was based on emotion and personal observation rather than divine revelation or objective fact. There is a common misconception that if people are good, good will flow to them, and if people are bad, they will reap bad things. This misconception was alive in Eliphaz's day, and it is certainly prevalent today. From national tragedies (natural disasters, wars, and economic collapses) to personal misfortune (career troubles, relationship difficulties, health concerns), people have a very real tendency to pin the cause for misfortune on the victim. It makes the world seem more orderly if we can find easy blame for trouble.

Here is how Eliphaz put it:

> *⁸"As I have seen, those who plow iniquity*
> *and sow trouble reap the same.*
> *⁹By the breath of God they perish,*
> *and by the blast of his anger they are consumed.*
> *¹⁰The roar of the lion, the voice of the fierce lion,*
> *the teeth of the young lions are broken.*
> *¹¹The strong lion perishes for lack of prey,*
> *and the cubs of the lioness are scattered."*
>
> JOB 4:8–11

"As I have seen"—those are fateful words. They are the words that well-meaning friends, relatives, preachers, and even political commentators the world over have spoken, and yet, really, how valuable are an individual's anecdotes? Suppose we limit our understanding of the world only to include that which we have experienced ourselves. Restricting our knowledge of the world to the pool of our own experiences—which is relatively small compared to the ocean of all human experience—is incredibly limiting. Our volume of experiences is limited, and our perspective and interpretations of them are limited as well.

I said earlier that if we had to pick a point where Eliphaz began to drift into trouble, this is it. He had formed a framework for interpreting Job's troubles, and the framework looked roughly like this:

- Good things happen to good people.
- Bad things happen to bad people.

The bad people might be really powerful. They might be as powerful as a lion, but God is more powerful than even a lion. No matter how scary—how lion-like—a bad person might be, and no matter how loud the bad person roars, God will break their teeth and starve out their pride. All this flows from the simple logic that:

- Good things happen to good people.
- Bad things happen to bad people.

For the sake of simplicity, we will call this the Standard View. This view has much support in the blessings and curses found in the book of Deuteronomy. Likewise, the prophets proclaim these general principles, and even in Jesus's words and Paul's letters, you see this reap-what-you-sow principle. It is comforting to expect just this kind of mathematical precision to shape justice in the world. In general, it is a very reliable principle: goodness produces good and evil produces evil. This is particularly true at the level of societies and nations.

But the book of Job is not about generalities or societies or nations. The book of Job is about trouble, at one specific time, in a particular person's life. And that person was a good soul. He did not deserve any of the trouble that came upon him. His case violates the principles of the Standard View. In Job's case, bad things happened to a good man, and his case is not unique. Many early Christians did not deserve to die horrific martyrs' deaths, but they died horribly just the same. Many innocent people were swept up in the Babylonian captivity of Jeremiah's day, and they were not guilty of the idolatry that led to the national disaster. Ezekiel and the heroes in the book of Daniel are just a few of the other examples of ill befalling good people in scripture. Many good people get debilitating or terminal illnesses or injuries or have car accidents or lose careers. This is not because of some latent sin but simply because we live in a fallen world where disease strikes, cars crash, and corporate decisions have real-life consequences. Many other unhappy events occur daily around the globe, and they cannot all be traced back to some fault of those suffering. An afternoon spent observing traffic in the local children's hospital should be all the evidence one needs to prove that the Standard View may be very true across a lifetime, as a principle for the outcome of society, as a statistical probability when applied to the majority of a large population, but it is not mathematically sound at the individual level. The numbers do not always add up. Cain murdered Abel, and there was no rationale or justification for it except to say that Cain was a sinner and committed a particularly terrible sin against his brother. No "blame Abel" spin applies to that tragic story.

The Standard View is simple.

The Standard View is too simple.

14

A MYSTERIOUS MESSENGER

FOR THOSE OF you who know the story of Job already, you know that Job's three friends become quite accusatory late into their speeches. They will insist that Job must be responsible for his trouble. But we're not quite to that stage in the dialogue between friends yet.

At this stage of the discussion, Eliphaz had not (yet) taken the Standard View's logic to its inevitable diagnostic conclusion. He had not (yet) tipped over into accusing Job of anything that would justify Job's sufferings. In future speeches, he will. But for now, he was still of the mindset that Job's piety and blameless ways should be the foundation of Job's confidence, and as Eliphaz will go on to relate, Job's present troubles must be just an aberration.

However, something interesting comes up in the next part of Eliphaz's speech that casts doubt on the validity of the Standard View. Eliphaz related a vision he had received in the night that contradicts with the Standard View, and he was honest enough to share its message.

It starts ominously:

> [12] *"Now a word was brought to me stealthily;*
> *my ear received the whisper of it.*
> [13] *Amid thoughts from visions of the night,*
> *when deep sleep falls on men,*
> [14] *dread came upon me, and trembling,*
> *which made all my bones shake.*
> [15] *A spirit glided past my face;*

> *the hair of my flesh stood up.*
> *¹⁶It stood still,*
> > *but I could not discern its appearance.*
> *A form was before my eyes;*
> > *there was silence, then I heard a voice…"*
>
> JOB 4:12–16

This is a spooky introduction, and the passage's poetic techniques serve to enhance the spooky effect. Recall our discussion on the unique qualities of Hebrew poetry, particularly regarding parallelism: ancient Hebrew poetry does not rhyme sounds. It rhymes ideas.

In the first line of verse twelve, it was a secret word that came to Eliphaz. It was brought "stealthily." There is something confidential and private about this word that is coming. In the second line, it was just a whisper that his ears caught. Both lines mean the same thing on the surface: Eliphaz received a message. But there is poetic movement from the specific (a stealthily delivered word) to the mysterious (a caught whisper).

Verse thirteen similarly moves from specificity to ominous mystery as the topic shifts from introducing the message to specifying the time of its arrival. Eliphaz described the message as having come in the night, and then he repeated the same idea in the next line in a more poetic rendering: "when deep sleep falls on men." This was a secret, mysteriously whispered message that came not just at night but in those magic hours of deepest sleep. There was a helplessness in Eliphaz's reception of this message. Like Scrooge's strange visitations in Charles Dickens's A Christmas Carol, Eliphaz received this ominous message from an uninvited and unidentified but already intimidating messenger at a time of great vulnerability.

Following this ominous introduction, there is no movement in verse fourteen. The parallelism is flat. Seized with fear and trembling, Eliphaz's bones shook. The poetry is deadpan to the ancient Hebrew ear, as jarring as an unrhymed stanza in a passage of Shakespearean poetry. It jumps out and startles the reader, underscoring the unsettling effect this uninvited messenger had on Eliphaz's nighttime slumber.

Eliphaz finally defined the messenger in verses fifteen and sixteen, but this definition did nothing to calm Eliphaz's unease. The word "spirit" used in verse fifteen can also be translated as "wind," and it is clearly in the feminine form. In other words, we could translate this verse one of two ways:

> *A spirit, she glided past my face*
> > *the hair of my flesh stood up.*

Or:

> *A wind, she glided past my face*
> > *and the hair of my flesh stood up.*

Either way, the effect for verse fifteen by itself is haunting. This wind/spirit heightened his fear. But the feminization of the wind/spirit has a deeper meaning when taken together with verse sixteen, which starts with "It stood still." It stood still. Not "she stood still." The word "it" in Hebrew is masculine. And so together, these verses read to the original Hebrew audience as follows:

> *A spirit, she glided past my face*
> > *and the hair of my flesh stood up.*
> *He stood still,*
> > *but I could not discern his appearance.*
> *A form was before my eyes;*
> > *Then there was silence, then I heard a voice…*

The spirit was a form. It was a voice coming stealthily, as a whisper, as a voice filling silence. It was a she. It was a he. Eliphaz could not tell what it was, but it had gotten his bones shaking and his hair standing on end. If there is a trivia category for "Most Gothic Passage in Scripture," this introduction by Eliphaz probably wins. It is a poetically charged introduction to a very serious message.

THE SPIRIT'S CONTRARY VIEW

Eliphaz went on to report this spirit's message:

> [17]*'Can mortal man be in the right before God?*
> > *Can a man be pure before his Maker?*
> [18]*Even in his servants he puts no trust,*

> *and his angels he charges with error;*
> ¹⁹*how much more those who dwell in houses of clay,*
> > *whose foundation is in the dust,*
> > *who are crushed like the moth.*
> ²⁰*Between morning and evening they are beaten to pieces;*
> > *they perish forever without anyone regarding it.*
> ²¹*Is not their tent-cord plucked up within them,*
> > *do they not die, and that without wisdom?'*
>
> ¹*"Call now; is there anyone who will answer you?*
> > *To which of the holy ones will you turn?*
> ²*Surely vexation kills the fool,*
> > *and jealousy slays the simple.*
> ³*I have seen the fool taking root,*
> > *but suddenly I cursed his dwelling.*
> ⁴*His children are far from safety;*
> > *they are crushed in the gate,*
> > *and there is no one to deliver them.*
> ⁵*The hungry eat his harvest,*
> > *and he takes it even out of thorns,*
> > *and the thirsty pant after his wealth.*
> ⁶*For affliction does not come from the dust,*
> > *nor does trouble sprout from the ground,*
> ⁷*but man is born to trouble*
> > *as the sparks fly upward."*

JOB 4:17–5:7

If you are a sharp observer of punctuation, you may have noticed that the spirit's quotation ends at 4:21. Some English translations abbreviate the quotation, allowing only 4:17 to be captured as a quote from the spirit. Other translations have different suggestions. Ancient Hebrew writing did not use quotation marks, so it is up to the reader to study a passage and determine what makes the most sense. With this in mind, extending the spirit's speech to encompass all of 4:12–5:7 makes the most sense. The logic is as follows:

- In 4:1–11, Eliphaz outlines the Standard View—the view he per-

sonally supported.
- In 4:12–5:7, Eliphaz outlines the spirit's Despairing View.
- In 5:8–27, Eliphaz restates the Standard View.

The above breakdown gives Eliphaz's speech a very clear structure: first, he stated the Standard View that he believed, then he described the mysterious spirit's contradictory opinion, and then he repeated and expanded upon the Standard View. This breakdown makes Eliphaz's personal beliefs very clear. Eliphaz and his two friends will build on the principles of the Standard View as they argue Job's case in future speeches.

Another element that equally supports this breakdown is that Job will later pick up on the spirit's disquieting Despairing View in response to his friends' arguments. Job will even directly quote the spirit's words to support his arguments.

THE SPIRIT'S VIEW VERSUS THE STANDARD VIEW

In essence, the Standard View will become Eliphaz and his two friends' position, and the Despairing View will become Job's position. The two sides will dig in as the book progresses, each defending their views of reality, and it is only when Elihu, a fourth friend, appears toward the end of the book that the stalemate is broken. But we're getting ahead of ourselves here. Since it will shape a great deal of the arguments to come, we need to take some time to understand the spirit's message in more detail.

> *¹⁷"Can mortal man be in the right before God?*
> *Can a man be pure before his Maker?"*
>
> JOB 4:17

This is a line that Job will pick up at the beginning of his third speech in chapter nine. We'll study that later, but it's worth noting as an example of where Job directly references the spirit's message.

The question is not whether we can beat God in a righteousness contest but rather whether we can ever be pure before him. The answer is uncertain at this opening-line stage of the spirit's message, but the phrasing gives the question the flavor of a challenge.

I have called the spirit's view the Despairing View because, when contrasted with the self-confident predictability of the Standard View, the Despairing View leaves little room for hope. There is no formula for guaranteed success in the Despairing View. This will become clear as we study it further, but from a less emotionally connected perspective, we might simply call this view the Realistic View. We will stick with despairing since it captures Job's emotional perspective, but we should not overlook the practical realism of the spirit's view as we study our way through it.

The Standard View says that good things happen to good people. The spirit responds by saying that nobody is good before God—even the angels get in trouble. People are even more prone to error. The angels are heavenly beings, but people are made of clay, their biological foundations are in the dust, they are as powerless and crushable before God as moths. They do not just perish—they perish "forever" without anyone noticing. There are elements of grim realism here that are hard to face.

In 5:1, the spirit asks, Who are you going to turn to? The spirit has already shown that the angels themselves get into trouble with God, so how are they going to be of any help?

In 5:2, the spirit told Eliphaz that there was no point in resenting trouble when it comes. Jealousy and resentment will just further destroy the sufferer. Resentment kills a fool, the spirit said. In context, this "fool" is a simple, silly person. The subsequent use of the word "fool" in this verse references someone easily led astray. These are not bad people. To use a somewhat informal modern term, these people are suckers.

THE SPIRIT SAYS: TROUBLE FOR HUMANS IS NORMAL

Eliphaz personally observed how he viewed the world as an orderly place: good things happened to good people, and bad things happened to bad people.

In response, in 5:3, the spirit also had some personal observations to share: such a view only takes root in a fool—not a bad person, not an evil person, but just a simple, perhaps silly, perhaps easily led astray, perhaps naive person—and makes this person's dwelling (which the original Hebrew means as the person's entire household) suddenly cursed.

Many modern translations follow the Syriac and Septuagint translations of scripture here and position this cursing as a passive affair. The original

Hebrew is not passive, and this comes out well in our English Standard Version (ESV) translation. The ESV states that "I cursed his dwelling."[29] What did this curse entail? His children were at risk, undefended and crushed unjustly. His possessions were stolen by mob-like invaders, plucking crops even from among the thorns, leaving not a shred of the harvest behind. It might be a fool who endures this fate, but he is not an evil person who deserves this trouble.

Remember how the spirit phrased this:

> *⁶"For affliction does not come from the dust,*
> *nor does trouble sprout from the ground,*
> *⁷but man is born to trouble*
> *as the sparks fly upward."*
>
> JOB 5:6–7

Affliction does not come from the dust. But as surely as a fire's sparks fly upward, people are born to trouble. This passage is pre-Newton and before any kind of modern understanding of gravity or thermodynamics. What the people of Job's day knew from practical experience, however, was that things fall down. They do not fall up. Except that sparks over a fire do fly up. Sparks do something that nearly nothing else in nature does: they go up. Affliction does not grow out of the ground, which would make it natural. It does not come from the dust, which would make it abundant and mundane and routine. Instead, trouble comes to humans the way sparks fly upward—it might seem unnatural, but it's an entirely reliable, predictable, and unchanging fact of life. Trouble, like sparks, does what you do not expect. Sparks go up. Trouble finds people.

ELIPHAZ AND THE SPIRIT DID NOT AGREE WITH EACH OTHER

Eliphaz relied on the Standard View: good things happen to good people, and bad things happen to bad people.

---

29 This is yet another piece of evidence supporting the extension of the spirit's quotation marks into chapter five. Eliphaz was many things, but he wasn't claiming to have a sorcerer's power to curse households. It is the spirit claiming to have cursed the fool's household.

The spirit said: nobody is good, and bad things happen to everybody, good or bad.

We have discussed how the Standard View can be useful as a statistical generality, but it is not mathematically precise. There are countless exceptions to the Standard View's expected conclusions.[30] The spirit took it a step further and stated that if you want a view that does lend itself to a kind of mathematical predictability, then the Despairing View is closer to reality: trouble happens to everybody. Humanity is born to trouble. It may be unnatural, since hardship does not come from the dust, but natural or not, it happens. You can count on it. No one is exempt. Trouble comes.

If we stop right here and consider these two views, I am sure you will agree that Eliphaz's Standard View feels better. It gives people some sense of control over their fate. Good things happen to good people, so be good and good will come to you. But let's take a step back and consider the spirit's view of reality. As uncomfortable as the conclusion might be, one has to admit that the evidence of both history and personal experience favors the spirit's gloomy view: trouble comes, and it does not always have an explanation. Cain was the one who sinned, and he did have some judgment levied against him, but Abel was just as dead. Trouble came to Abel through no fault of his own. As we have seen, trouble came to Job despite his exemplary record both morally and spiritually. He was a person who God repeatedly commended for his good life and character. Trouble came, and Job's reality did not support Eliphaz's cause-and-effect certainty.

---

30 The exceptions work two ways. Bad things do happen to good people, but good things also happen to bad people. Psalm 73 offers an intimate view of Asaph's frustration with the prosperity and happiness of the wicked, people who "have no struggles," whose "bodies are healthy and strong," people who are "free from common human burdens" (Ps. 73:4–5, NIV). Asaph does go on to acknowledge that his observations are limited and that God likely does eventually deal with the wicked, but that in a time span humans can reasonably observe, the apparent success and happiness of the wicked is more apparent.

15
ELIPHAZ RESTATES HIS CASE FOR THE STANDARD VIEW

Eliphaz was not having any of this gloomy spirit-revealed realism. His response to the spirit's view in the original Hebrew starts with the word "but" to signal his disagreement, and then he goes on to restate the Standard View again.

> [8] "As for me, I would seek God,
>   and to God would I commit my cause,
> [9] who does great things and unsearchable,
>   marvelous things without number:
> [10] he gives rain on the earth
>   and sends waters on the fields;
> [11] he sets on high those who are lowly,
>   and those who mourn are lifted to safety.
> [12] He frustrates the devices of the crafty,
>   so that their hands achieve no success.
> [13] He catches the wise in their own craftiness,
>   and the schemes of the wily are brought to a quick end.
> [14] They meet with darkness in the daytime
>   and grope at noonday as in the night.
> [15] But he saves the needy from the sword of their mouth
>   and from the hand of the mighty.

> ¹⁶*So the poor have hope,*
> *and injustice shuts her mouth."*
>
> JOB 5:8–16

The picture Eliphaz presented would encapsulate reality beautifully if the Standard View were perfectly true: if you are good, good things will happen to you; if you are bad, bad things will happen to you. The lowly are exalted, and the oppressors are crushed. This is true on an eternal scale when the final judgment renders its verdict, but Eliphaz was talking about this life, not some ultimate event at the end of time. The Standard View was his view for this life, and he prefaces this restatement with verse eight, in which he told Job to appeal to God.

On what basis would Job have appealed to God? Was Eliphaz suggesting that perhaps there had been a failure in the reliability of the Standard View that Job needed to bring to God's attention so that God could put it right?

ELIPHAZ'S PRACTICAL ADVICE FOR JOB

In 4:6, Eliphaz had told Job to put his confidence and hope in his fear of God and the integrity of his life. Now in 5:8, Eliphaz suggested that, as an antidote to the spirit's Despairing View, Job should appeal to God. Was it true that something had gone wrong in the world, that the Standard View had been violated, and that Job needed to get God on the case to put things right? Was that Eliphaz's point? Unfortunately, it was not. He went on from here to start drawing inferences that the Standard View naturally leads to: if bad things only happen to bad people, and if bad things were happening to Job, then Job must have done something bad.

This is how he phrased it:

> ¹⁷*"Behold, blessed is the one whom God reproves;*
> *therefore despise not the discipline of the Almighty.*
> ¹⁸*For he wounds, but he binds up;*
> *he shatters, but his hands heal."*
>
> JOB 5:17–18

Eliphaz's speech has just become transparently evil. Those evil effects had been subtle in 4:6–8 as he had started to introduce the Standard View. The Standard View sounds nice. If true, it would make for a fair, orderly world. We described 4:6–8 as the point where Eliphaz's speech had started to tilt. It had not gone entirely off course yet, but he had introduced a bias that could lead to hurtful interpretative results if Eliphaz were not careful with his conclusions.

In 4:12–5:7, Eliphaz described the spirit's appearance and its message. With this new perspective, Eliphaz opened a window onto an alternative viewpoint that could explain Job's trial without blaming Job somehow. But that Despairing View was not one that Eliphaz continued to support. In 5:8, Eliphaz further leaned toward a flawed conclusion by responding to the spirit's view not with reflection but with contradiction and another appeal to the Standard View.

In 4:8, Eliphaz's authority was "as I have seen," and similarly, in 5:8, Eliphaz's advice was based on an if-it-were-me logic. Eliphaz was a man convinced he had something to offer, and what he offered was the Standard View. His unsolicited advice was for Job to appeal to and put things right with God, and then God would bring healing. In a word, Job should repent. In later speeches, he will specify what Job should repent of, but for now, Eliphaz was content to be vague and speak in generalities.

A PRACTICAL LESSON FOR US

There is a very practical lesson here for us today. There are times when people do sin, and their sin results in trouble. A spendthrift ruins their finances and is chased by debt collectors. An unfaithful spouse destroys a marriage. An alcoholic ruins their career, relationships, and even physical health with a bottle. The list goes on, and there are significant commands throughout scripture for Christians to repent from these sorts of sins. In Luke 17:3, Jesus himself tells us that "If your brother sins, rebuke him, and if he repents, forgive him." In 2 Timothy 4:2 and Titus 2:15, young ministers are given the charge to rebuke where required. Jude 23 describes this kind of sin-addressing diligence as snatching people from the fire. There are many Proverbs on this theme—one of my favorites is Proverbs 27:6, which describes wounds from a friend as something to be trusted. Numerous other Proverbs describe the wise as people who can listen to and heed correction. The NIV translation of

Acts 3:20 describes repentance as producing "times of refreshing," a concept that is surely in keeping with what Eliphaz was trying to communicate.

So how could I have used a phrase such as "transparently evil" to describe Eliphaz's words in 5:17–18? Was he not just trying to turn Job from whatever sin might have led to this apparent judgment? Can we really hold it against him that he did not know the background found in Job chapters one and two? Was he not just doing his best to help?

BLAMING THE VICTIM

As I stated earlier, Eliphaz had not come to hurt Job. He had come to help. But an old expression applies here: the road to hell is paved with good intentions.

Eliphaz's error was not to rebuke sin. Eliphaz's error was to rebuke sin that was not there. His personal philosophy for interpreting the world led him to draw critical spiritual conclusions: trouble could only have come upon Job if Job had committed a grievous sin that justified this overwhelming discipline and correction. Eliphaz's error was not his intent to help Job repent by calling him out on a specific sin. His error was assuming that personal sin is always the root cause of affliction. He saw Job's troubles and assumed that there must be some kind of sin hidden within Job that had caused this trouble because, in Eliphaz's view, contrary to the spirit's words, trouble does not come from the dust. It comes only as a consequence of sin. Eliphaz assumed that Job deserved what he was getting.

Eliphaz assumed that the victim was to blame.

That judgment is still relatively subtle in Eliphaz's first speech, but he has laid the foundation. In future speeches, Eliphaz will insist even more blatantly on the rightness of this position. He will even begin to speculatively charge Job with various crimes to find something that will stick. But for now, in his introductory speech, he merely states the general principle and the logical conclusions:

- Trouble only comes when you've been bad;
- Job had trouble;
- so Job must have been bad;
- therefore, Job should make things right with God;

- then good things will come again.

Eliphaz promised that once Job gets things squared away with God, his life will be a picture of peace, security, prosperity, and contentment. Here's how he described this blessed state:

> ^{19}"He will deliver you from six troubles;
>   in seven no evil shall touch you.
> ^{20}In famine he will redeem you from death,
>   and in war from the power of the sword.
> ^{21}You shall be hidden from the lash of the tongue,
>   and shall not fear destruction when it comes.
> ^{22}At destruction and famine you shall laugh,
>   and shall not fear the beasts of the earth.
> ^{23}For you shall be in league with the stones of the field,
>   and the beasts of the field shall be at peace with you.
> ^{24}You shall know that your tent is at peace,
>   and you shall inspect your fold and miss nothing.
> ^{25}You shall know also that your offspring shall be many,
>   and your descendants as the grass of the earth.
> ^{26}You shall come to your grave in ripe old age,
>   like a sheaf gathered up in its season."
>
> JOB 5:19–26

Lest we mistakenly conclude that Eliphaz was simply proposing some kind of "good karma" theology, let's be clear that he was describing something much more deliberate and divine. Once right with God, Job's blessings would extend even to him being "in league with the stones of the field." What does that mean?

From an urban-dweller's perspective, stones in a field might appear to be a strange kind of partner to be in league with. But from the point of view of a farmer in the Bronze or early Iron Age, a stone in a field is a hidden threat to your plow. A chipped or broken plow blade puts an end to large-scale farming. A stone in a field can mean hunger for not just one person but an entire community. Eliphaz promised Job an arrangement even with the stones in the field. In other words, God would eliminate the everyday hassles of life and the threats to economic survival for the person who does good. That was the message.

Eliphaz's message was more than just a mistaken absolutist theology that promised freedom from life's troubles for the godly. Eliphaz's message also contained two thinly veiled, indirect charges:

1. The person right with God will take stock of his property and find nothing missing—but everything Job owned had been stolen or destroyed.
2. The person right with God will have many children and descendants as numerous as the grass in the field—but all of Job's children were dead.

Job could read between the lines here.

WRAPPING UP ELIPHAZ'S FIRST SPEECH

Eliphaz had a politician's knack for careful wording. Since he spoke first, he might very well have been the oldest of Job's friends, and his words reveal a gifted orator's thoughtful presentation:

- He started with a tentative, gentle beginning;
- then introduced the supportive-with-a-subtle-edge first overview of the Standard View;
- then offered the appearance of a balanced argument through the spirit's Despairing View;
- then reiterated the Standard View with additional supporting arguments;
- and finally provided Job with practical next steps to help him move beyond his current trials.

Some genuine oratory effort had gone into Eliphaz's speech, and doubtless, he assumed that his words were on target and helpful if only Job would heed the wisdom contained therein. At the end of his remarks, Eliphaz's confidence, based on personal observations, extended as he added an appeal to the authority of the general public:

> *²⁷"Behold, this we have searched out; it is true.*
> *Hear, and know it for your good."*
>
> JOB 5:27

"Hear, and know it for your good." The Hebrew word for knowing here means not just understanding but applying that understanding. In other words, repent and get right with God. If there had been any doubt that Eliphaz's carefully worded speech was a charge and call to repentance, Eliphaz's conclusion erased all doubt: Apply this logic to yourself. Apply this theology to yourself. Bad things only happen to bad people. Bad things have happened to you, so you do the math.

God will do the math in the final chapter of this book and call Eliphaz out for his words here. We will study that scene in detail when we get to it, but we can take a sobering lesson for our purposes now: just because everybody believes something to be true does not make it actually true.

There are things in the Bible that are black and white. Murder is a sin. It is wrong. That's very clear. Adultery is wrong. It is a sin. Also very clear. The idea that trouble is always the result of your sin in a perfectly balanced, cause-and-effect, mathematical-equation version of cosmic justice—that this cosmic justice is so reliable that an observer can judge people in trouble—that is not clear. That is not true. Sometimes the wicked get what they deserve in this life. Sometimes they do not. Sometimes a person is down because they were sinful, stupid, or bad—and sometimes a person is down because somebody else sinned or because of external forces that have nothing to do with anybody's sin. The reverse is true: those experiencing temporal success and joy are not always experiencing the rewards of a life lived in holiness. But the book of Job is about the truly righteous who suffer despite their good life, so we will stick to that theme for this study.[31]

So where did this leave Job? He had voiced his intense emotional pain

---

31 Some have argued that Ecclesiastes is in fact a record of the opposite imbalance, as it chronicles the life of a self-indulgent king who, despite many unholy actions and priorities, somehow experiences health, wealth, and success in nearly every endeavor. The purpose of Ecclesiastes, however, is not to document the opposite imbalance but to show the ultimate dissatisfaction that comes from success without God. The writer of Ecclesiastes finds that, despite unfettered access to all the world's offerings, worldly satisfactions come up short, and in the end the writer seeks and finds his comfort only in God and godly living.

in chapter three, and the response he received had been Eliphaz's carefully worded exhortation to assume guilt on top of the existent pain. It appeared in chapter two that both heaven and earth had been against Job. Eliphaz only succeeded in adding to Job's pain. And Job, being Job, will respond next by expressing that hurt.

16

RIGHTEOUS ANGER

¹Then Job answered and said:
²"Oh that my vexation were weighed,
*   and all my calamity laid in the balances!*
³For then it would be heavier than the sand of the sea;
*   therefore my words have been rash.*
⁴For the arrows of the Almighty are in me;
*   my spirit drinks their poison;*
*   the terrors of God are arrayed against me."*

JOB 6:1–4

THE WORD VEXATION in Hebrew can be translated as anger, passion, or resentment. Job's vexation—his passionate resentment, his anger—was something that he wished could be weighed. Job was not calmly enduring these trials but was becoming angry about them.

Life had dealt Job some of the most crushing blows possible for any person to endure. In one day, he had faced monumental tragedies that had then been topped by his illness and resulting physical torment. His honest response to this pain had been met with religious insensitivity from one of his closest friends. Anger was Job's response both to Eliphaz and his circumstances, and anger accounted for his previous outburst in chapter three. This isn't my judgment on Job's words—Job himself called his language rash and justified it by what he had endured.

There is something else in this word vexation worth noting. In Hebrew, it is the same word that is translated as "vexation" in the spirit's speech:

> *²"Surely vexation kills the fool,*
> > *and jealousy slays the simple.*
> *³I have seen the fool taking root,*
> > *but suddenly I cursed his dwelling."*
>
> Job 5:2–3

As discussed previously, the spirit was not talking about an evil person but a simple or naive person. This person was becoming established ("taking root"), and then the spirit cursed his house.

Lord knows my wife and I had moments of venting at our lot (having a medically fragile, special-needs child was never a part of our plan!). Our emotions sometimes led to confused and unhappy responses when we saw healthy children running and laughing while our child suffered in a hospital ward.

In 6:2, Job states, "Oh that my vexation were weighed"—if only my anger, my passion, could be weighed.

Job connected his circumstances with that of the victim the spirit had discussed in chapter five. Job's house had suddenly been cursed, just like the fool in 5:3. Job's children had been crushed, not in a courtroom, as in the NIV version of 5:4, but in a collapsed house. Job's possessions had been stolen, but not by the hungry, as in 5:5, but by the greedy and murderous. Job's passion, anger, and resentment boil like that victim in chapter five. It is no wonder that his "words have been rash" (6:3).

Job went on:

> *⁵"Does the wild donkey bray when he has grass,*
> > *or the ox low over his fodder?*
> *⁶Can that which is tasteless be eaten without salt,*
> > *or is there any taste in the juice of the mallow?*[32]
> *⁷My appetite refuses to touch them;*

---

32 "Mallow" has been variously identified as one of a variety of plants, but in general it is understood to be a plant that produces an edible but thick and tasteless juice.

> *they are as food that is loathsome to me."*
>
> JOB 6:5–7

Donkeys and oxen—which Job the farmer was very familiar with—do not make a racket when well fed. But when not fed, they bray and low. If Eliphaz had been looking for straightforward cause-and-effect principles, this was one Job could ascribe to. Does a person cry out in pain when he is happy and unhurt? Of course not. Instead of interpreting Job's trial as proof of guilt, Job told Eliphaz to interpret his cry as proof of his pain and not to feed him lines that added to his sorrow.

HELP THAT DOESN'T HELP

Job went on to describe Eliphaz's input as food that is disgusting. The idea is that Job expected better quality input from his friend. But the Hebrew for verse seven can also be translated as:

> *I refuse to touch it;*
> *it is like food when I am ill.*[33]

In other words, his circumstances made Job unable to accept this "food." Eliphaz's message was one that Job might find tasteless and unhelpful at the best of times, but in a crisis, it was like food to someone with the stomach flu. Job's ability to absorb what was unpalatable at the best of times completely failed him now that he was at his emotional limits. In a calm moment, he might have been able to grin and bear Eliphaz's words, but in this crisis, all he could do was vomit out Eliphaz's suggestions.

> *⁸"Oh that I might have my request,*
> *and that God would fulfill my hope…"*
>
> JOB 6:8

Amid such a trial, what could Job possibly hope for? What was his earnest request that he reached out to God for?

---

33 Reyburn, 129-130.

Here was what he wanted:

> ^{9}*"that it would please God to crush me,*
> *that he would let loose his hand and cut me off!*
> ^{10}*This would be my comfort;*
> *I would even exult in pain unsparing,*
> *for I have not denied the words of the Holy One."*
>
> JOB 6:9–10

FAITH'S DEATH WISH

Until this point, I have tried to draw some kind of parallel between Job's trials and the ones my wife and I experienced to help bridge the emotional gap between this ancient poem and modern circumstances. As we progress in our study, I will continue to add illustrative personal stories, but at a deep level, this is where the path Job took and the path I took part ways. Job longed for death in chapter three, and that sentiment was closely paralleled in my heart. I longed for escape from the endless crises, emergency rooms, needles, tests, false diagnoses, bad news, and new rounds of investigations and hospitalizations.

But in these two verses in chapter six, Job clarified his death wish. Death was his wish, but unlike my own heart, escape was not Job's purpose. Job was not quitting. Escape was what his wife had suggested in chapter two, a suggestion that had earned her the designation as a "foolish woman." Here Job clarified that he longed for death not for an escape but for his faith. He longed for this one consolation, one satisfaction, one joy amid "pain unsparing": the knowledge that he had remained faithful until death.

Job was not a quitter. Job was solid. But even solid characters grow weary and run the risk of succumbing to the weight of a burden that is too heavy to bear forever. That was Job's fear: that over time, the weight would become too much, and that under such a heavy load, he would eventually prove unfaithful, stumble, fall, and commit the very sin Satan had claimed Job would embrace from the beginning. Job wanted to die so that he would not fail. I had moments where I wanted to die so that I would not have to endure.

There is a big difference.

17

DIFFERENT KINDS OF TRIALS

CHRISTIANS ARE NOT universally and automatically faithful in a crisis. However, those who do survive the opening notes of a crisis with their faith intact outnumber those whose faith endures after trials that drag on and on.

Short-term heroism is much easier than long-term endurance. A crisis is challenging. Faith-testing crises that first stretch from a moment to a day, then move beyond a day to a week, and then build into weeks, months, years, and decades is another matter altogether. Difficult or incurable diseases, permanent injuries, divorces, deaths, tragedies, and abuses that leave unhealed wounds that drag across a lifetime are a completely different category of trial.

The sprinter and the marathon runner are built differently. That building comes from training, but once trained, those abilities do not necessarily transfer between distances. The marathon runner might not win a sprint race. The sprinter, suddenly tasked with a full marathon, might find the seventh or the tenth or the twentieth mile to be a mile too far and collapse, the race unfinished, the body injured.

Most of us are sprinters by nature. Our attention spans are short from childhood, when our boundless energy comes in bursts rather than in focused endurance. In the shopping mall, you are apt to see a three-year-old either running amok or collapsed, sleeping in a cart or a stroller while mom or dad carries on with the shopping. You will rarely see the three-year-old trudging diligently along for an entire afternoon wearing a child-sized backpack weighted with a fair share of the day's shopping load, conserving energy for the stairs and the lines. Endurance is something we learn, not something we are born to.

Emotional burdens are similarly loads that we have to learn how to carry over distance. For some of us, even a happy load is one we more easily handle in short bursts.

But Job's situation was unbearable to him. He carried a seemingly impossible emotional burden: too many deaths, too much destruction, too much financial pressure, too many widows and fatherless children surrounding him.

And he bore his physical torment on top of the emotional. It was too much.

WHEN IT ALL BECOMES TOO MUCH

Listen to Job's heart here:

> *¹¹"What is my strength, that I should wait?*
> *And what is my end, that I should be patient?*
> *¹²Is my strength the strength of stones, or is my flesh bronze?*
> *¹³Have I any help in me,*
> *when resource is driven from me?"*
>
> JOB 6:11–13

The translation choice in verse thirteen here is odd. A clearer translation would be:

> *Do I have any ability to help myself,*
> *when all hope for success is gone?*[34]

Job's call for death at God's hands was not, after all, a call for escape. It was not a quitter's plea. It was a call for victory: take me while I am still enduring this faithfully. The load was too great for Job to bear forever.

Job despaired that "resource [or success] is driven" from him. The Hebrew word translated as "resource," which I have suggested should instead be trans-

---

34 Adapted from Janzen, 79.

lated as "success," also implies a sense of deliverance or salvation.[35] Job was not despairing that his retirement plan looked anemic. He was despairing that his entire life had collapsed, and he despaired that there appeared to be no hope at all of any deliverance from this new reality. All avenues of rescue were cut off, all reasons for hope extinguished. There was nothing left but endurance. His existence had a terminal diagnosis in all categories: material, relational, health, financial. All were in ruins and without hope of rescue.

Job was not made of stone or metal, and his heart weakened at the sight of this long, dark road in front of him.

THE NEED FOR FRIENDSHIP

A person in these circumstances needs, if nothing else, a friend to share the load. That was Job's next request.

> *[14] "He who withholds kindness from a friend*
>   *forsakes the fear of the Almighty.*
> *[15] My brothers are treacherous as a torrent-bed,*
>   *as torrential streams that pass away,*
> *[16] which are dark with ice,*
>   *and where the snow hides itself.*
> *[17] When they melt, they disappear;*
>   *when it is hot, they vanish from their place.*
> *[18] The caravans turn aside from their course;*
>   *they go up into the waste and perish.*
> *[19] The caravans of Tema look,*
>   *the travelers of Sheba hope.*
> *[20] They are ashamed because they were confident;*
>   *they come there and are disappointed.*
> *[21] For you have now become nothing;*
>   *you see my calamity and are afraid."*
>
> JOB 6:14–21

Verse fourteen can also be translated as "a man in deep despair should

---

35 Reyburn, 133.

have the devoted attention of his friends." Verse fifteen follows up this statement of need by saying "My brothers are treacherous as a torrent-bed," which in the original Hebrew carries more strongly the idea that his brothers are undependable, like a stream that flows, then dries up, then flows again.

Job specified his expectation for his friends and then described his brothers. He described two layers of relationship here: friends, whose devotion you can count on, and brothers, who you can expect an even deeper level of commitment from.

Verse 2:11 describes Eliphaz, Bildad, and Zophar as Job's friends, and verse 6:15 implies that they were also like brothers to him. Job then told them that to withhold kindness is an offense against God himself. Job's concept of friendship, in other words, contained a significant component of selflessness. Job may not have been much fun right then, and his spiritual pain may have led him to say reckless things, but he was communicating that he expected his friends to bear with him during this time.

That is friendship. Then Job went on to state "But my brothers have proven undependable." Job seems to be saying that "even if all we had were just a friendship, I would expect you to be devoted to me, but you guys are even closer than that—you're like brothers to me, and therefore I expect an even a higher level of devotion."

Is that what Job was saying? Or was he sharing a big-picture observation that his actual flesh-and-blood brothers had also failed him in his moment of crisis? Job did have brothers. They will finally appear, along with his sisters, in the last chapter of Job.

I do not think that Job intended to speak about his actual flesh-and-blood brothers. We do not know anything about their involvement in Job's life until chapter forty-two, so we cannot say how they initially responded to Job's crisis. In the context of chapter six, Job was responding to Eliphaz's speech. In 6:1–7, Job was upset with Eliphaz's tasteless, even nauseating advice. Eliphaz's presumption that the Standard View applies to Job's crisis was upsetting, and Job said so. In verses 11–13, he expressed how hopeless he felt. And then, in verses 14–21, he expressed his unhappiness at being let down by his friends.

Like a traveler expecting to find a spring in the desert only to find that it has dried up, Job had likewise hoped to find comfort in his friends only to receive, after a long week of silent suspense, a hurtful recounting of the Standard View with its implied insult to Job's character.

A FAILURE OF FRIENDSHIP

Job summarized how his friends have failed him in this way:

> *"For you have now become nothing;*
> *you see my calamity and are afraid."*
>
> JOB 6:21

"For now you have become nothing." The idea the Hebrew is trying to get across here is "now you too have offered no help or refreshment." You too. You too, like my flesh-and-blood brothers. Or you too, like those desert streams. Either way, the point is the same: Job felt let down by Eliphaz's "wisdom." You have failed to help me.

To make it clear that Job's complaint was personal, directed against Eliphaz, Job chose his illustration carefully. We know that there were sections around Job's farm that were desert,[36] and perhaps Eliphaz had crossed that desert on his way to meet with Job at the end of chapter two. More particularly, the devastated caravans Job used in his illustration came from Tema. And Eliphaz was a Temanite. Perhaps Eliphaz had known people who had traveled in those caravans, who had stopped by mapped streams in the desert only to find them dry, who had suffered as Job was now suffering as a result of Eliphaz's words. Eliphaz should have offered refreshment, and instead, he left Job parched and in more pain as some of Eliphaz's fellow Temanites may have experienced.

Additionally, Job described a second group of disappointed desert travelers: people from Sheba. Sabeans were from Sheba. Sabeans had been responsible for the first assault on Job's farm. They had stolen the oxen and donkeys and had killed the men tending those animals along with the plowmen in the fields. Job's illustration not only linked his personal pain to the pain that Eliphaz's countrymen would have experienced in the desert but also linked Eliphaz's first speech to the first attack on Job's farm.

---

36 NIV translation of Job 1:19.

Job is a very literary book. It pays rich dividends to the reader who reads carefully. However, even at the surface, Job's message is easy to understand: I deserve better from you, Eliphaz.

> ²¹ *"For you have now become nothing;*
> *you see my calamity and are afraid."*
>
> JOB 6:21

The word see here, in Hebrew, is tir'u. The word afraid is tir'a.³⁷

> ²¹ *"For you have now become nothing;*
> *you tir'u my calamity and are tir'a."*
>
> JOB 6:21

Hebrew poetry rhymes ideas. Hebrew poetry also loves to make connections with puns and other forms of wordplay. "You tir'u and are tir'a." In other words, you're not thinking at all. You are in pure reaction mode, overcome by the dread of what you see in my life and responding with knee-jerk thoughtlessness—with Standard View drivel that shows your failure to think through the particulars of my unique circumstances.

Job continued:

> ²² *"Have I said, 'Make me a gift'?*
> *Or, 'From your wealth offer a bribe for me'?*
> ²³ *Or, 'Deliver me from the adversary's hand'?*
> *Or, 'Redeem me from the hand of the ruthless'?"*
>
> JOB 6:22–23

Job asked straightforward questions here: Have I ever tried to borrow money from you? Have I ever failed to take responsibility for my own messes? Even in this situation, have I asked you to bail me out?

Eliphaz challenged Job to take responsibility for some vague, unstated sin that had somehow caused these tragedies. Job's response was: I have no issue with taking responsibility. I pay my own debts.

---

37 Reyburn, 138-139.

JOB WAS OPEN TO GENUINE CORRECTION

There was a chance that somewhere, somehow, the Standard View did apply to Job's situation. Job was confident that this was not the case, but he was willing to be corrected if, by chance, there was some lurking sin that he had overlooked:

> [24] *"Teach me, and I will be silent;*
> *make me understand how I have gone astray.*
> [25] *How forceful are upright words!*
> *But what does reproof from you reprove?"*
>
> Job 6:24–25

The answer, of course, was that Eliphaz's arguments proved nothing. Eliphaz argued against the spirit's Contrary View and in favor of the Standard View, and he made general judgments against Job without ever proving anything. Eliphaz put a great deal of weight on an abstract philosophy. None of his inferences applied to Job. Honest words can be painful. Correction can be painful. But Eliphaz's words were painful for different reasons. Eliphaz's words hurt not because they were true—they hurt because they were false.

As he put it:

> [26] *"Do you think that you can reprove words,*
> *when the speech of a despairing man is wind?*
> [27] *You would even cast lots over the fatherless,*
> *and bargain over your friend.*
> [28] *But now, be pleased to look at me,*
> *for I will not lie to your face."*
>
> Job 6:26–28

The ESV's translation of verse twenty-six is awkward. A more straightforward translation that reflects the Hebrew would be:

> *Do you intend to correct what I have said,*
> *and treat my words as if they were just wind?*[38]

---

38 Reyburn, 142.

This might seem like a harsh assessment of Eliphaz's speech, but Job read his friends well: Bildad will latch onto this idea that Job's words were just wind later on in chapter eight.

STUBBORNNESS REVEALED

Job's specific charge against Eliphaz was that he would do anything to support the Standard View. Eliphaz would prefer to gamble away the futures of the fatherless (i.e., all the orphans on Job's farm that Eliphaz inadvertently included in his diagnosis) and bargain over a friend (speaking of Job in particular here) rather than rethink the Standard View.

Eliphaz's error was very human. Once locked into a mental paradigm, people are notorious in the literature of social psychology for blinding themselves to all contrary evidence.

Whether the effects of a firmly embedded idea are good or bad, and whether an embedded idea is proven right or wrong, it can be tough to shake once established. Biases, prejudices, loyalties, and resultant decisions are shaped by mental frameworks.

Choose your beliefs and worldview carefully because they will unrelentingly shape what you do from that point onward. They will even shape what you allow yourself to see. They will shape what you can see. Cognitive dissonance is the technical term for what I'm describing here. It is a basic principle of human psychology, and its effects were what Job was challenging here.

Job tried to get through to his friend with the next few verses.

> *28"But now, be pleased to look at me,*
> *for I will not lie to your face.*
> *29Please turn; let no injustice be done.*
> *Turn now; my vindication is at stake.*
> *30Is there any injustice on my tongue?*
> *Cannot my palate discern the cause of calamity?"*
>
> JOB 6:28–30

What's sad here is that Job was speaking to someone who, as we will see, had dug himself into a stubborn position. It will soon become clear that Eliphaz could not be just. For the sake of kindness and friendship, Job's case deserved reconsideration, but Eliphaz will not reconsider. He had a worldview that he would cling to in the face of all evidence, and we will see him become increasingly irrational in his fierce defense of the Standard View. Watch for it in Eliphaz's future speeches.

Note as well here that Job did not talk about his ears discerning malice. Job referenced his palate, that is, his tongue and mouth in general. Job was talking about his own words. He was challenging Eliphaz. He was disputing the implications of Eliphaz's speech, and he was pleading for Eliphaz's devotion (6:14), for him to take Job seriously (6:26), to treat Job kindly and assume that Job was being honest (6:27). Though Job's words may have been strong as he called for this change in Eliphaz's position, they were not unjust. Job could taste the difference. He was correcting and redirecting Eliphaz, but he was not insulting or being malicious toward Eliphaz. Job's mouth knew the taste of malice, and there was no malice in his speech to Eliphaz. His heart was pure even in this rebuke.

Job's speech exemplified a convicting mixture of honest candor and verbal self-control. He spoke openly but not wrongly. Too often it is easy to display emotional honesty through the medium of insults. This passage offers a model of self-control as in it Job expressed both his vulnerability and anger without sinning.

There is much to learn from Job's example.

18

A TURN INWARD

AFTER JOB'S CRY for friendship and his rebuke of Eliphaz's thoughtless Standard View speech, Job's thoughts turned inward. The act of maintaining the self-discipline required to be vulnerable and honest yet malice-free had been exhausting. His own emotional needs required attention. In the next part of Job's speech, he won't talk to Eliphaz or his other friends. He will talk instead to God.

WHEN LIFE BECOMES SURREAL

There is something surreal about an unexpected trial. Countless times after Mackenzie's birth, while in a hospital room, a surgery or CT-scan prep room, or an emergency room, I would pause, completely self-aware and at the same time utterly disoriented. Is this my life? I was not destined to be the parent of a medically fragile child. While the world dealt with the events of September 11, 2001, I juggled the collapse of my wife's health and my daughter's struggle for survival.

In the months shortly after Mackenzie's birth and just before 9/11, in May of that year, we checked into BC Children's Hospital. Carolyn's health had stabilized without a medical explanation. Occasionally she would collapse in public with more of those unexplained blackouts and mini seizures, but she always recovered on her own. Medical intervention merely counted heartbeats and measured oxygen levels—nothing done in a hospital or by paramedics had any effect whatsoever on her recovery. As a result, her stroke-like attacks—which we were assured were not actually strokes—took attention's back seat. Mackenzie was the center of our concern and likewise the only real focus for our medical team.

Once we were checked into BC Children's Hospital, the chief of staff came to visit us personally. He had been a pediatrician before his leadership and administrative role. He informed us that everyone in the hospital worked for him and that he was now taking on the role of Mackenzie's personal pediatrician.

She was that interesting.

We discovered that we would not leave the hospital until he found a diagnosis. If Mackenzie needed a scan, test, or procedure, it would be scheduled for that day, not for weeks down the road. The chief of staff had that authority and that degree of personal investment. We interpreted this visit to mean that the cavalry had arrived and that a solution was days away.

A CT scan did not produce any clues to her illness. Medical staff forced barium sulfate through a tube and down her throat so that they could take X-rays of her digestive tract. Then came ultrasounds and blood and urine tests. All the results were normal.

The stakes were further raised—because the cavalry was here, after all—and her infant body was hooked up to a machine that cycled her blood out, through a testing device, and back into her body to study her hormone levels. She was injected with drugs to stimulate hormone production, and then her blood was tested to measure the elevation in hormones expected to accompany each drug within the appropriate amount of elapsed time. The test took six hours, during which her blood flowed from her body to the machine and then back into her body. She was cycled through the entire catalog of hormones and produced them all on cue. There were no problems there.

Next, she was given not one but several spinal taps. I delivered her to her tormentors, stood outside the door while they did the procedure, and collected her afterward. I overheard the upset technician during one of these procedures complaining, "I've got her blood all over me," as Mackenzie wailed and I paced. Afterward, I collected my infant daughter's tiny bandaged body and held her while she cried, and she tried to hold me back, but her hands were covered with oversized gloves meant to keep her from pulling the tube from her nose.

Before the summer was over, the chief of staff came back for another visit.

He apologized to us. Every medical test had come back normal, but she was still failing. Her diagnosis was literally "failure to thrive," which meant "we don't know what's wrong, but she's not doing well and might not make it." The cavalry had failed. The general raised his white flag and sent us home.

We went home with a tube taped to our daughter's cheek that entered her nose and ended in her stomach. We were to feed her through that tube. She promptly pulled it out, and we spent four hours back in the emergency room of the hospital we had just checked out of to get it put back in.

She pulled it out again. We restrained her hands to stop her from repeating this trial, and she learned how to throw it up—it went in her nose and came out her mouth. She was five months old and willful.

We eventually learned how to put the tube in ourselves to save the three to four hours of hospital time several times each week. We would lay her on a blanket and then bind her up in it like they had taught us in prenatal class (for a very different purpose). My wife then held her head back and steady and looked away. I inserted the tube into Mackenzie's five-month-old nose, threaded it back to her throat, paused for her gagging and protesting and crying until she opened her throat to breathe, and then quickly pushed the tube through that gap, down her throat, and into her stomach. We then tested it with a stethoscope by blowing bubbles down the tube and hearing them gurgle in her tiny stomach to ensure it was where it was supposed to be. And we drew back stomach acid into a syringe and tested its pH to ensure the tube was where it was supposed to be and not in her colon or a lung. Once we were sure, we taped the tube to her cheek again.

Then we did it all over again the next day—sometimes the same day. Sometimes we would get a three or four day reprieve and call that happiness.

No one told us about the little pumps used to push food through that tube at a steady rate. We hung IV bags of baby formula from a camera tripod and tried to guess the right height to get the proper gravity-assisted flow. Too fast, and she would throw up, and with it, the tube again. Too slow, and we were feeding her all day. She was still skeletal and failing.

After six months of this, after we had reinserted the tube ourselves around seventy to eighty times, she had surgery to install a gastrostomy (G) tube—what we described as a little gas cap on her stomach. That was how we were to feed her now—no more tubes taped to her face.

With Mackenzie at nine months old, this new bit of hardware permanently affixed to her little belly looked like an off-center second navel. I remember thinking that the G-tube hole was going to leave a scar one day and that, as a teenager, she was going to be self-conscious about it and always wear one-piece bathing suits. I was secretly relieved that I would never have to have a bikini argument with my sixteen-year-old. That thought illustrates how little I grasped what was happening.

Her first word was not "momma" or "dada." Her first word came while recovering from surgery in her hospital bed, nine months old, looking at a game on the hospital room TV. She said, "hockeee." I grew up in California. I can't skate and don't really care for hockey, but my Canadian-born girl said "hockey" before saying "dada."

Everything about life had become surreal. Walking away from the neon hospital glow and into Vancouver's natural beauty was surreal. The medical procedures were surreal. Inserting tubes into my daughter's body was surreal. Nothing was believable.

My wife's ongoing collapses, her fainting in a coffee shop we had gone to for respite, collapsing at the dinner table and needing to be carried to the next room, were just another layer of the unreal. Every door we walked through, every street we walked on, every place I went with her, I carried with me the question of Will she suddenly collapse and go into a seizure here? Where is the nearest phone if that happens? We didn't have cell phones back then.

Leaving my wife alone simply changed the complexity of the concerns. Who will help her? Will I come home and find her healthy? Or in tears because of our daughter? Or maybe unconscious on the floor?

The occurrence of 9/11 seven months into this nightmare was a foggy reminder that the world beyond my immediate horizon was also unreal. When we were sent home from the hospital with a tube taped to Mackenzie's face, our response was "You're sending us home with that?" By "that," we meant the tube and the fear of it coming out on our watch. The human psyche can get used to a lot and still have it feel surreal.

With the G-tube, we got a pump. That was a vast improvement over the tripod and gravity routine. Unfortunately, we were starting to measure progress by sleep improvements rather than health improvements. Months later, after surgery, the surgically installed G-tube fell out in the night. Somehow the anchor balloon had deflated. My wife discovered it in the dark and cried out. I came running. We had been taught how to change it—an additional layer of unreality: removing a device from your daughter's abdomen, seeing a hole in its place, and then reinserting a fresh device. We had been warned to be quick about it. The muscles in the abdominal and stomach walls would close very quickly, after which she would need surgery to reinstall the device. But this G-tube fell out on its own, defective somehow, and we had no way of knowing how long it had been out.

In seconds, we had her out of the crib, onto the changing table, clothes off, the hole in her abdomen puckered and horrifyingly closed. We found the replacement G-tube, prepped it, cried out to God for help, and then, while Carolyn held Mackenzie, I tried to put the device back. It would not go. Every second was another second in which tissues tightened up further. A trip to the hospital would have been defeat—it would have meant another surgery. One more time, I shouted at my wife through our stress to hold her still, positioned the device over the puckered wound and pushed, and kept pushing as my frail girl cried out and twisted and then something gave way. I had forced a mechanical device through my daughter's abdomen across the abdominal cavity and (I hoped) into her stomach. I'd been sleeping three minutes before. Now I'd just accomplished home surgery.

I reinflated the anchor balloon inside with sterile water like we had been taught. Mackenzie stopped wailing and went willingly into mommy's arms for comfort. Mommy did not faint. She still mysteriously seized and blacked out over dinner or coffee, but not that early, early morning while it was still dark and our baby girl cried quietly into her shoulder.

I was still shaking when we were seen in the emergency room thirty minutes later. Everything was fine. The tube was properly secured inside her stomach. It was in the stomach, not free somewhere in the abdomen as I had feared. X-rays confirmed its location. She was fine. We had executed the procedure properly for what, it turned out, wouldn't be the last time.

We were home in time for me to shower, change, and still get to work to unlock the office doors to let the staff and customers in for the day and pretend that nothing had happened.

Inside, I was jelly—outside, professional. Our lives had become inhuman and surreal.

JOB'S COMPLAINT—TO GOD

¹"Has not man a hard service on earth,
*   and are not his days like the days of a hired hand?*
²Like a slave who longs for the shadow,
*   and like a hired hand who looks for his wages,*
³so I am allotted months of emptiness,
*   and nights of misery are apportioned to me.*
⁴When I lie down I say, 'When shall I arise?'
*   But the night is long,*
*   and I am full of tossing till the dawn.*
⁵My flesh is clothed with worms[39] and dirt;[40]
*   my skin hardens, then breaks out afresh.*
⁶My days are swifter than a weaver's shuttle
*   and come to their end without hope."*

JOB 7:1–6

There is a vivid poetic effect happening here in these last two lines that is lost in English. A weaver's shuttle is an amazingly fast tool. Its actions are a blur to the eye, and so the first line is readily understood: Job's life was speeding by.

The second line, however, uses a unique word for "hope." It is a word that does mean hope but can also mean thread.[41] The weaver's shuttle—Job's life—was pounding by in a blur, and then suddenly thwack-thwack-thwack-thwack: the shuttle was out of thread. It was out of hope. Life had been passing like a blur, and now it was over. That's a neat bit of poetry.

Before the bit about the weaver's shuttle, Job asked, Does not man have hard service on earth? The Hebrew phrase "hard service" is a Hebrew idiom that means "forced military service." Job was relating a person's life to being press-ganged into an army.

---

39 This same word, "worms," is rendered "maggots" in Exodus 16:24 where it describes maggots in food. Likewise, Isaiah 14:11 uses the word to identify maggots on a dead body.

40 An alternative rendering of the Hebrew "dirt" here is "scabs." Job's problem was not hygiene but disease.

41 Reyburn, 153-154.

The "hired hand" in the following sentence refers to a day laborer who would expect payment at the end of each day. The slave's respite is shade. The day laborer's respite is their pay. Like both of these hard-pressed people, Job too longed for an end to his toil and suffering.

In all these poetic images, Job was using common (for his day) illustrations to paint a picture of how his brief life had been assigned not hours but nights and months of agony. Time stretched mercilessly on. This was an existential cry from a soul that saw no hope in his future and did not want his life to be extended. He wanted the peace that comes with the end.

THE BEGINNING OF A DISCOVERY

Let's continue to listen in on Job's prayer to God.

> *⁷"Remember that my life is a breath;*
> *my eye will never again see good.*
> *⁸The eye of him who sees me will behold me no more;*
> *while your eyes are on me, I shall be gone.*
> *⁹As the cloud fades and vanishes,*
> *so he who goes down to Sheol does not come up;*
> *¹⁰he returns no more to his house,*
> *nor does his place know him anymore."*
>
> JOB 7:7–10

These four verses sketch the theology of afterlife that existed in Job's day. This was a theology based not on divine revelation but on personal observation and a general lack of information. For Job and his contemporaries, the end of life on this earth was the end of life, period.

Even in light of the work of the prophets after Job, this subject was still debated in Jesus's day. A clear understanding of heaven and eternity waited on Jesus and the Apostles to make clear. In the Old Testament, the details are very unclear. Death, as far as anyone knew for sure, was the end. Period.

The Pharisees in Jesus's day did believe in an afterlife, and their belief was founded on the Old Testament scriptures. But in Job's day, the Old Testament scriptures had not yet been written. Job did not have David's Psalms, the books of the prophets, and so on to help develop potential ideas of an afterlife. Even in Jesus's day, when the Pharisees held significant authority, the idea of an afterlife was still debated. The Pharisees believed in it. The Sadducees were another prominent school of theological thought, and they did not believe in it. Clarity, before Christ and the Apostles, was not yet available. However, in Job's day, there were not even grounds for a debate: death was the end.

As far as Job and his contemporaries were concerned, God himself would not be able to connect with Job again once Job died. God himself would look for Job but would not be able to find him. Like a dissipated cloud that cannot be reconstituted, the human personality "returns no more to his house." This passage refers to a person physically coming home, but in context, it also refers to a person's soul, the personality and innate being of a person, vacating its earthly home—their body—and never returning. At death, existence becomes nonexistence. In this context, the miracles of Jesus raising people from the dead (and a similar miracle by Elijah) are more than medical miracles. In the eyes of the contemporary audiences, they represented a reversal of the irreversible. They were not a demonstration of better medicine. They turned nonexistence into existence. This was an idea that in Job's day was, at best, a groundless fantasy.

The implications of these four verses will lead Job toward bitterness and complaint as he sees his remaining life as a pointless exercise in futile torture. However, in future chapters, he will begin to ask profound questions as he tests the soundness of these assumptions about mortality. Job makes two groundbreaking theological discoveries in this book. This discussion about life and death is the seed that eventually leads to the first of those discoveries.

19

AN EXISTENTIAL CRY

As we hinted in the last chapter, Job did not know that he had just touched the edge of revelation and profound discovery. At present, he saw only pain, and here was how he expressed that pain to God:

> [11]"Therefore I will not restrain my mouth;
> I will speak in the anguish of my spirit;
> I will complain in the bitterness of my soul.
> [12]Am I the sea, or a sea monster,
> that you set a guard over me?
> [13]When I say, 'My bed will comfort me,
> my couch will ease my complaint,'
> [14]then you scare me with dreams
> and terrify me with visions,
> [15]so that I would choose strangling
> and death rather than my bones.
> [16]I loathe my life; I would not live forever.
> Leave me alone, for my days are a breath.
> [17]What is man, that you make so much of him,
> and that you set your heart on him,
> [18]visit him every morning
> and test him every moment?
> [19]How long will you not look away from me,

> *nor leave me alone till I swallow my spit?*[42]
> [20] *If I sin, what do I do to you, you watcher of mankind?*
> *Why have you made me your mark?*
> *Why have I become a burden to you?*
> [21] *Why do you not pardon my transgression*
> *and take away my iniquity?*
> *For now I shall lie in the earth;*
> *you will seek me, but I shall not be."*
>
> JOB 7:11–21

Notice what had happened here: Job's situation had created a collision between limited theology (about death), false theology (the Standard View), and Job's tragic circumstances. Despite being influenced by Eliphaz's Standard View arguments, Job knows that he is personally innocent, and this raises serious questions about God's justice.

If bad things only happen to bad people, and if bad things were happening to Job but Job was good, then the judge was making a mistake. Bad advice can work evil. Do you start to see how Eliphaz's speech, while subtle, had been so wrong? A dispute between Job and God was developing here, not shaped by Job's original disposition and character but by the lousy counsel of Eliphaz.

"Am I a sea monster?" Job asked. "Can't you just leave me alone? Why have I become your target? What is your problem with me?" In verse twenty-one, Job acknowledged that maybe he had missed some kind of sin. If that is the case, he asked God why he could not just be pardoned. After all, Job will not live forever (7:16), and he will soon be gone and unreachable, even by God (7:21).

---

42 The ESV provides a literal translation here. This is a Hebrew figure of speech that a modern English reader might not initially understand. In fact, in English it come across as kind of gross with its reference to swallowing spit. This figure of speech originally meant "leave me alone for a brief period of time." That is, Job wanted to have a moment of peace for at least as long as it would take him to swallow. In modern English, we might say something like "leave me alone so I can catch my breath" or "give me a minute's peace" or "give me a break for a second."

HOW DID WE GET HERE?

Job's first speech in chapter three was just emotional—he had wished he had never been born.

In Job's second speech, he had been upset with Eliphaz's lack of empathy.

Now here in chapter seven, Job started his soliloquy by asking general existential questions again, but seven verses in, he switched to addressing God directly. He took the logic of Eliphaz's Standard View and voiced his complaint against God, questioning his poor administration of justice in light not only of Job's righteousness but also of the limited span of a human's existence.[43] In other words, led by Eliphaz's argument, Job was starting to get upset with God.

Job might have gotten around to complaining against God on his own, but we will never know for sure. He did very well dealing with these trials and not turning against God before Eliphaz showed up. It was only following Eliphaz's confident articulation of the Standard View that the discussion started to shift from Job's pain and despair to questions about who to blame.

Eliphaz wanted to blame Job—blame the victim. This approach makes the world feel safe and predictable for people who are observing other peoples' hardship rather than experiencing hardship themselves.

Job knew that he was innocent, which, if the Standard View was accurate, left God in the bad-guy chair. The Standard View only offers two options: either the condemned person is guilty or the judge is wrong. The premise is false, to begin with, but it will take some time for Job to recapture the spirit's less black-and-white interpretation of reality and start to debate

---

[43] In verse sixteen, Job said, "Leave me alone; my days are a breath," which is a good translation of the original Hebrew. "Breath" is, of course, a poetic metaphor. It is the translator's task to either translate the word directly…and leave the reader to interpret its meaning or to interpret its meaning and translate their conclusion. In this case, the ESV has chosen to translate the word "breath" directly, without poetic interpretation. A clearer translation might interpret that poetic meaning for the reader and come up with something like "Leave me alone, for my days are short" or "Leave me alone, for my days are insubstantial." Remember what we learned about parallelism: the meaning of the second line will usually rhyme with the meaning of the first line. In the first line Job acknowledged that he will not live forever. In the second line he asked to be left alone because his days were short. "Not forever" parallels with "not long." In light of this, Job wanted God to leave him alone. God had become an opponent because Eliphaz had set the argument up that way.

Eliphaz's philosophy coherently. In the meantime, Job was still a whirl of emotion, hurt by circumstances, hurt by friends, and beginning to feel hurt in his relationship with God.

PRACTICAL APPLICATION: DON'T BE ELIPHAZ

Beware of the advice you give a friend.

Beware of overly confident, overly dogmatic conclusions, interpretations, and judgments. Eliphaz's boldness added to Job's pain not only within his friendship with Eliphaz but also within his relationship with God. For the first time, Job lashed out at God: "Leave me alone. What is your problem with me? Why can't you give me a break, O watcher of men? Why have I become your target?"

God have mercy on the person who hurts another soul's relationship with God.

Beware: the more religious you are, the more at risk you are of committing Eliphaz's error. There is much to be said for love and humility. There is very little to be said for big but unwise opinions.

As Job said in 6:14, a despairing man should have the devotion of his friends. It is not always easy to be devoted to someone who is suffering. It is usually very, very hard. It is much easier to make snap judgments that make the speaker feel better.

Despite these words, I suspect many of you may still commit Eliphaz's mistake. I did. And the injury I inflicted with that mistake hurt both my wife and me.

Beware.

Be devoted.

Don't be Eliphaz.

20

BILDAD THE RUDE

We described the first half of Job's last speech as a rebuke to Eliphaz and a cry for steadfast friendship. In part of that speech, Job said:

> ²⁶"Do you think that you can reprove words,
>   when the speech of a despairing man is wind?"
>
> Job 6:26

We learned that Job was not saying that his words were wind but rather that his words were being treated like wind. In other words: "Please take my words seriously."

Eliphaz did not immediately respond to this plea.

Instead, Bildad entered the conversation.

> ¹Then Bildad the Shuhite answered and said:
> ²"How long will you say these things,
>   and the words of your mouth be a great wind?
> ³Does God pervert justice?
>   Or does the Almighty pervert the right?"
>
> Job 8:1–3

Job had asked for his words not to be treated like wind, and Bildad replied by calling Job's words not just wind but "a great wind."

If Eliphaz could be characterized as the religious traditionalist, Bildad could be described as the mouthy one. It helps to distinguish these friends with nicknames. I remember Bildad most easily as Bildad the Rude.

BILDAD THE RUDE UNLEASHED

In 6:29, Job asked his friend to reconsider the Standard View, to "turn now; my vindication is at stake." The word "vindication" in 6:29 is the same word translated as "right" in 8:3. Bildad responded that God does not pervert the course of vindication; therefore, there was no need for Eliphaz or Bildad or anyone to turn from anything.

Oh, but listen to what Bildad said next:

> [4]"*If your children have sinned against him,*
> *he has delivered them into the hand of their transgression.*"
>
> JOB 8:4

Whoa! What Eliphaz had only hinted at and drawn general boxes around, Bildad the Rude stated plainly: your kids were killed because they deserved it.

The Hebrew here is even blunter than our ESV translation. It essentially says "Your children got what they deserved." [44]

Some people's mouths have a filter that prevents them from saying stupid things. Bildad was not one of those people.

Bildad's mouth brings to mind the famous words of James:

> [5]*So also the tongue is a small member, yet it boasts of great things.*
>
> *How great a forest is set ablaze by such a small fire!* [6]*And the tongue is a fire, a world of unrighteousness. The tongue is set among our members, staining the whole body, setting on fire the entire course of life, and set on fire by hell.*
>
> JAMES 3:5–6

---

44 Reyburn, 164.

NO FACTS REQUIRED

Bildad was a firm believer in the Standard View, but unlike Eliphaz, who had taken a moment to consider the spirit's view before discounting it, Bildad chose to see the Standard View and nothing else. With that as his lens, he prescribed an easy solution to Job's problems:

> [5] "If you will seek God
> and plead with the Almighty for mercy,
> [6] if you are pure and upright,
> surely then he will rouse himself for you
> and restore your rightful habitation.
> [7] And though your beginning was small,
> your latter days will be very great.
> [8] For inquire, please, of bygone ages,
> and consider what the fathers have searched out.
> [9] For we are but of yesterday and know nothing,
> for our days on earth are a shadow.
> [10] Will they not teach you and tell you
> and utter words out of their understanding?"
>
> JOB 8:5–10

In 6:24, Job had opened himself up to the possibility that maybe there was some sin in his life that he was unaware of. He had asked to be taught, to be shown where he was wrong.

Bildad's response was a general appeal to the tradition of the Standard View, and in response to Job's request for teaching, Bildad told Job to ask "bygone ages"—that is, older generations—and they would instruct Job.

But here was the problem: nobody so far had told Job what it was that he had supposedly done wrong.

His friends were applying the Standard View by inference alone: bad things were happening to Job, so Job must have been bad. And his children likewise. The philosophy was dictating the interpretation of reality. No facts appear to have been required.

ARTFULLY CRUEL

Bildad then went on to paint a detailed, poetic caricature of Job's situation:

> [11] *"Can papyrus grow where there is no marsh?*
> *   Can reeds flourish where there is no water?*
> [12] *While yet in flower and not cut down,*
> *   they wither before any other plant.*
> [13] *Such are the paths of all who forget God;*
> *   the hope of the godless shall perish.*
> [14] *His confidence is severed,*
> *   and his trust is a spider's web.*
> [15] *He leans against his house, but it does not stand;*
> *   he lays hold of it, but it does not endure.*
> [16] *He is a lush plant before the sun,*
> *   and his shoots spread over his garden.*
> [17] *His roots entwine the stone heap;*
> *   he looks upon a house of stones.*
> [18] *If he is destroyed from his place,*
> *   then it will deny him, saying, 'I have never seen you.'*
> [19] *Behold, this is the joy of his way,*
> *   and out of the soil others will spring."*
>
>   Job 8:11–19

Eliphaz's carefully worded Standard View had been both artful and hurtful. Bildad's articulation of the same view went beyond just hurtful and became cruel.

The marsh plant without water withers.

The well-watered plant flourishes in the garden, but when torn from the garden, it too withers.

And then the garden disowns the plant with the words, "I have never seen you."

Other plants take the place of the dead plant.

Job, of course, was the one torn from his garden and left to wither. God had been Job's water, God had left him, and so the fault must have been with Job:

> ²⁰*"Behold, God will not reject a blameless man,*
> *nor take the hand of evildoers."*
>
> JOB 8:20

According to the Standard View, God could not have possibly allowed trouble into Job's life unless Job was guilty.

What had happened in Job's life, according to Bildad, could never have happened. Reality was irrelevant in the face of such a firmly held philosophical position.

But even with the Standard View, there is hope:

> ²¹*"He will yet fill your mouth with laughter,*
> *and your lips with shouting.*
> ²²*Those who hate you will be clothed with shame,*
> *and the tent of the wicked will be no more."*
>
> JOB 8:21–22

The ending of Bildad's speech is plain enough to the casual reader, but like Eliphaz before him, Bildad has some poetic artistry of his own to demonstrate. Bildad promised that in the end, success will be restored to Job's life, and his enemies will be "no more." These final two words echo how Job himself ended his last speech in 7:21 with his own "no more."[45]

Job had appealed to God for pardon from whatever sin he might have committed and reminded God that without this pardon, Job would die and God would search for him, but he would be "no more." Bildad's response was that Job's enemies will be the ones who will be "no more," just as soon as Job returned to God.

His philosophy may have blinded Bildad, but he was aware of Job's words and able to turn them back on the suffering soul. There was a clever eloquence here, an articulate craft, but a complete lack of kindness or wisdom.

The principled person is often on solid ground when relying on the truism that all actions have consequences. Still, applying a principle without

---

45 The ESV translates the end of 7:21 as "I shall not be." The wording in 7:21 and 8:22 are actually identical in the Hebrew. Job's complaint had been that he would "be no more," and Bildad's promise was that the wicked would "be no more." Bildad was quoting Job, though some English translations obscure this detail.

thinking—without considering the exceptional circumstances, the nuances of real life, or the hearts of those receiving the message—is a recipe for trouble.

Bildad's message is spot on for the one who is guilty of sin and clearly being punished by God. Applied to Job, Bildad's message was very wrong,[46] and God himself will pass a very strong judgment on Bildad and his message at the end of the book.

RESPONDING TO THE RUDE

Have you ever had a friend parrot a party line to you, quote a general philosophical principle, try to force-fit this principle onto your unique circumstances, and by doing so cause you hurt? Have you ever struggled with outrage at their misapplied argument, knowing there is some truth to their words but that they're entirely unjust and inappropriate in your exceptional situation of hardship? There is a special hurt in these situations. In addition to feeling unloved and isolated, you can also feel the tension of knowing that the general rule is both applicable in many circumstances and utterly inapplicable in this particular moment.

How do you respond?

Do you argue?

Do you agree with the general statement while fighting to overcome your protest that the conclusion is invalid in your particular case?

Do you focus on how the conclusion does not apply to you and therefore risk appearing to fight against a general principle that—on a different day, in other circumstances—you might agree with?

Do you ride the pendulum to one logical extreme or the other?

Or do you get frustrated, abandon the conversation, and walk away?

This latter response could be the first step to severing a relationship, and it is the one thing that Job explicitly did not do throughout this book.

---

46 Beyond being very wrong, Bildad's message was arguably even stupid. You might question my calling Bildad's argument "stupid," as it may sound like I'm repeating Bildad's own mouthiness error. In actual fact, when we study the Hebrew of Job 42:8 toward the end of this book, we will see that God himself will assess the value of Eliphaz, Bildad, and Zophar's arguments as pure "folly." God himself thought the application of these principles to Job and his situation was not just mistaken or misguided but stupid, the kind of dangerous stupidity that was subject to divine judgment and punishment. More on this when we get to chapter forty-two.

As much as his friends frustrated and even hurt him, he never walked away from them.

Job responded next to Bildad the Rude.

21

THE SPIRIT'S CONTRARY VIEW EXPANDED

¹Then Job answered and said:
²"Truly I know that it is so:
   But how can a man be in the right before God?"

JOB 9:1–2

THIS SHOULD SOUND familiar to the reader. "How can a man be in the right before God?" is a paraphrase of the spirit's Contrary View in 4:17.[47]

Job went on:

³"If one wished to contend with him,
   one could not answer him once in a thousand times.
⁴He is wise in heart and mighty in strength
   —who has hardened himself against him, and succeeded?—
⁵he who removes mountains, and they know it not,
   when he overturns them in his anger,
⁶who shakes the earth out of its place,
   and its pillars tremble;

---

47 I transitioned from calling the spirit's view the Despairing View to the term Contrary View for reasons that will become apparent later. The Realistic View is another term that might usefully characterize the spirit's idea.

> ^{7}who commands the sun, and it does not rise;
>   who seals up the stars;
> ^{8}who alone stretched out the heavens
>   and trampled the waves of the sea;
> ^{9}who made the Bear and Orion,
>   the Pleiades and the chambers of the south;
> ^{10}who does great things beyond searching out,
>   and marvelous things beyond number.
> ^{11}Behold, he passes by me, and I see him not;
>   he moves on, but I do not perceive him.
> ^{12}Behold, he snatches away; who can turn him back?
>   Who will say to him, 'What are you doing?'"
>
> JOB 9:3–12

What Job was doing here was expanding on the implications of the spirit's Contrary View.

First, because people cannot be righteous on their own before God (9:2), people do not have a leg to stand on when they try to dispute God (9:3). There are no arguments sufficient to defend the guilty when you're arguing with God, and since everyone is guilty relative to God, arguments are pointless right from the start.

Second, God is both all-powerful (9:4–10) and invisible (9:11). Nobody can stop God. Nobody can say to him, "What are you doing?" (9:12). Nobody calls God to account. He is God. He is unaccountable to anyone but himself.

As a general principle on another day, in different circumstances, Job might have agreed with Bildad's Standard View arguments, but applying it to Job's own life, at this specific stage of his life, Job could not agree to do. In Job's case, there was evidence of an arbitrary and unpredictable principle at work, something that the spirit had referred to in their secret nighttime whisper. The Standard View was no help in Job's case.

Bildad had directed Job to plead his case before God on the basis of the Standard View (8:5–6), but Job responded that a human can neither out-argue God nor force God to change his direction (9:12). Job could not even nail down exactly where God was at any particular moment to provoke such a confrontation (9:11). Job's case did not conform to the Standard

View's simple definitions, and the view's simple solutions could not help his situation either. Job's case seemed altogether hopeless.

INTRODUCING A MONSTER

Job's next verse plants a seed that will grow into a full-fledged image later in his book.

> *¹³"God will not turn back his anger;*
> *beneath him bowed the helpers of Rahab."*
>
> JOB 9:13

This is one of those verses that the casual reader might quickly skip over. Rahab, in this case, is not the Rahab from Joshua 2 (as is clear in Hebrew). Here in chapter nine, and elsewhere in Job, Rahab may refer to one of two entities:

- a mythical monster from the sea, which appears to be the intended meaning in one of Job's later speeches (see Job 26:12);
- or it might refer to Egypt, which was most definitely the case in the book of Isaiah (see Isa. 30:7).

In this particular instance, I'm inclined to interpret the verse as referencing a sea monster, as Egypt is irrelevant to the setting and plot of Job, and as Job will explicitly reference a sea monster later in Job 26:12. In addition, this interpretation aligns with other monster imagery Job uses elsewhere, both in his first speech (3:8) and in other places, which we will come to throughout our study. Verse 7:12 also hints at this sea-monster imagery when Job asks "Am I the sea, or a monster of the deep, that you put me under guard?" (NIV).

The monster imagery in Job's speeches is subtle at this early stage of the book, but as we move along, it will become more pronounced, and God himself will take up this monster theme in his speeches toward the end of the book.

What purpose does this reference to a sea monster serve in the immediate context of chapter nine? On the surface, it underscores Job's point: God cannot be opposed. Even the helpers of a mythical sea monster cower before him. At a deeper literary level, this passage is foreshadowing darker ideas to come. We will see the full development of this monster imagery more clearly in later chapters.

In the meantime, this passage has resurfaced the idea of a sea monster. But for the moment, Job returns to speaking plainly about the hopelessness of attempting to challenge God.

THE FUTILITY OF ARGUING WITH GOD

> *¹⁴"How then can I answer him,*
> *choosing my words with him?*
> *¹⁵Though I am in the right, I cannot answer him;*
> *I must appeal for mercy to my accuser.*
> *¹⁶If I summoned him and he answered me,*
> *I would not believe that he was listening to my voice.*
> *¹⁷For he crushes me with a tempest*
> *and multiplies my wounds without cause…"*
>
> JOB 9:14–17

We might be tempted to be offended by Job's candor and passion. In particular, the charge that God would hurt Job "without cause" seems indefensible and possibly even blasphemous. Certainly, Job's friends had an issue with this phrasing.

We could choose to defend Job on the same grounds that we extended interpretative grace toward Job's wife, understanding that emotional language can be permissibly exaggerated or careless. But in this particular case, there is no need for this kind of clever handling. God has already used the same phrase to describe his own actions in 2:3.

But Job was not done with his raw observations. Job continued:

> *¹⁸"he will not let me get my breath,*
> *but fills me with bitterness.*
> *¹⁹If it is a contest of strength, behold, he is mighty!*

> *If it is a matter of justice, who can summon him?*[48]
> ²⁰ *Though I am in the right, my own mouth would condemn me;*
> *though I am blameless, he would prove me perverse.*
> ²¹ *I am blameless; I regard not myself;*
> *I loathe my life.*
> ²² *It is all one; therefore I say,*
> *'He destroys both the blameless and the wicked.'*
> ²³ *When disaster brings sudden death,*
> *he mocks at the calamity of the innocent.*
> ²⁴ *The earth is given into the hand of the wicked;*
> *he covers the faces of its judges—*
> *if it is not he, who then is it?"*
>
> JOB 9:18–24

If Job's previous emotional honesty had upset his companions, then this latest outpouring added fuel to the fire: God overwhelms people with misery; God does not even bother to explain himself; the innocent are speechless and helpless before him, and he destroys them alongside the wicked; and even worse, God mocks the despair of the innocent, and he handicaps those who might provide earthly help.

This is a terrible record. It is a bill of charges that pictures God as evil. How could a person like Job have said such things?

I struggled a great deal with passages like this in Job when I restarted my studies of this book. I was also determined to be unflinchingly thorough and find out if there was anything in Job that could help a father struggling as I was. When I encountered Job's candor in verses twenty-one and twenty-two, it made me struggle, but it also made my heart sing.

Let's look at this again:

---

48 The word translated as "him" in the original Hebrew is actually "me," i.e., "Who can summon me?" The rendering in the ESV follows the Septuagint and seems to fit the context better by making the statement a question of who will call God to justice rather than who will call Job. But the actual Hebrew *me* can create a similar image, the implication being that God was now ready for a hearing and was summoning Job to the trial. Either way, the point is the same: who is going to arrange a trial with God as the judge and Job as the defendant? The implied answer is, of course, no one.

> ^{21}*"I am blameless; I regard not myself;*
> *I loathe my life.*
> ^{22}*It is all one; therefore I say,*
> *'He destroys both the blameless and the wicked.'"*
>
> JOB 9:21–22

Here was someone who had been pushed to the edge of reason and stripped of every last vestige of support for his former faith and hope, who was now spiritually and emotionally naked. He was willing to think anything and question anything and no longer cared even for his own life.

In pain, I needed to hear Job say what he really thought because my religious self hid the doubts that had started to build within me. Job said things I secretly felt.

But is what Job said true? Is this really what God is like?

Well, what did the spirit say?

A DARK VIEW OF GOD?

> ^{3}*"I have seen the fool taking root,*
> *but suddenly I cursed his dwelling.*
> ^{4}*His children are far from safety;*
> *they are crushed in the gate,*
> *and there is no one to deliver them.*
> ^{5}*The hungry eat his harvest,*
> *and he takes it even out of thorns,*
> *and the thirsty pant after his wealth.*
> ^{6}*For affliction does not come from the dust,*
> *nor does trouble sprout from the ground,*
> ^{7}*but man is born to trouble*
> *as the sparks fly upward."*
>
> JOB 5:3–7

So is what Job said true? The spirit would seem to think so.

What is our judgment in this regard?

We have secret knowledge. We have access to the behind-the-scenes preface to Job's trials in the first two chapters of Job. Was God to blame?

God had called Satan's attention to Job. Twice. And God had given Satan leave to carry out his evil designs. Twice. And God had taken responsibility as well, referring to Satan's first request to torment Job as inciting God against Job "without reason" (2:3).

So is what Job said in these verses true?

I fought the implications of this question on both traditional religious grounds and out of emotional desperation. If God were truly this evil, then what business did I have being a Christian?

But as I studied, I also fought for this position out of deep need, amid deep pain, to wipe away the foggy feel-good and patently false optimism that had colored my previous understanding of God and religion—to lay hold of something heartbreaking and painful but true. Like wanting the truth about a diagnosis, no matter how bad, I wanted no false comfort. Sell me no lies.

If God could be cruel, so be it. I wanted no more hope or faith based on false pretense.

But remember: Satan is the enemy. Over and over again, chapters one and two identify Satan only by a description: the enemy. Satan is the enemy. Not God.

FIRST SIGNS OF DEPRESSION

Up until verse twenty-four of chapter nine, Job had been unrelentingly honest, and his focus had been very nearly an attack on God himself. We can credit Eliphaz and Bildad for tilting the discussion in such a manner that Job's pain became a fight for an honest evaluation of reality and appeal for justice, with Job on one side of Eliphaz and Bildad's arguments and God on the other. But with this searing cry of unanswerable candor, Job's speech now changed gears, pulling back from the outward fight and turning inward.

Job stayed honest, but his focus shifted as his emotional energies waned. He turned on himself, and we will start to see signs of a spiral. Emotionally wounded and in despair, his vision narrowed. The rest of Job's speech and his next two speeches record a slow slide into deep personal darkness.

For Job, the truth turned out to be grimmer than initially suspected. There is danger found in honesty.

Some psychologists describe the depressed as having a propensity for negativity that brings them down and is the root cause of their illness. Other psychologists posit an alternative interpretation: the depressed simply see the world more realistically. Negativity in this view is not a cause of depression but rather a clear-eyed, rational response to a negative reality combined with a perceived inability to make any changes to improve that reality.

Job had become very realistic, both emotionally and spiritually. As he explored the implications of this realism and dealt with his sense of helplessness, he slid into a state that looks very much like our modern definition of major depression.

Here are Job's own words on this topic:

> ^{25}"My days are swifter than a runner;
>   they flee away; they see no good.
> ^{26}They go by like skiffs of reed,
>   like an eagle swooping on the prey.
> ^{27}If I say, 'I will forget my complaint,
>   I will put off my sad face, and be of good cheer,'
> ^{28}I become afraid of all my suffering,
>   for I know you will not hold me innocent."
>
> JOB 9:25–28

Notice how the language of guilt and punishment had entered Job's words. He had refuted Eliphaz and Bildad's arguments, but the persuasiveness of a false but familiar interpretation was dangerously influential, and it colored Job's thinking. Job knew he was innocent but had begun to believe that God counted him as guilty.

THE NEED FOR HELP

Job continued:

> ^{29}"I shall be condemned;
>   why then do I labor in vain?
> ^{30}If I wash myself with snow
>   and cleanse my hands with lye,
> ^{31}yet you will plunge me into a pit,
>   and my own clothes will abhor me.
> ^{32}For he is not a man, as I am, that I might answer him,

> *that we should come to trial together.*
> *³³There is no arbiter between us,*
> *who might lay his hand on us both.*
> *³⁴Let him take his rod away from me,*
> *and let not dread of him terrify me.*
> *³⁵Then I would speak without fear of him,*
> *for I am not so in myself."*
>
> JOB 9:29–35

"There is no arbiter between us."

Was Job looking for someone like Jesus? Yes, he was. Job, of course, did not know anything about Jesus specifically. But he understood that he could not argue with God personally, and as a result, he needed someone to step in between him and God, to "lay his hand on us both" and take away Job's burgeoning fear of God. With this kind of profound intervention, Job believed that he could speak without fear and approach God with confidence—exactly what Hebrews 4:14–16 and many other scriptures point out as some of the blessings that are a consequence of Jesus's ministry.

Job was on the edge of a profound theological discovery here. He had not crossed over from identifying a need to developing a conviction about a solution. Still, the need shaped itself as he worked through the disconnect between the Standard View espoused by Eliphaz and Bildad and the reality of his own experiences. An arbiter was needed to settle the differences between God and humankind.

From this expressed need, Job will eventually discover a new faith—but not yet. These hints at inspiration and hope remain the exception as Job continued to struggle beneath the hurt that dominated his reality.

Focus on the words of Job now that follow in the final part of this speech. This was a prayer from Job to God. Hear the emotion that is the point of this poetic prayer and the candor of a soul crying out to his Maker for comfort. Other than a few footnotes, I won't comment on what follows but rather leave you to read slowly and absorb the poetry. Try to feel and relate to what Job expresses in this prayer:

> *¹"I loathe my life;*

Even the Monsters

> *I will give free utterance to my complaint;*
> *I will speak in the bitterness of my soul.*
> ²*I will say to God,*⁴⁹ *Do not condemn me;*
> *let me know why you contend against me.*
> ³*Does it seem good to you to oppress,*
> *to despise the work of your hands*
> *and favor the designs of the wicked?*
> ⁴*Have you eyes of flesh?*
> *Do you see as man sees?*
> ⁵*Are your days as the days of man,*
> *or your years as a man's years,*
> ⁶*that you seek out my iniquity*
> *and search for my sin,*
> ⁷*although you know that I am not guilty,*
> *and there is none to deliver out of your hand?*
> ⁸*Your hands fashioned and made me,*
> *and now you have destroyed me altogether.*
> ⁹*Remember that you have made me like clay;*
> *and will you return me to the dust?*
> ¹⁰*Did you not pour me out like milk*
> *and curdle me like cheese?*
> ¹¹*You clothed me with skin and flesh,*
> *and knit me together with bones and sinews.*
> ¹²*You have granted me life and steadfast love,*
> *and your care has preserved my spirit.*
> ¹³*Yet these things you hid in your heart;*
> *I know that this was your purpose.*⁵⁰
> ¹⁴*If I sin, you watch me*
> *and do not acquit me of my iniquity.*

---

49 Instead of "I *will* say to God," the Hebrew reads, "I *would* say to God." Chapter ten is a continuation of chapter nine. In chapter nine, Job identifies the need for an intercessor to aid him in his discussion with God. In chapter ten, Job is stating what he *would* say to God if he had such an intercessor.

50 What follows next is what Job felt was God's secret purpose for creating him. Punctuating this line with a colon rather than a period in our translation might have made the Hebrew intention here clearer.

¹⁵If I am guilty, woe to me!
>*If I am in the right, I cannot lift up my head,*
>*for I am filled with disgrace*
>*and look on my affliction.*

¹⁶And were my head lifted up, you would hunt me like a lion
>*and again work wonders against me.*

¹⁷You renew your witnesses against me
>*and increase your vexation toward me;*
>*you bring fresh troops against me.*

¹⁸Why did you bring me out from the womb?
>*Would that I had died before any eye had seen me*

¹⁹and were as though I had not been,
>*carried from the womb to the grave.*

²⁰Are not my days few?
>*Then cease, and leave me alone, that I may find a little cheer*

²¹before I go—and I shall not return—
>*to the land of darkness and deep shadow,*

²²the land of gloom like thick darkness,
>*like deep shadow without any order,*
>*where light is as thick darkness."*[51]

JOB 10:1–22

---

51 The understanding of death in Job's time as hopeless and final is well articulated here. There is no heaven in this formulation, only darkness, gloom, and finality.

22

THE STORY SO FAR

Two friends had spoken so far. First, Eliphaz had presented the Standard View and then the spirit's Contrary View. Eliphaz had concluded that the Standard View was the correct lens through which to view Job's tragedies.

Next, Bildad had spoken. He, too, had been a true believer in the Standard View, and he had taken Eliphaz's generalities to their logical conclusion, assigning blame for the death of Job's children to some set of unspecified sins that they had committed.[52] Bildad had assured Job that, with repentance, there was still time for him to escape his children's fate and be restored to a happy state.

We have seen how this well-meaning input had been, although unwittingly,[53] a very effective spiritual attack on Job's relationship with God. Job's initial submission to receiving both trouble and blessing from God,[54] and his initial outpouring of pain that did not blame,[55] had twisted into an integrity contest with Job pitted against God.[56] A division had developed between Job and God. Spiritual injury and the associated emotional distress had been added to Job's emotional and physical pain.

We have seen how Job had considered the finality of death as both

---

52 Recall 8:4.

53 Recall 2:11—these friends came with good intentions.

54 See 1:21.

55 See chapter three.

56 See 6:29 for Job's description of the stakes in exactly this manner.

positive and negative. Negatively, death was a source of despair, a place of darkness, and an ending place where even God could not find Job. Positively, death was an escape from pain and a way to avoid the risk of eventual unfaithfulness—death as an exit before failure.

In these speeches, Job had also considered the intimidating holiness of God and identified a new need: the need for an intercessor to bridge the gap between God and people.

TWO (FALSE) CHARGES

Into this mix came Zophar. One might expect the third friend and fourth speaker to start consolidating the issues and moving the conversation forward. Instead, we will find Zophar to be a somewhat distracted listener, a poor diagnostician, and a careless speaker.

> *¹Then Zophar the Naamathite answered and said:*
> *²"Should a multitude of words go unanswered,*
>   *and a man full of talk be judged right?*
> *³Should your babble silence men,*
>   *and when you mock, shall no one shame you?*
> *⁴For you say, 'My doctrine is pure,*
>   *and I am clean in God's eyes.'"*
>
>   JOB 11:1–4

It is easy to get caught up in the emotion of the poetry in Job. Getting caught up in the emotion is part of the point of writing something in poetry to begin with. But it is important to also give proper due to the literary considerations beyond just the poetic. In particular, Zophar had leveled a charge here—two charges, in fact.

The first charge was that Job had been mocking his friends, and the second, that Job had declared to God that he considered himself to be flawless in his doctrine and pure even in God's eyes.

Were these charges true? By this, I mean: did Job actually mock his friends and make these boastful statements about his beliefs and status before God?

Consider first the mocking charge. Job's first speech in chapter three was clearly a mock-free zone as he had struggled with despair over his existence and had said nothing about his friends. But what about his other two speeches: his response to Eliphaz in chapters six and seven, then his response to Bildad in chapters nine and ten?

In chapter six, Job had called for the devotion of his friends and described them as undependable streams. He had not been mocking them but instead rebuking them. Likewise, at the end of the chapter, Job had accused his friends of treating his words as wind (6:26) and had pleaded with them to reconsider the Standard View in light of Job's exceptional circumstances. In chapter seven, Job had not addressed his friends at all but started to express his pain in a soliloquy. His soliloquy had quickly turned into a prayer for kindness and consideration from God, lest Job perish in misery and not be found again by his Maker.

There is nothing in chapters six and seven that could be described as mockery.

What about his response to Bildad in chapters nine and ten? At one point, Job had expressed outrage that it appeared to him that God himself "mocks at the calamity of the innocent" (9:23). Still, he had quickly gone on to follow this charge with the statement that "if it is not he, who then is it?" (9:24). Job had asked questions, expressed his pain, and made incredibly bold observations about how the world truly works (contrasting with how the Standard View suggests it should work). But regarding Zophar's charge, there is still no mockery in these verses.

Chapter ten is similarly personal and emotional, containing Job's renewed plea for mercy and kindness from God before his few remaining days were over—again, no mockery.

So why would Zophar charge Job with mockery?

Before we answer this, consider his second charge: that Job had claimed to have flawless beliefs and purity in God's sight. Even if Job had claimed these positions for himself, we could look back to chapters one and two to see that Job had been in a very good place in God's sight. If we jump to the book's final chapter, we see God vindicating not only Job's life but also his beliefs.[57] With this outside knowledge, it might be tempting not to bother

---

57 See 42:8.

investigating whether Job had said this stuff since it appears that God would have agreed with his statements anyway.

Let's skip nothing in this study. Let's find out everything. Did Job claim to have flawless beliefs and purity in God's sight?

Chapter three gives us nothing in this regard as it continues to express Job's pain and emotional turmoil. So what about Job's response to Eliphaz?

In 6:3, Job had excused the emotional intensity of his words as "rash," the result of his deep anguish and misery. In other words, he had already been hedging his phrasing, aware that his emotions had been boiling over. He had hardly been claiming flawlessness. In 6:10, Job had longed for death to escape this life before the pressures of his situation caused him to turn against God. Again, he had hardly been claiming flawlessness. In 6:14, he had again admitted to his potential weakness, and in 6:24, he had asked to be taught where his understanding of his situation was in error. Instead of claiming to have flawless beliefs, Job had opened himself up to criticism and correction. In 7:21, Job had asked God to pardon his offenses and forgive his sins. Job had not claimed personal purity before God. Instead, he admitted that the opposite could be true.

What about Job's response to Bildad?

Job had started his response to Bildad by immediately asking, "How can a man be in the right before God?" (9:2). In 9:15, Job admitted that even if he were innocent (an admission that there may be gaps in his personal righteousness somewhere), he could not argue with God—this isn't a claim of having flawless beliefs but a claim of being unable to debate with God.

In 9:21, Job had said something bold: "I am blameless…" This statement would appear to vindicate the "clean in God's eyes" part of Zophar's charge, except that verse twenty-one follows verse twenty. In the previous verse, Job stated that even though he believed he was "in the right" and "blameless," God would still find cause to condemn him. Job had been expressing his belief that he did not deserve this punishment and that, nevertheless, he was apparently unclean in God's eyes—the opposite of what Zophar was charging here. Zophar's charge was not that Job claimed innocence in his own eyes but that Job claimed to be clean in God's eyes. Job had never said that. As a matter of fact, he had followed his own assertion of blamelessness by saying that God will not hold him innocent regardless (9:28), and that God had already found him guilty (9:29). Job's conclusion here had been based on not divine revelation but the logic of Eliphaz's Standard View—Job was suffering the punishment of the wicked, according to the Standard View. So even though Job knew he was not wicked, God must have already judged him to be so. From this conclusion had come Job's cry for an arbiter to sort out the problem between him and God—a problem that did not actually exist but had been manufactured by the misleading Standard View.

In 10:2, Job had asked God not to condemn him. In 10:15, Job had questioned whether he was guilty or whether he was in the right. Thus, Job had not been claiming to be pure in God's sight; he had been acknowledging his uncertainty and fear that the opposite was God's actual opinion.

So Zophar charged Job with mockery. But Job hadn't mocked anybody. And Zophar charged Job with claiming to have flawless beliefs and purity in the sight of God when Job had never said that and had even asserted the opposite as the more likely case.

Zophar had made several charges about things Job had said—which Job had not actually said.

WHO SAID WHAT

So who said these things?

> [27] "Behold, this [i.e., the Standard View] we have searched out; it is true.
> Hear, and know it for your good."
>
> Job 5:27

The closest anyone had come to claiming flawless beliefs had been in this line from Eliphaz. He had apparently taken a poll. The three friends had all agreed and had the Standard View down cold. All that had been left to do was explain it to Job and apply it to his situation. The view had been solid and brooked no debate.

Bildad had echoed this confidence in the Standard View when he had told Job to ask those from previous generations (8:8), when he had assured Job that the Standard View had held even in those previous generations and therefore should not be questioned further.

Job's "crime" had not been claiming to have a flawless set of beliefs but rather daring to question the reliability of the Standard View. He had questioned tradition, and that was a recipe for hostility and social exclusion. It was the same "crime" Jesus committed when he crossed the traditions of the Pharisees in the Gospels. To question the unquestionable is to set yourself up as a target for serious charges. Even the softest of questions can be perceived as bold pridefulness to those invested in insecure beliefs.

And what about the charge of cleanness in God's eyes? No one had claimed this position so far in these chapters.

What about the charge of mockery? Only Bildad the Rude had engaged in mockery when he had described Job's words as "a great wind" (8:2).

ZOPHAR THE WITLESS

So was Zophar just a true believer in the Standard View, reacting emotionally to Job's challenge of the status quo and misinterpreting Job's questions as claims of having flawless beliefs? Was Zophar demonstrating a classic defensiveness in the face of observations that contradicted his worldview? And did Zophar simply morph Job's belief in his own innocence into claims of innocence even in God's eyes? Possibly. Or maybe Zophar was just clued out: Zophar the Witless.

As we will see, Zophar's oratory skills were weaker than his other two friends', as was his attention span. As a result, not only were his speeches shorter, but later in the book, he will appear to forget his role and will simply fail to supply his third speech and final rebuttal as the other two friends had. In addition, this will not be the last time in his two short speeches that he will misunderstand or misquote the words of others.

Suppose we can roughly characterize the first two friends as Eliphaz the Religious and Bildad the Rude. In that case, Zophar will have to go down as Zophar the Witless. Or to be kinder: Zophar the Clued Out. Or gentler yet: Zophar the Distracted. Or more descriptively: Zophar the Guy Who Was Only Partially Paying Attention to This Conversation and Occasionally Interrupted It to Talk Nonsense.

A DEMONSTRATION OF IRONY

Zophar did not seem to be at all aware of his errors and continued on:

> ^{5}*"But oh, that God would speak*
> *and open his lips to you,*
> ^{6}*and that he would tell you the secrets of wisdom!*
> *For he is manifold in understanding.*
> *Know then that God exacts of you less than your guilt deserves."*
>
> JOB 11:5–6

There are two ironies here in Zophar's words. The first irony is clear in our translation: he had called on God to condemn Job, yet Zophar himself will be the one God condemns for these words at the end of the book.

The second source of irony here is obscured in the ESV translation. Where ESV states "for he is manifold in understanding," the original Hebrew states "for wisdom is double sided" or "has two sides," meaning that wisdom is "double what you think it is" or "it is more complicated than you know."[58] In other words, Zophar was not describing God's grasp of wisdom ("manifold in understanding") but instead describing the nature of wisdom itself. Wisdom is complicated and difficult—this idea came from the guy who was only half paying attention in these discussions!

Zophar's description of wisdom's double-sided nature would be a nice preface to refuting the Standard View's overly simplistic explanations. If Zophar had moved to create a framework for understanding Job's situation that accepted the unclear exceptions of Job's irregular reality, perhaps God might have viewed him more favorably at the end of the book. But knowing that wisdom is double sided did not, unfortunately, lead Zophar to humbly reconsider Job's guilt. Instead, he remained a committed Standard View supporter and continued along this line:

> ^{7}*"Can you find out the deep things of God?*
> *Can you find out the limit of the Almighty?*
> ^{8}*It is higher than heaven—what can you do?*
> *Deeper than Sheol—what can you know?*
> ^{9}*Its measure is longer than the earth*
> *and broader than the sea.*
> ^{10}*If he passes through and imprisons*

---

58 Reyburn, 218.

> *and summons the court, who can turn him back?*
> *¹¹ For he knows worthless men;*
> > *when he sees iniquity, will he not consider it?"*
>
> JOB 11:7–11

These are Job's own words from chapters nine and ten.[59] Zophar was simply restating the problem of the unsearchable holiness of God, which had been the root of Job's desire for an intercessor. Zophar had restated the problem, but he had no solution to it.

He went on:

> *¹¹ "For he knows worthless men;*
> > *when he sees iniquity, will he not consider it?*
> *¹² But a stupid man will get understanding*
> > *when a wild donkey's colt is born a man!"*
>
> JOB 11:11–12

What was Zophar's point?

Was he saying that the Standard View holds and only a stupid person would fail to understand this—and that a stupid person has no hope of becoming wise?

Yes, that would appear to be his point.

How did this help the suffering Job?

One would imagine that this was no help at all but was just insulting and discouraging. But there is a bit more to this speech than meets the eye. Job himself had used a donkey image to describe himself in his first response to Eliphaz.

WHERE THE DONKEY IMAGERY COMES IN

Here is how Job had originally referenced donkey imagery earlier in the book:

> *⁵ "Does the wild donkey bray when he has grass,*

---

59 These are not word-for-word quotes, but the idea Zophar expressed in 11:7–9 can be found coming first from Job's lips in 9:3–4, 10–11. Zophar's idea in 11:10 can also be viewed as restatements of 9:12–20, 32–35.

> *or the ox low over his fodder?*
> *⁶Can that which is tasteless be eaten without salt,*
> *or is there any taste in the juice of the mallow?*
> *⁷My appetite refuses to touch them;*
> *they are as food that is loathsome to me."*
>
> JOB 6:5–7

Recall that Job's point in chapter six had been to explain his response to Eliphaz's recitation of the Standard View. Just as a donkey makes noise when hungry, he too had been justified in crying out against a view that did not meet his need. Job could not accept Eliphaz's advice any more than a donkey could accept its hunger.

Zophar resurrected that donkey illustration and continued to place Job in the donkey's role (as Job did), but Zophar was now using the donkey as an image of stupidity to illustrate the hopelessness of Job ever becoming wise.

In this metaphor, Zophar was taking the image Job had used to illustrate his distress and was using it to claim that Job's underlying problem was his stupidity. The donkey's colt cannot be born as a human, and thus Job the donkey was unable to grasp—and would never be able to grasp—what was evident to everyone else. Job was too stupid to understand the Standard View.

For a friend who came to "comfort and console" Job in his suffering, Zophar appears determined to make a miserable job of it.

THE OPPOSITE OF WHAT JOB HAD SAID

Despite this negativity, however, Zophar did give Job the same offer of hope that both Eliphaz and Bildad had proffered. Here was Zophar's spin on this material:

> *¹³"If you prepare your heart,*
> *you will stretch out your hands toward him.*
> *¹⁴If iniquity is in your hand, put it far away,*
> *and let not injustice dwell in your tents.*
> *¹⁵Surely then you will lift up your face without blemish;*
> *you will be secure and will not fear.*
> *¹⁶You will forget your misery;*

> *you will remember it as waters that have passed away.*
> *¹⁷And your life will be brighter than the noonday;*
> *its darkness will be like the morning.*
> *¹⁸And you will feel secure, because there is hope;*
> *you will look around and take your rest in security.*
> *¹⁹You will lie down, and none will make you afraid;*
> *many will court your favor."*
>
> JOB 11:13–19

Zophar was not just restating the Standard View for Job. He was restating the Standard View by taking Job's own words and inverting them. A rough sketch of the provenance of these verses is as follows:

- Verse 11:14 is a reversal of Job's thoughts in 3:25 and 10:15–16.
- In 3:10, Job asked why his conception had not been prevented to "hide trouble from [his] eyes." The Hebrew word translated as "trouble" here is translated as "misery" in 11:16. In 3:10, Job had wished he'd never seen trouble. Job did see it, but in 11:15, Zophar assured Job he would surely forget it.
- In 10:20–22, Job had foreseen a future of only darkness and gloom, and so in 11:17 Zophar assured Job that bright light would come if Job submitted to the Standard View.
- Job had expressed his condition of hopelessness in 3:26 and 6:11. In 7:6, 13–15, he had expressed his unrelenting distress and insecurity. In response, Eliphaz assured Job that he would experience the opposite of these conditions: hope and security (11:18–19).

To achieve these reversals of circumstance, Job needed to repent. Zophar instructed Job to put away his sin, but like the two previous friends, he identified no specific sin that Job needed to address. He assumed Job was guilty of sin based on the apparent surplus of punishment in Job's life. Despite Zophar's acknowledgment of wisdom's double-sided nature, Zophar could not imagine exceptions to the formula first articulated by Eliphaz.

RELIGIOUS BLINDNESS

A misguided theology can be a very blinding thing. Tradition can be blinding. Philosophies, templates for viewing the world, ideologies—these are all useful tools, but reality can expose them as rigid and clumsy. The mind calcifies within a framework, and what is obvious to an innocent observer is simply not seen by "the wise."

A misguided theology can also be a cruel thing. Zophar's assurance was that Job would forget his trouble, remembering "it as waters that have passed away" (11:16). These were Job's children Zophar was talking about. These were also the hundreds of murdered people who had worked for him and the widows and fatherless children around him, whose lives had been irrevocably traumatized by loss and grief. So not only can a wrong theology be cruel, but it can also lead to monstrous unkindness.

If there is a donkey in this chapter, it is Zophar, not Job. Zophar had come to help, but like Bildad, who had blamed the deaths of Job's children on some unidentified sin, Zophar forgot that he had come to comfort and console. Instead, he delivered an unthinking and unfeeling blanket application of a view that did not apply to Job's situation.

The friends had come to help, but so far, they had only managed to hurt.

A HARSH CONCLUSION

Here was how Zophar wrapped up his lecture:

> *"But the eyes of the wicked will fail;*
> *all way of escape will be lost to them,*
> *and their hope is to breathe their last."*
>
> Job 11:20

The only positive thing that can be said about Zophar's speech is that it was short. A less positive observation is that, where Eliphaz and Bildad had at least attempted to end on a positive note, Zophar closed his speech with a threat. The implication was that if Job did not take the vague steps toward repentance that Zophar had identified in 11:13–14, then 11:20 would be

Job's fate. Unless Job dealt with his unidentified sin, his only hope would be death. That was Zophar's concluding thought.

Indeed, death already looked like the only thing Job could hope for. Job had already immersed himself too much in thoughts of death.

Like his previous two friends, Zophar made a bad situation worse by witlessly applying a broad principle to a context it did not apply to. In his opening statement, he had charged Job with mockery. Job was starting to have enough of these "friends." In his response to Zophar, we will see him open with the very mockery Zophar had accused him of indulging in. Zophar's charge had been uncalled for before, but in the next chapter, it will become a self-fulfilling prophecy as Job will level his tongue at his useless counselors.

23

JOB STARTS MOCKING

¹Then Job answered and said:
²"No doubt you are the people,
and wisdom will die with you.
³But I have understanding as well as you;
I am not inferior to you.
Who does not know such things as these?
⁴I am a laughingstock to my friends;
I, who called to God and he answered me,
a just and blameless man, am a laughingstock."

JOB 12:1–4[60]

ZOPHAR HAD ACCUSED Job of mocking them in the previous chapter. He had also accused Job of claiming to have flawless beliefs and purity in the sight of God. They had been unfounded charges. Once Job was saddled with these charges, however, his immediate response was to make them true. He

---

60 There is a lot of emotion in this opening response by Job, but the poetry underneath the actual words further emphasizes this emotion. Both verses three and four are awkward three-line verses in Hebrew. "Who does not know all these things?" in verse three and "a mere laughingstock, though righteous and blameless" in verse four both stand out as out of place, like extra out-of-rhythm lines in an otherwise rhythmic English poem. These lines break the rhythm and draw attention to themselves, emphasizing Job's emotional discomfort with lines that would sound uncomfortable to the original reader.

mocked the friends' useless wisdom. He described his former relationship with God as one where he called and God answered. And Job stated that he was just and blameless—it is worth saying again that God himself agrees with this position at both the beginning and end of the book.

What was Job's strategy here? Why, rather than refuting Zophar, did Job appear to make Zophar's false charges come true?

Eliphaz had implied that Job deserved his punishment. Bildad had skipped Eliphaz's subtleties and stated plainly that Job's children had been killed for their (unspecified) sin. There had been very little that Job could do in his emotional state to counter these men other than to appeal for them to reconsider their underlying Standard View premise.

Zophar's charges, however, were different, and they were demonstrably wrong to everyone present. They were stuffed with inaccuracies and one major misattribution. Beyond getting the diagnosis for Job's overall situation wrong, Zophar was not even accurately following the conversation and keeping track of who said what.

Zophar's speech did not inspire an intellectual discussion or an emotional appeal for understanding but instead a verbal slap in the face. "No doubt you are the people, and wisdom will die with you" (12:2). Job was still descending into the depression that we identified as developing in his previous speech, but on his way down, Zophar's foolishness provoked a spark, and that spark showed Zophar what mockery really looks like; it showed Zophar what a claim of self-righteousness looks like; and it showed Zophar that, even if Job had claimed to have flawless beliefs, Job had a mind just as fitted for thinking as they have and just as much of a right to use it to interpret his situation.

A VARIATION ON THE STANDARD VIEW: TROUBLE AS TRAINING INSTEAD OF PUNISHMENT

JOB'S SPARK FLASHED with something else as well. He made a very poignant observation.

> "In the thought of one who is at ease there is contempt for misfortune;

Even the Monsters

it is ready for those whose feet slip."

Job 12:5

How much easier it is for people to believe that everyone who suffers is experiencing what they deserve. The human mind wants a tidy package, a balanced equation, a predictable and therefore manageable reality. Those whose feet slip deserve that slip. Misfortune only comes to those who deserve it. That this Standard View is a lie that only comforts people who aren't suffering themselves—that was the charge Job leveled at his friends.

My wife and I were spared these sorts of accusations after the birth of our daughter. Our lives up until then had been too community-oriented, too apparently successful, not just on a worldly level but on a spiritual one as well, with church responsibilities reliably completed and the spiritual fruit from our efforts in the service of others too apparent. We helped strengthen marriages, helped singles in our ministry find purity and then marriage, welcomed outsiders who then studied the Bible and became Christians, confessed our sins, helped heal hearts, and served and encouraged the poor. The church group we were responsible for had literally experienced birth, marriage, and death (by cancer) as well as spiritual rebirth and hidden sins uncovered and overcome, all while the two of us held down full-time secular careers. We were not perfect—but no one charged us with deserving our daughter's medical issues. If anything, some struggled with the very thing Job struggled with: how could God allow harm to come to a family that worked hard in his service?

However, we were still confronted with a variation on the Standard View at every turn. If we did not deserve these challenges, then perhaps God had given us these challenges not to punish but to train.

"What is God teaching you through this?" was an innocent and apparently spiritual question that others asked of us—a lot. There was certainly no evil intent in those who asked that question. But asking this of a father and mother whose hearts have been irrevocably captured by just a few pounds of a frail and fragile baby girl who was struggling for life, clinging to mommy and daddy, victimized by needles and tubes and million-dollar machines—asking that of those heart-torn parents teetering on the edge of emotional collapse—asking that of the father, when not only his daughter but also his wife goes down for unknown reasons (An aneurysm? Maybe a series of small strokes?)—what is God trying to teach you through this?—the question was not just well meaning but also, practically speaking, evil. What is God teaching me? What is God teaching me? How about I hit you, and then you tell me what God is teaching you through this.

Of course, I never hit anyone. But I felt like it nearly every time I heard that pious phrase. What do you think God is teaching you through this?

But why the anger? Why the sudden rage? Why did that simple question make me apoplectic inside as I maintained a calm exterior?

Like the Standard View implications that Job confronted, the what-is-God-teaching-you question blames the victim. In Job's case, the assumption was that Job was guilty of sin and therefore deserved his punishment. By logical deduction, then, the solution to his crises was to repent. The sooner he repented, the sooner his trials would cease.

In our case, the assumption was that we needed to learn something, and therefore there was nothing truly tragic about our circumstances. It was just training. By logical deduction then the solution to our daughter's crises was to be a good student and learn quickly. The sooner we learned the lessons God had for us, the sooner our daughter would be restored to health. What we experienced was just a slightly altered version of the Standard View: punishment was traded for training, but the important thing was that this belief preserved the underlying orderliness and predictability of reality. The solution to the crisis was in our hands, if only we would respond to God's enigmatic actions appropriately.

There is truth in the Standard View, which makes it seductive. Sometimes God is punishing (or training). As Job faced the idea that bad things often happen to bad people, he slipped into confusion, which led to his depression. You see, the burden was now on Job to figure out what he'd done wrong.

Like Job, I had moments when the interpretative power of the Standard View was very persuasive. After all, David learned to be king by leading men on the run through the desert. Joseph went through slavery and prison before rising to be the second-in-command of Egypt. Even Jesus went through suffering, and as the book of Hebrews makes clear, he learned, the Son of God learned, and was made perfect through suffering.[61] So like Job, all I had to do was figure out what I was missing, and all of this suffering would stop.

---

61 See Hebrews 5:8–10.

Believing that a solution is within our power to act on can be comforting. When pain is sufficiently great, even false comfort can serve as a refuge.

When Mackenzie was less than six months old, I preached a midweek sermon entitled "The Rare Jewel of Christian Contentment," based on a seventeenth-century book of the same name. The book contains a series of sermons by an English preacher named Jeremiah Burroughs, in which one of the most memorable lines (from both the book and my sermon) was the statement that "Christ's school is a school of suffering." It is a true statement. My sermon on it was popular enough that I was asked to preach it again at a church in Calgary. I was flown in to deliver the message.

Mackenzie was just a training course for my wife and me. All we had to do was apply ourselves to the lessons and graduate, and then the course would be over. The sermon was just as much of a hit the second time as it had been the first. Now I just needed to figure out how to make it real in my own life.

THE STANDARD VIEW AS A PSYCHOLOGICAL TRAP

As I talked about in chapter two, after the trouble with our daughter started, I adopted a false optimism in an earnest effort to project faithfulness. My choice to wear this mask was driven by a misguided fear that any sign of emotional stumbling would somehow jeopardize her chance of God giving her a favorable response to our prayers. So I added a new stoic and very prideful idea to this religious artificiality: "God must be preparing us for some important mission."

God bless my wife for parting ways with me and my own divided heart on this point. She would have none of it. While, like Job, she protested and argued with God and eventually with me on this topic, I disappeared further into a surface-level calm and an even more conflicted internal state.

What happens to the soul that buys into the Standard View that suffering is always punishment? What happens to the soul that then tortures itself into a faith collapse trying to root out, confess, and repent of phantom sins that might be the cause of their suffering?

And what happens to the soul that buys into the version that God is always teaching us something through trouble—that learning the lesson will prepare them for a higher calling in God's service?

What happens to that soul when trouble, in the end, is just trouble, and there was no glorious mission? What happens when the lessons frantically studied prove to be just figments created by our desire to find comfort by seeing order where there is none?

What if God is not teaching the suffering soul anything?

COMFORT FOR EVERYONE BUT THE AFFLICTED

In its various forms, the Standard View is seductive, but its comforts wear out as time passes. Repentance results in no relief, and lessons remain elusive. It is a view that simply adds an additional burden onto a suffering soul.

It turns out that the comforts of the Standard View are not comforts for the sufferer. They are only comforting for "one who is at ease" (12:5). Furthermore, the Standard View teaches that misfortune is the sufferer's fault (or for the benefit of the sufferer). As a result, there is nothing to fear in the world and little that needs to be done to help people who are suffering.

The Standard View absolves the comfortable from needing to exercise inconvenient compassion.

The Standard View makes action optional and perhaps not even advisable. This is because action might get in the way of God's discipline (or the lesson God is trying to teach).

The Standard View is wrong. Job knew it, and now so do we.

24

REALITY IS A MESS

The Standard View did not distract Job for long. It did start to sour his thinking about God, but it did not succeed in drawing him completely into a fantastical view of reality. Job knew from personal experience that reality is not neat. The Standard View formula is not a law of physics. Exceptions are the norm.

Here is how Job further expressed this idea:

> *⁵"In the thought of one who is at ease there is contempt for misfortune;*
> > *it is ready for those whose feet slip.*
> *⁶The tents of robbers are at peace,*
> > *and those who provoke God are secure,*
> > *who bring their god in their hand.*
> *⁷But ask the beasts, and they will teach you;*
> > *the birds of the heavens, and they will tell you;*
> *⁸or the bushes of the earth, and they will teach you;*
> > *and the fish of the sea will declare to you.*
> *⁹Who among all these does not know*
> > *that the hand of the Lord has done this?"*
>
> Job 12:5–9

Remember how, earlier in our study of Job, we discussed the importance of parallelism in Hebrew poetry? The first line of a verse says something, and the second line says something parallel to it—the second line expands on, focuses, or somehow, in a parallel fashion, builds on the first line and, by so doing, rhymes ideas.

Sometimes in English poetry, amid a rhyming poem, a line in the middle will not rhyme. Perhaps the meter will be off as well, and both rhythm and rhyme fail. It is not a mistake. It is intentional. It jars the pattern and, by doing so, brings focus to a key verse.

In this same way, Job 12:6 would have been jarring to the original Hebrew ear. First of all, it is a three-line verse in the original rather than the traditional two lines we have mostly seen so far. Second, of the three lines, only two of the lines "rhyme" an idea. The first line states that robbers (who at the time would have been rapists, murders, and thieves) live undisturbed lives. Their lives are a contradiction of the Standard View because they get away with their crimes. In Job's day, there was no international police force to chase down the Sabean and Chaldean raiders that had murdered the people on Job's farm and stolen its wealth. These marauders had returned home content and even now feasted on the livestock taken from Job's farm as they celebrated and toasted their successes.

We would expect the second line of verse six to build on this idea of the marauders living undisturbed lives in defiance of the Standard View's predictions. This is exactly what we get: the marauders are redefined as people who provoke God—further emphasizing how doomed they should be—and yet they remain secure.

But then along comes line number three.

As a final stamp on this theme, the third line simply redefines these marauders yet again—this time not only as people who kill and steal, not only as people who provoke God with their actions, but as people who "bring [or carry] their god in their hand." They were idol worshippers. There is no justification anywhere in the Standard View for the success of idol-worshipping peoples—and yet in Job's world, these were the dominant people. They were dominant in terms of population size, power, and overall wealth and success.

The third line fails to reference that these people are undisturbed and secure, and so the parallelism fails. The last line does not rhyme properly. Instead, it focuses just on identifying these people as idol worshippers because that is the jarring part. People living undisturbed lives is not jarring. But these people were evil, and these evil people lived undisturbed lives—that is what is jarring. So the poetic parallelism fails and, in this way, emphasizes the failure of the Standard View.

The unfortunate thing for us as modern English readers is that we have to pick this poetic language apart so carefully to understand what is going on at the literary level that we wind up cauterizing our emotional connection to the verse.

The key thing that Job was trying to communicate emotionally is that the world is broken. Evil people are successful people.

GOD IS IN CHARGE OF THE MESS

It is worth noting at this point that the "you" in verse seven is singular. The other two friends were likely listening, but Job was talking directly face-to-face with Zophar here.

Job made his argument in this three-line verse. No further evidence was required.

From here, Job told Zophar just to ask the animals, the birds, the earth itself (or "the bushes of the earth," as the ESV has it)—even the fish. Ask the fish. They will tell you. The hand of the Lord has done this.

The hand of the Lord. "The LORD" here in Hebrew is "Yahweh," which was God's holiest name. This rare name for God appears in the prose introduction and conclusion of Job, but outside of God's own speeches, this is the only time the name "Yahweh" is used in the poetry of Job. The friends never used this holiest of names. Job only used it once, here, in an inflammatory context: nature itself teaches that Yahweh is responsible for the success of killers, rapists, and thieves. That was what Job had just said, and he used the name "Yahweh" to say it.

Wow. This is a dare. This is bold language. This is something that should make us sit up straight, open our eyes wide, and really pay attention. If this were a movie, at this point, the soundtrack would suddenly get intense.

But this was not just irrational emotion talking. Job had a very solid reason for his statement:

"In his hand is the life of every living thing

> *and the breath of all mankind."*
>
> JOB 12:10

Job had stated the truth. Every life is in God's hands—both the life of the murderer and the life of their victims. It is something, then, when God does nothing, and very often, God does nothing.

That's worth repeating: It is something when God does nothing, and very often, God does nothing.

The Standard View does not hold.

Job continued:

> *^{11}"Does not the ear test words*
>   *as the palate tastes food?*
> *^{12}Wisdom is with the aged,*
>   *and understanding in length of days."*
>
> JOB 12:11–12

Job expected that his friends would be able to discern the truth in what he was saying. He expected that they would also be able to discern the untruth in what they were saying. They ought to have been able to observe that their own words were not true. What they said should have tasted funny to them. They should not have needed Job to point out the flaws in their arguments.

A TOUGH PORTRAIT OF GOD

Job's next words paint a picture of God that some might find offensive, though they start out innocently enough. Here's how they start:

> *^{13}"With God are wisdom and might;*
>   *he has counsel and understanding.*
> *^{14}If he tears down, none can rebuild;*
>   *if he shuts a man in, none can open.*
> *^{15}If he withholds the waters, they dry up;*

> *if he sends them out, they overwhelm the land."*
>
> JOB 12:13–15

The basic idea of God's wisdom and power that Job presented here was one that Job's friends would not have argued with. They would have seen Job as someone torn down and imprisoned—someone who needed to get right with God to gain relief from this situation. But Job did not deliver these few verses to support their thesis. Instead, he delivered these few verses as a buildup to what follows.

What follows is a horrible articulation of God's actions in the world, foreshadowed by Job's analysis of how God manages water: he either gives not enough and therefore creates a drought, or he gives too much and creates a flood. Whatever God does, there is a horrible quality to it. God's actions, in reality, defy the Standard View's theories.

Rather than depicting God as one who creates order, Job charged that God uses his wisdom and power to create disorder. Job's point was that the Standard View is not true and that God is much more unpredictable, even horrible, than Job's friends would like to admit.

Job continued to build out his thesis:

> *16"With him are strength and sound wisdom;*
> *the deceived and the deceiver are his.*
> *17He leads counselors away stripped,*
> *and judges he makes fools.*
> *18He looses the bonds of kings*
> *and binds a waistcloth on their hips.*
> *19He leads priests away stripped*
> *and overthrows the mighty.*
> *20He deprives of speech those who are trusted*
> *and takes away the discernment of the elders.*
> *21He pours contempt on princes*
> *and loosens the belt of the strong.*
> *22He uncovers the deeps out of darkness*
> *and brings deep darkness to light.*
> *23He makes nations great, and he destroys them;*

> *he enlarges nations, and leads them away.*
> *²⁴He takes away understanding from the chiefs of the people of the earth*
> *and makes them wander in a trackless waste.*
> *²⁵They grope in the dark without light,*
> *and he makes them stagger like a drunken man."*
>
> JOB 12:16–25

In verse seventeen, it says that God leads counselors away "stripped." What did God strip them of? In English, I think we would assume clothes, and if not clothes, then perhaps honor or dignity.

One clue to understanding this verse more accurately is to remember that Hebrew poetry rhymes ideas. The second half of the verse should make the first half clear. In the second half of verse seventeen, Job charged God with turning judges into fools. In Hebrew, the word literally means madmen.

With this as our parallel, we can understand that God does not strip counselors of their clothes (or dignity) but rather of something like their sanity. Perhaps reason, good judgment, or clear thinking.

Job was claiming that God is responsible for the dysfunction in civic life.

This was a very intense charge but not a random one. Three verses later, Job repeated himself by claiming that God silences those trusted to provide good advice and removes the discernment of elders responsible for providing social direction. Again, in verse twenty-four, God deprives the earth's leaders of their reason. He sends them wandering across the landscape and makes them lost. In verse twenty-five, they "stagger like a drunken man." They are not drunk. But they stagger like they are drunk. Are they suffering from dehydration in the wasteland? Are they suffering some kind of dizziness from low blood sugar? Are they uncoordinated like a drunk person or suffering from some kind of physical ailment (Parkinson's disease? Alzheimer's?) that makes them lost and unstable? It does not really matter. It is poetry, and the point is to make the reader feel something, and that something, in this case, is that the world is messed up and that somehow God is responsible for the mess.

In chapter three, Job had been upset that God gives light to those in misery (3:20). Here Job was distressed that God removes light and lets the leaders of society grope about in darkness (12:25).

Job had said similar things in chapter nine, speaking there from the victim's point of view. He had concluded a brief run of charges by accusing God of blindfolding the judges in the land, but then he had added, "if it is not he, who then is it?" (9:24). In chapter nine, Job had left an opening in his charges for an alternate source of the world's troubles. Here in chapter twelve, having been provoked by Zophar into making the mocking and self-righteous statements that Zophar had accused him of, Job returned to his baldly honest assessment of God's responsibility for the world's troubles. However, this time, he did not end with a conciliatory "if not he, then who?"

This time Job was not backing down. And he had a few things to say to his friends as well.

25

JOB REBUKES HIS FRIENDS

> *¹"Behold, my eye has seen all this,*
> *my ear has heard and understood it.*
> *²What you know, I also know;*
> *I am not inferior to you."*
>
> JOB 13:1–2

THE "YOU" IN these verses is singular. Job was still talking directly to Zophar in verses one and two.

> *³"But I would speak to the Almighty,*
> *and I desire to argue my case with God."*
>
> JOB 13:3

Job had been talking directly to Zophar. But—and in the Hebrew, this is a big but, as the original phrasing made the contrast very pronounced—Job didn't want to talk to Zophar. Job wanted to talk to God. He wanted to talk to God despite 7:16–21, where Job had asked God to leave him alone. Despite 9:3–13, where Job had despaired that it was impossible to win a dispute with God. And despite 9:14–22 and 9:29–35, where his helpless inadequacy to dispute with God had caused him to cry out for an arbiter to intervene on his behalf.

Even though there was no arbiter and he could not conduct a trial on his own, Job still desired to speak with and even argue his case with God.

He wanted this even despite 12:14, where Job had indicated that he understood that God's judgments could never be reversed. Despite this seemingly insurmountable lineup of obstacles and even terrors, Job wanted a hearing with God. Not with Zophar—and not with his other friends either.

As Job moved into the next verse, the Zophar-focused singular you becomes a more all-encompassing plural you. Job had had it with all three friends, not just Zophar.

> *⁴"As for you, you whitewash with lies;*
> *worthless physicians are you all.*
> *⁵Oh that you would keep silent,*
> *and it would be your wisdom!*
> *⁶Hear now my argument*
> *and listen to the pleadings of my lips.*
> *⁷Will you speak falsely for God*
> *and speak deceitfully for him?"*
>
> Job 13:4–7

Will you speak falsely and deceitfully for God? What was Job saying here?

Job had seen and experienced the ill effects of how the world operates. His eyes had seen, his ears had heard, and he had understood what he had observed (13:1). The friends presumably had seen the horror and evil in the world as well, and yet, despite the objective reality around them, they sought to force Job's circumstances into the Standard View model. They would even "whitewash with lies" to make their model of the world work.

My wife has a vinyl tape measure. If a strip of fabric measures half an inch too long, you can stretch the vinyl, and voilà! The fabric is now the right length. Reality has been altered (due to poor tape measure design) to suit the demands of the measurer. Job's point was that you can stretch the tape measure all you want—his friends could smear him with lies as much as they wanted—but in the end, reality was still reality.

Were Job's friends really going to stretch the tape measure by speaking wickedly—that is, falsely—on God's behalf? Were they going to paint Job as evil just to make God look good?[62]

---

[62] Notice the three-way tug-of-war here between Job's righteousness, God's justice,

The next verse is particularly revealing:

> [8] *"Will you show partiality toward him?*
> *Will you plead the case for God?"*
>
> JOB 13:8

The phrase "show partiality toward him" is sarcastic. Job was portraying his friends as acting as God's superior and doing him a favor. They were forcing reality through the Standard View filter, but this view was bumping up against Job's seemingly paradoxical mix of troubles and righteousness, which either called the Standard View into question or called God's justice into question. Job suggested that, rather than rethink the Standard View, his friends were planning to do God a favor and bail him out of this awkward jam by somehow finding false fault with Job, thus exonerating God.

The Hebrew in the second half of verse eight uses the legal language of courtrooms and trials. The idea is that Job's friends were offering to be God's defense attorney. Job turned the tables instead and asked how these false witnesses for God would fare if God examined them.

> [9] *"Will it be well with you when he searches you out?*
> *Or can you deceive him, as one deceives a man?"*
>
> JOB 13:9

Clever arguments might fool people into believing that Job was wrong and God is vindicated, but these arguments cannot fool God himself. God knows his actions. God knew Job's righteousness and innocence.

GOD IS NOT A SPIN DOCTOR

In 3:20, Job had asked why light was "given to him who is in misery." In 12:22, Job told his friends that God "uncovers [or reveals] the deeps out of

---

and the absolute and universal truth of the Standard View. Only two of these three things could survive the test of reality. Job at times argued that God's justice needed reconsidering, but mostly he argued that the Standard View was the flawed factor that needed rethinking. The three friends never budged from the assumption that the problem lay with Job alone.

darkness and brings deep darkness to light." God gives light to those in deep pain, and that light reveals deep, dark, sometimes even ugly things. God gives light not to banish darkness but to reveal what the darkness was hiding. And God also gives this light, perhaps even especially, to those in misery.

There is no spin doctor in God. He does not make the ugly look pretty. God is about truth, even when the truth is unsavory, contradictory, unhappy, and chaotic.

Job's friends were striving for a sense of order that mollified their mental stress—it would be better to find their close friend Job guilty of some heinous sin than to discover that disorder and unfairness are inherent in the world's reality.

Regardless of their reasons for attempting to defend God and make the world appear orderly, the three friends will not hoodwink God with their clever verbiage. And he will not be happy with the dishonesty this false defense of God required either.

SHIELDS OF CLAY

A little understanding of ancient warfare will make this next bit of Job's speech clearer, but first, let's listen to the poetry:

> *[10]"He will surely rebuke you*
> *if in secret you show partiality.*
> *[11]Will not his majesty terrify you,*
> *and the dread of him fall upon you?*
> *[12]Your maxims are proverbs of ashes;*
> *your defenses are defenses of clay.*
> *[13]Let me have silence, and I will speak,*
> *and let come on me what may.*
> *[14]Why should I take my flesh in my teeth*
> *and put my life in my hand?"*
>
> JOB 13:10–14

God is about the truth, and likewise, Job was determined to seek and expose the truth, regardless of the consequences. Job insisted here that the lies that brought his friends comfort were useless in reality. They were defenses of clay. The Hebrew phrasing is even more precise—it states that they were "shields" of clay.

Clay makes for a lousy shield. Clay is unmanageably heavy. As a shield, it would make the warrior practically immobile. Clay is also fragile. In battle, one solid blow would not just breach its defense but would likely shatter it.

The Standard View, like a clay shield, is unwieldy and fragile. It requires vast effort to support and swing into action and then disintegrates at the first real contest.

26

GOING FOR BROKE

Job was under no illusions that the truth is comfortable. Reality is dangerous—the truth is dangerous. Job, however, was determined to speak the truth, after which "let come on me what may" (13:13). He was willing to take his own life in his hands if need be—whatever it took. He would, whatever the cost, speak the truth.

He continued:

> *15 "Though he slay me, I will hope in him;*
>   *yet I will argue my ways to his face.*
> *16 This will be my salvation,*
>   *that the godless shall not come before him."*
>
> Job 13:15–16

What was it exactly that would be Job's salvation? The theme of honesty versus false posturing runs through these verses. Job's honesty was what would be Job's salvation. Hebrew parallelism within poetic verses supports this interpretation—the second half of the verse repeats or elaborates on the message in the first half. In this case, the reason for Job's salvation was that no godless person would come before God. In other words, Job's willingness and ability to approach God candidly, with the raw truth exposed, was the proof of Job's righteousness and guarantee of deliverance.

Job was honest. Job was insistent that the ugliness the light revealed should not be papered over or downplayed. He saw that the truth was ugly, but there was still a flicker of hope even within his unhappy candor and insistence on the unvarnished truth. God was slaying him, yet he would still hope in God. That seems to be the point Job was making.

But is this really what Job was saying?

Our English translation of verse fifteen puts a gentle interpretational spin on the original Hebrew that slightly distorts Job's meaning. The Hebrew, as opposed to the ESV, is raw. It is impolite. The sense in Hebrew is something more like:

> *Let God kill me. What more do I have to lose?*
> *I will surely defend my ways to his face.*[63]

This is not some melodramatic, pious, or passive "let God slay me—I'll still hope in him" coming from Job's mouth. The Hebrew is "let God kill me—I've got nothing left to lose." Job, in extreme circumstances, was determined to tell the truth, regardless of the consequences, not because he was heroic but because he has nothing left to defend. What more do I have to lose? What more can you take from me? Life? I don't even want to live.

So how does verse sixteen fit with this reconsidered verse fifteen?

> *Let God kill me. What more do I have to lose?*
> *I will surely defend my ways to his face.*
> *This will be my salvation,*
> *that the godless shall not come before him.*

Job had a go-for-broke relationship with the truth now. Nothing was holding him back from reporting things exactly as they were. He had lost his children, friends, material possessions, and even his health. He bore the burden of overwhelming grief and financial devastation as well as the surrounding social pressure to care for the survivors he was responsible for, plus his own medical torment and the weight of his remaining friends increasingly suspecting that he was somehow, due to some secret sin, responsible for these many tragedies. The theology of Job's friends was beginning to call into question his status before God himself. Job had nothing left to live or

---

63 Reyburn, 256.

fight for and, in this state, saw no reason to tell anything but the truth. And the truth was on Job's side.

THE COMFORT OF INNOCENCE

Job continued his speech with these lines:

> *¹⁷"Keep listening to my words,*
> *and let my declaration be in your ears.*
> *¹⁸Behold, I have prepared my case;*
> *I know that I shall be in the right.*
> *¹⁹Who is there who will contend with me?*
> *For then I would be silent and die."*
>
> JOB 13:17–19

Several times in our study, we have referenced the fact that sometimes the Standard View is true. Sometimes trouble does come to a person as punishment for sin or, put less forcibly, as the consequences of sin. But there is something very powerful about going through trouble while knowing that you do not deserve it.

Job knew he did not deserve this trouble. That knowledge is powerful. Even amid pain, turmoil, grief, and a slide into depression, it is deeply meaningful to know that, as the storms crash upon you, you did not do this to yourself. Job might never know the cause of these trials, and he might never escape their consequences, but he did not bear the added burden of culpability.

TWO REQUESTS

Job's friends had succeeded in turning his troubles into a contest between Job's righteousness and God's justice, and so Job now turned away from his friends and for the rest of this speech addressed God directly:

> *²⁰"Only grant me these two things, God,*
> *and then I will not hide from you:*
> *²¹Withdraw your hand far from me,*

> *and stop frightening me with your terrors.*
> *²² Then summon me and I will answer,*
> *or let me speak, and you reply to me."*
>
> Job 13:20–22, NIV

If we read Job's requests here like a Western English-speaking reader, we are apt to think that he had two requests for God:

1. Withdraw your hand from me;
2. and stop frightening me with your terrors.

A closer reading might get us to four requests:

1. Withdraw your hand from me;
2. stop frightening me with your terrors;
3. summon me, and I will answer;
4. or let me speak first, and then you answer.

Both readings are close to the meaning in the original Hebrew, but not exactly right. We have to go back to our discussion on Hebrew parallelism and remember that these verses are designed to rhyme ideas.

Job's first request was for God to stop tormenting him. "Withdraw your hand far from me" and "stop frightening me with your terrors" are saying the same thing. In this case, the repetition heightens the idea's intensity by moving from a physical hand to the more emotionally evocative word "terrors." Job was placing the sole responsibility for these trials and associated terrors on God. Job was calling on God to leave him alone and stop tormenting him.

Job's second request was for a hearing before God. Job would not be satisfied with just relief from his pain—he also wanted a meeting. He did not have the intercessor he needed, but he wanted a hearing anyway. He did not care if God would talk first and Job defend, or if Job would make the opening argument and God defend—Job just wanted to hash this out. Job did not want a pardon. He wanted God to articulate the charges against him clearly and then declare Job's innocence and full acquittal.

The two requests that Job had then were:

1. Give me a break from these undeserved punishments;
2. and set up a meeting so we can clear the air between us.

HEBREW WORDPLAY: JOB BECOMES THE ENEMY

Listen to what Job said next:

> ^{23}"How many wrongs and sins have I committed?
> Show me my offense and my sin.
> ^{24}Why do you hide your face
> and consider me your enemy?"
>
> JOB 13:23–24, NIV

The first part of verse twenty-four, "Why do you hide your face," is an expression in Hebrew that is translated literally here. But the meaning behind the phrase in Hebrew is essentially "Why are you acting unfriendly?"

The parallelism then kicks in with the reference to an enemy in the second half of the verse. In this parallelism, the second line is intensifying the first line. Why are you acting unfriendly? In fact, why are you treating me like your enemy?

There is another Hebrew poetic device at work here. As we have already stated, wordplay, including puns and similarly spelled words, is a favored Hebrew literary device. The phonetic spelling of the Hebrew word Job is actually 'eyob. This name 'eyob sounds a great deal like one of the Hebrew words for enemy, which in English would be spelled out as 'oyeb. The vowels are just switched around: 'eyob is Job; 'oyeb is enemy.[64]

Why are you treating 'eyob as though he were your 'oyeb?

GOD AS A PRISON WARDEN

Job was not done with his complaint to God. Here is what he had to say to his Maker next:

---

64 Reyburn, 261-262.

> ^{25}*"Will you torment a windblown leaf?*
> *Will you chase after dry chaff?*
> ^{26}*For you write down bitter things against me*
> *and make me reap the sins of my youth."*
>
> JOB 13:25–26, NIV

God, of course, did not write down bitter things against Job, and God was not trying to make Job pay for any sins, youthful or otherwise, but with the Standard View superimposed on Job's life, this was the logical conclusion. And the logical conclusion tormented Job.

Job continued:

> ^{27}*"You fasten my feet in shackles;*
> *you keep close watch on all my paths*
> *by putting marks on the soles of my feet."*
>
> JOB 13:27, NIV

Putting marks on the soles of someone's feet may not be a meaningful image for us in the twenty-first century, but for Job's contemporaries living several millennia BCE, marking Job's soles functionally meant that God had put a tracking device on him. The idea is that God was closely monitoring Job and logging each of his infractions for retribution purposes, so the logic of the Standard View would imply. If this view were accurate, Job's complaint was that the effort to monitor, pass judgment, and enforce punishments on Job was so over the top that he truly was a tormented, windblown leaf—a target not worthy of God's corrective energy.

This is bold language. Job felt that he had nothing to lose, and he was calling reality as he saw it. But amid this raw expression of pain, he rather suddenly had a positive idea.

A new idea sparked within him, and that is what comes next.

27

HOPE FROM A TREE AND A MISSING QUESTION

AT FIRST, AS Job continued his prayer, he further built his case that the feebleness and insignificance of humankind made it an unworthy target of God's perfectionist torment. Here is how he put it:

> ^{28}"So man wastes away like something rotten,
>   like a garment eaten by moths.
>
> ^{1}"Mortals, born of woman,
>   are of few days and full of trouble.
> ^{2}They spring up like flowers and wither away;
>   like a fleeting shadow, they do not endure.
> ^{3}Do you fix your eye on them?
>   Will you bring them before you for judgment?
> ^{4}Who can bring what is pure from the impure?
>   No one!
> ^{5}A person's days are determined;
>   you have decreed the number of his months
>   and have set limits he cannot exceed.
> ^{6}So look away from him and let him alone,

> *till he has put in his time like a hired laborer."*
>
> Job 13:28–14:6, NIV

Verse five of chapter fourteen is deliberately unbalanced.

First, the parallelism goes from days to months, which is an unusual progression as it broadens the scope rather than focusing it. Stylistically, we might instead expect the opposite: God not only decrees a person's months but also decrees their every day, even their every hour, minute, second. But instead of narrowing the view on God's control over our lifetime, the poem broadens the vista from days to months: God not only decrees a person's days but also decrees their months, even their years, decades, whole life span.

The second thing that stands out about this verse is that it is three lines, even in the original text. God determines peoples' days and decrees their months, and if we really must have a third line, we would expect the parallel progression to extend to something larger, like years or decades. But the verse doesn't do that. Instead of another time period that extends this progression into a poetic eternity, we get limits. There is an endpoint.

The verse is deliberately unbalanced as it points to a new direction that Job was about to take with his prayer. This unbalanced ending tells a powerful story in three lines: God sets the length of each person's life span, and it seems, especially at the beginning, that life will go on forever—then it's suddenly over. The poetry that seemed poised to extend into eternity crashes into the limit that God has set.

Isn't that exactly how we experience our lives? They go on and on, and so do the lives of the people we know—and then they are suddenly, shockingly, over and gone.

Job closed off this train of thought with verse six: leave humankind alone. Let us poor souls live out our short lifespans like the tired, wage-hungry hired hand in the opening verses of chapter seven.

There is discouragement and even depression here. There is a plea not for salvation or vindication but just for isolation and an escape from God's attention. It is a gloomy wish and a depressed goal.

But the strange progression of verse five seems to haunt Job. The progression from days to months to years implied that Job's own thought process was heading toward eternity, not limits. It seems, and I'm speculating here, that those three awkward lines did not rest easily in Job's mind. And so he continued his prayer with another three-line verse.

> ⁷"At least there is hope for a tree:
>   If it is cut down, it will sprout again,
>   and its new shoots will not fail.
> ⁸Its roots may grow old in the ground
>   and its stump die in the soil,
> ⁹yet at the scent of water it will bud
>   and put forth shoots like a plant.
> ¹⁰But a man dies and is laid low;
>   he breathes his last and is no more.
> ¹¹As the water of a lake dries up
>   or a riverbed becomes parched and dry,
> ¹²so he lies down and does not rise;
>   till the heavens are no more, people will not awake
>   or be roused from their sleep.
> ¹³If only you would hide me in the grave
>   and conceal me till your anger has passed!
> If only you would set me a time
>   and then remember me!
> ¹⁴If someone dies, will they live again?
>   All the days of my hard service
>   I will wait for my renewal to come.
> ¹⁵You will call and I will answer you;
>   you will long for the creature your hands have made.
> ¹⁶Surely then you will count my steps
>   but not keep track of my sin.
> ¹⁷My offenses will be sealed up in a bag;
>   you will cover over my sin."
>
> Job 14:7–17, NIV

Job came amazingly far in these eleven verses.

First, he described a tree's miraculous ability to recover after being cut down. It is true that many trees can recover from severe damage and live for a long time, but that reality would have been even more pronounced for Job if his natural environment in any way related to the olive tree rich Mediterranean we are familiar with today. There are olive trees still growing there that may have borne fruit when Caesar waged his wars. It is well documented that olive trees can live for over a thousand years.

I grew up in California. I was born in Canada and went to university, got married, and had my children in Canada, but I lived in Northern California from age eleven to nineteen. One of my early jobs was working in walnut orchards as a teenager. The white walnut is the walnut we are familiar with in the grocery store. It has good fruit but weak roots. The black walnut has a stellar root system but an undesirable nut. The solution is to plant orchards of black walnut trees and then cut them down and graft white walnut saplings to the stumps. There are hundreds of miles of walnut orchards in California with tall whitish trunks that suddenly turn dark, almost black, six to twelve inches from the ground as the black roots plunge into the soil. And the black walnut roots, even while they nourish their white walnut tops, continue to reassert themselves by throwing green shoots up from the junction between white and black at the tree trunk base. Left unattended, these green shoots would grow into solid branches. The farmers called these ground-level fledgling branches "suckers." My teenage job was to walk the orchards each year, armed with a small hatchet or machete, and chop down each new season's crop of suckers so that, for the rest of the season, the black walnut roots would focus their resources on feeding the white walnut top and its cash crop of nuts. But every year, the black walnut roots would try to grow their own branches again.

Verse ten takes this simple principle that life can reassert itself in trees and asks, Why can't people experience rebirth after death too? In the original text, this happens to be yet another three-line verse—the third line is unfortunately missing in many English translations. Together with the missing line, the verse reads:

> [10] "But a man dies and is laid low;
> he breathes his last and is no more.
> *[And then where is he?]*"[65]
>
> JOB 14:10, NIV

---

65 Reyburn, 274 and Janzen, 108.

Verse five is a three-line verse, the third line stating that human lives have time limits.

Verse seven is the second three-line verse that essentially says, Wait a minute—trees don't have the same kind of absolute limits.

And now verse ten gives us the last of this trilogy of three-line verses, which now questions the logic of verse five: are we sure that life is over for people when they appear to be gone? The finality of death in the theology of Job's day is missing here. There is instead this question: And then where is he?

The example of the tree had opened Job's mind to a new idea. Trees offer a potential answer to this question. Maybe there is the possibility of life after apparent death. Maybe, like a cut-down tree, a person does not breathe a last breath and then is no more. Maybe there is something else. And so the question, missing in most English translations but preserved in the original, stands out: then where is he?

Following this creative and hopeful idea, verses eleven and twelve seem to close the door on this bit of light. Like evaporated water, a dead person is a vanished soul who will not rise again. But the analogy Job used is revealing: streambeds do get restored. Job did not make this counterpoint obvious, but his stream analogy parallels the tree as an illustration of life after death. When the rain comes, tree stumps sprout again, and dry streambeds are restored with flowing water.

Job stated in verses eleven and twelve that a person lies down and is no more, but he used imagery that contradicted his statement (14:11) and further undermined this view by describing death as sleep (14:12).

Early in his speeches, before the deep depression had settled in, Job had also used sleep as a metaphor for death, such as in 3:11–17. But this poetic language had darkened as his depression had set in, and the images he had used for death became abruptly negative. He had begun describing death as a place without hope and of no return, where even God would not be able to find him (7:6–10, 21). It was a place of gloom, night, deep shadow, and disorder (10:21–22). It was only now in chapter fourteen that the idea of life after apparent death started to reshape Job's doom-ridden death language, and he went back again to describing death as merely sleep.

From these subtle and poetic hints at something beyond this life, Job got explicit, even prescriptive, in the following verses. Job proposed that God select a date in the future to return to Job's grave and revive him. This was crazy talk in the context of the theology available in Job's day. This was beyond speculation and became fantasy, and so in verse fourteen, Job will confess to the strangeness of this idea: "If someone dies, will they live again?" (NIV). It was a question, but maybe one Job was willing to put some hope in. Job committed to waiting on that future date of revival. The end result of this revival will be a renewed relationship with God, one in which Job's offenses, whatever they may have been, will have been cast away and forgotten.

DEALING WITH REALITY

But all of this was just imagination at work. Trees and streams are not people. Job was aware of this. Hope had sparked, but he had not taken leave of the reality that he observed.

> *¹⁸"But the mountain falls and crumbles away,*
> *and the rock is removed from its place;*
> *¹⁹the waters wear away the stones;*
> *the torrents wash away the soil of the earth;*
> *so you destroy the hope of man."*
>
> JOB 14:18–19, NIV

This verse is oddly structured. We would expect verse nineteen to read something like:

> *Humanity's hope is destroyed as water wears away stone;*
> *as torrents wash away the soil, so hope is ruined.*

With my suggested rewording, the parallelism would be even, and the rhyming of ideas would be balanced. But that is not how the verse is written. The original, as captured in the NIV, is unbalanced. It reads fine in English, but the rhythm would have been off for the original Hebrew readers. The first two lines are in parallel, and then the startling third line jars not only the rhythm of the poem but also the flow of ideas. Job's speculation of life beyond death was shattered by the hard statement that you, God, destroy humanity's hope.

In Job's previous imagery, water was the reviving force that brought a tree back from death and restored the dried-up stream. Water was the catalyst for revival and the trigger for hope.

Faced with human reality and no divine revelation on the topic, Job was left with the hard truth: water is also a force for destruction. It gives rebirth, but it also destroys. In such a case, a person's hope is washed away and ruined.

Job believed this to be true, so he said it:

> [20]*"You prevail forever against him, and he passes;*
>   *you change his countenance, and send him away.*
> [21]*His sons come to honor, and he does not know it;*
>   *they are brought low, and he perceives it not.*
> [22]*He feels only the pain of his own body,*
>   *and he mourns only for himself."*
>
> JOB 14:20–22

As I write this, I'm in my late forties. Job's sentiments did not resonate with me a year ago, or five years ago, but somehow, now, as I more clearly contemplate that this mortal journey has an end, his statements touch a place that was not open to contact when I was a younger man. (Now, giving this second edition a review in my fifties, these verses resonate even more with me—I can only imagine that they will move me at an even deeper level in later decades.)

Job's troubles did not come to a young person who might only rail against his pain. They came to an older person who would experience them differently, through the lens not just of grief and loss but also of a shortened future horizon. Time had become an issue. Hope had sparked and eternal life had been imagined, but in the absence of anything more substantial than speculation, Job was left with his shattered life. That life was winding down in a state of physical, emotional, and spiritual pain.

Job needed something more than what he was finding so far. Eliphaz will come back on stage next and try to fulfill that need.

28

ELIPHAZ IS INSPIRED TO RUDENESS

In the previous chapter, Job found a spark of hope in his imaginative vision of trees and streambeds coming back to life. This spark, however, was quickly snuffed out. All Job had before him was evidence of declining health and the meaningless emptiness of his future. Whether the end of his life came quickly or after many more torturous years, in the end, the conclusion would be the same. With this knowledge, Job settled back into gloom.

Eliphaz now took the stage with a second chance to address Job's despair. How do you suppose this strict traditionalist might respond to Job's emotional candor and theological speculation?

> ^{1}*Then Eliphaz the Temanite answered and said:*
> ^{2}*"Should a wise man answer with windy knowledge,*
> *and fill his belly with the east wind?*
> ^{3}*Should he argue in unprofitable talk,*
> *or in words with which he can do no good?"*
>
> Job 15:1–3

Oh boy. We have heard these ideas before: Zophar had referred to Job's words as "babble" (11:3), and Bildad had referred to them as "a great wind" (8:2). Eliphaz had used no such language in his first diplomatic speech, but now Bildad and Zophar had inspired him with their rudeness, and Eliphaz adopted their approach.

Zophar had used the word "babble," and so now Eliphaz said, "unprofitable talk."

Bildad had referenced "a great wind," and so now Eliphaz talked about "windy knowledge" and "the east wind."

Eliphaz had taught his friends to talk in the language of the Standard View. The friends had taught Eliphaz, in turn, to talk in the language of rudeness.

Just because many people smoothly agree as they exchange ideas does not mean their ideas are true. It is more than even groupthink (to use a modern psychology term)—it's groupescape (to invent a term). In plain language: it is easier to collectively blame the victim than to collectively admit wrongdoing, so any direction (Standard View theology, lack of compassion, rudeness, etc.) is a good direction provided it offers an escape from an uncomfortable reality. Back in more psychological terms, it's a collective response to shared cognitive dissonance.

It is a shame when bad thinking inspires further bad thinking and the innocent continue to suffer the consequences.

ASSUMPTIONS OF JOB'S INNOCENCE ABANDONED

Eliphaz did not just imitate his friends' aggressive posture. He also took on another aspect of Bildad's and Zophar's speeches—that of vague accusations.

In Eliphaz's first speech, he had stated:

> *⁶"Is not your fear of God your confidence,*
> *and the integrity of your ways your hope?"*
>
> Job 4:6

This had been Eliphaz's introduction to a series of verses expounding on Job's integrity and fear of God, which naturally flowed into an initial description of how the Standard View operates. In short, Job's righteousness was to be the basis for his hope and confidence.

Now, in his second speech, in light of Standard View assumptions, Eliphaz readdressed the topic of Job's blamelessness. Eliphaz could not continue to support the idea of Job's integrity and fear of God and also read the world through the Standard View. Only one of the two could be true—something had to give. As Eliphaz adopted his friends' rudeness, he also reversed his earlier assumptions of Job's innocence.

Here is how Eliphaz did his best Bildad imitation:

> [4] "But you are doing away with the fear of God
> and hindering meditation before God.
> [5] For your iniquity teaches your mouth,
> and you choose the tongue of the crafty.
> [6] Your own mouth condemns you, and not I;
> your own lips testify against you."
>
> JOB 15:4–6

With this updated view of Job, Eliphaz concluded that Job's fear of God did not exist after all. Eliphaz now believed the opposite: Job's words did away with the fear of God, and even worse, they hindered the spiritual health of others as well.

BREAKING TRADITION TWICE

In Eliphaz's first speech, he had not just articulated the Standard View—he had also described the spirit's Contrary View and discounted it.

In his speeches, Job had echoed the spirit's view. Job's observations on the cruelty and arbitrariness of life from a human perspective had been frightening and shocking in their candor. This honesty, it turned out, was too much for Eliphaz's strict religious traditionalism. To Eliphaz, the irreverence of some of Job's observations was proof of Job's secret sinfulness. Eliphaz's view of appropriate fear of God called for a willingness to be blind to the things that did not fit.

Adding to these marks against Job, his imagining life after death and calling God to solve his crisis through some kind of eternal-life miracle struck Eliphaz as "unprofitable talk" (15:3). Beyond being useless, Job's words were even a form of craftiness and sin. Eliphaz saw Job's imaginations as an evil that hindered his meditation before God and did away with the fear of God.

Job had broken the logic of Eliphaz's Standard View in two ways.

First, Job said that the Standard View did not hold because the world is often harder and more cruel than a righteous person's sinful mistakes can justify. This argument was offensive to Eliphaz's tradition. It said that the hardships of life exceed a fair recompense for sins committed. Job's trials illustrated this principle, and if Job's innocence was maintained, then the Standard View didn't add up. Reality was too negative to support this view for long.

Second, Job's ideas about life after death suggested grace on a scale that staggers the imagination and beggars the rigid cause-and-effect fierceness of the Standard View. In the Standard View, you earn your blessings—but eternal life is beyond earning. It can only be a gift, and gifts are not given in the Standard View, and therefore these imaginations are fantasies that lead to evil. If Job's ideas were accepted, the human soul might hope for more than it can earn and that would shatter the Standard View's math.

Both Job's negative (but realistic) observations and positive imaginations were offensive to Eliphaz's understanding of how the world works. If not all trouble is deserved and eternity is a potential gift, then these two extremes blow apart the tight reliability of the Standard View tradition and pose a threat to Eliphaz's narrow religion. Job's proposed universe was wider in both positive and negative directions than Eliphaz could accept.

Eliphaz wanted to earn every positive that he got, and he wanted to get absolutely nothing negative that he did not deserve. In other words, Eliphaz wanted to be in control.

TRADITION DIGS IN (AND COUNTERS THE SPIRIT)

Eliphaz was on a roll and not stopping now.

> *⁷"Are you the first man who was born?*
> > *Or were you brought forth before the hills?*
> *⁸Have you listened in the council of God?*
> > *And do you limit wisdom to yourself?*
> *⁹What do you know that we do not know?*
> > *What do you understand that is not clear to us?*
> *¹⁰Both the gray-haired and the aged are among us,*
> > *older than your father.*
> *¹¹Are the comforts of God too small for you,*[66]

---

66 The Hebrew word translated as "comfort" here carries the idea of not just comfort but also consolation.

> *or the word that deals gently with you?"*
>
> JOB 15:7–11

Now, here is a frank question: what comforts and gentle words were Eliphaz referring to?

God had not yet directly spoken in this story to Job, so Eliphaz could not be referencing God's actual spoken words.

The scriptures had not yet been written, so he was not referencing God's written words either.

So, presumably, Eliphaz was either referring to the words the three friends had spoken and ascribing their ultimate authorship to God, or he was referencing God's words in a metaphorical sense (i.e., God spoke words of comfort through the events that occurred in Job's life). The metaphorical argument fails when we consider that comfort comes after pain, not before, and that the events of Job's life since his first tragedies had not brought comfort but only increasing physical, emotional, and spiritual distress. In verse nine, though, Eliphaz laid claim to meaningful insights that, in verse ten, he assured Job were supported even by those older (and presumably wiser) than Job's own father.

Let the consolations—the predictability and control that the Standard View provides—be enough for you. That was Eliphaz's argument. According to Eliphaz, the solution was all in the interpretation. If Job would just surrender and confess to a sin that justified these trials (and, by implication, give up his ideas of eternity as well), then the Standard View would provide false but definable comfort. The world can feel safer if you're willing to strap on emotional blinders and lie about your own guilt. Just buy the lie, Job, and ignore the contrary evidence. Then we can all achieve a kind of existential peace.

But Job was not that kind of person. The spirit within him was honest and craved real comfort and not the stupor of self-deception, and this spirit flashed within him. This offended Eliphaz, who responded as follows:

> *[12]"Why does your heart carry you away,*
> *and why do your eyes flash,*
> *[13]that you turn your spirit against God*
> *and bring such words out of your mouth?*

> *14What is man, that he can be pure?*
>> *Or he who is born of a woman, that he can be righteous?*
> *15Behold, God puts no trust in his holy ones,*
>> *and the heavens are not pure in his sight;*
> *16how much less one who is abominable and corrupt,*
>> *a man who drinks injustice like water!"*
>
> JOB 15:12–16

Wait a minute! These are the spirit's words from chapters four and five![67]

Had Eliphaz converted away from the Standard View and started to reconsider the spirit's Contrary View?

No. As we will see in the following verses, Eliphaz was still very rooted in the Standard View. But he saw Job's eyes flash, and he heard Job's words. Eliphaz recognized that—having passed on the spirit's message in chapters four and five as a counterpoint to the Standard View, having done so only to use it as a ridiculous foil to support the bookends of his Standard View explication—Job had actually adopted this view as his own position. "Such words" now also poured from Job's mouth, particularly in chapters nine, ten, and twelve. Job had heard both views in Eliphaz's first speech and adopted the wrong one. As the original spokesperson for the spirit's Contrary View, Eliphaz's self-appointed role was to steer Job away from the spirit's view and back to the common opinion.

He did so this way:

> *17"I will show you; hear me,*
>> *and what I have seen I will declare*
> *18(what wise men have told,*
>> *without hiding it from their fathers,*
> *19to whom alone the land was given,*
>> *and no stranger passed among them)."*
>
> JOB 15:17–19

This was all just buildup. This was the foundational authority upon

---

67 See 4:16–5:7.

which Eliphaz based his argument that Job should ignore the spirit and put his beliefs exclusively in the Standard View. And now the argument:

> *[20] "The wicked man writhes in pain all his days,*
> > *through all the years that are laid up for the ruthless.*
> *[21] Dreadful sounds are in his ears;*
> > *in prosperity the destroyer will come upon him.*
> *[22] He does not believe that he will return out of darkness,*
> > *and he is marked for the sword.*
> *[23] He wanders abroad for bread, saying, 'Where is it?'*
> > *He knows that a day of darkness is ready at his hand;*
> *[24] distress and anguish terrify him;*
> > *they prevail against him, like a king ready for battle.*
> *[25] Because he has stretched out his hand against God*
> > *and defies the Almighty,*
> *[26] running stubbornly against him*
> > *with a thickly bossed shield;*
> *[27] because he has covered his face with his fat*
> > *and gathered fat upon his waist[68]*
> *[28] and has lived in desolate cities,*
> > *in houses that none should inhabit,*
> > *which were ready to become heaps of ruins;*
> *[29] he will not be rich, and his wealth will not endure,*
> > *nor will his possessions spread over the earth;*
> *[30] he will not depart from darkness;*
> > *the flame will dry up his shoots,[69]*
> > *and by the breath of his mouth he will depart.*
> *[31] Let him not trust in emptiness,[70] deceiving himself,*
> > *for emptiness will be his payment.*

---

68 The English translation of "waist" is a polite choice. The original Hebrew word refers not to the waist but the buttocks. This might come across as an extra level of rudeness to twenty-first century readers, but the point was not aesthetics but rather success: the wicked man's fat bottom is proof of his wealth and comfortable status.

69 Recall that a good bit of the destruction on Job's farm was caused by fire.

70 "Trust in emptiness," that is, trust in his wealth and success which are ultimately empty and unreliable.

> ^{32}*It will be paid in full before his time,*[71]
> *and his branch will not be green.*
> ^{33}*He will shake off his unripe grape like the vine,*
> *and cast off his blossom like the olive tree.*
> ^{34}*For the company of the godless is barren,*
> *and fire consumes the tents of bribery.*
> ^{35}*They conceive trouble and give birth to evil,*
> *and their womb prepares deceit."*
>
> Job 15:20–35

This was the wisdom that Eliphaz came up with from his own observations and the collective wisdom of previous generations: bad things happen to bad people. He was right: bad things do happen to bad people—but bad things also happen to good people. And good things also happen to both good and bad people. Trying to work backward from an ambiguous event, be it positive or negative, to judge the character of the people impacted is a path strewn with assumptions, pitfalls, and potentially disastrous errors.

Eliphaz's observations and the collective wisdom of generations were not wrong because they were inaccurate. Rather, they were wrong because they were incomplete. And this incompleteness, when applied to Job's tragic circumstances, became not just mistaken but cruel and had the potential to drive a wedge between Job and his God.

An incomplete ideology forcefully applied to a wounded heart can be an effective agent of evil. Where a soul might more readily resist the force of an undisguised assault, the authoritative predictability of the Standard View makes it an attack that is much harder to identify and defend against. It is an assault on faith that works from within. It tears down either one's own confidence and hope or undermines trust in the attentiveness and integrity of God himself. Or it does both, and a soul is completely ruined not by blatant sin but by ideas wrapped in spiritual language.

False truth can slyly erode the foundations of faith.

But Job was not just a righteous person. He was also a wise one. He saw through the misguided counsel he received and will address this bad advice head-on in the next chapter.

---

71 "Paid in full," that is, by the calculus of the Standard View.

29

MISERABLE COMFORTERS

> ¹*Then Job answered and said:*
> ²*"I have heard many such things;*
>   *miserable comforters are you all.*
> ³*Shall windy words have an end?*
>   *Or what provokes you that you answer?*
> ⁴*I also could speak as you do,*
>   *if you were in my place;*
> *I could join words together against you*
>   *and shake my head at you.*
> ⁵*I could strengthen you with my mouth,*
>   *and the solace of my lips would assuage your pain."*
>
> Job 16:1–5

AFTER ELIPHAZ'S FIRST speech, Job had cried out for empathy (6:14). In response to Bildad's speech, Job had turned to God for relief (10:20 in light of 10:8–12). Finally, responding to Zophar, Job had decried the lack of empathy he had received from his friends and the ease with which his comfortable friends could heap contempt onto him and his situation (12:4–5).

In chapter sixteen, we see this pattern continue: Job asking for help, not judgment. After dismissing his friends' "comfort" as miserable and long-winded, Job sarcastically described how, if he were in their shoes, it would also be easy for him to shake his head and make fine speeches. He then told his friends that he, too, could exercise a lack of compassion if he were in their place. Verse five is trying to bring across the idea that the very movement of Job's lips would somehow provide comfort. The tone is bitingly sarcastic.

We do not get a soundtrack with ancient poetry, and we do not get facial expressions or stage directions in the margins either, but the following verses make it very clear that as Job went on, he was speaking in anger, pain, and even a bit of despair:

> ^{6}"*If I speak, my pain is not assuaged,*
>   *and if I forebear, how much of it leaves me?*
> ^{7}*Surely now God has worn me out;*
>   *he has made desolate all my company.*
> ^{8}*And he has shriveled me up,*
>   *which is a witness against me,*
> *and my leanness has risen up against me;*
>   *it testifies to my face.*[72]
> ^{9}*He has torn me in his wrath and hated me;*
>   *he has gnashed his teeth at me;* [73]
>   *my adversary sharpens his eyes against me.*
> ^{10}*Men have gaped at me with their mouth;*
>   *they have struck me insolently on the cheek;*
>   *they mass themselves together against me.*
> ^{11}*God gives me up to the ungodly*
>   *and casts me into the hands of the wicked.*
> ^{12}*I was at ease, and he broke me apart;*
>   *he seized me by the neck and dashed me to pieces;*
> *he set me up as his target;*
> ^{13}*his archers surround me.*
> *He slashes open my kidneys and does not spare;*
>   *he pours out my gall on the ground.*
> ^{14}*He breaks me with breach upon breach;*

---

72 Notice how the "witness" and "testimony" are rooted in the Standard View. If the view is true, then Job admits that the evidence against him is irrefutable.

73 We know that this is not what is happening in Job's life, but once again, if the Standard View is true, then this is the only way to interpret the tragedies that have befallen Job and those around him.

> *he runs upon me like a warrior.*
> *¹⁵I have sewed sackcloth upon my skin*
> *   and have laid my strength in the dust."*
>
> JOB 16:6–15

"Laid my strength in the dust." The Hebrew literally says "thrust my horn into the dust." A horn in Job's day was a symbol of strength. Job said that he had sewn the garment of mourning and grief over himself and had buried his strength.

Eliphaz had charged him with letting his eyes "flash" and turning his "spirit against God" (15:12–13). Job's response was to ascribe his passion to how deeply he mourns, and he qualified that it was a passion without strength. God was the warrior, and Job was the wholly conquered subject.

LOOKING FOR A WITNESS

Job's words from here mark the start of a new discovery. Pay close attention to what he said next:

> *¹⁶"My face is red with weeping,*
> *   and on my eyelids is deep darkness,*
> *¹⁷although there is no violence in my hands,*
> *   and my prayer is pure.*
> *¹⁸O earth, cover not my blood,*
> *   and let my cry find no resting place.*
> *¹⁹Even now, behold, my witness is in heaven,*
> *   and he who testifies for me is on high.*
> *²⁰My friends scorn me;*
> *   my eye pours out tears to God,*
> *²¹that he would argue the case of a man with God,*
> *   as a son of man does with his neighbor."*
>
> JOB 16:16–21

Back in 9:32, Job had expressed his unhappiness that God was "not a man, as I am… that we should come to trial together." Following this expression of helplessness, Job had wished for a lawyer or advocate, someone to "lay his hand on us both" (9:33) and cause God to change his course of action.

This longing had gone without a solution at the time.

After this expression of desire for an arbiter, Job had moved on to the contemplation of mortality. Initially, this had led to despair, but after considering life-after-death examples in nature, Job began to imagine the possibility of life after his own death. This idea would address the lack of an arbiter to remove God's hand from Job and still allow Job to be reunified with God again (at some point after death). However, as neat a solution as it was, this idea was without theological basis in Job's day. As a result, at the end of chapter fourteen, he could not put faith in it.

An arbiter and eternity—these are the two great needs that Job's tragedies had revealed to him. But there was no precedent in the theology of Job's day to justify either of these ideas.

From wishing for an arbiter in chapter nine, Job now in chapter sixteen began not just to consider another idea but to put faith in it. He said that someone was looking out for him in heaven, a witness who testified for him.

Notice that this figure is no longer an arbiter, one who would judge between God and Job, but rather a witness on Job's behalf. God may well be all-powerful and not subject to an arbiter's decisions, but God will listen to a star witness and a powerful defense lawyer together, speaking on Job's behalf "as one pleads for a friend" (Job 16:21, NIV). Job's advocate was not an impersonal gun for hire but a compassionate friend.

This was not just imagination anymore. Job had added faith to this vision: "Even now my witness is in heaven" (16:19, NIV). Job suddenly had confidence that his witness was there. "My intercessor is my friend" (16:20, NIV). And Job's ideas were not just fantasy. They will have ultimate fulfillment, of course, in the form of Christ.

Here is how the apostle John put it:

> [15]*No longer do I call you servants, for the servant does not know what his master is doing; but I have called you friends...*
>
> JOHN 15:15A

These are Jesus's own words to his disciples. But the parallels between what Job wished for and who Jesus is are even more pronounced than just this idea of divine friendship. Let's consider a few other New Testament references along this line:

> *¹⁴Since then we have a great high priest who has passed through the heavens, Jesus, the Son of God, let us hold fast our confession. ¹⁵For we do not have a high priest who is unable to sympathize with our weaknesses, but one who in every respect has been tempted as we are, yet without sin. ¹⁶Let us then with confidence draw near to the throne of grace, that we may receive mercy and find grace to help in time of need.*
>
> HEBREWS 4:14–16

> *⁵For there is one God, and there is one mediator between God and men, the man Christ Jesus.*
>
> 1 TIMOTHY 2:5

> *²⁶Likewise the Spirit helps us in our weakness. For we do not know what to pray for as we ought, but the Spirit himself intercedes for us with groanings too deep for words. ²⁷And he who searches hearts knows what is the mind of the Spirit, because the Spirit intercedes for the saints according to the will of God.*
>
> ROMANS 8:26–27

Did Job know about Jesus? We have no evidence that Job knew anything specifically about Jesus. The events of his life occurred well before Moses wrote down the first five books of the Bible, so Job was without even the heavily veiled references and foreshadowing that do occur in the Garden of Eden, the Law, and elsewhere. As far as we know, Job had no foreknowledge about Jesus.

But was there another source of divine revelation about Jesus that is simply absent from the text of the book of Job? It is possible. The spirit spoke the truth to Eliphaz, although Eliphaz chose to dismiss that revelation. But there is no need to attribute some secret source for Job's revelation. The knowledge of God, of righteousness, and of God's divine attitude toward people was handed down orally from the time of Adam onward. Noah was not a righteous person by accident. He learned from those before him. The details were imprecise; certainly, God had not given us the Law yet, and none had recorded the prophets, but in Noah's day, and Job's as well, the idea of God's overall involvement in the world was clear for those with access to good teachers and with hearts willing to learn and respond.

Job had taken the basic concepts of God's righteousness and power, as revealed orally and through creation, and paired those concepts with a human's inability to argue with God or force upon God any kind of change in action or decision. From these two concepts, the helplessness of humanity's position before God is apparent. The suffering soul is then led either to despair or to the hope of finding some kind of intermediary who can effectively bridge the human-divine gap. Job's thinking started with the idea of an arbiter, then he backed off from this heavy-handed position and settled on the idea of a witness and a mediator. This is a position that faith finds reasonable and begins to take root in.

Job believed that there must be a witness-mediator because he so badly needed such a person and because the idea of a witness-mediator does not contradict God's omniscient authority. It fits with the principle of God's love and compassion for his creation. God allowed Abraham to argue on behalf of Sodom. Moses may not have written the story down yet, but God's people would have orally passed down the story for years before Moses formally documented it. Abraham's defense of Sodom was hopeless given the evil nature of that city. But a witness-mediator working with Job rather than Sodom would have had a solid case to work with.

But will Job's witness-mediator—will Job's friend in heaven—arrive in time? The question of eternity was still outstanding; Job had articulated the need and explored the grounds for considering it, but he had yet to state his conviction in any life-beyond-the-grave hope. While Job was waiting for his witness-mediator, his mortal clock was ticking.

UPPING THE ANTE FROM WITNESS AND MEDIATOR TO REDEEMER

While Job waited, perhaps in vain, he was not getting any younger. And he knew it. So he expressed it:

> ²²*"For when a few years have come*
> *I shall go the way from which I shall not return.*
>
> ¹*"My spirit is broken; my days are extinct;*
> *the graveyard is ready for me.*
> ²*Surely there are mockers about me,*
> *and my eye dwells on their provocation.*
> ³*Lay down a pledge for me with you;*
> *who is there who will put up security for me?"*
>
> JOB 16:22–17:3

A theologian could go wild over verse three. Job had articulated that he needed and had faith in the existence of a witness-mediator. Still, in this verse, despite his faith in this friend in heaven, Job knew that ultimately, even a witness-mediator could not pay Job's bill on Job's behalf.

Suppose the Standard View is true, and Job was suffering because of some sin, even a minor sin that was not proportional to Job's suffering and that God could be convinced made Job worthy of a reduced sentence. In that case, there was still likely a debt (Job never claimed to be perfect), and who could pay on his behalf? Only God can pay on Job's behalf. This foreshadowing of Jesus, not just as witness-mediator and friend but also as the Christian's debt payer, is amazing.

But Job's insight ended here. Job recognized the principle, but the mystery is not revealed in the pages of this book. The prophets speak to this, and the Gospels reveal the full solution to this mystery—and it is a mystery. The New Testament uses exactly that language of mystery to describe Christ's work in redeeming humanity.[74]

The book of Job foreshadows the mystery and ministry of Christ, but it is not ultimately about that. What it is about is a righteous person suffering. That soul suffered even more as his friends' misguided theology led them to blame the victim and drive a wedge both between Job and God and between Job and his friends. The consequences of those wedges will appear in what Job said next.

---

74 Look up the word *mystery* in a concordance and you will see that nearly all of the verses with that word are referring to Christ. Throughout the Old Testament period, this mystery was a matter that even angels longed to look into (1 Peter 1:12).

30

ACCUSING GOD

JOB WENT ON from here to lay a new charge against God.

> *⁴"Since you have closed their hearts to understanding,*
> *therefore you will not let them triumph.*
> *⁵He who informs against his friends to get a share of their property—*
> *the eyes of his children will fail.*
> *⁶He has made me a byword of the peoples,*
> *and I am one before whom men spit."*
>
> JOB 17:4–6

These are fighting words. Job had now charged God with responsibility for the religious blindness of his friends. By extension, Job had declared that God was also responsible for preventing their ultimate triumph since the path was not the way of truth.

The ESV speaks in verse five about friends wanting a share of property, but this translation doesn't align with the original Hebrew idea. In the original language, the phrase is proverbial, not literal, and it refers to the idea of a person violating their integrity for gain. That literal phrase uses material language, but the people at the time would have understood this proverb as a metaphor for social gain, for things such as flattery, good standing, being proven right, and so on.

For clarity and to better capture the poetry of the original, we would have to drop the word-for-word and idea-for-idea translation priority and instead go for a translational focus on the emotional intent, which might look something like this:

> *⁴Since you, God, have prevented them from emotionally connecting to the truth,*
> > *you will not let them ultimately triumph with their wrong judgment about me.*
> *⁵People may sell out their friends to gain emotional or social status,*
> > *but their children and ideas will fail in the long run.*
> *⁶But still, God has ruined my reputation among people,*
> > *and I am now someone that people disrespect in public.*[75]

Was Job referencing just the judgmental words that his three friends had brought to bear against him? Was he concerned that the three friends had only voiced what many others in his community were thinking? Or, out of the hundreds of widows, had some turned against Job and blamed him for their tragedies?

Whatever the background to Job's complaint, Job felt isolated and additionally injured by the responses of those around him. And he put the responsibility for this social backlash on God.

If the Standard View is true and bad things only happen to bad people, and Job knew he was not bad, then the only logical conclusion for Job to make was that God had not been a righteous judge. God had made a mistake. Society was observing the evil that had come into Job's life and made the only conclusion they could reasonably make: Job must have done something wrong.

But Job knew his own behavior and heart, and therefore, from Job's

---

[75] This is my own translation that I've written after distilling pages of commentary on these verses as well as a translator's handbook on the technical details. I've included it here to provide a summarized version of the passage that the reader can easily digest. It violates all the word-for-word and idea-for-idea translation principles of modern English translations in order to get across what the poetry is emotionally trying to convey. The poetry focuses on God's accountability for what was occurring and the resulting emotion Job felt as a result of the social fallout of God's actions.

perspective, it would appear that God had made an error. God was to blame. And the friends were also to blame for failing to believe in Job's integrity and see that something must be wrong with the Standard View's conclusions.

JOB BECOMES COMBATIVE BUT DOES NOT QUIT ON HIS FRIENDS

> *⁷"My eye has grown dim from vexation,*
> *and all my members are like a shadow.*
> *⁸The upright are appalled at this,*
> *and the innocent stirs himself up against the godless.*
> *⁹Yet the righteous holds to his way,*
> *and he who has clean hands grows stronger and stronger.*
> *¹⁰But you, come on again, all of you,*
> *and I shall not find a wise man among you."*
>
> Job 17:7–10

When faced with the quality of friendships that Job had as his source of "comfort," how many of us would have simply abandoned those friendships, casting them off as unnecessary baggage, frustrating an already difficult life? Alternatively, how many of us, exhausted physically and emotionally, might have surrendered to the lie, confessed to what society demanded of us, and so bought social peace at the price of our integrity?

Job did neither of these things. He was emotionally exhausted, but he would not surrender his integrity to fit his society's image of what would make sense of his tragedies. Upright men may be appalled, and good people might stick to their ways and thoughts and leave Job far behind, but Job would not give in to this social pressure. He was innocent. He would not lie and falsely confess to make his society happy.

But he would not despise and reject his peers either, despite their error. Job still called them upright and righteous. Job did not just put up with them. He challenged them to continue to engage with him. Try again, he said. But Job was not under any illusions that he would find wisdom among them.

Despite everything that had happened so far in these dialogues, Job continued to engage with these friends.

NO PATIENCE FOR FALSE POSITIVITY

Job was not Jesus. But he had Christlike qualities in how he dealt with his less-than-ideal friendships. Yet having all the good virtues in the world did not change Job's emotional pain and exhaustion. He hurt. He was tired. He had no hope. Hope had sparked, perhaps, in his idea of life after death and his faith in a heavenly friend, but only dimly. It flickered. It went out. It will be re-sparked, but first, Job stumbled emotionally. Grief comes in waves, and for the rest of this speech, the wave crested and swamped his suffering soul.

Hear the emotion in how Job expressed himself in these next few verses.

> *[11] "My days are past; my plans are broken off,*
> *the desires of my heart.[76]*
> *[12] They make night into day:*
> *'The light,' they say, 'is near to the darkness.'*
> *[13] If I hope for Sheol as my house,*
> *if I make my bed in darkness,*
> *[14] if I say to the pit, 'You are my father,'*
> *and to the worm, 'My mother,' or 'My sister,'*
> *[15] where then is my hope?*
> *Who will see my hope?*
> *[16] Will it go down to the bars of Sheol?*
> *Shall we descend together into the dust?"*
>
> JOB 17:11–16

Amid my pain and fear that I was losing my wife and daughter, verse twelve resonated deeply with me. Job expresses his idea in poetry, essentially saying that "these people turn night into day and say that the dawn is near." A close modern version of this line is the expression that "it's always darkest just before the dawn."

Whenever somebody told me, "Don't worry—things will turn out okay," I would hurt inside. My wife once turned on a well-wisher uttering similar thoughtless promises with a sharp response: "How do you know? How do

---

76 The ESV translation here leaves the last line hanging awkwardly. The idea is less abrupt in the original, with the basic idea being that "my days are over, my plans are ruined, and the desires of my heart are denied to me."

you know? Can you promise that things will turn out okay? Can you guarantee it? If things don't turn out okay, then what will you do?"

Job was no fan of empty platitudes, and neither was my wife. It is a rare, and perhaps temporarily impaired, soul that can find comfort in assurances without substance. There is a reason people want the truth, even in a crisis—especially in a crisis. Give us the bad news, doctor.

People do not usually want to be lied to.

Do not say "The dawn is near" if you are just guessing.

31

BILDAD AND THE PLURAL YOU

> ¹*Then Bildad the Shuhite answered and said:*
> ²*"How long will you hunt for words?*
>   *Consider, and then we will speak.*
> ³*Why are we counted as cattle?*
>   *Why are we stupid in your sight?"*
>
> Job 18:1–3

THE YOU IN verse two, in Hebrew, is plural. It is as though Bildad wanted everyone to shut up, not just Job. If all we had were this plural you in verse two, we would probably be safe to put this down to more Bildad rudeness. But in verse three, the word your is also plural. "Why are we [plural] considered stupid in your [plural] sight?" So who was Bildad talking to? The we is clearly Bildad, Eliphaz, and Zophar. So who are the other people on Job's side of this plurality? Who else did Bildad feel was considering the three friends to be stupid?

There are a few possibilities. One is that this could be an obscure literary device, similar to the royal we in English.

If Bildad's your is meant in a royal fashion, talking to a single person as though he were a multitude, then this line is sarcastic. Why are we considered stupid in your most eminent and honorable sight? There is a ring to this interpretation that sounds like something Bildad would say, and it certainly clears up the plural confusion.

Another possibility is less literary and more literal. There were likely other people listening to this conversation. Elihu was Job's fourth friend who had not spoken yet but we'll learn later had been listening all along. Perhaps there were other onlookers, some who might have nodded sympathetically at Job's cries and complaints, silently indicating their support for his pain and opinion. It is possible that Bildad felt this silent support and so was not addressing Job alone in a sarcastic or royal plural but was literally addressing numerous people who were present.

Whatever the interpretation of these plurals, Bildad went on from here in the singular, addressing Job directly.

FAITH IN A TRADITION VERSUS FAITH IN GOD

> ⁴"You who tear yourself in your anger,
>   shall the earth be forsaken for you,
>   or the rock be removed out of its place?"
>
> JOB 18:4

In other words, the Standard View is bedrock. God cannot be wrong, and the Standard View cannot be wrong. Therefore, it has to be Job who was wrong. Bildad was saying that Job's insistence on his innocence was like Job expecting his friends to dismantle the earth—abandon the bedrock of their philosophy—to support Job's claims.

Faced with facts that proved his faith wrong, Bildad could not grasp that he needed to rethink his faith. Bildad had confused faith in his personal interpretations (that is, the Standard View) with faith in God himself. A philosophy for interpreting the world had replaced Bildad's devotion to the personal God.

This is an easy thing to do. It is a common thing to see. Unfortunately, people whose faith is in a denomination, a tradition, a particular interpretation of personal life events, or even a cultural mindset can allow this baggage to become superimposed on top of scripture and faith in God. The result is a tainted view of God where these ideas, traditions, methods, and cultural habits replace the real thing. It is idolatry without the obvious physical idols.

A HEARTLESS CRITIC

A rude person is a natural critic, and in this next section, Bildad went after many things that Job had said, turning them around and using Job's own words against him. He started with this bit:

> [5] "Indeed, the light of the wicked is put out,
>   and the flame of his fire does not shine.
> [6] The light is dark in his tent,
>   and his lamp above him is put out."
>
> JOB 18:5–6

In 10:20–22, Job had decried his fate, which he said was doomed to darkness, deepest night, deep shadow, and the place where even light is darkness.

Here, Bildad assured Job that it was the wicked whose lamp is snuffed out, whose flame goes out, and whose light and lamp goes dark. It is the wicked who are driven from light into darkness. In other words, not only did Job's kids get what they deserve, but Job was getting the fate of the wicked as well.

Bildad continued:

> [7] "His strong steps are shortened,
>   and his own schemes throw him down.
> [8] For he is cast into a net by his own feet,
>   and he walks on its mesh.
> [9] A trap seizes him by the heel;
>   a snare lays hold of him.
> [10] A rope is hidden for him in the ground,
>   a trap for him in the path.
> [11] Terrors frighten him on every side,
>   and chase him at his heels."
>
> JOB 18:7–11

In 13:27, Job had complained that God had shackled his feet, monitored his paths, and tracked him unrelentingly. In response, Bildad assured Job that his path was tracked even more doggedly than he had ever imagined. It was a path strewn with nets, meshes, nooses, and traps. Calamity and disaster were ready and waiting and hungry for him.

Bildad was not done with quoting Job. Here's another emotional arrow fired at the suffering man:

> *¹²"His strength is famished,*
> *and calamity is ready for his stumbling.*
> *¹³It consumes the parts of his skin;*
> *the firstborn of death consumes his limbs."*
>
> JOB 18:12–13

In 7:5, Job had described his physical state as one in which his body was "clothed with worms," his skin "broken and festering" (NIV). Yes, confirmed Bildad, this is just what the wicked should expect. Calamity and disaster will "eat away parts of his skin… and devour his limbs" (NIV).

Bildad was unrelenting. He had more to say along this line:

> *¹⁴"He is torn from the tent in which he trusted*
> *and is brought to the king of terrors.*
> *¹⁵In his tent dwells that which is none of his;*
> *sulfur is scattered over his habitation."*
>
> JOB 18:14–15

Bildad was now referencing the ancient practice of sterilizing a disaster site with fire and sulfur, something that in some form or another had in all likelihood happened on Job's farm.[77] He continued on with this theme:

> *¹⁶"His roots dry up beneath,*
> *and his branches wither above.*

---

[77] The scattering of sulfur was not a form of judgment but rather a testament that judgment had already been executed. In particular, sulfur was used in ancient times as a disinfectant post-tragedy to clean up a horror scene. It is possible—some might argue likely—that sulfur was used as part of the cleanup process on Job's farm. If this is an accurate interpretation, then Bildad's rudeness was not just theoretical but was referencing the actual activity (and smells) present on Job's land where this speech was occurring.

> ^{17}*His memory perishes from the earth,*
>   *and he has no name in the street.*
> ^{18}*He is thrust from light into darkness,*
>   *and driven out of the world.*
> ^{19}*He has no posterity or progeny among his people,*
>   *and no survivor where he used to live.*
> ^{20}*They of the west are appalled at his day,*
>   *and horror seizes them of the east.*
> ^{21}*Surely such are the dwellings of the unrighteous,*
>   *such is the place of him who knows not God."*
>
> JOB 18:16–21

In Job's previous speech, he had complained of the tendency of the comfortable to utter platitudes to those in real trouble. These people would attempt to "make night into day" and say, "The light… is near to the darkness" (17:12). Bildad had the opposite information to share: he focused on how the wicked are "thrust from light into darkness" (18:18). And in case the metaphor was lost on his audience, he interpreted it as well: the evil will be "driven from the world…. such is the place of him who knows not God" (18:18, 21).

Bildad also described how the wicked would be erased from all memory by the elimination of their descendants. He started poetically: the roots and branches of the wicked dry up and wither (18:16). Bildad then stated that all memory of the wicked and their family's name would be erased (18:17). And then, just in case this poetry had been too subtle, Bildad, ever rude and blunt, spelled it out even more clearly: the children of the wicked will all be destroyed (18:19). I'm sure I don't need to remind you that all of Job's children had been killed.

Bildad's words were intentional. His statements were pointed. He based each of his descriptions of the fate of the wicked either on something Job had said to describe his own hurt and grief or on what had physically happened around them. He was describing the circumstances and emotions that Job had openly and vulnerably shared, and then he turned every one of those details into evidence to support the Standard View and further crush Job.

In his first speech, Bildad had stated that Job's kids got what they deserved

(8:4), and in this one, he ran through a list of the pains that had come upon Job and then concluded that these were exactly what Job also deserved.

Wow, with friends like this, who needs enemies? When I first really understood what Bildad was saying in these speeches, I grew livid with anger. How could someone treat another friend this way? Then I wondered how a righteous person should respond to a friend like this. The next chapter in Job is a showcase demonstrating a beautiful answer to that very question.

32

JOB'S MATURITY

IN THE HEART of a weaker person, like myself, Bildad's words might have inspired rage or despair, hate or collapse. A reasonable, still emotional, but balanced response would seem like far too much to ask of someone in Job's position. Job, however, stood against even this assault. He did not hate, and he did not collapse either. Instead, he demonstrated openness and a startling maturity.

> *¹Then Job answered and said:*
> *²"How long will you torment me*
>   *and break me in pieces with words?*
> *³These ten times you have cast reproach upon me;*
>   *are you not ashamed to wrong me?*
> *⁴And even if it be true that I have erred,*
>   *my error remains with myself.*
> *⁵If indeed you magnify yourselves against me*
>   *and make my disgrace an argument against me,*[78]
> *⁶know then that God has put me in the wrong*
>   *and closed his net about me.*
> *⁷Behold, I cry out, 'Violence!' but I am not answered;*
>   *I call for help, but there is no justice.*

---

[78] Notice that Job was very aware of how Bildad had used Job's own words and circumstances against him. What we discussed in the last chapter did not escape the suffering man's notice in the moment.

> *⁸He has walled up my way, so that I cannot pass,*
>   *and he has set darkness upon my paths.*
> *⁹He has stripped from me my glory*
>   *and taken the crown from my head.*
> *¹⁰He breaks me down on every side, and I am gone,*
>   *and my hope has he pulled up like a tree.*
> *¹¹He has kindled his wrath against me*
>   *and counts me as his adversary.*
> *¹²His troops come on together;*
>   *they have cast up their siege ramp against me*
>   *and encamp around my tent."*
>
> Job 19:1–12

The imagery here is poetic, and Job was trying to emotionally convey that not only had God wronged him, but God had done so using excessive force. God had brought troops and built siege works against him. Troops and siege works—against a single person. He described God as having torn him down on every side. Blocked his way. Torn up his hope. Burning with anger against one individual, God had counted Job as a personal enemy.

These were Job's conclusions based on the trouble that had come into his life, interpreted through the lens of the Standard View.

But notice something crucial here. Not only was Job's response to Bildad's rudeness measured and mature, but his response to God's apparent rejection was also careful. God had counted Job, it would appear, to be among his enemies. This was how things looked. God may have turned against Job (so it appeared), but Job had not turned against God. Job also did not reject Bildad as a friend for his rudeness. Job did not reject Bildad or God, despite the events that had occurred and his friends' harsh interpretation of them. Job felt isolated, but he bore no responsibility for his isolation. He had not contributed to this state of affairs by any initial sin. Nor had he sinned against his friends as a result of this painful dialogue.

For me, this is a stunning demonstration of character. I can slip into resentments easily. The term ghosting may have been invented by the generation after me in the context of social media, but this cold-shoulder response to hurt relationships is very old. My generation just didn't have a good name for it. People ghost friends. People ghost family. People ghost God.

Job's ability to be open about his hurt, even his anger, but not turn away from his friends or God despite that hurt and anger is truly remarkable.

JOB DESCRIBES HIS ISOLATION

¹³"He has put my brothers far from me,
  and those who knew me are wholly estranged from me.
¹⁴My relatives have failed me,
  my close friends have forgotten me.
¹⁵The guests in my house and my maidservants count me as a stranger;
  I have become a foreigner in their eyes.
¹⁶I call to my servant, but he gives me no answer;
  I must plead with him with my mouth for mercy.
¹⁷My breath is strange to my wife,
  and I am a stench to the children of my own mother.
¹⁸Even young children despise me;
  when I rise they talk against me.
¹⁹All my intimate friends abhor me,
  and those whom I loved have turned against me.
²⁰My bones stick to my skin and to my flesh,
  and I have escaped by the skin of my teeth.
²¹Have mercy on me, have mercy on me, O you my friends,
  for the hand of God has touched me!
²²Why do you, like God, pursue me?
  Why are you not satisfied with my flesh?"

JOB 19:13–22

A CRY FOR A SAVIOR

Job's plea for compassion and his refusal to reject both God and friends is a fine example and model to emulate. But there is more. Job did not just avoid rejecting God and his friends but also reached out to both for help and, in faith, reached even beyond the looming grave for a savior.

Here is how Job expressed this:

²³"Oh that my words were written!
    Oh that they were inscribed in a book!
²⁴Oh that with an iron pen and lead
    they were engraved in the rock forever!
²⁵For I know that my Redeemer lives,
    and at the last he will stand upon the earth.
²⁶And after my skin has been thus destroyed,
    yet in my flesh I shall see God,
²⁷whom I shall see for myself,
    and my eyes shall behold, and not another.
    My heart faints within me!"

                                                JOB 19:23–27

WAIT, WHERE DID THIS COME FROM?

IN 9:33–35, JOB had spoken about his need for an arbiter to resolve the apparent dispute between Job and God. This had been just the beginning of an idea, conceived in response to his need but not backed by concrete evidence.

In chapter fourteen, Job had stepped out on another imaginative limb, speaking about another need. Faced with his life's grim reality, he had imagined hope as existing in a life beyond the grave. It had only been a partially conceived hope, but it had been rooted in concrete examples of trees and streams, and from these examples, Job had posed a scenario where God could seek Job out after his death and revive him. However, the chapter had ended on a down note as Job had acknowledged that, instead of rewatering and reviving him, reality was more likely to erode and wash him away (14:18–21), sealing his fate permanently. The water of hopeful life was really the water of erosive death. But the seed of an idea had been planted. Eternity was now out in the open.

An arbiter and eternity—Job had described both ideas as a result not of revelation but of need.

Then at the end of chapter sixteen, Job had returned to his arbiter idea and downgraded it from arbiter to advocate—a person who would plead Job's case rather than directly fix it. But Job expected this advocate to be effective. This advocate was heavenly and someone that Job had faith in.

And now, in chapter nineteen, Job's mediator-turned-advocate had changed again and was now a Redeemer—one that that would speak to Job beyond the grave and bring him into God's presence. This was no longer a wish but something that Job had developed confidence and faith in: "I know that my Redeemer lives."

But it was not just Job's Redeemer that lived. Job also had confidence that he would also see God—he himself and not someone reporting on his behalf—and that this meeting would occur despite an impossibility: Job's flesh might be destroyed, but in his flesh he would see God. Job was now confident in his hope that he would be revived. There will be life beyond the grave for Job and, with that life, redemption. His heart yearned within him for this future.

Hope that had been gone was now restored, rooted in a deeper and more permanent place. Job was no longer looking for some kind of earthly restoration as a basis for hope but was looking for something that reached even beyond death itself.

AGAIN, WHERE DID THIS COME FROM?

Was there something in the oral traditions handed down from the days of Noah, from the teachings of Melchizedek, or from a special revelation revealed personally to Job that served as grounds for this confidence? There is nothing in the text to explain it. But Job's statement is clear. "I know that my Redeemer lives," Job said. He wanted those words recorded in lead engravings or stone carvings. I know. I will see God; I myself will see him with my own eyes—I, and not another.

ON BEHALF OF DUST

This is such a fantastic confession of faith—and for it to be pre–New Testament makes it even more amazing. Is there anything else revealed in Job's confession about this Redeemer that we can learn from before we move on?

Verse twenty-five states that "at the last he will stand upon the earth."

The Hebrew reads slightly differently. Rather than standing "upon" the earth, the Hebrew reads that this Redeemer will stand "on behalf of" the earth.[79]

The Redeemer will stand on behalf of the earth. As that wording stands, the meaning is fairly clear: the Redeemer will redeem the earth. But there is more. The Hebrew word that the ESV translates as earth is elsewhere translated as dust.

In the end, the Redeemer will stand on behalf of dust. Why dust?

In chapters four and five, Eliphaz had quoted the spirit's contrary revelation. Specifically, in 4:19, the spirit had referenced the feebleness of humanity, noting that they "dwell in houses of clay, whose foundation is in the dust." This verse is referencing not mud buildings but rather human bodies. People are made of basic earthly stuff: dust. In Genesis 2:7, God formed Adam from dust. In Job 7:21, Job had stated that soon his body would return to the dust. Later, Job had pulled the spirit's revelation and his fear of returning to dust together, perhaps even with oral-tradition versions of Genesis, in prayer to God:

> *⁹"Remember that you have made me like clay;*
> *and will you return me to the dust?"*
>
> JOB 10:9

And then we come to Job's confession about his Redeemer, which, as it reads literally in Hebrew, states:

> *²⁵"For I know that my Redeemer lives,*
> *and at the last he will stand [on behalf of dust.]"*
>
> JOB 19:25

THE TURNING POINT: JOB'S LEAP OF FAITH

Job had started with an arbiter—someone to set God straight.

Then he had moved to an advocate—someone to plead with God "as one pleads for a friend" (16:21, NIV).

---

79 Janzen, 140-141.

And finally, we come to a Redeemer—someone who will stand on behalf of humanity, even though people are just dust.

Job had first wanted God set straight. Then he had just wanted God persuaded. But finally, it was not about arbitration or arguing the merits of a case—in the end, he bypassed all arguments and adopted redemption as his solid ground. As Job shifted from I hope to I know, his faith now had found solid ground not in himself and his own righteousness—the very place where his friends insisted that he was placing his confidence—but rather in his Redeemer.

Job would have enjoyed reading the book of Romans. The Gospels fulfill many things, and Job's faith was certainly one of the things that the Gospels provide the reality for.

It is not accidental that Job's faith in eternity also began to take a more solid form when Job also placed his faith in redemption rather than arbitration or advocacy. Job did not follow up his statement of hope beyond the grave with gloomy backtracking as his original eternity speculations had in chapters fourteen and seventeen. Instead, Job's hope in eternity went up against even logical contradictions without flinching: "And after my skin has been destroyed, yet in my flesh I will see God… how my heart yearns within me!" (19:26–27, NIV). This was no longer a logical debate, nor was this is a flutter of speculation. This was a confident hope that created a yearning expectation within him.

A WARNING FOR JOB'S FRIENDS

Job did not end this speech by undercutting his hope as he had done previously. He did, however, still have his friends to deal with. As he turned his attention back toward them, he did so knowing he was now finally through his own dark woods. The depression was over. He had come out into the sunshine. He had a real hope now that inspired a deep yearning within him.

However, coming into daylight, he saw how dangerous his friends' Standard View stubbornness was. It was dangerous for him—and it remained dangerous for them. So he warned them with these lines:

> [28]*"If you say, 'How we will pursue him!'*
> *and, 'The root of the matter is found in him,'*

> *²⁹be afraid of the sword,*
> *for wrath brings the punishment of the sword,*
> *that you may know there is a judgment."*
>
> JOB 19:28–29

Redemption is real. The Standard View is not a permanent law of reality that can be used to judge ambiguous or exceptional cases. "The root of the matter" was not found in Job's actions that had somehow earned his troubles. Job was warning his friends to watch out. He was a few thousand years early, but his words echo similar New Testament warnings, including Jesus the Redeemer's own words of warning:

> ¹¹*"Judge not, that you be not judged. ²²For with the judgment you pronounce you will be judged, and with the measure you use it will be measured to you."*
>
> MATTHEW 7:1–2

Job was telling his friends to pull back. They needed to stop hounding him for their own sake, or they could find themselves subject to the same kind of retributive justice that they had been expounding.

There is an important lesson here. The Standard View is seductive. Natural observations bolster its promise of predictability and control, and in many cases, the expectations of the Standard View do come to pass. For those observing trouble in a comfortable place, it is much easier to remain comfortable by blaming the victim than to become uncomfortable and help. There is something in the misapplied Standard View that feels pious but is sinful, and that self-deception makes it all the more dangerous.

33

ZOPHAR'S "THEREFORE"

Zophar was next in line to speak, and he did not like the implications of Job's warning in the previous chapter. As far as Zophar was concerned, there was no fault with the three friends.

> *¹Then Zophar the Naamathite answered and said:*
> *²"Therefore my thoughts answer me,*
>   *because of my haste within me.*
> *³I hear censure that insults me,*
>   *and out of my understanding a spirit answers me."*
>
> Job 20:1–3

In English, it is awkward for someone to start a speech with the word *therefore*. But the original Hebrew word served to explicitly link Zophar's speech with the last thing that Job had said. In the English translation, it is obvious that Zophar was responding to Job's rebuke, but in the original Hebrew, this is even more obvious.

ZOPHAR TO JOB: DON'T ARGUE WITH US

> *⁴"Do you not know this from of old,*
>   *since man was placed on earth,*
> *⁵that the exulting of the wicked is short,*
>   *and the joy of the godless but for a moment?*

> *⁶Though his height mount up to the heavens,*
>   *and his head reach to the clouds,*
> *⁷he will perish forever like his own dung;*
>   *those who have seen him will say, 'Where is he?'"*
>
> JOB 20:4–7

Just like in Bildad's last speech, these lines in Zophar's speech deliberately pull from Job's own words as Zophar tried to turn the tables on Job's rebuke and refocus the spotlight away from the three friends.

In 19:25–26, Job was able to state his faith in his Redeemer: "I know that my Redeemer lives."

In verse four, Zophar said, "Do you not know," and went on to articulate yet again what he saw as the relentless reliability of the Standard View. Don't you know this stuff already?

We can see the connection between Job's words and Zophar's response in our English translations, but the connection in the original Hebrew phrasing is even more explicit. Zophar essentially said: What you know is that the Standard View is irrefutable. That is what you should know. Not this Redeemer business.

In 14:10, Job had talked about the fate of people who do not have eternity to hope for, and then, as we noted, there is that important third line in the original Hebrew text: "where is he?"

In 20:7, Zophar picked up on the plaintive query and applied it specifically to the wicked, likewise asking, "Where is he?" Job had been concerned with the fate of all people after death. Zophar was only concerned with the hopelessness of the wicked. Zophar had subverted Job's words for his own purposes as he tried to dismantle these ideas of redemption and eternity.

ZOPHAR TO JOB: STOP TALKING ABOUT NIGHT VISIONS AND ETERNITY

Job's confession in 19:25–26 and his vision of life after death were imaginative exercises born of need, hope, and faith. They were not based on the Standard View but the spirit's Contrary View, which had been revealed in a vision in the night. Zophar had had enough of life-after-death talk and night visions, and so he laid down these next verses like some kind of cruel curse.

> ⁸"He will fly away like a dream and not be found;
>   he will be chased away like a vision of the night.
> ⁹The eye that saw him will see him no more,
>   nor will his place any more behold him.
> ¹⁰His children will seek the favor of the poor,
>   and his hands will give back his wealth.
> ¹¹His bones are full of his youthful vigor,
>   but it will lie down with him in the dust."
>
> JOB 20:8–11

ZOPHAR TO JOB: AND STOP WITH THE REDEEMER TALK AS WELL

Zophar really had it in for Job. He had it in for him personally, and he also had it in for his ideas about a Redeemer. In 7:21, Job had cried out to God for help because he feared he would die and be buried and never be seen again—God himself would look for Job and not be able to find him. In response, Zophar informed Job that the wicked are the sort that are seen no more and buried in the earth.

In 19:25, Job had spoken about this Redeemer as one who will stand on behalf of dust. Zophar was not into this at all. Rather than be saved by a Redeemer who defies the Standard View and stands on behalf of dust, Zophar proclaimed that Job's youthful vigor would lie (not stand) with him in the dust. There was no Redeemer for dust. There was only decay in Zophar's conception of dust.

A TARGETED ASSAULT ON JOB'S SITUATION

Here is how Zophar tried to counter Job's hopeful ideas:

> ¹²"Though evil is sweet in his mouth,
>   though he hides it under his tongue,
> ¹³though he is loath to let it go
>   and holds it in his mouth,
> ¹⁴yet his food is turned in his stomach;

> *it is the venom of cobras within him.*
> *¹⁵He swallows down riches and vomits them up again;*
> *God casts them out of his belly.*
> *¹⁶He will suck the poison of cobras;*
> *the tongue of a viper will kill him.*
> *¹⁷He will not look upon the rivers,*
> *the streams flowing with honey and curds.*
> *¹⁸He will give back the fruit of his toil*
> *and will not swallow it down;*
> *from the profit of his trading*
> *he will get no enjoyment.*
> *¹⁹For he has crushed and abandoned the poor;*
> *he has seized a house that he did not build.*
> *²⁰Because he knew no contentment in his belly,*
> *he will not let anything in which he delights escape him.*
> *²¹There was nothing left after he had eaten;*
> *therefore his prosperity will not endure.*
> *²²In the fullness of his sufficiency he will be in distress;*
> *the hand of everyone in misery will come against him.*
> *²³To fill his belly to the full,*
> *God will send his burning anger against him*
> *and rain it upon him into his body.*
> *²⁴He will flee from an iron weapon;*
> *a bronze arrow will strike him through.*
> *²⁵It is drawn forth and comes out of his body;*
> *the glittering point comes out of his gallbladder;*
> *terrors come upon him.*
> *²⁶Utter darkness is laid up for his treasures;*
> *a fire not fanned will devour him;*
> *what is left in his tent will be consumed."*
>
> JOB 20:12–26

On the surface, these fifteen verses read like a Standard View exposé and, from an informational perspective, that is what they are. But as usual in this book of poetry, there is also something poetic and literary going on here.

Recall our discussion of chapter one. Job's kids were at a feast, eating, when suddenly the Sabeans attacked and killed many of Job's staff "with the mouth of the sword" (1:15). Then fire from the sky "ate up" the sheep and servants in another section of the farm (1:16), and the Chaldeans put to death another portion of Job's operation, killing the staff there also "with the mouth of the sword" (1:17). All this happened while Job's kids were eating. And then they too were killed while at a feast table. So there was an eating motif in chapter one that was awful.

Later, after Job had sampled Eliphaz's first introduction of the Standard View as an interpretative framework for these tragedies, Job's response was to describe this view and its implications for his situation as nauseating. The Standard View was food that made him ill (6:5–7).

Zophar had now picked up on this eating theme. Zophar informed Job that evil might taste sweet, but it will turn sour in the stomach. In other words, swallow the Standard View. It might not taste good, but it is the right stuff. Evil, by contrast, will become venomous once consumed.

As a basic teaching, Zophar's point is hard to disagree with. But when applied to Job's particular circumstances to counter his resistance to the Standard View, Zophar's point was wrong. It was another example of the false dilemma that the friends had created. Their worldview was black and white and could only grasp either/or propositions; nuance escaped them.

Zophar described the wicked as greedy, consuming even their own treasures, unable to stop themselves from gorging on wickedness until finally, full to bursting, God attacks, beating the overfull sinner, piercing him with the arrows tipped with iron, the most advanced military technology of the era. As verse twenty-six makes clear, the devourer will finally be devoured.

BEYOND ALL THE EATING AND FOOD POETRY, WHAT DID ZOPHAR JUST SAY?

Said plainly, Zophar was claiming that Job's tragedies were just what he deserved. Job was very wealthy (recall chapter one). Assuming the Standard View is correct, and that bad things only happen to bad people, Job must have also been a bad person. And so Job and his farm were devoured.

In 7:5, Job had described his physical state as one in which his body was "clothed with worms and scabs," and his skin was "broken and festering" (NIV). According to Zophar, Job was even now, during these discussions, being devoured in a manner perfectly fitting his status as a former devourer who had finally been brought to justice before God.

Do you see now how Zophar's speech was more than just impersonally restating his worldview? Do you see how it was an unrelenting personal assault on Job himself? Zophar had gone so far into the Standard View that he could see nothing except that which could be filtered through his worldview's framework.

A RIGID WORLDVIEW CAN MAKE YOU BLIND

This is an easy trap. Democrat or Republican. Socialist or Capitalist. Liberal or Conservative. City-centric or country folk. Western, eastern, northern, southern. Our culture, family background, and even our own philosophies—all developed by personal experiences in our own short lives—can become rigid frameworks that provide a useful structure for filtering and interpreting the world around us. But these filters can also become traps and blinders that support and justify both personal and mass stupidity.

The Standard View had become so embedded into the way Zophar thought that he could not really think at all anymore. God himself had said that Job was a blameless and upright man, but Zophar couldn't see that.

The friends had not come to judge Job. They had come to comfort and console him, but their defense of the Standard View had overwhelmed their good intentions. Defending a worldview under threat had swamped Zophar's original intentions for this conversation. Zophar could not see anymore. But that didn't stop him from speaking. Here's what he said next:

> ^{27}*"The heavens will reveal his iniquity*
> *and the earth will rise up against him.*
> ^{28}*The possessions of his house will be carried away,*
> *dragged off in the day of God's wrath.*
> ^{29}*This is the wicked man's portion from God,*
> *the heritage decreed for him by God."*
>
> JOB 20:27–29

Job had no heritage left except for the remains of robbery, murder, tragic deaths, and his own destroyed health. That was his heritage—and that was

Zophar's point. Job's heritage was the heritage of the wicked, and in this, Zophar did not see injustice but rather evidence that Job's sin had yet to be revealed. His was a textbook punishment. The only thing hidden here was the evil Job must have concealed.

34

REDEFINING COMFORT

First, Eliphaz had spoken. Job had responded. Then Bildad. Job. Zophar. Job. And the first cycle of speeches was complete. Chapters 4–14 covered this first cycle of speeches, with the final two chapters, 12–14, containing Job's concluding thoughts. In the middle of this response, Job had called on his friends to "keep listening to my words" (13:17). This specific phrase in Hebrew can be literally translated as "hear, hear." The repetition is for emphasis. A clearer English translation may be "listen carefully" or "pay attention." Job had not felt heard after the first cycle of speeches.

Then Eliphaz had spoken again. Job had responded. Then Bildad. Job. Zophar. Job. With the same speaking order, this second cycle of speeches cover chapters 15–21. The second cycle was shorter than the first. And at the beginning of Job's final speech in this cycle, he once again used the Hebrew phrase "hear, hear," which the ESV translates as "keep listening."

As the second cycle concluded, Job still had not felt heard by his friends.

> *¹Then Job answered and said:*
> *²"Keep listening to my words,*
> *and let this be your comfort."*[80]
>
> Job 21:1–2

In Eliphaz's first speech of this second cycle, he had said that "the com-

---

80 That is, the comfort that the friends brought to Job. Job wanted to be heard.

forts of God" should be enough for Job—they were "the word that deals gently" (15:11). As we discussed when looking at that speech, it is somewhat ambiguous whether Eliphaz was referring to some divine words already spoken but not recorded in the book so far, or if Eliphaz was referring to the words of the friends as though they were somehow God's own words. If the latter was Eliphaz's intended meaning, Job had no patience for crediting divine authorship to these friends' words. Taken together, they were "miserable comforters" (16:2).

Now, in 21:2, wrapping up this second cycle of speeches, Job took his audience back to the first speech in the cycle by once again proscribing words of comfort. Job now asked that his friends console him not with the work of mouths—which have been miserably ineffective—but rather with the work of ears. Job wanted to be heard, not lectured.

PEOPLE NEED TO BE HEARD

Job's request was not just personal to Job—it is very good advice for anyone dealing with a friend in pain. There is a reason why professional counselors spend more time listening than they do talking.

It is a stereotype that the typical male is a lousy listener, needing to fix something and having no patience to just listen to the emotions that cannot be solved. It was an issue in my marriage that the events following the birth of our daughter made all the more acute.

This is not, however, just a male thing. Very often, men too do not feel heard. Perhaps because of genetics, perhaps because of culture or upbringing, reinforced by habit, men, in particular, are often very slow at understanding their own emotions and often even slower at finding ways to articulate those feelings, even to those they are closest to. All this delay and slowness make it all the more important for the person listening to a stereotypical male to be patient. When many men (and some women) try to speak about what is deepest in their hearts, false starts will be the norm. Misspoken emotions are common when an inexperienced soul tries to clumsily discover itself in addition to the monumental task of communicating that self to someone else. Both men and women in a crisis need to be heard.

Regardless of whether the suffering soul is a man or woman, an emotionally skilled communicator or nearly inarticulate fumbler, they do not need a lecture. Even if the suffering soul is the author of their own trouble, a lecture is not usually the right medicine in the moment. As Job himself said, responding to Bildad in cycle two:

> *⁴"And even if it be true that I have erred,*
> *my error remains with myself."*
>
> Job 19:4

Or as Job said even further back in the speeches, responding to Eliphaz's first speech in cycle one:

> *¹⁴"He who withholds kindness from a friend*
> *forsakes the fear of the Almighty."*
>
> Job 6:14

Job, a person highly commended by God, had specific expectations for his friendships. What he expected was kindness, not lectures and judgment. The consolation he called for was to "hear, hear"—to listen carefully—not to lecture.

Ah, but it is easier to lecture. To lecture is the natural posture of those embedded in the Standard View. And if the Standard View listener wisely seals their lips—perhaps due to a painful experience after speaking inadvisably in previous situations—their natural fallback position is to judge silently. But neither lecturing nor silently judging is listening. The Standard View seals ears. The suffering soul needs not a stubbornly closed ear but an open, listening ear. Even if the suffering soul has made mistakes or is a bad communicator, they need kind and patient ears, not the lectures or judgments of tradition and principle.

THE IMPATIENCE OF JOB

Job said something next that surprised me when I first read it.

> *³"Bear with me, and I will speak,*
> *and after I have spoken, mock on.*
> *⁴As for me, is my complaint against man?*

> *Why should I not be impatient?"*
>
> JOB 21:3–4

Impatient? Do we not talk in our society about someone having "the patience of Job"? But Job was not patient. Job had communicated his frustration, anger, and even resentment so far throughout this book.

Job expressing his submission to God's will in 1:21 is often interpreted as a bold statement of calm in the face of tragedy, but as we discussed when studying chapter one, verse twenty-one follows verse twenty. After exploring the cultural significance of torn clothes and shaved heads, it is clear that verse twenty depicts the exact opposite of calm resignation.

Here, in chapter twenty-one, Job explicitly said that he was not patient, and why should he be? Yet this self-proclaimed impatience seems to conflict with James's assessment of Job in the New Testament:

> *[10] Brothers and sisters, as an example of patience in the face of suffering, take the prophets who spoke in the name of the Lord. [11] As you know, we count as blessed those who have persevered. You have heard of Job's perseverance and have seen what the Lord finally brought about. The Lord is full of compassion and mercy.*
>
> JAMES 5:10–11, NIV

The passage starts off talking about patience, but then it moves on to perseverance. The two are different, and in Job's case, the focus is on perseverance. Job lasted. Job did not quit. But just like we saw in 1:20, his example is not one of inhuman and impossible calm. His example is one of candid honesty, prayerful earnestness, and intense engagement with God and his friends. He opposed the philosophies and theologies that informed his culture and contributed to his confusion, pain, and despair. But he was not patient through all of this. He wanted it to all be over. Now. At times he even longed for an early death just to escape his suffering.

He was not patient, but he was very perseverant—he never quit. Not on God. Not on his friends. Not even on life, despite his longing to escape it.

Job was not a quitter. But he was no calm stoic either. He endured, but he felt no compulsion to pretend to be happy about it, as we have seen.

If we can rid ourselves of the misconception that Job was patient through his trials, it may go a long way to helping us learn more from his good example instead of being overwhelmed, turned off, or dismayed by the impossible bar he seems to set in the face of tragedy. Job was many things, including perseverant, but he was not patient. He said so himself.

A STUNNING STATEMENT OF FAITH (AND A BIT OF BLASPHEMY)

> ⁵"Look at me and be appalled,
>   and lay your hand over your mouth.
> ⁶When I remember, I am dismayed,
>   and shuddering seizes my flesh.
> ⁷Why do the wicked live,
>   reach old age, and grow mighty in power?
> ⁸Their offspring are established in their presence,
>   and their descendants before their eyes.
> ⁹Their houses are safe from fear,
>   and no rod of God is upon them.
> ¹⁰Their bull breeds without fail;
>   their cow calves and does not miscarry.
> ¹¹They send out their little boys like a flock,
>   and their children dance.
> ¹²They sing to the tambourine and the lyre
>   and rejoice to the sound of the pipe.
> ¹³They spend their days in prosperity,
>   and in peace they go down to Sheol.
> ¹⁴They say to God, 'Depart from us!
>   We do not desire the knowledge of your ways.
> ¹⁵What is the Almighty, that we should serve him?
>   And what profit do we get if we pray to him?'
> ¹⁶Behold, is not their prosperity in their hand?
>   The counsel of the wicked is far from me."
>
>   Job 21:5–16

Something very big in the history of faith just happened here. Did you catch it?

The first section of this passage is fairly straightforward. Verses five through six highlight the horror of Job's circumstances. Recall that those circumstances included property theft, the murders of his staff, the deaths of his children, the abundance of widows and fatherless children, and the burial sites that now surrounded him. Those circumstances also included his wretched physical disease, which was visually awful, smelled bad, and was a physical and social source of pain. It was a state that horrified Job and should horrify anyone observing him. "Lay your hand over your mouth" is a poetic image that resonates with us even today.

By contrast, the following few verses describe the happy state of the wicked. Undoubtedly, Job was not suggesting that the exact opposite of the Standard View is always true: that wickedness is a guaranteed path to happiness and success. But what he was doing was highlighting the contrast between the horror of his personal circumstances and the apparent happiness and success of many who did not serve God and scorned the idea of doing so. His statements here are very bold. They are so bold that in the Septuagint version of this book (a Greek pre-Christ version of the Hebrew scriptures), verse fifteen was deleted. It was too blasphemous, and the devout Hebrew scholars tasked with translating their scriptures into the Greek language apparently could not bring themselves to include such a harsh statement.

But Job followed the wicked's bold blasphemy with his own contrasting statement of faith:

> ^{16}*"Behold, is not their prosperity in their hand?*
> *The counsel of the wicked is far from me."*
>
> JOB 21:16

As we see at the beginning of verse sixteen, rhetorical questions can sometimes trip a reader up. I like the original Hebrew of verse sixteen better, which is easier to understand and not phrased as a question at all.

The verse in Hebrew reads as follows:

> *"Behold, their prosperity is in their hand,[81]*
> *so I stand aloof from the counsel of the wicked."*
>
> JOB 21:16

Their prosperity is in their hand. They are prosperous and free from fear, and they defy God, seeing no value in him. They are the masters of their own fates. Their prosperity is something they control. That is what Job was saying. Their confidence and success is absolute. They own it. And it is precisely because of this that Job stood aloof from them.

What? Who would not want success, happiness, and security, as well as the joy of knowing that your success, happiness, and security were a product of your own power that you yourself controlled? Who would not want that?

Job—that's who!

Something big had happened here in the history of faith.

Eliphaz, Bildad, and Zophar had been preaching the Standard View of faith. Underneath all the cause-and-effect calculus and the predictability and control this view offers, there is a deeply selfish motive for adhering to this philosophy: the Standard View is a formula for success and happiness. The Standard View, at its heart, is about controlling your life and getting what you want (and explaining away the bad things that happen to other people). It is a fine piece of philosophy as long as nothing accidental or unjustified happens in your own life, as it did in Job's. The Standard View is, at its root, selfish.

Job's case shattered the Standard View. He had seen the lie, and he had discovered something else—or perhaps he had always known that something else, and these circumstances were merely providing him with a stage on which to articulate what he had always known.

Here is Job's secret: beyond assurance of a Redeemer, beyond a promise for eternity, Job wanted a relationship with God. Job would take God before all else.

Job would take suffering with God before he took peace, security, and success without God.

Job would choose disaster with God over success without God.

---

81 Janzen, 155-156.

The wicked were successful without God—so Job stood aloof from their counsel. What they had was not what he wanted. He wanted God.

This declaration is a landmark in the history of faith.

Job's deeply imaginative insights into eternity and redemption are very important, but they were speculative. It would not be until much later that Christ would bring substance to these ideas. Before eternity and redemption were made clear in Christ, one individual wanted God above all else—above even his success and happiness.

35

DEBUNKING THE LOGIC OF THE STANDARD VIEW

JOB HAD EXPRESSED a devotion to God that was separate from the rewards he might get from God for that devotion. To him, having a relationship with God was not about stacking the odds in his favor and securing his own success. He was genuinely invested in God for the sake of their relationship.

Job's friends, however, were not there yet. The friends clung to their faith in the Standard View, and so Job left this profound expression of personal devotion and addressed once again the illogic of the Standard View.

> ^{17}"How often is it that the lamp of the wicked is put out?
> That their calamity comes upon them?
> That God distributes pains in his anger?
> ^{18}That they are like straw before the wind,
> and like chaff that the storm carries away?"
>
> JOB 21:17–18

The Hebrew makes it clear that the answer to these questions is either seldom or never.

Job went on:

> ^{19}"You say, 'God stores up their iniquity for their children.'

> Let him pay it out to them, that they may know it.
> ^{20}Let their own eyes see their destruction,
>> and let them drink of the wrath of the Almighty.
> ^{21}For what do they care for their houses after them,
>> when the number of their months is cut off?
> ^{22}Will any teach God knowledge,
>> seeing that he judges those who are on high?
> ^{23}One dies in his full vigor,
>> being wholly at ease and secure,
> ^{24}his pails full of milk
>> and the marrow of his bones moist.
> ^{25}Another dies in bitterness of soul,
>> never having tasted of prosperity.
> ^{26}They lie down alike in the dust,
>> and the worms cover them.
> ^{27}Behold, I know your thoughts
>> and your schemes to wrong me.
> ^{28}For you say, 'Where is the house of the prince?
>> Where is the tent in which the wicked lived?'
> ^{29}Have you not asked those who travel the roads,
>> and do you not accept their testimony
> ^{30}that the evil man is spared in the day of calamity,
>> that he is rescued in the day of wrath?
> ^{31}Who declares his way to his face,
>> and who repays him for what he has done?
> ^{32}When he is carried to the grave,
>> watch is kept over his tomb.
> ^{33}The clods of the valley are sweet to him;
>> all mankind follows after him,
>> and those who go before him are innumerable.
> ^{34}How then will you comfort me with empty nothings?
>> There is nothing left of your answers but falsehood."
>
> JOB 21:19–34

Job's rebuttal of the Standard View would appear to be complete. He concluded this speech by charging that his friends' answers have been nothing but "falsehood." The actual Hebrew word is better translated as treachery or faithlessness. The friends' philosophy was dangerous, as it threatened to damage Job's spiritual and even psychological health.

REFUTING THE CONSENSUS

In 18:20, Bildad had commented on the fate of the wicked. He had stated that they were subject to the unalterable and inevitable punishments that the Standard View requires. Theirs was a fate that appalled people from both the west and the east. Bildad had been attempting to drag in public opinion and peer observations from even beyond the circle of friends discussing these matters with Job.

Eliphaz had started consolidating this consensus in 5:27 when he had informed Job that those gathered had examined the Standard View and found it to be true.

Bildad had carried on this theme in 8:8–10, calling on the former generations as witnesses. Likewise, in 18:20, he claimed that both east and west all agreed with this view. In these two passages, Bildad had expanded this consensus both back in time and across geographical borders.

Job's response to these claims that the Standard View is universally acknowledged truth was to ask in 21:29, "Have you not asked those who travel the roads, and do you not accept their testimony?" In chapter twelve, Job protested the friends' consensus by calling on them to examine their own experiences and observations and even consult the animals, birds, fish, and even the earth.[82] Job's point in chapter twelve had been logical, but it had been in poetic and hyperbolic language. At the end of chapter twenty-one, Job was more plainspoken: you ought to actually talk to people who travel if you plan on quoting them.

JOB IS DONE WITH STUMBLING

The arguments of Job's friends were nonsense and faithless treachery. They failed before the evidence of reality based on both personal experience and the witness of the well-traveled. And they were dangerous—they nearly cost

---

82 Recall 12:7–8.

Job his faith as the Standard View's logic had temporarily gained standing in Job's mind and thrust a wedge between Job and God.

But the wedge was dislodged. If it came down to it, Job would choose disaster with God over success without God. Job chose God. He had developed faith in some form of life after death. He now had confident hope not just in a witness and advocate but in a Redeemer. Come what may, Job was for God—whatever the personal cost.

This new stand had been hard won over twenty-one chapters. To gain this insight, Job had gone on a journey through spiritual alienation, personal desperation, and deep depression. Now, having come out the other side, Job could see the treachery in his friends' arguments and call it out with confidence and with evidence. He will stumble no more over the Standard View's confusions.

36

THE HARDENING OF THE CATEGORIES

WHEN A PERSON locks themself into a worldview, and that worldview is repeatedly shown to be false, it is appropriate for that person, however painful it might be, to reexamine the basis for their view and make the necessary adjustments.

However, once people lock into a worldview, it seems to be a common human trait to resist any inducements to change at all costs. My father used to refer to the "hardening of the categories" as a trait of middle age. Eliphaz's categories were irreparably hardened if his next speech is any indication.

The Standard View rests on three foundational pillars: the reliable justice of God, the binary categories of humans being either sinful or righteous, and the punishments and blessings meted out accordingly. Job's case suggested a failure of one of those pillars. Job had argued for a hearing with God to defend his case. This was something that Eliphaz had initially supported (5:8), but once he realized that Job's intent for this hearing was to overthrow the Standard View, he began to oppose this idea (15:2–13). Since Eliphaz's last speech, Job had risen from his depression and embraced his vision of eternity and a Redeemer. He had gone all in on his relationship with God, even if that relationship resulted not in mathematically reliable blessings but instead in uncertain suffering. He was loyal regardless of formulas. That, combined with his ideas about eternity and a Redeemer, completely unbalanced the Standard View's calculus.

For a person with hardened categories, this was unbearable, and so in this third speech, Eliphaz went after Job one last time. This time the gloves were off. Eliphaz dropped his verbal niceties, and like Bildad before him, he went on the speculative attack, inventing sins to paste onto Job in the hope that something would stick. The goal here appears to have been to puncture Job's shield of innocence. If Eliphaz could expose Job's secret sins, then Job's tragedies could be viewed as just punishments, and the Standard View would be salvaged.

Eliphaz was a man committed to his worldview. He was willing to destroy a friendship to preserve the integrity of his philosophy. Some would argue that religion can do that to people, but in fact, people do that to themselves. Philosophies, ways of interpreting the world, personal criteria for filtering reality—these might be based on religious or cultural or economic or personal history; they might even have multiple roots. Rigid dogma is not unique to the religious. But the common denominator across all people is that old wineskins aggressively resist new wine, even when reality evidences the need for change. Hardened categories resist softening.

THREE REFERENCES TO PIETY

> *¹Then Eliphaz the Temanite answered and said:*
> *²"Can a man be profitable to God?*
>   *Surely he who is wise is profitable to himself.*
> *³Is it any pleasure to the Almighty if you are in the right,*
>   *or is it gain to him if you make your ways blameless?*
> *⁴Is it for your fear of him that he reproves you*
>   *and enters into judgment with you?"*
>
> JOB 22:1–4

All three of Eliphaz's speeches begin with a word that the NIV translates as "piety" and the ESV translates as "fear of God."

His first use of this word is in 4:6, where Eliphaz first introduced the Standard View and referenced Job's fear of God as the foundation upon which Job should place his confidence. Eliphaz did not yet see Job as a threat to the status quo, so he was willing to describe Job as righteously fearing God.

Eliphaz's second use of this word occurs in his second speech. In 15:3–4, he returned to the topic of Job's fear of God, or his piety, but this time he warned Job that he was undermining piety. This was a reversal of his previous suggestion that Job's fear of God should be his grounds for confidence. Eliphaz had come to view Job's words as sinful and crafty (15:5). As Job insisted on his innocence, he undermined the Standard View, which to Eliphaz was the same as Job undermining his fear of and devotion to God. Who would be devoted to God if the Standard View proved false? If there was no prize, what was the point of pursuing the Almighty? In Eliphaz's mind, the Standard View had become equal to piety itself. Philosophy had displaced relationship.

Eliphaz's view of piety was, at its heart, selfish. It was a conditioned response to a reward, the very thing Satan had charged Job with in his discussions with God at the beginning of this book.[83] Job did not support the Standard View, but Satan was a big believer in it!

Now in his last speech, Eliphaz addressed Job's piety and fear of God for the third time (22:4). In this passage, he functionally asked Job, "Have these trials come into your life because of your righteousness?" This is, of course, sarcasm.

As a practical note here, if you're using sarcasm to comfort someone in pain, you're on the wrong track.

Let's ignore Eliphaz's sarcasm and focus on his underlying point. Eliphaz seems to be saying that, by suggesting that God would allow bad things to happen to a good person, Job was injecting a dangerous dose of cynicism into religious life. But as Job said so eloquently in the previous chapter, bad things do happen to good people. In our modern society, we have a common expression that aligns with Job's realistic point of view: no good deed goes unpunished. For readers of my generation, you'll remember that Billy Joel used to sing about how only the good die young.

These lines expose how obvious it is that the Standard View is not reliable as a predictive tool. The opposite of the Standard View at times seems more reliable. The good die young rather than living long lives. Bad deeds often go unpunished.

Eliphaz feared this thinking. He believed it would undermine piety and distract people from the appropriate fear of God. In Eliphaz's mind, God is

---

83 Recall 1:9–11 and 2:4–5.

just an impersonal judge handing out justice according to a formula and gets nothing personal from the transaction (see verses two and three).

From Eliphaz's point of view, then, there was only one solution to this conflict: someone had to uncover Job's sin.

DIGGING FOR SIN

Zophar had wished that God would step in and reveal what was hidden,[84] but God had not done so.

Job had declared that he had nothing to hide.

So far, the friends had been vague with their charges, speaking to principles but not directly to Job's circumstances. Job had called on witnesses near and far to support his proposition that the Standard View is rubbish—good things do happen to bad people, and bad things also happen to good people. The world is so much more complicated than the Standard View's simplistic theology will allow. But Job had not stopped there. In addition to assaulting Eliphaz's theology directly, he had also undermined it indirectly with his ideas of life after death, redemption, and grace that beggars the cause-and-effect boundaries imposed by the Standard View.

From Eliphaz's perspective, something had to be done before this runaway train of thought derailed everything Eliphaz believed in. Eliphaz needed to bury Job's ideas. He needed to ruin Job's credibility and find that hidden sin that would collapse Job's arguments and return things to their simple, predictable, and controllable state. If God would not reveal Job's sin and Job would not confess to it, then Eliphaz would just have to go and dig it out. But how does one go about discovering concealed sin?

Eliphaz's method of discovery will be to start laying charges, overwhelm his victim with accusations, however outlandish, and expect that something will eventually come to light. The Standard View says that sin had to be there—so Eliphaz will go looking for it.

That's what comes next: Eliphaz's Great Sin Hunt.

---

84 See 11:4–5.

37

MOTIVATION MATTERS

ELIPHAZ WILL GO on a sin hunt with Job next, but he will reveal something about his own motivations for following God in the process. Let's hear it first in his own words:

> ^{5}"Is not your evil abundant?
>   There is no end to your iniquities.
> ^{6}For you have exacted pledges of your brothers for nothing
>   and stripped the naked of their clothing.
> ^{7}You have given no water to the weary to drink,
>   and you have withheld bread from the hungry.
> ^{8}The man with power possessed the land,
>   and the favored man lived in it.
> ^{9}You have sent widows away empty,
>   and the arms of the fatherless were crushed.
> ^{10}Therefore snares are all around you,
>   and sudden terror overwhelms you,
> ^{11}or darkness, so that you cannot see,
>   and a flood of water covers you.
> ^{12}Is not God high in the heavens?
>   See the highest stars, how lofty they are!
> ^{13}But you say, 'What does God know?
>   Can he judge through the deep darkness?
> ^{14}Thick clouds veil him, so that he does not see,

> *and he walks on the vault of heaven.'*
> *¹⁵ Will you keep to the old way*
> *that wicked men have trod?*
> *¹⁶ They were snatched away before their time;*
> *their foundation was washed away.*
> *¹⁷ They said to God, 'Depart from us,'*
> *and 'What can the Almighty do to us?'*
> *¹⁸ Yet he filled their houses with good things—*
> *but the counsel of the wicked is far from me."*
>
> JOB 22:5–18

Wait. We have heard something similar before.

In 21:16, we encountered a landmark in the history of faith. In that verse, Job declared that the success of the wicked is something they control, but without God, so Job would stand aloof from their counsel. In other words, Job would take disaster with God rather than success with the wicked. This idea that Job wanted God for God was a profound statement of faith. Job was truly committed to a relationship and not to material rewards. Satan had it wrong.

This kind of devotion completely ignores the reward-based principles of the Standard View. Job had also repeatedly shown that the wicked often prosper. This fact is contrary to the Standard View, so Eliphaz acknowledged that yes, the wicked do seem to prosper for limited periods of time, but it is only temporary. They are "snatched away before their time" (22:16). In other words, according to Eliphaz, the bad, not the good, die young. In the meantime, the bad fail to acknowledge God, despite the fact that their good things came from God. It is for this reason that Eliphaz stood apart from the counsel of the wicked.

Job stood apart from the successful wicked because he did not want any success that would come without God. Eliphaz stood apart from the successful wicked because their success is temporary and doomed. Job's position was one of relationship. Eliphaz's was one of calculation. According to Eliphaz, based on the Standard View's logic, it makes more sense to avoid the counsel of the successful wicked because their success will be short-lived. Eliphaz's stance implies that if the wicked's success were to be long-lived, well, then maybe their counsel would be worth considering. But given that their success is short-lived, their counsel is not worth following. That is the logical extension of Eliphaz's argument.

Whether their success is long or short, Job would have nothing to do with the counsel of the wicked because it comes without God. Job loved God. Job's priority was God. Eliphaz's priority was whatever most benefited Eliphaz.

Eliphaz would have been shattered to have endured Job's trials. He would have been unable to pretend that these trials were justified without compromising his grip on reality. With the Standard View so thoroughly fractured, his devotion to God would have been left without any motivation at all. Without reward, there would have been no point in Eliphaz's perseverance. In contrast, Job endured because his faith was based on relationship, not reward.

That's worth repeating: Job endured because his faith was based on relationship, not reward.

As Job himself said right at the beginning of his trials, "Shall we accept good from God, and not trouble?" (2:10, NIV).

A PREACHER'S RHYTHM

Eliphaz apparently did not realize what his statements in verse eighteen said about his motivations, character, and shallow devotion to God. Oblivious, he continued to lecture Job:

> [19]"*The righteous see it and are glad;*
> *the innocent one mocks at them,*
> [20]*saying, 'Surely our adversaries are cut off,*
> *and what they left the fire has consumed.'*
> [21]*Agree with God, and be at peace;*
> *thereby good will come to you.*
> [22]*Receive instruction from his mouth,*
> *and lay up his words in your heart.*
> [23]*If you return to the Almighty you will be built up;*
> *if you remove injustice far from your tents,*
> [24]*if you lay gold in the dust,*
> *and gold of Ophir among the stones of the torrent-bed,*
> [25]*then the Almighty will be your gold*

>   *and your precious silver.*
> *²⁶For then you will delight yourself in the Almighty*
>   *and lift up your face to God.*
> *²⁷You will make your prayer to him, and he will hear you,*
>   *and you will pay your vows.*
> *²⁸You will decide on a matter, and it will be established for you,*
>   *and light will shine on your ways.*
> *²⁹For when they are humbled you say, 'It is because of pride';*
>   *but he saves the lowly.*
> *³⁰He delivers even the one who is not innocent,*
>   *who will be delivered through the cleanness of your hands."*
>
>   JOB 22:19–30

In the original Hebrew text, there are two ifs in verse twenty-three and a third if in verse twenty-four (all captured by the ESV translation). These three ifs are followed by three thens. The first two thens are captured by the ESV in verses twenty-five and twenty-six. The third then is found at the beginning of verse twenty-seven in the Hebrew text but is missing in the ESV translation.

The three if statements followed by three then statements create a kind of preacher's rhythm in the original Hebrew that builds momentum toward Eliphaz's conclusion. His conclusion, ironically, turned out to be accurate. Job, once restored, was able to intercede for those who were not innocent. Eliphaz got Job's unique role right but got the basis for that role completely wrong. At this point, he would have been very surprised to find himself as one of those people requiring Job's effective intercession before an angry God—angry, that is, at Eliphaz. But we are getting ahead of ourselves. We are on chapter twenty-two, not forty-two, so hold that thought.

WRAPPING UP ELIPHAZ'S SPEECHES

This is the last we will hear from Eliphaz. In his first speech, Eliphaz's wording was gentle and cautious. He introduced two interpretations of Job's distress: the Standard View and the spirit's Contrary View. He guided Job toward the Standard View and offered hope for the future founded on the predictability of this simple cause-and-effect way of seeing the world. Eliphaz identified

Job's fear of God as what made Eliphaz confident that things would turn out okay.

God did inject a contrary viewpoint by way of the spirit's revelation, but Eliphaz was sufficiently secure in his wisdom to ignore the spirit's input.

By the time Eliphaz got to his second speech, the conversation had deteriorated remarkably. Contrary to expectations, Job had come down in favor of the spirit's interpretation of events. Bildad had declared that Job's children had died due to some unspecified sins, and Zophar had concluded that Job had no more hope of grasping this wisdom than a donkey's colt could have of being born a person.

In response, Job had started to dive into a deep depression, but visions of life after death, of mediation and advocacy, had also begun to take root.

Job's thoughts were now so far beyond Eliphaz's perspective in his first speech that he now had to either disavow his own Standard View position or reject his original confidence in Job's fear of God. In his second speech, Eliphaz chose to defend the view and renounce Job's good character. He charged that, by voicing dangerous and unconventional ideas with emotional candor, Job had undermined his piety.

The way forward, however, was already becoming apparent to Job. Eliphaz's reversal and charges did not crush him. On the contrary, his slide into depression halted, and Job turned his tongue not only on the false assumptions of the Standard View but also on the poor showing his friends had made in its defense.

Before the conversation got back around to Eliphaz for the third time, Job's ideas about eternity and intercession had turned into the deep conviction that he would stand before God after death and find redemption. Job had come so far from his previously beaten state that he also warned his friends that they risked their own judgment if they persisted with this Standard View nonsense.

This was not the crushed submission Eliphaz had expected. In this final speech, Eliphaz's passionate attack was a last attempt to puncture Job's appearance of righteousness. He slung false charges with reckless abandon and, in the process, exposed his own insecurity and selfish materialism. Eliphaz, it turned out, was not the stalwart man of God that he had projected to be in his first speech. Eliphaz was wrapped in a facade of religion for worldly and materialistic purposes (i.e., it was good business), but when faced with

Job's reality, he failed to exercise the compassion and kindness that even basic friendship demanded. Adherence to a philosophy overruled love.

PRACTICAL LESSONS FOR THE TWENTY-FIRST CENTURY

For us today, it is essential to reflect on how easy it is to be Eliphaz.

The older you get, the easier it gets.

The closer you get to amassing a sufficient amount of worldly experience and achieving financial stability (or comfort with your state of instability), the easier it is to assume you know everything and start making judgments. As Job said, those who are comfortable have contempt for those who slip (Job 12:5). It is more comfortable to believe that the unfortunate cause their own problems than to acknowledge the discomfort of reality and do something to relieve its pains in those around you. Believing in Eliphaz's cause-and-effect religion makes your own life seem more safe and secure. It allows you to believe that, by being righteous, you can prevent similar trouble from happening to you. This narrow-mindedness removes our conviction to get uncomfortable and help others who are suffering. The proverb "there, but for the grace of God, go I" is replaced with "there, by their own stupid choices, go they—and therefore I don't have any responsibility but to heap scorn on them."

But recessions happen. Car accidents happen. Diseases happen. Crimes have victims who did not invite their abuse. Adults carry childhood wounds into adulthood, wounds that make them create more suffering for others, suffering that they did not start by themselves. The Standard View is always true except when it is not, and as Job has clearly articulated, the Standard View is not true a lot.

If I sin and suffer for it, the Standard View is true, and I have no one but myself to blame. I then need to take personal responsibility, submit to God, and repent—many of the things Eliphaz and his friends had advocated for Job to do. Whether or not I am blessed in a measurable material way for my change of heart and behavior is God's business. There is no formulaic guarantee of blessing as a result. Like Job's, my actions need to be motivated by my relationship with God, not by the return of my stuff.

But if I see someone else suffer, it is not my job, nor is it even a wise or frequently accurate posture, to work backward and assume that sin is the root cause of the suffering I'm observing. If, when faced with others' distress, our instinct is to take our emotional reactions and strike out at the one who suffers, then maybe there is some of Eliphaz in us. If a loved one reveals sudden trouble—trouble with a relationship, with grades, with work, with health, and so on—and our first response is to cross-examine how this loved one's actions contributed to their trouble, then Eliphaz is revealed within us.

Even if your judgment is accurate and your loved one is at least partially responsible for their distress, we are tasked to love, not to judge. From that love may eventually come counsel, correction, observations, or even warnings and direction to steer the loved one away from future harms, but our role is not to be a judge first and comforter second. And we are never to be a speculative critic. Our corrections are to come from a place of love, not from the desire to remove our own discomfort.

The role of comforter requires a maturity that eluded Eliphaz—but that maturity is not optional. As we will see, Eliphaz will get in trouble for his words, and we will also have to answer one day for the careless words we may have spoken.[85]

These were Eliphaz's final words in the book of Job. And it was now Job's turn to speak again.

---

85 See Matthew 12:36.

38

THE PRIVATE EFFORT OF SELF-CONTROL

> *¹Then Job answered and said:*
> *²"Today also my 1complaint is bitter;*[86]
>   *my hand is heavy on account of my groaning."*
>
> JOB 23:1–2

RIGHT AWAY, WE encounter a problem with our translation that needs attention.

First of all, Job's complaint was not bitter. The word rebellious is a better translation of the original Hebrew word Job used.[87] A new day had dawned, and despite his more positive view of his relationship with God, he still had a rebellious complaint.

Some English translations suggest that it is God's hand that is heavy on Job, a position that the Septuagint version of Job (a Greek pre-Jesus translation of the Hebrew scriptures) takes as well. But the original Hebrew reads "my hand," as does our ESV version here. God did not oppress Job, but rather Job had been trying to muzzle himself. His own hand is heavy upon him.

---

86 The phrase "today also" may indicate that this is a new day. I originally envisioned these speeches as having taken place during one marathon discussion, but what we are reading may be a condensed accounting of several days' worth of conversation. This is not a certain interpretation but one that the Hebrew word choice does appear to suggest.

87 Reyburn, 430-431.

The idea that Job was muzzling himself does not initially sound plausible considering his candor thus far, but it is important to remember that, amid his candor, Job had not turned against God or chased off his friends either. Instead, Job had, despite his circumstances, continued to reaffirm his devotion to God and to engage with his friends. What we do not see, and what Job alluded to here, is the effort that this self-control required of him.

I am sure many of us could take a significant practical lesson away from just this one verse. Candor, mixed with self-control, is a kind of heroism that does not get a lot of press but takes a lot of effort. Job was not a stoic—but he did not sin as he expressed his pain.

SEEKING GOD BOLDLY

Job continued to cry out to whoever would hear him:

> *³"Oh, that I knew where I might find him,*
> *that I might come even to his seat!*
> *⁴I would lay my case before him*
> *and fill my mouth with arguments.*
> *⁵I would know what he would answer me*
> *and understand what he would say to me.*
> *⁶Would he contend with me in the greatness of his power?*
> *No; he would pay attention to me.*
> *⁷There an upright man could argue with him,*
> *and I would be acquitted forever by my judge."*
>
> Job 23:3–7

What a change from chapter nine! There, Job had felt that he could not hope to speak with God at all—that even if he were granted a hearing, God would crush him, multiply his wounds for no reason, and somehow find him guilty anyway.[88] But since chapter nine, Job had explored life after death. He had weighed the ideas of defense and advocacy and found faith finally in redemption beyond the grave. These changes not only lifted Job out of his depression but also allowed him to "approach God's throne of grace with

---

88 See 9:14–24.

confidence" (Heb. 4:16, NIV). Job now expected that God would say things that Job could truly consider, that God would not come at him with great power and a raft of charges but with grace. In approaching God's presence, he would find deliverance. Redemption. Job now believed that God "would pay attention to me" (Job 23:6).

FEARFUL, BUT NOT SILENCED

This faith, however, did not change Job's immediate circumstances. Job was not high on drugs. He had hope and faith, but he still lived in reality. Job had faith in how things would turn out if he could approach God, but God's address is not so easily located in actual practice.

Here is how Job explained the problem:

> ⁸*"Behold, I go forward, but he is not there,*
> *and backward, but I do not perceive him;*
> ⁹*on the left hand when he is working, I do not behold him;*
> *he turns to the right hand, but I do not see him.*
> ¹⁰*But he knows the way that I take;*
> *when he has tried me, I shall come out as gold.*
> ¹¹*My foot has held fast to his steps;*
> *I have kept his way and have not turned aside.*
> ¹²*I have not departed from the commandment of his lips;*
> *I have treasured the words of his mouth more than my portion of food.*
> ¹³*But he is unchangeable, and who can turn him back?*
> *What he desires, that he does.*
> ¹⁴*For he will complete what he appoints for me,*
> *and many such things are in his mind.*
> ¹⁵*Therefore I am terrified at his presence;*
> *when I consider, I am in dread of him.*
> ¹⁶*God has made my heart faint;*
> *the Almighty has terrified me;*
> ¹⁷*yet I am not silenced because of the darkness,*

> *nor because thick darkness covers my face."*
>
> Job 23:8–17

These last few verses initially sound like a return to Job's former despair: God is inaccessible and has terrible plans for me. I am terrified of him. But with careful reading, it becomes clear that Job was actually in a much better state of mind than he had been previously.

First, he described how God is inaccessible and not readily summoned to a hearing. That idea is consistent with some of Job's original concerns.

Job next restated his loyalty and innocence. This is also not new material, except for the line regarding God's testing (23:10). Job had previously assumed that God would prioritize judging and punishing humanity according to their deeds—typical Standard View fare. Now Job was viewing his trials not as a punishment but as a test. God was not punishing Job's actions but examining them.

Verses thirteen through fourteen sound like a return to the old helplessness from chapter nine: God cannot be opposed; God has terrible things in mind for me. Verses fifteen and sixteen further support this reading as Job repeated twice that he was terrified. But then in the final verse, while acknowledging the darkness that still gripped him, Job spoke to his undaunted stance: "yet I am not silenced" (23:17). In chapter nine, Job had also been terrified, but in that stage, he had felt silenced and bitter as well.[89] Here, Job was still wrapped in darkness but was not silenced. He now viewed these trials as tests and not punishments, and he knew that he would come out well—as gold pulled forth from the crucible's heat—once these tests concluded.

Job was intimately aware of the sovereignty of God in his life. God could do whatever he wanted. God was all-powerful, none could oppose him, and some of his plans were truly terrifying. But there was nothing that Job could do about this reality except look with hope beyond the immediate horizon and believe that, in the end, in eternity, he would come through these trials refined like pure gold.

---

89 See 9:33–10:1.

GRIM REFLECTIONS ON INJUSTICE AND GOD'S INACTION

At this point, one might expect Job to branch off into an eloquent expression of the hope that gives him the boldness to continue to engage with religion and faith. However, terrified yet hopeful, Job was not an academic poet considering trouble from a theoretical point of view. The direction of Job's speech from here on will be dictated not by what might have a nice literary direction but rather by the ache in his heart for his dead children, the ongoing stress and pain of other lost lives around him, economic pressures, and the incessant physical pain for which he still had not found relief. Job's existential pain had diminished, but his emotional and physical pain was still all too vivid and affected his spiritual outlook. As a result, despite his newfound convictions and hopes, Job also had gloomy questions and observations. He posed those questions next:

> *¹"Why are not times of judgment kept by the Almighty,*
> *and why do those who know him never see his days?*
> *²Some move landmarks;*
> *they seize flocks and pasture them.*
> *³They drive away the donkey of the fatherless;*
> *they take the widow's ox for a pledge.*
> *⁴They thrust the poor off the road;*
> *the poor of the earth all hide themselves."*
>
> JOB 24:1–4

The crimes here are not the crimes of marauders but the crimes of a civil society working abusively to benefit those with money and power.

Moving boundary stones is not an act of overt violence. Instead, it is an act of neighbors playing with property lines—stealing just a few extra inches or feet from the property next door.

Pasturing flocks is a peaceful and productive way to make a living and contribute to society. But these flocks are of an unrighteous provenance. The orphan's donkey is stolen. Notice that the word donkey is singular—the orphan only had one. The orphan is alone and is a child. The donkey is a beast of burden and also a plow animal. How much land does a child likely have to plow? How abundant are a child's goods that they cannot just carry them themself? This is like a child with their own pickup truck and trailer. The orphan has no need of a donkey—or so parts of society would judge. As a result, what some might consider surplus is taken away from the orphan, perhaps for the good of those with actual properties and families to feed. But it is still theft.

The widow needs financial help. Someone offers her a loan. This is a good deed. But the lender takes the widow's sole ox as a pledge. It is not marked as security for a loan in the way that banks today simply list a piece of the debtor's property as collateral that would only be taken away should the debtor not pay. No, this passage describes a case where the lender takes the ox away from the widow so that she cannot use it until she pays the loan back. The lender can now use the ox instead. But the ox might be the widow's sole source of income. Without the ox, she cannot repay the loan. The lender essentially bought the ox for the price of a loan. This is theft of the clever type: theft by financial manipulation, theft by offering a vulnerable person a terrible trade that they could not refuse. It is legal and therefore moral in the eyes of the greedy, but it is evil in the eyes of God.[90]

These observations do not jive nicely with Job's hope, but they do speak candidly about how the world operates.

Job continued:

> [5] *"Behold, like wild donkeys in the desert*
>   *the poor go out to their toil, seeking game;*
>   *the wasteland yields food for their children.*
> [6] *They gather their fodder in the field,*
>   *and they glean the vineyard of the wicked man.*
> [7] *They lie all night naked, without clothing,*
>   *and have no covering in the cold.*
> [8] *They are wet with the rain of the mountains*
>   *and cling to the rock for lack of shelter.*
> [9] *(There are those who snatch the fatherless child from the breast,*
>   *and they take a pledge against the poor.)*

---

90 For a more explicit discussion of righteousness in lending finance, consider the laws that God wrote regarding these transactions. A couple of key passages can be found in Deuteronomy 24:6 and 24:10–13 and in Exodus 22:25–27. Legalized theft through clever legal loopholes, in God's eyes, is still theft.

> *¹⁰They go about naked, without clothing;*
>> *hungry, they carry the sheaves;*
> *¹¹among the olive rows of the wicked they make oil;*
>> *they tread the winepresses, but suffer thirst.*
> *¹²From out of the city the dying groan,*
>> *and the soul of the wounded cries for help;*
>> *yet God charges no one with wrong."*
>
> JOB 24:5–12

Part of what terrified Job was God's inaction. God could not be opposed and did whatever he pleased (23:13), but he allowed the world to persist with injustice unaddressed and failed to set a time for judgment (24:1). And then verse twelve offers up that unbalanced third line, which you should be used to noticing by now. That unbalanced third line doesn't rhyme with the previous ideas, and so it stands out in the poetry as jarring: "God charges no one with wrong" (24:12).

But there was more. It was not just the victims that Job had in view in this frank appraisal of society but also those who deliberately flaunt their rebellion against God.

He explained this in the following verses:

> *¹³"There are those who rebel against the light,*
>> *who are not acquainted with its ways,*
>> *and do not stay in its paths.*
> *¹⁴The murderer rises before it is light,*
>> *that he may kill the poor and needy,*
>> *and in the night he is like a thief.*
> *¹⁵The eye of the adulterer also waits for the twilight,*
>> *saying, 'No eye will see me';*
>> *and he veils his face.*
> *¹⁶In the dark they dig through houses;[91]*
>> *by day they shut themselves up;*
>> *they do not know the light.*

---

91 To break into a mudbrick house, you don't pick the lock. You simply dig through the wall.

> ¹⁷*For deep darkness is morning to all of them;*
> *for they are friends with the terrors of deep darkness."*
>
> Job 24:13–17

Having gone from considering the victim to looking at the perpetrators of oppression, deceit, and betrayal, Job appears to be heading straight down the depression road that had consumed him in previous speeches. But Job didn't go down that path. The darkness no longer silenced and depressed him. Instead, he had hope that there was something beyond this life where redemption would be found. With this belief as his new solid ground, he embarked on an act of faith no less hopeful than his longing for personal redemption—Job looked at the successful unrepenting wicked and by faith saw an ultimate judgment. The darkness is terrifying, but it is not ultimately triumphant. Job waited in expectation of redemption while the wicked should only expect what their sins have earned them.

JUDGMENT BEYOND THE GRAVE

Job continued his speech:

> ¹⁸*"You say, 'Swift are they on the face of the waters;*
> *their portion is cursed in the land;*
> *no treader turns toward their vineyards.*
> ¹⁹*Drought and heat snatch away the snow waters;*
> *so does Sheol those who have sinned.*
> ²⁰*The womb forgets them;*
> *the worm finds them sweet;*
> *they are no longer remembered,*
> *so wickedness is broken like a tree.'*
> ²¹*They wrong the barren, childless woman,*
> *and do no good to the widow.*
> ²²*Yet God prolongs the life of the mighty by his power;*
> *they rise up when they despair of life.*
> ²³*He gives them security, and they are supported,*
> *and his eyes are upon their ways.*
> ²⁴*They are exalted a little while, and then are gone;*

> *they are brought low and gathered up like all others;*
> *they are cut off like the heads of grain.*
> ^{25}*If it is not so, who will prove me a liar*
> *and show that there is nothing in what I say?"*
>
> Job 24:18–25

On the surface, Job appears to have just articulated the judgment side of the Standard View. Not only were Job's friends unlikely to try to prove him false, but one interpretation of Bildad's abbreviated response in the next chapter is that this speech from Job had confused his friends. Had Job just switched sides in this argument?

But there is a key difference between what Job was saying here and the message his friends had been pushing. The formula the friends subscribed to was mathematical and surgical. As Bildad had put it in his last speech, the wicked person is "torn from the tent in which he trusted and is brought to the king of terrors" (18:14). The friends believed that God's judgment of the wicked would be precise, focused, and dramatic. Job's own case would fit this formula perfectly if they could only find the sin that precipitated his judgment.

WHAT JOB WAS REALLY SAYING?

The judgment that Job spoke of here was different than what the friends imagined within the Standard View framework. Job said that the wicked feel secure, but they eventually "are brought low and gathered up like all the others" (24:23–24). Like all the others. What others? Other people. Other people who are brought low and gathered up and cut off like heads of grain. In other words, the wicked are exalted for a while, but then they die like everyone else.

Job was not forecasting a surgical judgment for the wicked but rather describing the reality of what happens to everyone in the end, to both the wicked and the righteous. Everybody dies. There is no difference between the wicked and the righteous in this regard. In this, Job is one with the writer of Ecclesiastes.[92]

---

92 See Ecclesiastes 9:2.

However, what changed from Job's previous perspective is that Job now had something beyond this life in view. While this common doomed fate had caused Job to despair in previous speeches (e.g., see 14:1–6), Job now saw death not as a dark end after a difficult life but rather as the doorway that led to the righteous being redeemed by their Maker. The fate of death was still common, touching all people, but its implications were now different.

The wicked can seem secure and content and established—for now—but when God prolongs their life here, that's not always a good thing for the wicked (24:22). Judgment awaits.

On the other hand, Job knew that he would stand before his God and be redeemed after death. For him, death was not the end but a new beginning. He had assurance in this life of eternal life.

Unfortunately, Bildad the Rude will speak next, and he was not persuaded.

39

BILDAD'S BEFUDDLED THIRD SPEECH

Job's theological insights, emotional candor, and practical applications were too much for Bildad the Rude. From his perspective, the conversation since his last speech had gone horribly awry. Job had only revealed his strong convictions about eternity and redemption after Bildad's second speech. Eliphaz had attempted to halt Job's digression into joy by casting a bucketful of spurious charges at Job, none of which were credible. The false charges just made the inaccuracy of the Standard View that much more apparent (not to mention the shallow motivations of Eliphaz's faith).

After discharging their doomsday weapon of actual, concrete charges and having it misfire, the friends were now on poor debate ground. In his final speech, Bildad will attempt to recover the Standard View as sound philosophy, pulling back from trying to find Job's nonexistent sin and sticking with the theory's general principles. After all, these kinds of philosophies work better in the abstract. However, the thunder of his speech was now gone. The Standard View looked pretty shaky now that the actual charges laid against Job had resulted in a fizzled prosecution.

> *¹Then Bildad the Shuhite answered and said:*
> *²"Dominion and fear are with God;*
> *   he makes peace in his high heaven.*
> *³Is there any number to his armies?*
> *   Upon whom does his light not arise?*
> *⁴How then can man be in the right before God?*

> *How can he who is born of woman be pure?*
> *⁵Behold, even the moon is not bright,*
> *and the stars are not pure in his eyes;*
> *⁶how much less man, who is a maggot,*
> *and the son of man, who is a worm!"*
>
> JOB 25:1–6

This was Bildad's entire third speech, and it turned out to be his last. The first thing that stands out is that it was rather short.

It is easy not to take this speech seriously. It is too short. On its own, it does not appear to have a deeply thoughtful arc, and it ends with Bildad's characteristic rudeness as he compared men to maggots and worms. But, really, who needs to spend any serious study time on this little poem?

But this is the Bible. God wrote it down because it is important. He preserved the text across thousands of years because he wants its message to be read, absorbed, understood, and responded to. So let's not take the easy route. Instead, let's try to understand what Bildad was going on about here.

BILDAD'S UNEXPECTED BEGINNING

The first thing worth considering is that Bildad had opened his previous two speeches with harsh and dismissive words:

> *²"How long will you say these things,*
> *and the words of your mouth be a great wind?"*
>
> JOB 8:2

> *²"How long will you hunt for words?*
> *Consider, and then we will speak."*
>
> JOB 18:2

However, he opened this third speech not by being dismissively rude but rather by acknowledging God's ultimate dominion and authority.

> *²"Dominion and fear are with God;*
> *he makes peace in his high heaven.*

> *³Is there any number to his armies?*
> *Upon whom does his light not arise?"*
>
> Job 25:2–3

This speech was immediately different. From the outset, Bildad's posture had meaningfully improved, as he now focused on God's power rather than Job's inadequacy. Rather than maintaining his former posture of harsh judgment (recall his claim in 8:4 that Job's children got what they deserved), Bildad appears to be adopting a somewhat humbler tone. God is center here, not Bildad's diagnoses.

BILDAD SEEMS LIKE A CHANGED MAN

In previous speeches, after his rudely dismissive introductions, Bildad had gone on to tout the authority and reliability of the Standard View. In his first speech, Bildad had argued in favor of the Standard View by referring to the testimony of former generations and by applying sentimental logic.[93] In his second speech, Bildad used horror-story imagery and contemporary but vague secondhand confirmations to support the Standard View.[94]

This pattern was broken as well in Bildad's tiny third speech. Instead of backing the Standard View, he quoted the voice of its opposition. In 4:17, the spirit had spoken to Eliphaz about the impossibility of a mortal achieving a righteous and pure standing before God. This simple statement cuts the legs out from under the Standard View. If a person cannot be righteous and pure before God on their own, then their condition within the Standard View framework is hopeless. This simple statement was spoken by the spirit and supported by Job in subsequent speeches but vehemently countered by Eliphaz and the other friends.[95] The spirit's Contrary View was unacceptably arbitrary to the defenders of the Standard View. But here, instead of defending the Standard View yet again, Bildad quoted the spirit and even elaborated on the spirit's imagery to paint a vivid picture of the hopelessness of humanity's position.

---

93 See 8:8–10 and 8:20.

94 See 18:12–14 and 18:20.

95 For example, see 14:4.

He said:
> [4] "How then can man be in the right before God?
> How can he who is born of woman be pure?
> [5] Behold, even the moon is not bright,
> and the stars are not pure in his eyes;
> [6] how much less man, who is a maggot,
> and the son of man, who is a worm!"

JOB 25:4–6

Was Bildad now, in his last speech, coming around to the spirit's point of view? Unfortunately, there is not enough speech here to say for sure what Bildad's intention was. He started well enough. But after his good start, he quickly slipped into his characteristically rude manner, equating people to maggots and worms, perhaps in a rough effort to support the spirit's less-than-complimentary assessment of humanity's spiritual qualities.

AN ABRUPT CONCLUSION

So why did Bildad's speech end here?

In the next verse we get a very clear "Then Job replied" (26:1). There can be no doubt that Bildad's speech was over. The question we might ask is this: did Bildad voluntarily end his speech? Was he troubled and confused about where his own words were going and so awkwardly halted on this maggot illustration? Did he start well, inspired by the need for a different approach to the discussions with Job but then get tangled in his own rude habits and convictions about the Standard View, which left him unsure how to proceed after verse six? Changing one's way of interpreting the world is not an easy task. Perhaps Bildad had started to change but was not sufficiently mature enough to articulate his newfound insights clearly.

On the other hand, perhaps his convictions had reached a semblance of maturity. Maybe the problem was that his communication style had not yet caught up to the grace and hope that the spirit's Contrary View required. Perhaps Bildad had started well with reasonably stable new convictions, but then the contradiction between his new outlook and his old personality met crossways in verse six, and he stopped talking on that account. Maybe Bildad was like a new convert to Christianity who attempts to share his faith by using foul language to disavow his former way of life, catches himself in the contradiction, and winds up tongue-tied. This realization—that repentance is not over with salvation but instead just beginning—is a milestone discovery for those just commencing their spiritual journey. This suddenly revealed new need for personal application and focus can leave a speaker speechless.

This last interpretation might seem like a stretch. Perhaps it is too charitable to Bildad the Rude. Whatever interpretation we accept, it has to account for Bildad's change in tone at the beginning of his speech, his sudden about-face support of the spirit's Contrary View, and his oddly short delivery.

Something else that further supports my speculation is the contrast between the ending of this speech and the conclusion of Bildad's first two speeches. Bildad had ended his first speech by formulaically assuring Job that he had hope as long as he repented. In chapter eighteen, Bildad had closed his speech by soberly articulating the doomed fate of those who fail to repent. In both cases, the endings were Standard View approved and logical conclusions, but here in chapter twenty-five, the ending wraps up nothing. His introduction abruptly stops and leaves the reader waiting for the body of the speech that never comes. Perhaps he did shut his mouth voluntarily, preferring an aborted thought to further error.

Another interpretation is that Bildad merely paused, and Job, noting the pause, had had enough. Whether or not he perceived Bildad's conflicted change of heart, he wanted no more from his friends, and indeed, this is the last we will hear from any of the three friends in this book. Job jumped in, perhaps cutting Bildad off, and embarked on his longest speech yet.

40

JOB GOES ON THE OFFENSIVE

¹Then Job answered and said:
²"How you have helped him who has no power!
How you have saved the arm that has no strength!
³How you have counseled him who has no wisdom,
and plentifully declared sound knowledge!
⁴With whose help have you uttered words,
and whose breath has come out from you?"

JOB 26:1–4

IF JOB WAS cutting Bildad off here, it seems apparent that he did so without perceiving any kind of change, or changing, of Bildad's heart. Instead, Job's speech appears to be directed at Bildad's maggot imagery. Adding to Bildad's disdainful depiction of humanity as equivalent to worms and maggots, Job described people as powerless, feeble, and without wisdom. If Bildad truly was starting to change his tune but got tongue-tied in his rude habits, then Job's response was to rebuke the already chastened Bildad.

In chapter twenty-six, Job reinforced Bildad's self-correction from chapter twenty-five (if that's indeed what it was) with sarcasm that almost parodied Bildad's own rude communication style. Job's words were offensive, but Bildad would also recognize them as his own style mirrored back at him. This can be an effective approach for rebuking an already softened heart, but it is a recipe for escalation when tried on a hardened opponent.

Given Bildad's silence in response to chapter twenty-six, it would appear that Job's rebuke was heard by a softer heart than Bildad had displayed in previous speeches.[96]

EXPOSING BILDAD'S SOURCE

However, the introduction to this ninth speech of Job's was not just a rebuke of Bildad's rude style. It also contained rhetorical questions that highlighted the source of Bildad's changed heart.

As Job put it:

> [4]"*With whose help have you uttered words,*
> *and whose breath has come out from you?"*
>
> JOB 26:4

It seems clear that it was the spirit that helped Bildad utter some of his last words. This was the spirit that had appeared to Eliphaz in his vision from chapters four and five. Were Job's questions here ironic? Was he pointing out to Bildad what Bildad already knew or had at least begun to perceive? Or were Job's questions intended not for Bildad, who knew who he was quoting, but rather for Eliphaz and Zophar, so that these two, who were slower to accept the spirit's message, might realize who had originally authored Bildad's words? Or was Job even referring to Bildad's arguments at all? Was he instead actually referring to Bildad's rudeness, essentially asking, Who helped you be so rude?

Bildad's abbreviated speech contained a hint of good and a taste of bad, so Job's question perhaps had more than one answer. It seems to me that Job is revealing the divided nature of Bildad's words through sarcasm.

DEATH IS NOT SCARY AFTER ALL

Regardless of who and what Job was questioning, Job had effectively stopped the rudeness and drawn his listeners' attention to the wisdom of the spirit's original position.

---

96 See 8:2 and 18:2–3.

From this introduction, he went on to finish the spirit-inspired thought that Bildad had started before slipping into his talk of maggots and worms. Job said:

> [5] *"The dead tremble*
> *under the waters and their inhabitants.*
> [6] *Sheol is naked before God,*
> *and Abaddon has no covering."*
>
> Job 26:5–6

The place of the dead was naked before God.

Previously, death was a place of darkness where God would search for Job but be unable to find him. Then Job's thinking had begun to change, and this "deep darkness" became something that God would shine a light into to reveal hidden secrets. Able now to envision God searching the darkness and finding that which was hidden, Job imagined God searching the darkness of death and finding the lost Job.

As we have seen, this new idea had become a firmly settled conviction. Bringing the topic full circle, Job now affirmed that death itself is not a cloaked, dark mystery at all but is, in fact, naked before God.

MONSTER IMAGERY INVERTED

In the verses that follow, Job brought up the monster imagery he had touched on previously:

> [7] *"He stretches out the north over the void*
> *and hangs the earth on nothing.*
> [8] *He binds up the waters in his thick clouds,*
> *and the cloud is not split open under them.*
> [9] *He covers the face of the full moon*
> *and spreads over it his cloud.*
> [10] *He has inscribed a circle on the face of the waters*
> *at the boundary between light and darkness.*
> [11] *The pillars of heaven tremble*
> *and are astounded at his rebuke.*

> ^{12}*By his power he stilled the sea;*
> *by his understanding he shattered Rahab.*
> ^{13}*By his wind the heavens were made fair;*
> *his hand pierced the fleeing serpent.*
> ^{14}*Behold, these are but the outskirts of his ways,*
> *and how small a whisper do we hear of him!*
> *But the thunder of his power who can understand?"*
>
> Job 26:7–14

This God shattered even Rahab, or as the NIV puts it, he cut this monster "to pieces" (26:12).[97] Rahab, remember, is a mythical sea serpent, and in the original Hebrew, the word Rahab can also mean storm or arrogance. So this arrogant and stormy creature of death is helpless before God, and God hacks it to pieces, not by God's brute strength (which Job had already established could shake the very earth) but by his wisdom. Without lifting a finger, God dispatches monsters.

This reference to Rahab is significant. First, this language was unique to Job. The friends did not talk about monsters. Monster imagery helped Job to articulate the depths of his emotions in the same way that apocalyptic language seemed to help express the intense feelings of some of the later poet-prophets.

Job originally referenced Rahab in 9:13. In chapter nine, he used the image of this monster and its cohorts cowering before God to illustrate Job's comparative helplessness before God. The point was that even Rahab was helpless before God. Job had used this poetic and colorful image to underscore God's power. In chapter nine, Job did not have a chance against such a God as this. Remember, poetry primarily aims to elicit emotion, and so this monster imagery is not literal but figurative and designed to evoke a feeling.

Now, here in chapter twenty-six, Job redeployed the image of Rahab with a similar effect. Rahab was not just cowering but being hacked to pieces by

---

[97] It is worth pointing out that Joshua 2 uses a different Hebrew word for the prostitute Rahab than the word Job uses for Rahab here. In our English translations, Job and Joshua seem to be referencing the same person. But the Rahab used in Job was not a person's name but a mythical sea monster. Later texts use this word as a symbol for Egypt, equating Egypt to an arrogant monster (e.g., see Isaiah 30:7).

this God. But this time, Job did not use the image to illustrate his helplessness before God. He was now using the image to illustrate that death itself is no match for God. God, by his wisdom alone, hacks monsters to pieces. The monster, whose name also means storm, is calmed and "made fair" by God's breath alone (26:13),[98] and then this gliding serpent is pierced by God's own hand.

These, Job says, were just the outskirts and whisper of God's work. This was the God that Job no longer cowered before. This was the God that Job had confidence would find him and redeem him even after death. It was now death, not Job, that was naked and helpless before the power and wisdom of God.

This bears repeating: It was now death, not Job, that was naked and helpless before the power and wisdom of God.

God himself will use monster imagery when he speaks. Job's gliding serpent imagery in chapter twenty-six sounds a bit like the leviathan in chapter forty-one and even more like the leviathan in Isaiah 27:1. We will come back to this monster imagery again.

For purposes of chapter twenty-six, it is worth simply noting how the monster had evolved from symbolizing Job's despair before an all-powerful God to symbolizing death's powerlessness before God and Job's basis for confidence in redemption. The tables had turned. Nothing could prevent God from achieving Job's resurrection and redemption.

---

98 Remember that Hebrew poetry rhymes ideas, not sounds. In verse twelve, God stilled the sea and shattered the monster. These ideas rhyme because Rahab was a sea monster. In verse thirteen, the heavens are made fair (i.e., calm) and the monster is pierced. These ideas also rhyme because the monster's name, Rahab, is a Hebrew word that also means *storm*. In this context, "the heavens" refer not to the Christian afterlife but rather to the sky itself, where the storm (Rahab) thrives. By making the heavens "fair," God had banished the storm (Rahab). The monster then attempting to glide away is caught and pierced. Thus, in these two verses, the sea monster was stilled and shattered and the storm form of this monster was cancelled out and then pierced. And then, as verse fourteen goes on to explain, these are just the outskirts and a small whisper of God's ways.

41
JOB IS UNCOMPROMISING

¹And Job again took up his discourse, and said:
²"As God lives, who has taken away my right,
  and the Almighty, who has made my soul bitter,
³as long as my breath is in me,
  and the spirit of God is in my nostrils,
⁴my lips will not speak falsehood,
  and my tongue will not utter deceit.
⁵Far be it from me to say that you are right;
  till I die I will not put away my integrity from me.
⁶I hold fast my righteousness and will not let it go;
  my heart does not reproach me for any of my days."

JOB 27:1–6

JOB CALLED THINGS as he saw them. Job had been denied justice—by God. This was a charge that Job had not let go of and one that, as we have seen, God himself did not deny. But Job's integrity and his faithfulness were not based on getting a good deal from God. Till I die, I will not deny my integrity. Where Job's wife had felt that integrity was pointless at death's door (in the language of finance, this effort would have no return on investment), Job committed here to be righteous for as long as he lived. The commitment here was not casual. Verses two through six use the traditional Hebrew phrases for swearing an oath. This was Job making a vow. Despite the apparent gaps (from Job's mortal point of view) in God's side of this relationship, Job's commitment to God was unyielding.

JOB REBUKES HIS FRIENDS

⁷"Let my enemy be as the wicked,
  and let him who rises up against me be as the unrighteous.
⁸For what is the hope of the godless when God cuts him off,
  when God takes away his life?
⁹Will God hear his cry
  when distress comes upon him?
¹⁰Will he take delight in the Almighty?
  Will he call upon God at all times?"

JOB 27:7–10

Job was not referring here to the Chaldeans or Sabeans who had attacked his farm. Instead, Job was talking about his friends. Rather than accept ambiguity and even mystery, they had attempted to force Job's reality into an artificial framework and, in doing so, added to Job's trials. Thus they had become "as the wicked" and "as the unrighteous." The friends had wound up acting like Chaldean and Sabean raiders, making Job's bad situation worse.

REDEFINING HOPE

The wording of 27:8 is accurate: the godless have no hope beyond the grave. The original Hebrew text, however, is a little more precise and could be translated as:

For what hope has the godless one when he makes an illicit profit,
  when God takes away his life?

The ESV offers a better parallel between the two lines than the above translation, but the Hebrew actually does read in this somewhat unbalanced way. The two parts to this verse, in Hebrew, don't rhyme ideas as they normally should. In this unbalanced but closer-to-the-Hebrew version, the reader's expectation, that the two lines will contain parallel ideas, compresses the two events this verse describes—the godless making an illicit profit and God taking away their life—as if the two are nearly simultaneous events. Both the profit and the death beg the question: what is our hope now? Illicit profit, in this formulation, is as hope-destroying as death itself.

Job had hope. The ungodly do not, not even when they appear to profit. This idea goes back to Job's response to the success of the godless in 21:16. In chapter twenty-one, Job had chosen poverty and trial with God rather than prosperity without God. Here in chapter twenty-seven, Job equated the success of the wicked with their hopelessness.

Perhaps the worst thing that can happen to the godless is for them to experience success after blinding success, so that only after death, when it is too late, do they realize that worldly success was a destructive mirage.

DOES JOB REALLY NEED TO TEACH HIS FRIENDS ANYTHING?

Here's what Job had to say to his friends now:

> ¹¹*"I will teach you concerning the hand of God;*
> *what is with the Almighty I will not conceal.*
> ¹²*Behold, all of you have seen it yourselves;*
> *why then have you become altogether vain?"*
>
> JOB 27:11–12

There really was no need for Job to teach the friends anything further. Job's speeches so far had thoroughly debunked any credibility the Standard View might have held.

No matter how many different ways the friends evaluated the Standard View, Job exposed the failure of their logic. As Job said in chapter twenty-one:

> ²⁹*"Have you not asked those who travel the roads,*
> *and do you not accept their testimony…?"*
>
> JOB 21:29

There really was no need for Job to teach his friends these things.

¹²"Behold, all of you have seen it yourselves;
*   why then have you become altogether vain?"*

JOB 27:12

JOB SAYS SOME SURPRISING THINGS

What came next in Job's speech, though, is very interesting. Job proceeded to make not the spirit's argument again but rather a case in favor of the Standard View. This was a decidedly unexpected turn for Job. Listen to this next bit:

¹³"This is the portion of a wicked man with God,
*   and the heritage that oppressors receive from the Almighty:*
¹⁴If his children are multiplied, it is for the sword,
*   and his descendants have not enough bread.*
¹⁵Those who survive him the pestilence buries,
*   and his widows do not weep.*
¹⁶Though he heap up silver like dust,
*   and pile up clothing like clay,*
¹⁷he may pile it up, but the righteous will wear it,
*   and the innocent will divide the silver.*
¹⁸He builds his house like a moth's,
*   like a booth that a watchman makes.*
¹⁹He goes to bed rich, but will do so no more;
*   he opens his eyes, and his wealth is gone.*
²⁰Terrors overtake him like a flood;
*   in the night a whirlwind carries him off.*
²¹The east wind lifts him up and he is gone;
*   it sweeps him out of his place.*
²²It hurls at him without pity;
*   he flees from its power in headlong flight.*
²³It claps its hands at him
*   and hisses at him from its place."*

JOB 27:13–23

THE COPYIST'S ERROR THEORY

Why would Job say these things? These are the kinds of words that Job's friends have been using.[99] The similarity is so striking that, when I first struggled through this book in my studies and consulted various commentaries for guidance, I discovered that some scholars interpret these words as the misplaced remainder of Bildad's aborted speech. In this interpretation, Bildad had started down the road of supporting the spirit's Contrary View, and then he reverted back to rudeness and resumed his Standard View position. The theory is that some early copyists shuffled the paragraphs when working on the book, and so now we are left with Bildad's words buried amid Job's long final speech. Not only would this theory solve the riddle of why Bildad's last speech is so abruptly brief, but it would also shorten Job's last speech, which is unusually long, and remove Job's difficult-to-interpret sudden shift in rhetoric.

The problem with this theory is that Job was not written in a book format where a page or two could be easily shuffled. In this era, people wrote texts on single-page scrolls, not multi-page books. Furthermore, if we accept this error theory, we also have to accept that somehow this error made its way into every ancient manuscript we have ever unearthed: we have not found any ancient copies of Job that contain the supposedly "original" order of the verses.

The last issue with this scholarly explanation is that it is unnecessary. Job had a perfectly good reason to say what he said.

THE CASE FOR SARCASM

A better explanation for these verses is that Job did say these words, but he said them sarcastically. In this view, Job cut Bildad's rudeness off and proceeded to finish his speech for him, stitching portions of what the three friends had said into a summary of the Standard View. This interpretation makes more sense to me. Certainly, it makes more sense than the copyist's-

---

99 There is a particular similarity between the ideas Job expressed here and those Eliphaz had expressed in 5:12–14 and 15:20–35, those Bildad had expressed in 8:11–19 and 18:5–21, and those Zophar had expressed in 20:4–29.

error view that fails to account for how the error occurred and why we have no alternative versions of Job to support the thesis.[100]

The challenge, however, with this sarcasm interpretation is that it fails to acknowledge the change in Bildad's posture. His speech, though very brief, did start very differently than his other speeches. His beginning was not naturally building toward yet another Standard View exposé.

It turns out that reading sarcasm into this passage is also unnecessary. There is a very good reason for Job to say these words sincerely and not sarcastically. We don't need to use sarcasm to explain the passage away. So why would Job suddenly say the very things that he had been refuting throughout this book so far?

A THIRD SOLUTION

Before we answer why Job would say these things, it is helpful to ask whether the things he said here are ever true. Does God ever punish the wicked? Does God ever deal with the unrighteous in this life?

If the question is whether God always punishes the wicked in this life according to their evil deeds, the answer, of course, is no. Job had provided many examples of bad people dying rich and in peace in their old age.

But does God sometimes (or many times or often or occasionally) deal with evil in the moment? The answer here, of course, is yes. The plagues on Egypt, the judgments on many of Israel's evil kings, Herod's death in the book of Acts, and so on—there are numerous examples of God dealing swiftly and justly with the wicked in this life.

So sometimes, the Standard View is true. As a system for predicting how bad actions may lead to a disastrous end, the Standard View is useful. Much of Proverbs is founded on the general applicability of this cause-and-effect view of reality.

---

100 It's reasonable to assume that any human copyist might mix up individual letters or words when copying out a text. In the modern context, mixing up whole pages of a document could also reasonably happen, particularly in word processing programs where you can simply cut and paste whole pages with a few clicks. But when copying a scroll by hand, an absentminded copyist would have no reason to return to the skipped section, let alone to then knowingly copy it out in the wrong place.

However, as an infallible work-backward method for deducing evil based on apparent punishment, it fails. Sometimes (in this life), the innocent suffer unjustly.

Job's speeches had focused on dismantling the Standard View as a backward-looking forensic tool. This focus was a direct consequence of Job's situation. But there was danger in his one-sided focus. Job's arguments could be misinterpreted to suggest that the Standard View is never true—that God never addresses sin in this life.

Here is an idea: was Bildad so at risk of tossing the Standard View completely overboard with his characteristic harshness that Job felt a need to cut him off and balance out the picture a little?

Yes, God is awesome and all-powerful. Bildad described God as such in 25:2–3, and in 26:5–14, Job supported and expanded upon Bildad's depiction of God as all-powerful. But lest Bildad throw the baby out with the bathwater with his descent into a maggoty disrespect for any hope for order in the universe, Job pulled Bildad back and acknowledged that sometimes the Standard View does hold up. The wicked may escape this life unscathed, but not all will do so. Those who choose unrighteousness have no cause for hope, even if they appear to have escaped the consequences of their sin, at least in this life. Job reminds us that God is still the judge. Chaos is not the rule.

With this conclusion to chapter twenty-seven, Job appears to be acknowledging that sometimes the Standard View is true. What is a suffering soul then to make of reality? Is all hope for clarity lost? Is life just a collection of competing, contrary philosophies, none of which are ever infallibly reliable? Who can make sense of this? We're twenty-seven chapters into this book, and we seem to be no closer to understanding Job's trials. Where can wisdom be found to make sense of all this? That is the question that Job will ask and answer next.

42

WHERE CAN WISDOM BE FOUND?

THIS NEXT SPEECH is one of my favorite passages in the Bible. Bring your full imagination to the imagery that Job expounded here:

> ^{1}"Surely there is a mine for silver,
>   and a place for gold that they refine.
> ^{2}Iron is taken out of the earth,
>   and copper is smelted from the ore.
> ^{3}Man puts an end to darkness
>   and searches out to the farthest limit
>   the ore in gloom and deep darkness.
> ^{4}He opens shafts in a valley away from where anyone lives;
>   they are forgotten by travelers;
>   they hang in the air, far away from mankind; they swing to and fro.
> ^{5}As for the earth, out of it comes bread,
>   but underneath it is turned up as by fire.
> ^{6}Its stones are the place of sapphires,
>   and it has dust of gold.
> ^{7}That path no bird of prey knows,
>   and the falcon's eye has not seen it.
> ^{8}The proud beasts have not trodden it;
>   the lion has not passed over it.
> ^{9}Man puts his hand to the flinty rock

> *and overturns mountains by the roots.*
> ¹⁰*He cuts out channels in the rocks,*
>   *and his eye sees every precious thing.*
> ¹¹*He dams up the streams so that they do not trickle,*
>   *and the thing that is hidden he brings out to light.*
> ¹²*But where shall wisdom be found?*
>   *And where is the place of understanding?"*
>
> Job 28:1–12

This is where twenty-seven chapters had led Job. He had acknowledged a deep appreciation for humanity's exploits and brave deeds—we have revealed mysteries, unearthed treasures, uncovered hidden things—but Job's need went beyond humanity's capacity. Job needed wisdom—not the courageous wisdom of the underground cartographer mapping the locations of precious metals and the sources of rivers, but the wisdom that could interpret the events that had afflicted Job's life and the lives of those around him. People can dangle at the end of ancient woven ropes with lit torches in hand to discover mysteries—such incredibly bold spelunkers existed long before National Geographic was around to record their deeds. But Job's situation, and the situation of others like him, defied the tools of even the bravest and wisest.

Where can wisdom be found?

WISDOM BEYOND PLATITUDES

If Job had been dealing with just one loss, then perhaps he could have simply mourned and moved on, leaving behind unanswered questions but able to let go. Job's suffering, however, was absolute. Ten children had died, and with them his future line. Nearly everyone who worked for him had been murdered or killed by the firestorm. He was economically destroyed. Hundreds of widows and fatherless children were at his door with not only their grief but also their financial need and perhaps questions about Job's part in causing this disaster. His skin disease was consuming him—it robbed him of sleep, tormented his waking hours, and made him socially repulsive. Added to all this, his friends had focused on blaming Job for all his troubles.

Job's pain was not one he could mourn and put behind him. It was fresh every day.

MARRIAGE COUNSELING FOR THE POTTERS

It became clear early on that Mackenzie, although undiagnosed, would not be typical. I expressed to many that I did not care if my daughter ever made it to the Olympics—I just wanted to have a conversation with her. If she was physically frail, even medically fragile, I could live with that. Just let me talk with her. We could read books together and go on walks.

At the recommendation of a distant and concerned friend, I read a couple of books on mourning and grief. I was not mourning Mackenzie's death but the death of the daughter who might have been and some of the normal things in life that might not come true for her. My bottled-up calm had been unhealthy, and the reading helped. As I dealt with my sorrow, I began to weep, and I began to recognize the distance that had been growing between my wife and me. We began to search for a marriage counselor.

About eight months after Mackenzie was born, my wife and I met with a marriage counselor for the first time. It was a failed appointment. We did not connect with her in any way. This professional's values, outlook, and skills were all at odds with our own. If anything, we left the appointment more connected with each other because of our mutual disregard for the counselor.

The very next day, my wife met a social worker who had a counseling background and twenty-five years of experience working with parents of special needs kids. We started meeting with her within the week.

This social worker was a wealth of wise advice and insight. There was nothing explicitly biblical or even generally spiritual about her approach. Still, she was a good listener and able to cut through a lot of noise. She gave us practical feedback and exercises to improve our communication, and she helped my wife and me see and understand basic things about each other. We dealt with grief differently. We expressed fear differently. We needed comfort in different ways. The details of what we learned in those appointments are a story for another day, but suffice to say that they were the first light at the end of the tunnel for us. We found the lens to better interpret each other's behaviors and obtained the tools we needed to help each other. The light that went on in those sessions illuminated issues that had always been in our relationship, but it took the stress of multiple medical crises to drive them to the surface and address them. The strength we gained in those sessions remained with us throughout the years to come. Little did we know that our journey was just beginning. There was more to come. Our social worker gave us the tools we needed to keep our marriage intact while the rest of our lives collapsed.

MACKENZIE UPS THE STAKES

At one year old, Mackenzie caught the flu and nearly died. We spent a week living in a Pediatric Isolation Unit. She was only twelve pounds on her first birthday, and she lost 10 percent of her body weight in the first twenty-four hours in the hospital. Inexplicably, I had to fight with the resident doctor to let her stay in the hospital until she stabilized. Mackenzie had gone from being the personal patient of the chief of staff to a hopeless task for a dismissive intern. The medical establishment was giving up on our little girl. Eventually, she shook the bug and gained back some weight, and we returned home.

A few months later, we moved from British Columbia to Ontario as my company transferred me to a new location in Toronto. The new job, new city, new culture—the whole package—was initially a disaster. My career went from success to failure as I struggled not to be fired. I worked in Toronto, but we had moved to Hamilton because there was a children's hospital there with a good reputation and the housing prices were attractive. The commute from Hamilton to Toronto, on paper, seemed manageable. On good days it was just over an hour each way. In reality, I began to live with two-, three-, sometimes four-hour commutes each way.

Despite an army of medical specialists, physical therapists, and gifted practitioners from other disciplines, it was becoming clear that Mackenzie was not just developing slowly—she was not developing properly at all. At three years old, she had a vocabulary of only a few dozen nouns, and she still could not even crawl. Eventually, she began to deteriorate and lose most of the few words she had managed to accumulate.

Shortly after Mackenzie turned three, her baby brother Jackson was born. He was healthy. This should have been a cause for joy, but coinciding with his birth, and perhaps even during the pregnancy, Carolyn was overtaken with a severe depression. After the birth, postpartum depression was the official diagnosis. I came home each night after an unreasonable commute to a struggling daughter, an energetic infant boy, and a severely depressed wife. Through the accumulation of work and home issues, I, too, gradually became depressed. The move appeared to have been a huge mistake.

We fed Mackenzie through a tube connected to her G-tube—her little gas cap on her stomach—and one day, I picked her up, not realizing that I was standing on her tube, and pulled the tube and its balloon anchor right out of her stomach. The entire surgically installed apparatus was ripped through her abdomen and lying on the floor in front of me, still pumping her formula pointlessly across the living room floor. At the same time, a new hole in my daughter's abdomen leaked stomach fluids. As with the hundreds of other emergency room visits and crises to this point, nausea nearly knocked me down, but the crisis demanded focus and we addressed the problem. Later I shook and tried not to cry and tried not to let my distraction the next day at work get me dismissed from my job. How do you explain to people at work that you just accidentally ripped something out of your daughter's stomach through the abdominal wall? There is no explaining that. There is faking it throughout your professional workday and walling off that part of you so you can function, but there is no way to instantly recover from such an experience. If I took a sick day or a stress day for everything that happened with Mackenzie, I would have stopped working in my thirties and never gone back again.

After moving to Ontario, Mackenzie developed a new symptom: insomnia. As an infant, she had slept nearly round the clock. Now she managed to stay awake for thirty-six to forty-eight hours straight. She cried and made noise in her bed. She set off the alarm on her food pump. She kept us awake, and because of her medical problems, putting her somewhere on the opposite end of the house where we could not hear her was not an option. Sleeping three hours straight became a novelty. I took public transit to work at the time, so my commute became my one opportunity for sleep. My wife did not get even that relief. For the record, severe sleep deprivation makes depression worse.

LOVE WAS NOT ENOUGH

My wife's depression did not lift after the first few months as the doctors had expected. In the meantime, Jackson continued to grow and thrive and demand all the attention that an energetic baby boy demanded. He was crawling ahead of schedule, climbing stairs, and overcoming barriers we installed to keep him off the stairs, and he started walking exactly on his first birthday. Life was out there, and this little boy was going to have as much of it as babyhood would allow.

Instead of going away, my wife's depression deepened. She became hard to talk to. She began to struggle with suicidal thoughts regularly. I was putting in a day's work just commuting, underperforming on the job when I was there, dealing with our own financial strain from our cross-country move. I was terrified of losing my wife, scared that the counseling we had previously received would not be enough, overwhelmed by life and ongoing medical traumas, permanently sleep deprived, and, as a result of being new to the province, basically friendless. I knew a few ex-Vancouverites in the Toronto area, but my schedule and circumstances prevented any meaningful reconnection.

By the time my son turned two and Mackenzie was five, I was nearly finished. We moved again to Oakville just to shorten the commute. We could not financially afford to move, but we could not emotionally afford not to move either. Even in her depression, my wife looked at me and said, "We can live in a tent if we have to—whatever it takes to help you make it." Our lives had been unraveling for over half a decade now, but she and I were still partners in this. Our romantic life had grown remote with the depression and its antidepressant medications, and our friendship was stretched wire-thin by stress, grief, and months of sleep deprivation, but through it all, we still loved each other.

But love was not enough.

Love could not explain why our seemingly perfect life had been torn apart. Love could face a sudden one-shot crisis, but the challenge of ongoing, accumulating trials was a different matter. Time has a way of healing the grieving heart, according to songs in the top forty, but it also has a way of wearing down the long-suffering heart. "Hope deferred makes the heart sick" is how Proverbs 13:12 puts it.

DISCOVERING DEEPER ISOLATION

I can remember realizing more and more as the years passed that friends could not help me. They could offer respite, cheer us up with gifts or encouragement or assistance—but they could not fix any of our pain at the deepest heart level. Our families' help was similarly handicapped. My wife and I were each other's best support despite the depression, health challenges, commute issues, and so on. Of all the people in the world, she and I understood each other the best. We felt the same love and hurt for our only daughter; we experienced every hospital crisis together; we had the same stake in this mystery.

But in the end, we could not fix it for each other either. My wife could not deeply help me. And I could not deeply help her.

There was a proverb that I began to recite to myself. It had seemed very negative and depressing in previous years because of its message of existential isolation. It teaches that we are all irretrievably alone. It seemed like such an out-of-place message lost in the middle of the Bible.

> [10]*Each heart knows its own bitterness,*
> *and no one else can share its joy.*
>
> PROVERBS 14:10, NIV

As the years passed, those words meant more and more to me not because they fixed anything but because they were true. I wanted the truth. I wanted our lives fixed, but even beyond a miracle fix, I needed the truth.

Why was this happening? Where was this going? What were we supposed to do, not do, stop doing, start doing, learn, avoid, teach, overcome—what was our role in all this? Were we doing enough? Was there a solution to the medical mysteries out there, and we just had to do more, try harder, and research better to fix it?

Movies of medical mystery miracles like Lorenzo's Oil became a source not of inspiration but of torture. If we just did more, understood more, tried harder, like the people in that movie, we could give our daughter a normal life.

I needed a father who could take me aside like a kid and unveil reality for me, explain how I got to this place, and explain how to move forward.

I wanted wisdom.

Job wanted wisdom.

The Standard View had been trashed as an explanation for Job's circumstances, but where was the wisdom that could explain Job's particular circumstances? And mine?

People can do so much in the physical world, going places and doing things that even falcons and lions do not attempt, but so little progress has been made when it comes to wisdom. Wisdom is such a mystery to humanity that even the measurement of its worth eludes us.

TRYING TO VALUE WISDOM

Job explained things this way:

> *13 "Man does not know its worth,*
> *and it is not found in the land of the living.*
> *14 The deep says, 'It is not in me,'*
> *and the sea says, 'It is not with me.'*
> *15 It cannot be bought for gold,*
> *and silver cannot be weighed as its price.*
> *16 It cannot be valued in the gold of Ophir,*
> *in precious onyx or sapphire.*
> *17 Gold and glass cannot equal it,*
> *nor can it be exchanged for jewels of fine gold.*
> *18 No mention shall be made of coral or of crystal;*
> *the price of wisdom is above pearls.*
> *19 The topaz of Ethiopia cannot equal it,*
> *nor can it be valued in pure gold.*
> *20 From where, then, does wisdom come?*
> *And where is the place of understanding?*
> *21 It is hidden from the eyes of all living*
> *and concealed from the birds of the air.*
> *22 Abaddon and Death say,*
> *'We have heard a rumor of it with our ears.'"*
>
> JOB 28:13–22

TALK TO THE BOSS

Wisdom. You cannot buy it. You cannot compare it to gemstones or precious metals. You cannot place it on a map and journey to it. And even those personified forces of Death and Destruction,[101] the authors of Job's crises, even they cannot explain themselves. They act, but they act without knowledge. Suppose my daughter's medical condition and my wife's depression could speak. In that fantasy, I can imagine them explaining themselves like low-grade workers toiling witlessly: We don't know any more than you do. We just work here. This is what we were told to do. You'll have to talk to the boss about the details.

The boss. The one who knows what is going on.

Satan was the enemy at the beginning of this book, but God was the one who granted permission. God was the boss. And as we have already shown, he never denied his role in these events.

You've got to talk to the boss.

My friends could not help. Family could not help. My wife could not help—not at the level I needed. I needed to understand, and there is only one who understands what I needed to know.

Job went on:

> [23]*"God understands the way to it,*
>   *and he knows its place.*
> [24]*For he looks to the ends of the earth*
>   *and sees everything under the heavens."*
>
>   JOB 28:23–24

God alone knows.

It is not that God is one of the few who know the secret—God alone knows.

You have to talk to the boss.

---

101 Abaddon means "destruction" in Hebrew. See Reyburn, 512.

43

TRUE BUT NOT USEFUL

AFTER JOB RECOGNIZED that only God really knows what's going on—you have to talk to the boss—he paused to consider the basic truth that God is the starting point for wisdom and understanding. He put it this way:

> [25] "*When he gave to the wind its weight*
>   *and apportioned the waters by measure,*
> [26] *when he made a decree for the rain*
>   *and a way for the lightning of the thunder,*
> [27] *then he saw it and declared it;*
>   *he established it, and searched it out.*
> [28] *And he said to man,*
>   *'Behold, the fear of the Lord, that is wisdom,*
>   *and to turn away from evil is understanding.'"*
>
> JOB 28:25–28

In other words, fearing God and turning away from evil is as foundational to humanity's reality as the physics of the weather.

What Job said here is true—but it is true at ninety thousand feet. It is big-picture true. However, it did not meet Job's need in his distress, and it did not meet mine either.

JOB'S PRE-TROUBLE BIOGRAPHY

Job took an interesting detour next. He shifted from examining big-picture truths to reviewing his life before these trials had swamped his existence. This might seem like a strange detour, but he was setting the stage for a fresh look at his current troubles. But I'm getting ahead of the story here. Let's first hear from Job about the kind of person he was before these trials occurred.

By the way, this speech also serves as a delayed rebuttal to the speculative and wild charges in Eliphaz's third speech.

> *¹And Job again took up his discourse, and said:*
> *²"Oh, that I were as in the months of old,*
> > *as in the days when God watched over me,*
> *³when his lamp shone upon my head,*
> > *and by his light I walked through darkness,*
> *⁴as I was in my prime,*
> > *when the friendship of God was upon my tent,*
> *⁵when the Almighty was yet with me,*
> > *when my children were all around me,*
> *⁶when my steps were washed with butter,*
> > *and the rock poured out for me streams of oil!*
> *⁷When I went out to the gate of the city,*
> > *when I prepared my seat in the square,*
> *⁸the young men saw me and withdrew,*
> > *and the aged rose and stood;*
> *⁹the princes refrained from talking*
> > *and laid their hand on their mouth;*
> *¹⁰the voice of the nobles was hushed,*
> > *and their tongue stuck to the roof of their mouth.*
> *¹¹When the ear heard, it called me blessed,*
> > *and when the eye saw, it approved,*
> *¹²because I delivered the poor who cried for help,*
> > *and the fatherless who had none to help him.*
> *¹³The blessing of him who was about to perish came upon me,*
> > *and I caused the widow's heart to sing for joy.*
> *¹⁴I put on righteousness, and it clothed me;*

> *my justice was like a robe and a turban.*
> *¹⁵I was eyes to the blind*
> *and feet to the lame.*
> *¹⁶I was a father to the needy,*
> *and I searched out the cause of him whom I did not know.*
> *¹⁷I broke the fangs of the unrighteous*
> *and made him drop his prey from his teeth.*
> *¹⁸Then I thought, 'I shall die in my nest,*
> *and I shall multiply my days as the sand,*
> *¹⁹my roots spread out to the waters,*
> *with the dew all night on my branches,*
> *²⁰my glory fresh with me,*
> *and my bow ever new in my hand.'*
> *²¹Men listened to me and waited*
> *and kept silence for my counsel.*
> *²²After I spoke they did not speak again,*
> *and my word dropped upon them.*
> *²³They waited for me as for the rain,*
> *and they opened their mouths as for the spring rain.*
> *²⁴I smiled on them when they had no confidence,*
> *and the light of my face they did not cast down.*
> *²⁵I chose their way and sat as chief,*
> *and I lived like a king among his troops,*
> *like one who comforts mourners.*
>
> JOB 29:1–25

It is tempting with a chapter like this one to just skim through it and not examine the details closely. The basic points are clear: Job was a successful and good person who was well respected in this community and did a lot of good work for those in need. God had already said that Job was a good person, so it hardly seems necessary to dig into the details here. We might say to ourselves, We believe you, Job, and move on.

But we've come this far in our study of Job and discovered all kinds of hidden gems. There is a rich vein of material in these twenty-five verses that is worth exploring. So let's not start skipping the good stuff now. Instead, let's do a little mining, and what we'll discover is that there is a point to this chapter beyond just a defense of Job's former life.

Here we go.

LONGING FOR AUTUMN

As Job looked back on this former life, he longed for the days when "I was in my prime" (29:4). The Hebrew does not actually use a word that directly means Job's "prime." Instead, it states something more along the lines of "Oh, when I was in my autumn days." It was not his prime he longed for but his "autumn days."[102]

However, this more literal translation of the Hebrew runs the risk of sounding to a Western urban reader as though Job was longing for his declining years, his late-middle-age years. Shakespeare did much to influence how we relate the human lifespan to the annual calendar, with winter ultimately standing in for advanced old age. However, Job was not referencing autumn as the second-last season of the year—in fact, if Job was following a traditional Jewish calendar, he would have understood autumn to be the beginning of the new calendar year. Job was instead referencing autumn as the time of harvest.

Job was longing neither for his last days nor for his first days. He was longing for his most productive days, for the days when he was reaping the rewards of previous labor, and for the season of celebration and success. For us today, we might interpret prime as meaning youth (and the associated vigor and health), whereas Job was not speaking about age or health at all but about the joy of rewarding hard work and celebrating success. As he went on in the parallel second line to state, these autumn days were days when "the friendship of God was upon my tent" (29:4). God's friendship and those days of reaping the rewards of a life well lived were intimately linked. This is another example of the ancient Hebrew poetic convention of rhyming ideas rather than sounds: the image of Job's autumn days echoes and deepens into the image of God's encompassing and sheltering friendship.

The next verse describes how this was a time in Job's life when he had

---

[102] See the Revised Standard Version of the Bible for a translation that captures this well.

both God and his children with him. Now, his children were dead, and Job judged God to be absent because he had so far been silent.

CREAM AND OIL

Job went on to say that in these former times, "my path was drenched with cream and the rock poured out for me streams of olive oil" (29:6, NIV). Clearly, Job's paths were not literally muddy with milk (or the ESV's butter). The poetic image speaks to abundance.

The second line of this verse describes oil pouring from rocks, and unlike the cream and butter metaphor, this poetic image is partly figurative and partly literal. Rocks do not produce oil, but the olive presses of Job's day used very large stones to press the olives and cause their oil to pour out. Olives produced the oil, but oil poured from the rock, that is, the stone presses.

Recognizing that line two has both figurative and literal aspects makes you wonder about the first line (or at least it made me wonder). If you have ever witnessed a cow or goat being milked by hand, you'll have some idea where the verse's figurative paths of cream come from. Hand milking is not nearly as efficient as modern mechanical milking machines. When a farmer works by hand, milk sometimes squirts on the ground. Filled buckets also sometimes slop over. In a normal operation with a moderate amount of milking animals, not a lot gets wasted. But when the milking operation is a big as Job's was, then a little bit wasted here and there can quickly add up. Key paths on Job's farm actually could have been covered with creamy mud at times. Do not assume that all the poetic images in Job are inherently figurative. Job's book uses over-the-top imagery at times but not as often as the casual reader might suspect.

SOCIAL RESPECT

Job's former life, however, had not just been one of abundance and blessing. Job's former life had also been one where his community deeply respected him. In verse seven, Job described himself taking his seat in the city gate and public square.

We do not have city gates and public squares in this same sense anymore. Our cities don't have any such gates anymore, and our public spaces tend to be parks with benches for feeding pigeons. The imagery does not resonate with us anymore. In Job's day, public squares were places of social authority. They served as the courtroom for addressing legal grievances, the council chambers for bringing concerns forward to civic leaders, and the legal offices for transferring property, resolving disputes, and managing other vital civic functions. For the sake of helping us today relate to Job's words, imagine that these verses are set in a civic building with Job taking his seat on a city council or panel of court judges.

With this context in mind, we can now see that, in this period of his life, Job had been not just one voice among many but rather a respected leader. The young and old, rich and poor, noble and common all became silent and respectful when Job entered the room. That had been Job's former status. This elaboration on Job's former life aligns well with the initial description of Job in the first chapter.

Did Job have this status because he was rich? The next section goes on to clarify that as well. Verse twelve starts with "because." The reason his community granted Job this special status was because of his godly manliness.

GODLY MANLINESS

Godly manliness? What do verses twelve through seventeen have to do with godly manliness? Are we drifting into some kind of sexism here? Don't these verses speak instead to Job's basic righteousness?

This is important. Chapter twenty-nine does not stand alone. It is the first of three chapters that we are going to see describe a godly man.

Have you ever read Proverbs 31:10–31 on the Woman of Noble Character and wondered, Why is there a chapter in the Bible on the Woman of Noble Character but no particular chapter devoted to describing the Man of Noble Character? Why do women get the raw deal of such a focused high standard, and the men get away with generic generalities that apply to both sexes?

Well, first of all, both sexes can learn a lot from Proverbs 31. The Bible was written the way it was written, and if some passages focus more on one sex than the other, the Creator of both sexes has the privilege of writing that way.

But there's another answer to this question. We could take the view that men do not get one chapter (actually, Proverbs 31 offers women only two-thirds of a chapter) because men get three chapters.

Job chapter twenty-nine describes the Man of Noble Character in a healthy, successful, and satisfied state.

Job chapters thirty and thirty-one describe the Man of Noble Character under great trial. In particular, chapter thirty describes the great trial in social terms, and then chapter thirty-one describes the kinds of commitments the Man of Noble Character makes regardless of circumstances.

There are plenty of things for women to learn from these three chapters as well, just like men can learn from Proverbs 31. So let's take a look at these chapters on manly godliness next.

44

NOBLE CHARACTER

THE NEXT FEW chapters are critically important to absorb. They paint a portrait of what a godly man looks like in both good and bad circumstances—starting with the good, then moving on to circumstances such as Job's trials. These chapters are practical and blunt—exactly the sort of plainspoken direction that most men find helpful.

These are also critically important chapters for women to absorb. For single women, the measure of your future mate is not his haircut, paycheck, car, or abs. The measure of your future husband is found in Job 29–31. Are your expectations godly? Or are your expectations worldly? Married women can find value in understanding what qualities to support and encourage in their husbands, helping their sons know what to focus on, and helping to train their daughters to have godly eyes and expectations.

SUPERHEROES

Job chapter twenty-nine describes the Man of Noble Character during times of success. Success here is measured in both wealth and community respect. But what is the basis of this respect?

> [12] *"because I delivered the poor who cried for help,*
> *and the fatherless who had none to help him."*
>
> JOB 29:12

Any man, worldly or godly, should know to defend and look after his own family. It is the reason why even ungodly society finds men who abuse their spouse or children so repugnant. Failure to look after your own is the antithesis of fatherhood—even worldly fatherhood. Pick your culture: if a father does not care for his own offspring, the general social response is the same—this is not just unapproved behavior. It is fundamentally wrong, shameful, and almost always illegal.

But a Man of Noble Character is different. His natural paternal instinct and sense of compassionate responsibility extend beyond just the biological family unit and encompass the poor and fatherless unrelated to him.

The Man of Noble Character looks after the terminally ill (29:13). And yet, our society often delegates the care of the bedridden exclusively to women. Some men will not even enter a hospital, letting their personal discomfort override the opportunity to provide care.

The Man of Noble Character exercises practical and effective concern for widows (29:13), those with disabilities (29:15), the generally needy, and the stranger (i.e., the immigrant, the newcomer) (29:16). This work is not impersonal charity but the work of a proxy father (29:16).

The work is not just reactive bandaging. The Man of Noble Character actively identifies danger. He proactively defangs it (29:17), putting himself in harm's way to prevent future trouble for the weak and rescue those already in trouble.

The work of a Man of Noble Character is the work that today, in fiction, is done by superheroes. But the Man of Noble Character is expected to perform these feats without the benefit of superpowers. There is a reason Superman and Spiderman are popular: beyond the flashiness of their excessive powers, superheroes use their powers for good in the service of those in need, those unable to repay, those who are not of the superhero's social circle. Superheroes save everyone in need—not just their friends but all victims regardless of their circumstances, even the unworthy, wherever they may be found. However, the superhero is fiction. The Man of Noble Character is not.

NOBLE CHARACTER—IN RETIREMENT

Verses eighteen through twenty seem to shift to a new topic as Job mourned the loss of what he had anticipated would be the end of his life: a peaceful fading out as he died in his own house, full of years and happiness. But notice how these three verses end:

> ^{18}"Then I thought, 'I shall die in my nest,
>   and I shall multiply my days as the sand,
> ^{19}my roots spread out to the waters,
>   with the dew all night on my branches,
> ^{20}my glory fresh with me,
>   and my bow ever new in my hand.'"
>
> JOB 29:18–20

What do you use a bow for? To hunt. To go to battle. Where do you get glory from? Achievements. Successes. Job had hoped the end of his life would be a time when his glory remained fresh in him—not preserved as a memory of more youthfully ambitious times but fresh. Recent. The bow would not be on the wall as a memory aide but still be in current successful use.

Job had not changed topics but instead paused to emphasize that his former active role in society was one he had imagined he would continue up to the end of his long life. Job wanted to continue to be a superhero even into his frail gray years. He did not intend to wind down and spend his retirement years golfing. Instead, he intended for his glory to remain fresh and the bow to be ever new in his hand.

A DIFFERENT KIND OF SOCIAL AUTHORITY

Having clarified that this righteous role in his community was not just a brief phase for Job but part of his fundamental character, Job continued to describe his past.

> ^{21}"Men listened to me and waited
>   and kept silence for my counsel.
> ^{22}After I spoke they did not speak again,
>   and my word dropped upon them."
>
> JOB 29:21–22

We could misunderstand Job's authority and respect in the meetings at the city gates as the product of intimidation or power. So Job clarified the situation: "my words fell gently on their ears" is how the NIV phrases it. In Hebrew, the reference is less about gentleness and more about refreshment. "Like drops of rain on dry ground" is a little closer to the original Hebrew phrasing.[103] People weren't quiet when Job spoke because he intimidated them or drowned them out. They were quiet because they wanted to soak up his good, refreshing, and nourishing words.

Job went on to expand on this point:

> [23] *"They waited for me as for the rain,*
> *and they opened their mouths as for the spring rain.*
> [24] *I smiled on them when they had no confidence,*
> *and the light of my face they did not cast down.*
> [25] *I chose their way and sat as chief,*
> *and I lived like a king among his troops,*
> *like one who comforts mourners."*
>
> JOB 29:23–25

Perhaps by now you are starting to notice the three-line verses on your own and consider the importance of the broken meter or unrhymed extra line.

The first two lines of verse twenty-five are in parallel—the ideas rhyme. Job was like the chief or the king. But the third line upends this rhythm: he was also like one who comforts mourners.

Lines two and three also rhyme with each other in another way. Lines one and two rhyme the ideas of chief and king together. But lines two and three also rhyme in that they both elaborate on what kind of leader this chief is. Job was a leader who lived with his troops and who comforted mourners. He was not like a king who lived in a palace far away. He camped with his troops in the same hot and cold weather. And he was not like a chief who constantly harped on his success, ignored his failures, and tried to spin every setback as a learning opportunity or a goad to push his subordinates mercilessly. Instead, he was like a chief who recognized that after a hard battle, losses needed to be mourned. And he let his people mourn. He did not just

---

103 Reyburn, 534.

coldly give them some limited time to mourn, but he entered their space of sorrow and comforted them himself.

Job was like a chief and king among his people, and in this role, he not only led them but also lived with them and comforted those who needed it. He was a wise servant-leader for his people, and he intended to continue to provide this servant leadership even into his old age.

Job was a good man. He was a good man both morally and spiritually. Thus, chapter twenty-nine serves as both a template for the Man of Noble Character and a solid rebuttal of Eliphaz's wild accusations.

But this is who Job was. Job's past identity was in part shaped by his health and opportunities. Without his successful circumstances, Job would never have had the opportunity to serve his community in the many ways that he did. Unfortunately, this kind of service becomes increasingly difficult when personal circumstances change for the worse and commence upon a long season of deterioration.

So how does a Man of Noble Character operate when dealing with disaster followed by disaster and when his positive community standing becomes nonexistent? Job tackled that subject next.

45

HITTING BOTTOM

Job then described his current social standing, which was the exact opposite of his former position in his community.

> *¹"But now they laugh at me,*
>   *men who are younger than I,*
>   *whose fathers I would have disdained*
>   *to set with the dogs of my flock.*
> *²What could I gain from the strength of their hands,*
>   *men whose vigor is gone?*
> *³Through want and hard hunger*
>   *they gnaw the dry ground by night in waste and desolation;*
> *⁴they pick saltwort and the leaves of bushes,*
>   *and the roots of the broom tree for their food.*
> *⁵They are driven out from human company;*
>   *they shout after them as after a thief.*
> *⁶In the gullies of the torrents they must dwell,*
>   *in holes of the earth and of the rocks.*
> *⁷Among the bushes they bray;*
>   *under the nettles they huddle together.*
> *⁸A senseless, a nameless brood,*
>   *they have been whipped out of the land."*
>
>   Job 30:1–8

This is a really rough social sketch. These are not officials, chiefs, or nobles. These are not needy widows or orphans. These are men who have ceased to function as men. Job essentially said that he had too much respect for his sheepdogs to put these degraded men with them.

Unlike the needy and the victims in Job's community, who Job had a role in protecting and helping in chapter 29, these men were the authors of their own depravity. They were a banished, base, and nameless people. These men had lost their vigor, unlike Job, whose vision of his future had been one where his bow and glory would be ever fresh. The issue does not appear to be that of physical strength. Rather, the passage's focus is on their moral character. They still had strength in their hand, but that strength was of no use to anyone. They were voluntary slackers whose character decomposed even as they continued to breed. These are not unfortunate men but men who have chosen squalor and a grubbing subsistence.

A very rough social sketch indeed!

But remember, the point of this passage is not to pass judgment specifically on these men and their sons but to contrast Job's former life to his present circumstances. Previously chiefs and nobles, young and old, had held Job in the highest esteem. Now, even the offspring of a base and nameless brood mocked Job. Even the lowest looked down on him. And Job did nothing to deserve this. The previous chapter describes the Man of Noble Character in happy circumstances. This chapter paints a vivid picture of contrasting circumstances to set the stage for a look at the Man of Noble Character in unhappy circumstances.

Before we can get to those proper actions in distress, Job needed to finish his portrait of that distress.

> [9]*"And now I have become their song;*
>   *I am a byword to them.*
> [10]*They abhor me;*
>   *they keep aloof from me;*
>   *they do not hesitate to spit at the sight of me.*
> [11]*Because God has loosed my cord and humbled me,*
>   *they have cast off restraint in my presence.*
> [12]*On my right hand the rabble rise;*

> *they push away my feet;*
> *they cast up against me their ways of destruction.*
> ¹³ *They break up my path;*
> *they promote my calamity;*
> *they need no one to help them.*
> ¹⁴ *As through a wide breach they come;*
> *amid the crash they roll on.*
> ¹⁵ *Terrors are turned upon me;*
> *my honor is pursued as by the wind,*
> *and my prosperity has passed away like a cloud.*
> ¹⁶ *And now my soul is poured out within me;*
> *days of affliction have taken hold of me.*
> ¹⁷ *The night racks my bones,*
> *and the pain that gnaws me takes no rest.*
> ¹⁸ *With great force my garment is disfigured;*
> *it binds me about like the collar of my tunic.*
> ¹⁹ *God has cast me into the mire,*
> *and I have become like dust and ashes."*
>
> JOB 30:9–19

In the previous chapter, Job had expected that his bow would remain "ever new in his hand" (29:20), but now, God had unstrung his bow and afflicted Job himself.

The number of unbalanced three-line verses in this passage would have been awkward and unsettling to the original reader, keeping with the jarring nature of the material in the context of Job's life and character.

When Job said that "night racks my bones," the phrase in Hebrew can also be translated as "at night, my bones ache intensely." This image is one of pain so intense that it felt like his limbs would come off, which adds further force to the following line: "the pain that gnaws me takes no rest."

After describing his social disaster (30:9–10) and his sense of spiritual abandonment (30:11), Job went on to describe social attacks (30:12–14), his fear and insecurity (30:15), his physical agony (30:16–18), and then finally his feeling of spiritual assault (30:19). There was no aspect of Job's life that did not feel endangered and tormented.

The contrast to Job's former happy state could hardly be more stark.

UNHEEDED CRIES FOR HELP

As a result of these painful trials and his collapsed social standing, Job cried out with more than just physical or emotional pain—he also cried out from the social misery that was mounding additional unnecessary layers of psychological distress onto him. Job did not bottle this pain. He expressed it out loud in the following few verses:

> [20] *"I cry to you for help and you do not answer me;*
> *I stand, and you only look at me.*
> [21] *You have turned cruel to me;*
> *with the might of your hand you persecute me.*
> [22] *You lift me up on the wind; you make me ride on it,*
> *and you toss me about in the roar of the storm.*
> [23] *For I know that you will bring me to death*
> *and to the house appointed for all living.*
> [24] *Yet does not one in a heap of ruins stretch out his hand,*
> *and in his disaster cry for help?*
> [25] *Did not I weep for him whose day was hard?*
> *Was not my soul grieved for the needy?*
> [26] *But when I hoped for good, evil came,*
> *and when I waited for light, darkness came.*
> [27] *My inward parts are in turmoil and never still;*
> *days of affliction come to meet me.*
> [28] *I go about darkened, but not by the sun;*
> *I stand up in the assembly and cry for help.*
> [29] *I am a brother of jackals*
> *and a companion of ostriches.*
> [30] *My skin turns black and falls from me,*
> *and my bones burn with heat.*
> [31] *My lyre is turned to mourning,*
> *and my pipe to the voice of those who weep."*
>
> JOB 30:20–31

WHERE DOES A SUFFERING SOUL GO FROM HERE?

Chapter twenty-nine shows the Man of Noble Character in a successful state, actively engaged in the service and protection of those around him. But where does this man go when chapter thirty is his reality? How does this man function when immersed in disease, social denigration, loss, insecurity, depression, and spiritual isolation? Job's wife counseled him to quit. Job's friends tried to persuade him to believe in a false reality. Neither of these options were noble or honorable. To endure would appear to be Job's only option, but what aspects of his former character could he continue to commit to, even in these dire circumstances?

What follows is the answer to this question—the bare-bones standards for a Man of Noble Character.

46

MINIMUM STANDARDS

What follows is the last of Job's speeches to his friends, and in this final communication, he made plain something that is often hard to see during a trial. Grief, loss, and depression can be powerfully blinding forces. Some folks make excuses for themselves when pressure or pain mounts. They make harmful life choices and use their stress to justify them. The phrase mitigating circumstances is even used in many law courts in this and other countries.

But what are the minimum standards for a Man of Noble Character, regardless of how intense their current trial? I've heard doctors, professors, and counselors offer their own opinions on this question, but I found Job's opinion to carry the most weight during my own struggles. God himself commended Job as someone worth listening to—and I know from these pages that Job was not speaking about grief from a place of cold, distant theory but from a place of deep personal experience. If Job called these items out, then they are worth paying attention to. The standards that follow are worth clinging to regardless of how wild the storm gets.

STANDARD #1: HAVE PURE EYES

Here was Job's first commitment:

> *[1] "I have made a covenant with my eyes;*
> *how then could I gaze at a virgin?*
> *[2] What would be my portion from God above*

> *and my heritage from the Almighty on high?*
> *³Is not calamity for the unrighteous,*
>   *and disaster for the workers of iniquity?*
> *⁴Does not he see my ways*
>   *and number all my steps?"*
>
> JOB 31:1–4

Job started with purity. Job knew men. Job also knew that there was never any excuse for what women sometimes refer to as the "male gaze," that relentless undressing with the eyes that seems bred into the male half of our species. Trouble does not excuse objectifying another human being.

Even though men will sometimes try to self-medicate their unhappiness in life by turning to stare at strangers on the street, pornography, or some other form of visual lust fulfillment, this is always a wrong path, regardless of the level of stress. Empathizing with women and how the male gaze (or catcalling or unwanted advances) makes them feel is also an important aspect of Job's commitment here. On this topic, he's not just self-disciplined at the action level—he is noble at the heart level.

Victory in this area starts with one's eyes. If a man never stares, never goes for that second glance, never seeks the right angle to look unobserved—if a man stops the sin at the stage of sight, he is well on his way to stopping the sin altogether. Impurity is a path that starts, with most men, at the eyes. It is no accident that Proverbs 5 warns the young man against adultery by describing it as a path, one with stages, one that a man should avoid even starting down. As Job stated quite plainly, God knows the ways we take and counts our steps. He knows where our feet go. And he knows where our eyes go as well.

Note: Job wasn't saying he was perfect. He was saying he had committed to not staring. These are the minimum standards he was outlining here. Said differently, he had committed to respecting everyone around him, including women.

Sex is a powerful distraction and medication—many are the souls who sought temporary escape from the pain of suffering by the simple pleasure of giving unholy eyes free rein. But, whatever the circumstance, the Man of Noble Character makes a covenant with his eyes "not to look lustfully at a young woman" (Job 31:1, NIV). This is a commitment that can always be kept. It is simply a case of whether a man chooses to make that commitment or not. And then chooses to stick to it.

STANDARD #2: BE HONEST

> ⁵*"If I have walked with falsehood*
> *and my foot has hastened to deceit;*
> ⁶*(Let me be weighed in a just balance,*
> *and let God know my integrity!)*
> ⁷*if my step has turned aside from the way*
> *and my heart has gone after my eyes,*
> *and if any spot has stuck to my hands,*
> ⁸*then let me sow, and another eat,*
> *and let what grows for me be rooted out."*
>
> Job 31:5–8

Life can get rough. Job knew that as well as any man, but even amid his darkest trials, Job held to his commitment to be honest. His dealings with others were not sneaky, misleading, or fraudulent. Note here how, in addition to talking about temptations of sight, Job also talked about the temptations of the heart. Dishonesty is also a heart matter.

STANDARD #3: BE FAITHFUL AT THE HEART LEVEL

> ⁹*"If my heart has been enticed toward a woman,*
> *and I have lain in wait at my neighbor's door,*
> ¹⁰*then let my wife grind for another,*
> *and let others bow down on her.*
> ¹¹*For that would be a heinous crime;*
> *that would be an iniquity to be punished by the judges;*
> ¹²*for that would be a fire that consumes as far as Abaddon,*
> *and it would burn to the root all my increase."*
>
> Job 31:9–12

So the first commitment was to be pure and the second to be honest. The first was an eye problem, and the second was an eye-and-heart problem.

This third commitment married the two together, mixing the eye problem of purity with the eye-and-heart problem of dishonesty to expose a deeper purity issue: heart-level unfaithfulness. This passage does not reference the eyes here, just the heart. The lurking was not at a window to see but at a door to enter.

The marital faithfulness conversation in many Christian circles focuses on men looking and women relating. Men, so one popular stream goes, lust with eyes, but the heart is more at risk for women. There may be some truth to this, but it does tend to be an oversimplification of the human condition, both male and female. In the same way that women can lust with their eyes (it's not the exclusive domain of men), men's hearts are captured by desire as well. Verse one discusses casual lust—the kind of lust a contract with the eyes will overcome. There is also an emotional unfaithfulness that starts not with the eyes but with a relationship—that neighbor or co-worker with whom a simple conversation leads to lurking and waiting for another opportunity to talk.

Notice that Job never referenced an actual sexual affair. Job only referenced being enticed and lurking. Job was talking about playing with fire, not even going so far as adultery. That playing with fire is itself "a heinous crime" and "an iniquity to be punished by the judges" (31:11).

A DETOUR: THINGS GET A BIT GRAPHIC

Some may take offense at verse ten with the "then" part of these if-then statements. Verse ten describes the consequence of this potential sin as Job's own wife then having sex with other men.

This is not a translation problem. On the contrary, that is exactly what the original Hebrew version of this verse is trying to communicate. We should not, however, misunderstand; this verse is not about Job's wife. Instead, the verse is about a theoretical curse against Job for a sin that Job never actually committed. The point is to illustrate the intensity with which Job rejected this sin and committed to its opposite.

If you find the ESV translation sufficiently vague that you want to dodge this awkward and unsettling implication, let's unpack the Hebrew for a moment. In verse ten, the Hebrew doesn't have the word grain in it as some English translations do and the ESV implies. Instead, the Hebrew says "let her grind another"—the other man, not his grain. And then the ESV phrase "let others bow down on her" is a direct, literal translation of the Hebrew phrase, which in Hebrew is a euphemism for sexual relations. In plain English, we might translate this as "let other men have sex with her" or, using an English euphemism, "let other men sleep with her."[104]

The verse is graphically sexual in the original. Though many English translations try to sanitize the language for modern Christian sensibilities, a sanitized version is not what God originally inspired to have written down and included in his scriptures. If that offends us, we will have to take it up with God.

And now that we've unpacked this one verse, we can see that, as one would expect, the more accurate Hebrew rendering also shows a better parallel between the verse's first and second lines. They are both talking about the same shameful curse upon Job as a theoretical consequence of his unfaithfulness—had he, of course, been unfaithful, which he hadn't.

Again, this verse isn't about Job's wife. It's about Job emphasizing his innocence. The bottom line, graphically underscored by a disturbing "then" statement, is that Job is committed to both visual purity as well as faithfulness at the heart level.

STANDARD #4: BE APPROACHABLE AND JUST

> [13]*"If I have rejected the cause of my manservant or my maidservant,*
> *when they brought a complaint against me,*
> [14]*what then shall I do when God rises up?*
> *When he makes inquiry, what shall I answer him?*
> [15]*Did not he who made me in the womb make him?*
> *And did not one fashion us in the womb?"*
>
> JOB 31:13–15

In our modern age, with our human rights commitments at the national and legislative level and with our Human Resources policies at the organization and company level, we might be tempted to skim over these verses. Men of

---

104 For references through this Standard #3 section, see Reyburn, 564-568.

Noble Character in smaller operations without formal policies might take note, but larger corporations with complicated union rules might make Men of Noble Character in those organizations shrug and consider the entire bureaucracy beyond the responsibility of a single man. Even well-structured companies in nonunion contexts tend to come out in favor of strong and beneficial human resource policies (at least in principle) by making a business case for how these polices improve retention, morale, and ultimately productivity; help the business avoid lawsuits; create a positive branding image; and protect their reputation.

These modern-day considerations, however, run the risk of leading the Man of Noble Character astray. The verse here only briefly references the obligation to treat servants properly (in a modern context, "servants" could be read as "contractors" or "employees"). After this brief context-setting reference, this commitment is focused on treating employees properly for a particular reason: we are all God's children.

Union or nonunion, strong HR policies or not, the Man of Noble Character commits to treating those who work for him well and, even more specifically, granting them justice when they have a grievance against him—because of who they are. Notice that Job was not committing to being a perfect employer. He assumed that his servants would have grievances against him—whether Job might make mistakes as an employer was not even a question. How he would address those mistakes when brought to his attention is what was at issue.

The Man of Noble Character has committed here to be humble, approachable, and just. Job, however, committed to helping more than just those who worked for him.

STANDARD #5: COMMIT TO SOCIAL JUSTICE AND SERVICE

> [16]"If I have withheld anything that the poor desired,
>   or have caused the eyes of the widow to fail,
> [17]or have eaten my morsel alone,
>   and the fatherless has not eaten of it
> [18](for from my youth the fatherless grew up with me as with a father,
>   and from my mother's womb I guided the widow),

> *[19] if I have seen anyone perish for lack of clothing,*
> *or the needy without covering,*
> *[20] if his body has not blessed me,*
> *and if he was not warmed with the fleece of my sheep,*
> *[21] if I have raised my hand against the fatherless,*
> *because I saw my help in the gate,*
> *[22] then let my shoulder blade fall from my shoulder,*
> *and let my arm be broken from its socket.*
> *[23] For I was in terror of calamity from God,*
> *and I could not have faced his majesty."*
>
> Job 31:16–23

This passage expands the Man of Noble Character's responsibilities to a wider audience and impact, moving from treating servants justly to serving those in need across the wider society. He does not just advocate for justice for his staff but for everyone in need, ensuring that they not only have justice but also food, clothing, and even familial care.

IS THIS HYPERBOLE? OR SOMETHING ELSE?

Verse eighteen stands out, however, as improbable. From his youth Job reared orphans, and from birth he guided widows? From a purely stylistic point of view, we might criticize Job's words as a foolish and arrogant hyperbole that ruins the credibility of his overall point. If verse eighteen was just gross exaggeration, maybe we could use a poetic-license argument to justify it. But this poetry is from thousands of years ago. The events took place before the time of Moses, perhaps in Abraham's generation or even earlier. A verse that sounds to the modern ear like hyperbole might have had a very different intent originally. This is very likely the case with verse eighteen.

As some commentators suggest, commentators that I would agree with, this verse is not trying to suggest that Job, as an infant, led widows about (by crawling!) or that he, as a six-year-old boy, adopted orphans into his care. That would be a ridiculous claim. Instead, I believe this verse is trying to communicate that the overall principle of caring for those in need was part of Job's earliest upbringing and character. This was not a new idea he came to suddenly at age thirty-five due to some moving personal encounter or revelation. This was who Job was from birth onward, a trait he had in all likelihood learned and absorbed from the womb (so to speak) onward as he had observed how his parents conducted themselves. He had been raised to it, and it was part of his natural character as well. The modern nature-versus-nurture debate was not part of the cultural conversation in Job's day. Instead, the phrasing of verse eighteen skips the source of this character and simply communicates that it was there from his earliest days.

Job did not discover charity as a rich man or as part of a public-relations or conscience-salving strategy. On the contrary, charity, not just of money but of time, energy, and emotion, was a part of who he had always been, even before he was anyone of social significance.

STANDARD #6: KEEP MONEY IN ITS PLACE

Understanding that charity work for Job was not a rich man's hobby but part of his basic character opens up the topic of money in general. After all, Job was (or had been) a very rich man. So what was Job's attitude toward his wealth? What should be the Man of Noble Character's attitude toward money?

Here is Job's take on things:

> [24] "If I have made gold my trust
>   or called fine gold my confidence,
> [25] if I have rejoiced because my wealth was abundant
>   or because my hand had found much,
> [26] if I have looked at the sun when it shone,
>   or the moon moving in splendor,
> [27] and my heart has been secretly enticed,
>   and my mouth has kissed my hand,
> [28] this also would be an iniquity to be punished by the judges,
>   for I would have been false to God above."
>
> Job 31:24–28

What did appreciating the sun and the moon have to do with putting his trust in money? Everything.

In Job's day, the sun and the moon were dominant pagan gods. Most ancient cultures with an idolatry tradition found room for them in their pantheon. These were often the top gods, and in some cases, one nation might hold to multiple gods represented in these celestial bodies. Egypt, Rome, and Greece all had their celestial-object deities. The Babylonians and Assyrians did as well. The Hittites were famous for their one thousand gods, and they cataloged numerous sun and moon gods.

Job's point is that his security was in God, not money or any other false god. The Man of Noble Character finds his security in faithfulness to God.

STANDARD #7: BE GRACIOUS TOWARD ENEMIES

Security begs the question of enemies, and Job, in particular, had enemies who had destroyed his farm and murdered most of his staff. These enemies had also stolen not only his wealth but also his ability to make a living. How does the Man of Noble Character deal with enemies? We have Jesus's teachings on this matter in the New Testament, but was the Man of Noble Character different in the Old Testament?

Here is what Job said:

> ^{29}*"If I have rejoiced at the ruin of him who hated me,*
> *or exulted when evil overtook him*
> ^{30}*(I have not let my mouth sin*
> *by asking for his life with a curse),*
> ^{31}*if the men of my tent have not said,*
> *'Who is there that has not been filled with his meat?'*
> ^{32}*(the sojourner has not lodged in the street;*
> *I have opened my doors to the traveler)..."*
>
> JOB 31:29–32

These verses should be especially compelling if we take them into the usually less extreme social situations such as our homes, neighborhoods, and workplaces. Job committed to not hate another person in the face of pillage and murder. The challenges we are more likely to face are a mean-spirited boss, a backstabbing coworker, a meddling neighbor, or a hurtful relative.

Is it not easy to rejoice when this kind of "enemy" stumbles? Is it not vindicating when the one who "stole" a job from us fails at it or when the boss we quit working for in disgust finds only problems and disaster when they discover that they cannot easily find a replacement for you? Is it not easy, even satisfying in a worldly way, to rejoice in their trouble? But is it not also true that graciousness in these circumstances would be the godly response?

Graciousness is what Job was pointing to here, even when dealing with enemies. He does not simply refuse to rejoice when his enemies have trouble, but instead, he helps his enemy. That is why the people of Job's household could comment that everyone had their fill at Job's table. Everyone. Even enemies. Even strangers traveling through—strangers who were possible security threats—Job provided for.

Notice how Job pointed out that, even in his extreme experiences, he did not curse his enemies, not even the raiders that committed atrocities on his farm. We've seen Job's emotional candor over these past thirty-one chapters, but we have never seen his hate. He had mourned the lack of justice but not boiled with revenge fantasies. That balance, that emotional honesty without hate even in the most extreme trial, is a rare nobility.

Job's character here was truly exemplary. This is already a big list, but Job was not finished. He had two more items to put forward.

47

THE FINAL STANDARDS

Job's list of seven godly qualities outlined in the previous chapter is a super practical set of guidelines for anyone to follow—even in the darkest of trials. Cancer, loss, financial troubles, chronic illness—all the unfair and unwelcome trials of life come with their sorrows and pressures, but even amid these things, Job's list is a good guide to hang on to. Treating people with decency; being honest, faithful, approachable, and just; practicing social justice; and so on are a solid base for behavior.

Job was, however, under no illusions that either he or the Man of Noble Character is perfect. With that understanding in mind, Job offered two more items for consideration:

STANDARD #8: BE TRANSPARENT AND CONFESS YOUR MISTAKES

> [33]*"if I have concealed my transgressions as others do*
> *by hiding my iniquity in my heart,*
> [34]*because I stood in great fear of the multitude,*
> *and the contempt of families terrified me,*
> *so that I kept silence, and did not go out of doors—*
> [35]*Oh, that I had one to hear me!*
> *(Here is my signature! Let the Almighty answer me!)*
> *Oh, that I had the indictment written by my adversary!*
> [36]*Surely I would carry it on my shoulder;*

> *I would bind it on me as a crown;*
> *³⁷I would give him an account of all my steps;*
> *like a prince I would approach him."*
>
> JOB 31:33–37

The wealthy, socially prominent, and powerful man here is not only willing to have those who work for him point out his flaws (31:13) but committed to exposing his own guilt as well, even in the absence of charges. Fear of social contempt was not a barrier to confession for Job.

Where an indictment could be made public, Job was keen to present it in writing and make it public—and he was keen to defend himself as well. The principle here goes back to his original commitment to avoid falsehood and deceit (31:5). Silence itself can be a form of deceit. It's not a lie, strictly speaking, but it can still be deceptive.

Job was committed not to managing his public image but to being transparent. First John 1:8 teaches us that we are all sinners guilty of something. If we do not ever confess to anything, then we are following neither Job's example nor the directive of other verses such as James 5:16.

Transparency is a godly quality and an essential aspect of the Man of Noble Character.

Job had one other item to raise with us.

STANDARD #9: COMMIT TO (ANCIENT) ENVIRONMENTALISM

To the modern mind, Job's final commitment was to something that today we would call environmental concern. This is a complicated one, so let's read it carefully:

> *³⁸"If my land has cried out against me*
> *and its furrows have wept together,*
> *³⁹if I have eaten its yield without payment*
> *and made its owners breathe their last,*
> *⁴⁰let thorns grow instead of wheat,*
> *and foul weeds instead of barley."*

The words of Job are ended.

JOB 31:38–40

Job's opening line here suggests a kind of early environmentalism. However, the passage's reference to refusing to pay farmers for their produce, thus causing them to "breathe their last" (31:39), makes it sound like Job was more concerned for the tenant farmers who sublet his land than for the land itself. Perhaps Job operated his farm in a feudal system, requiring that he, as the owner of the land, got the first share of the crops and that the serfs below him, who farmed and were in many ways chained to the land, would only accrue any remaining leftovers. This subservient system would put a very different spin on the opening chapters of Job, but there is no evidence anywhere—in the opening chapters or elsewhere—to suggest that Job handled his estate in this kind of oppressive manner.

So was Job committing to some form of early environmentalism or to specific business ethics?

We can find the key to understanding this commitment in verse thirty-nine:

> [39]"*if I have eaten its yield without payment
> and made its owners breathe their last…*"

Remember what we have learned so far about parallelism in Hebrew poetry: the second line's meaning rhymes with the first line's. The two lines should explore the same idea in different ways, with the second line expanding or contracting on the first line's image in a way that heightens the overall meaning. Regardless of how the image progresses between the two lines, be it expanding or contracting, both lines should consistently be parallel ideas. Their meaning should still rhyme.

By itself, the second line of verse thirty-nine does suggest that this commitment was all about business ethics. But Job had already committed to being an ethical businessman in the fourth standard (39:13–15).

However, the first line's phrasing is interesting. The assertion here is that Job did not withhold payment. Payment to who?

In the preceding verse, it is the land itself that cries out and whose furrows are wet with tears. Why? Because payment was withheld. If the land were to cry out, if its furrows were wet with tears, if Job were to take from the land without payment or oppress its tenants, then what would happen?

The answer to "then what?" is the curse in verse forty:

> ^{40}"let thorns grow instead of wheat,
> and foul weeds instead of barley."

All of this chapter's curses contrast directly with the previously mentioned crime. Dishonest gain was to be met with the loss of goods (31:5–6). Unfaithfulness to his wife was to be matched with her unfaithfulness to him (31:9–12). Raising his hand against orphans was to be met with the removal of his entire arm (31:21–22).

If Job was simply reiterating his commitment to managerial ethics in verses thirty-eight through forty, then the subsequent curse would not only punish Job but also his victims. The oppressed tenants (oppressed by the lack of payment in this feudal system) would now face starvation due to massive crop failure. Thus, in this interpretation, the curse makes no sense.

But as we have seen, we can interpret Job's commitment here in two ways. To interpret it as a commitment to managerial ethics would require awkwardly ignoring verse thirty-eight, focusing only on verse thirty-nine, and then skimming over an incongruous verse forty. That interpretation does not work.

So if we interpret this passage as a commitment to environmental stewardship, what do we make of the withheld payment and breathless owners?

The crime that Job was talking about is the crime of abusing the land. Careful farmers know to rotate their crops. They know to let the land lie fallow. They know to leave the remains of last year's crop on the field as compost. They may know to fertilize the land with manure, or they may know that leaving the land fallow and letting sheep or cattle graze the wild grasses for a year or more is another way to fertilize the earth. These practices ensure that the soil can replenish the nutrients required to remain fertile and healthy for future generations. Moses's laws later written in Exodus and elsewhere will prescribe such maintenance of the land as a sacred duty.

Today, we address many of these agricultural concerns by pouring synthetic fertilizers over the land to drive artificial productivity. The wisdom and sustainability of this modern approach is a matter of ongoing debate and certainly not the focus of our study. In Job's day, however, this kind of artificial productivity was not possible, and therefore that debate is not relevant for this poem.

What was possible in Job's day was to skip the wise and forward-looking farmer's practices and simply abuse the land. Plant, harvest, plant, harvest, and repeat until the soil wore out and the crops thinned and eventually failed. The selfish, shortsighted businessperson could make money this way by avoiding the hassle of crop rotation, the expense of letting land lie fallow, the complexity of manure sourcing and distribution, and other practices of careful husbandry.

The land would continue to produce for many years in such a scenario, but poetically speaking, it would cry out.

Practically speaking, the knowledgeable worker would recognize what they were doing to the ground. They would see less reward for their efforts and feel discouraged, perhaps even depressed, about the degrading value of their labor.

Suddenly, this commitment is relevant for us today. Many modern workers have expressed in blogs, memoirs, and articles the deep emotional pain of engaging in what they know is damaging, futureless work. As Job put it, people become breathless not because of lack of payment (it's the land that's left without payment in Job's poem, not the owners or the workers) but because they are participating in a bad enterprise.

With this understanding, the curse makes perfect sense. The damaged and weeping land fights back. It fights back against the abusive farmer and his complicit associates.

The modern reader might be skeptical of this interpretation of Job's final words. Any skeptic must find another way to account for Job's words and explain how the following curse is an appropriate consequence of violating the preceding principle. Environmental stewardship is not a twenty-first-century invention. The Law of Moses gives instructions on how to handle even trivial details of environmental practice, such as a bird-hunting dilemma involving a mother bird and its young as well as crop management policies, proper sanitation practices, and so on. God's laws in the Old Testament were not just lists of rules about sacrifices and ceremonies.

With this commitment to look after the land fully stated, the words of Job are now ended.

But something is missing.

IS THAT ALL THERE IS?

Is there no way to find meaning in trials? Is blind hope the only way forward for Job and others who suffer? Is there no basis for interpreting life's trials in a way that provides meaning while still living this life? Is everything purely random, and can we only hope for redemption beyond the grave? In the meantime, are we just to live with a kind of dogged, righteous determination? Is that really the message of the book of Job?

48

ISN'T IT TIME FOR GOD TO SAY SOMETHING?

It would seem that this stage of Job's story would be a good time for God to interject a divine point of view into the conversation. Job was done talking. The three friends had exhausted their arguments, and one, if we have interpreted his short third speech correctly, had even been persuaded to rethink his original convictions. What else was left but for God to come in and reveal the outstanding mysteries?

THE PROBLEM WITH GOD SPEAKING TOO SOON

There is a problem with this otherwise natural next step. If the mystery of why in this book was suddenly, individually resolved, the book as a whole would suffer from a limiting specificity.

If God were to say, "These things occurred so that you, Job, could begin to open discovery's door onto eternity and redemption," then the book would be a closed argument. It would not be universally applicable to other innocent sufferers who may already understand heaven, eternity, and redemption well. In other words, the message of Job would be old news for readers of the New Testament.

Likewise, if God were to characterize the root cause of Job's troubles as an assault on the Standard View, or as a means of exposing and correcting the sins of the three friends, or for some other specific purpose, the book would again have limited applications. It would offer up a specific solution to a specific case and not provide a universally meaningful message.

The author's challenge (and by this, I am presuming God to be the ultimate author) is to make Job's story and example universally applicable, and therefore meaningful, to other people (like us) going through different things at other times.

Jesus used parables to keep his teachings open and applicable across a wide range of circumstances. They require interpretation, but the parable style keeps his teachings fresh and practical two thousand years later. However, Job's story is a real, specific story, and anything God says to resolve Job's particular case will immediately cast the story and its meaning in cultural and theological cement. Those who are innocent and suffer for reasons other than Job's would not find comfort or personally applicable meaning in his story.

OTHER BUSINESS TO ATTEND TO AS WELL

Outside of addressing the why of this book's events, there is some other business worth attending to as well.

For example, there were times in Job's speeches where he walked up to the line of accusing God and perhaps even crossed over that line.[105] How should the book of Job address this issue? If God were to correct some of these emotional statements, the reader would be tempted to interpret Job's occasionally edgy tone as sin. The reader might then begin to respond to their own troubles with a kind of plastic artificiality to avoid making what could be perceived as "Job's mistake." Religious denial of real emotions might become the standard for the follower of God. As a result, the reader could entirely misunderstand the book of Job.

But if God does not address the problematic elements of Job's tone at all, it might open the opposite door, making such harsh outbursts dangerously habitual. How can the Almighty best manage this complexity?

Here's another example: Job did a great job of tempering the intensity of his anti–Standard View message by using Bildad's conversion as a foil to ensure that the pendulum did not swing too far in the direction of the Contrary View. Both the Standard and Contrary Views are useful in their

---

[105] For example, see 23:13–17 and 24:12.

time and place. There is a need in this story to balance the emotional-honesty pendulum as well to make sure that candor does not become an excuse for irreverence. But here, God is also handicapped—any form of divine correction or sanction runs the risk of inciting wrong behaviors in later readers. Job had balanced the Standard View versus Contrary View dynamic himself, but he was not in a good position to defend any of his own overheated statements beyond his appeal in 6:2–3 that his rash words came from personal pain.

The three friends were in an even worse position on the subject of emotional balance as their credibility on this topic had long since been depleted. How could Job's emotional extremes be tempered and how could opposition to the Standard View be modulated without denying the validity of Job's emotions or the occasional accuracy of the Standard View?

ENTER ELIHU

There was a fourth friend, a silent witness until now, who played a very important role in this story. He essentially spoke for God without anyone explicitly introducing him as God's prophet. He was careful to position himself as only a person who was Job's friend and not his teacher. The narrator of Job serves up a lengthier and more meaningful introduction for this man than the other three friends enjoyed because Elihu was special. Elihu was the good friend. Elihu was God's opening act as he prepared the way for God's direct speeches.

It is a common mistake, however, to misread the text and think of all Job's friends as a collective who did everything wrong. As we have seen, the friends were not uniform in their response to Job's situation. They each had their own personalities and approaches. They each brought their own material to share, their own psychology and personal mistakes that flavored the conversation. One was stiff and traditional, one was rude, one barely paid attention to the flow of conversation. And as we have seen, it may very well be that one of the friends even started to change his mind by the end of his speeches. Whether or not we have interpreted Bildad's last speech correctly, what does stand out is that Elihu, the fourth friend, was a good person with wholly meaningful things to say.

There are, however, many commentators who give Elihu short shrift. In fact, only one commentator that I consulted, writing in the late 1800s, offered any kind of hint that Elihu was more than just another Job-critic.[106] Instead, the literature I consulted routinely wrote off Elihu as a parrot who invoked summaries of what the other three friends had already said.

These interpretations, however, fail to read closely. Elihu was the only friend that Job did not debate with and the only one of Job's friends that God did not rebuke at the end of this book.[107] So let's read closely and learn what Elihu had to say.

---

106 William Henry Green, Conflict and Triumph: The Argument of the Book of Job Unfolded, revised edition (New York: Robert Carter and Brothers, 1873; reprint, Carlisle: The Banner of Truth Trust, 1999).

107 See 42:7.

49
INTRODUCING THE FOURTH FRIEND: ELIHU

¹So these three men stopped answering Job, because he was righteous in his own eyes. ²But Elihu son of Barakel the Buzite, of the family of Ram, became very angry with Job for justifying himself rather than God. ³He was also angry with the three friends, because they had found no way to refute Job, and yet had condemned him.

Job 32:1–3, NIV[108]

The word "righteous" in verse one can also be translated as "innocent." So the three friends stopped talking to Job because he was innocent in his own eyes. Job was innocent, as chapters one and two made very clear, but the friends didn't know this background material and were convinced that Job's sin was simply yet to be discovered.

The first thing that stands out about Elihu's entrance into this story is that he is the only person in this book given a lineage. He was not Job from Uz, Eliphaz the Temanite, Bildad the Shuhite, or Zophar the Naamathite. He was Elihu, son of Barakel. No one else's father is identified in this book.

---

108 From this point forward, all scripture references are from the NIV. See the Appendix for an explanation regarding the use of Bible translations.

Introducing The Fourth Friend: Elihu

And the writer notes that Barakel was a Buzite. And Barakel was not just a Buzite but a descendant specifically from the family of Ram.

Abraham had a brother named Nahor. Nahor had sons—Abraham's nephews. Nahor had many children, but you should recognize two of them by name: Uz and Buz.[109] Job was from Uz. Elihu's family was from Buz. We have already said that the events of this book appear to be from around the time of Abraham. Definitely before Moses. Are these references to Uz and Buz coincidental (perhaps these were common names at the time)? Or is it possible that Elihu and Job were distantly related and from territories (and presumably tribes) named after Abraham's nephews? The facts fit, but the facts are sparse. We can build a thin circumstantial case in favor of this interpretation, but we do not know for sure.

What we do know is that the writer honors Elihu uniquely with a more elaborate introduction. He was not just Elihu. He was Elihu from a family line worth noting.

And he was angry with Job.

Angry?

With Job?

This is likely one of the reasons why most commentators write Elihu off as another ignorant and judgmental friend. He entered the story with a seemingly inappropriate anger at an innocently suffering soul.

Why carefully study the words of a character who, thirty-two chapters into this book, thought it was valid to be angry with Job?

He is worth studying carefully because he was the only friend Job did not argue with and God did not rebuke. Also, Elihu's speeches were important enough for God to record in his Word and preserve for thousands of years. All this suggests that we should read Elihu's words closely.

Why was he angry with Job? He was angry because Job had justified himself rather than God.

What does that mean?

The three friends were busy trying to justify God, and they did so based on the Standard View. They tried to bury Job's character and reputation to prove that God was a just judge. They created an either/or scenario: either Job was the bad guy, or God was, and they defended God.

---

109 See Genesis 22:21.

Job, on the other hand, defended himself. No one in these debates thought to defend God and Job. No one considered a third way. Job imagined an escape from the whole mess where he would be redeemed in the next life, but that was a wipe-the-slate-clean (some time in eternity) solution that never adequately explained the present. It left unanswered the very questions that we asked a few pages ago:

Is there no way to find meaning in trials?

Is blind hope the only way forward for Job and others who suffer?

Is there no basis at all for interpreting the trials of life?

Is everything purely random, and is redemption beyond the grave the only satisfaction we can hope for?

Is this really the message of Job's trials?

This conclusion made Elihu angry. The friends had set up an either/or paradigm, and Job had bought into it and chose to defend only himself. By doing so and still seeking God, he found his way to several fantastic discoveries and subsequent convictions. Still, this route failed to address the immediate existential crisis of the present. Job's newfound convictions promised that it would be better later but left no hope for any of this to mean anything in the present. Elihu wanted a better answer than that.

But Elihu was also angry at the three friends. They sought to find meaning in the present, but these men could only interpret suffering as punishment and search for the root-cause sin that was creating the pain. Sometimes the Standard View is correct, and a person in pain is suffering the consequences of their sin. In Job's case, however, the Standard View was wrong. The friends had failed to make their case but condemned Job anyway. They stuck to their philosophy even when their philosophy failed to fit the facts.

ELIHU'S ANGER

ALL THIS MADE Elihu angry. He was even angrier than the NIV translation lets on, as in verse two, there is another use of the word angry in the Hebrew that the NIV drops from the translation (perhaps for stylistic reasons?). So three times in two verses, the text says that Elihu was angry. And he was angry again in the next two verses:

> *⁴Now Elihu had waited before speaking to Job because they were older than he. ⁵But when he saw that the three men had nothing more to say, his anger was aroused.*
>
> JOB 32:4–5

Reading casually, we might view Elihu as an awfully angry young man.

Reading casually, we might have the impression that he had been angry but biding his time for all of these thirty-two chapters.

The text, however, does not say that. Instead, it says he had been quiet this whole time because the other men leading this conversation were older. He had been listening. He had let his elders retain the stage for as long as they required. It was only when the conversation was over—when the three friends had nothing more to say, and Job was done talking, and the entire debate was going to be left in this unfinished state—that his anger awoke.

Elihu had patiently listened through misdirection and error, but he could not stomach such a conclusion. Quitting without meaning for the here and now was unacceptable. The failure of his elders to do more than just run out of steam made him angry. He had witnessed a failure of leadership and wisdom. The failure started with Eliphaz, likely the eldest, the one from Teman, a territory proverbial for its wisdom.[110]

Now, into this gap, Elihu will speak with messages for both Job and the three friends.

ELIHU COMMITS TO A DIFFERENT APPROACH

> *⁶So Elihu son of Barakel the Buzite said:*
> *"I am young in years,*
> *and you are old;*
> *that is why I was fearful,*
> *not daring to tell you what I know.*
> *⁷I thought, 'Age should speak;*
> *advanced years should teach wisdom.'*
> *⁸But it is the spirit in a person,*

---

110 Cf. Jeremiah 49:7

> *the breath of the Almighty, that gives them understanding.*
> *⁹It is not only the old who are wise,*
> *not only the aged who understand what is right.*
> *¹⁰Therefore I say: Listen to me;*
> *I too will tell you what I know.*
> *¹¹I waited while you spoke,*
> *I listened to your reasoning;*
> *while you were searching for words,*
> *¹²I gave you my full attention.*
> *But not one of you has proved Job wrong;*
> *none of you has answered his arguments.*
> *¹³Do not say, 'We have found wisdom;*
> *let God, not a man, refute him.'*
> *¹⁴But Job has not marshaled his words against me,*
> *and I will not answer him with your arguments."*
>
> JOB 32:6–14

Elihu addressed this first section to Eliphaz, Bildad, and Zophar. He used the Hebrew plural you to address many instead of just one. Elihu explained that he had previously kept silent because these three men were older; his silence had been the silence of respect. He also explained that the reason he now entered the conversation was fourfold: First, wisdom is not found only in the aged but rather comes from the spirit of the Almighty working within a person. Second, Elihu's elders had failed to answer Job. Third, Elihu was the only friend that Job had not assembled arguments against. And fourth, Elihu's words will be different. He will not answer Job's concerns with the friends' arguments. The Standard View will not be Elihu's position.

This last point is very important. In every commentary I read that wrote off Elihu as just a parrot summarizing the three friends, I looked for how the commentary addressed verse fourteen. Consistently, I found the commentary lacking. Elihu's protest in verse fourteen is a direct statement against the interpretation that most modern commentators prefer. The failure of modern commentaries to address this verse is a weakness in those resources. Elihu's opening commitment was not to repeat the three friends' arguments, and as we read closely, we will discover that he honored this commitment.

Before Elihu started addressing Job's needs differently, he extended his introduction a bit by addressing a few opening words to Job himself:

> ^{15}"*They are dismayed and have no more to say;*
>   *words have failed them.*
> ^{16}*Must I wait, now that they are silent,*
>   *now that they stand there with no reply?*
> ^{17}*I too will have my say;*
>   *I too will tell what I know.*
> ^{18}*For I am full of words,*
>   *and the spirit within me compels me;*
> ^{19}*inside I am like bottled-up wine,*
>   *like new wineskins ready to burst.*
> ^{20}*I must speak and find relief;*
>   *I must open my lips and reply.*"
>
> JOB 32:15–20

Eliphaz had opened these debates in chapters four and five and referenced a message from the spirit—but Eliphaz had discounted that message. The spirit's message had been too ugly, too unpredictable. So Eliphaz had discarded the spirit's message in favor of the Standard View.

Elihu now opened a new phase in this dialogue, and he, too, spoke with the spirit's prompting. He briefly mentioned this source in verse eight, but now he was more explicit in verse eighteen. The spirit compelled him to speak. The pressure to speak welled up within him like new wine threatening to burst through its wineskin. The language here is not just that of a young buck chomping at the bit to have his say—the language is that of a prophet compelled by the spirit to speak and not be silent. Jeremiah used similar words to describe his ministry. Here is how he phrased it:

> ^{9}*But if I say, "I will not mention his word*
>   *or speak anymore in his name,"*
>   *his word is in my heart like a fire,*
>   *a fire shut up in my bones.*
>   *I am weary of holding it in;*

> *indeed, I cannot.*
>
> JEREMIAH 20:9

Other prophets expressed similar pressure to respond to the spirit's direction. Psalm 39:3 and Acts 4:20 provide more examples of this spirit-induced compulsion to speak on God's behalf. Such a spirit even compelled Saul (1 Samuel 19:23–24) and Balaam (Numbers 22–24) to become reluctant prophets.

ELIHU COMES AS A FRIEND

From what stance did Elihu speak? Was he a reluctant prophet? Was he a deranged prophet, compelled unwillingly to speak on God's behalf? Was he a judge? What sort of prophet was Elihu?

Elihu answered that question himself in the following verses:

> ^{21}*"I will show partiality to no one,*
> *nor will I flatter anyone;*
> ^{22}*for if I were skilled in flattery,*
> *my Maker would soon take me away.*
>
> ^{1}*"But now, Job, listen to my words;*
> *pay attention to everything I say.*
> ^{2}*I am about to open my mouth;*
> *my words are on the tip of my tongue.*
> ^{3}*My words come from an upright heart;*
> *my lips sincerely speak what I know.*
> ^{4}*The Spirit of God has made me;*
> *the breath of the Almighty gives me life.*
> ^{5}*Answer me then, if you can;*
> *stand up and argue your case before me.*
> ^{6}*I am the same as you in God's sight;*
> *I too am a piece of clay.*
> ^{7}*No fear of me should alarm you,*

nor should my hand be heavy upon you."

JOB 32:21–33:7

Elihu was not a prophet-judge or even a prophet-seer. Elihu was a friend.

He had not come to this discussion with a bias—partiality would not be part of his repertoire. Job should not be afraid of Elihu. Elihu's words are in part God's response, prompted by the spirit, but it is a response that came through Elihu and not from the divine voice itself. Elihu was merely human. Elihu's words should not weigh Job down. If Job had concerns with Elihu's words, Job should speak up.

This is a very different approach than that of the three friends. Eliphaz, Bildad, and Zophar gave authoritative speeches and would brook no debate. From the closing sentence of his first speech, Eliphaz made it very clear that the Standard View was the consensus view and that there was no room to disagree with that approach (5:27). Job's only option was to apply the consensus interpretation to his own life. From that opening, the three friends had denigrated Job's words (8:2; 11:2–3; 15:2–4), called on him to conform to the consensus view without further debate (8:8–10; 15:17–18; 20:4, 29), called upon God himself to shut Job up (11:5–6), insulted Job's intelligence (11:12), and exhorted him to stop talking (18:2).

Elihu had a completely different approach. He did not insult Job but befriended him: I am a man like you. We are the same before God. There is no cause to be afraid of me.

ELIHU LEAVES A DOOR OPEN FOR DISAGREEMENT

Elihu also did not call Job to be silent before his message but to instead speak if he had issues with anything Elihu said. He called upon Job to prepare a response and even confront Elihu if need be (33:5).

The first three friends had demanded conformity and silence, and in response, they got opposition and vigorous debate. On the other hand, Elihu invited open dialogue and disagreement—but as we will see, Job did not argue with Elihu. As a result, unlike the messages from mortals, Elihu's message from the spirit did not spark a passionate fight.

BOTH GENTLE AND FIRM

Elihu's approach here was gentle, but that does not mean that it was one of platitudes and generalities. On the contrary, Elihu had a strong message to share, which we'll get into in the next chapter. However, it is important to note that this strong message came from a place of equality before God. It came from a place of sincerity and uprightness, without bias, flattery, or judgment, and it was open to disagreement and invited discussion.

Notice in 33:1 that Elihu even called Job by name. It is a small thing, but Elihu was the only friend that used Job's name. Elihu approached Job with intimacy and kindness, but that intimacy did not prevent him from speaking the truth. Gentleness and firm clarity can intermingle.

This was a good start—but where was Elihu's speech going?

50

ELIHU HAS AN ISSUE WITH JOB

As we have seen, Elihu started his speech kindly, promising to be different than Job's other three friends and opening himself up to opposition if Job disagreed with anything Elihu had to say. So far, so good.

A kind and gentle beginning is a good start, but then Elihu did something that is rather surprising. Elihu had an issue with Job, and he didn't sugarcoat it. Elihu was a gentle soul, but he was also a passionate and direct person as well.

Here's what he had to say to Job:

> *⁸"But you have said in my hearing—*
> *I heard the very words—*
> *⁹'I am pure, I have done no wrong;*
> *I am clean and free from sin.*
> *¹⁰Yet God has found fault with me;*
> *he considers me his enemy.*
> *¹¹He fastens my feet in shackles;*
> *he keeps close watch on all my paths.'"*
>
> Job 33:8–11

Did Job really say these things?

It is easier to understand Elihu's statements here if we understand that he was not making three or four different charges against Job but rather one. Elihu's concern was that Job had said several things that together arrive at a dangerous conclusion. A summary of his charge is simply this: Job said that he was innocent but that God found fault with him, and therefore, there was something wrong with God's justice.[111]

This is the trap that the Standard View framework had led Job into. The Standard View posited a scenario where either Job deserved his trouble or God was an unfair judge. In 32:2, we read that Elihu was angry because Job had fallen into this trap, taken the self-defense posture in this artificial debate, and therefore tried to prove that God had made a mistake.

We don't have to wonder if Elihu was reasonable with this charge—Job had made a similar summary in 27:1–6. Ultimately, Job's error accepted the courtroom logic of the Standard View and agreed that someone had to be found guilty for what had happened in Job's life. This false dilemma was a trap, and Elihu was upset with Job for falling into it.

GOD IS NOT A HOLLYWOOD GENIE

The Standard View assumes that people can control God. According to this cause-and-effect philosophy, righteous behavior is a magical power that can force the divine Creator to act in the service of people. As a result, God becomes a person's private genie. Righteousness thus becomes the secret recipe for releasing and commanding the enslaved genie. (By the way, I am using genie here in the simplistic Hollywood animated movie sense, not the original Arabic sense, which has very different connotations.)

God is not, however, a genie. God is not under humanity's control in any circumstances. Job had accepted the Standard View's promise that humans could use righteousness to control the divine. He had complained that God had failed to live up to his obligations within that framework—and that framework was wrong. The friends were wrong to assume that Job deserved his fate, and Job was wrong to assume that his righteousness could earn him control of the divine.

Elihu addressed this issue directly:

> [12]*"But I tell you, in this you are not right,*

---

111 See Job 19:7 and 27:2 for comparison.

for God is greater than any mortal."

Job 33:12

God does not do humanity's bidding. God is greater than we are. And therein lies the fundamental flaw in the Standard View. The illusion of control that it offers is founded on a completely false premise.

WHAT A DIFFERENCE A FEW WORDS MAKE!

However, just because humanity does not control God, it does not mean that God fails to speak. God does speak to people in a variety of different ways. Elihu went on to articulate this very point:

> *¹³"Why do you complain to him*
>   *that he responds to no one's words?*
> *¹⁴For God does speak—now one way, now another—*
>   *though no one perceives it.*
> *¹⁵In a dream, in a vision of the night,*
>   *when deep sleep falls on people*
>   *as they slumber in their beds,*
> *¹⁶he may speak in their ears*
>   *and terrify them with warnings,*
> *¹⁷to turn them from wrongdoing*
>   *and keep them from pride,*
> *¹⁸to preserve them from the pit,*
>   *their lives from perishing by the sword."*

Job 33:13–18

God speaking to humanity through visions in the night sounds frightening, but the message is slightly different in Hebrew. In verse sixteen, the NIV describes God as speaking in a manner intended to "terrify them with warnings." The word in Hebrew does not mean "to terrify." The Hebrew word means "to seal." God sends these dreams to "seal" people with warnings. The idea is that through dreams, God leaves a seal, or a mark, noting the warning that God has provided.[112]

In the very next verse, the NIV speaks to this message as one designed "to turn them from wrongdoing" (33:17), but in Hebrew, the word also does not directly translate as "wrongdoing." The word in Hebrew literally means "deeds." God sends such messages to turn a person from their deeds. Those deeds may be wrong (thus the NIV's translation), but not necessarily so. They may simply be deeds headed in one direction, and for some reason, God wants the individual to go elsewhere. The second line of verse seventeen makes this point clearer as it describes how God intends these messages to "turn them from [their deeds]" and "keep them from pride." It does not say that this person has committed pride. Rather, God's message is preventive.

Applying what we have learned about parallelism to this passage makes it clear that these dreams are not meant to turn a soul from an already committed sin but to prevent that person from continuing down a path that could lead to pride and a bad end.

The first reading of the NIV (and many other modern translations) suggests that Elihu was describing harsh visions that rebuke and terrify already sinning people into returning to a righteous path. In that sense, the modern translations have bent the original Hebrew so that Elihu seems to be making a Standard View argument. But Elihu was describing not an angry God scaring people straight but a loving God delivering messages to help people avoid getting into trouble to begin with. God is not the judgmental terror of many modern English translations but a loving shepherd providing guidance.

What a difference a few words make!

PERHAPS A SUBTLE CORRECTION FOR ELIPHAZ?

It is interesting that Elihu's description of God speaking through dreams can also be read as a critique of Eliphaz's opening speech.

In chapter four, the spirit had come in the night with a warning for Eliphaz. The spirit had warned Eliphaz right at the beginning of this book not to go down the dogmatic Standard View road. The spirit had made a

---

112 See Reyburn, 613.

strong argument that the Standard View is not a universal truth—the world is more ambiguous and even darker than the Standard View allows.

God had spoken these warnings by way of a nighttime vision. Eliphaz, however, did not listen. Later, Job had warned Eliphaz (as well as the other two friends) that "you should fear the sword yourselves; for wrath will bring punishment by the sword" (19:29).

God had warned Eliphaz by the spirit's nighttime vision. Job had warned his three friends by referencing a sword.

Now Elihu warned the three friends a third time by linking the idea of nighttime visions with Job's use of sword imagery (33:15-18).

God, Job, and Elihu all had the same message of warning for Eliphaz. Elihu is the one that tied the language of all three speakers together.

ANOTHER WAY THAT GOD SPEAKS

God, however, does not speak only by way of dreams and mysterious visions. Instead, God speaks in various ways—"now one way, now another" (33:14)—and this dream warning is only one of God's ways.

The next way Elihu described is more challenging and sounds like a classic Standard View scenario:

> ^{19}*"Or someone may be chastened on a bed of pain*
> *with constant distress in their bones,*
> ^{20}*so that their body finds food repulsive*
> *and their soul loathes the choicest meal.*
> ^{21}*Their flesh wastes away to nothing,*
> *and their bones, once hidden, now stick out.*
> ^{22}*They draw near to the pit,*
> *and their life to the messengers of death."*
>
> JOB 33:19–22

This is classic Standard View language and hardly needs any commentary, but Elihu was not done with just these four simple verses. He was not positing the Standard View's cut-and-dried harshness as one of God's speaking styles. There are more than just these four verses to Elihu's message. He further expanded on this idea with these lines:

> [23] "Yet if there is an angel at their side,
>   a messenger, one out of a thousand,
>   sent to tell them how to be upright,
> [24] and he is gracious to that person and says to God,
>   'Spare them from going down to the pit;
>   I have found a ransom for them—
> [25] let their flesh be renewed like a child's;
>   it is restored as in the days of their youth'—
> [26] then that person can pray to God and find favor with him,
>   they will see God's face and shout for joy;
>   he will restore them to full well-being.
> [27] Then they will go to others and say,
>   'I sinned, I have perverted what is right,
>   but I did not get what I deserved.
> [28] God has delivered me from going down to the pit,
>   and I shall live to enjoy the light of life.'"
>
> JOB 33:23–28

Wow! Unlike the other three friends, Elihu bought into this idea of a Redeemer! He described not just a mediator but someone who would also provide a ransom: the Redeemer that Job longed for.

Redemption without punishment is not in the vocabulary of the Standard View. Notice that Elihu did not describe a scenario where the sinner had done something to earn their forgiveness. Rather, he described a scene where a person needed redemption and a heavenly mediator sought and found the required payment.

Redemption was where Job finally put his faith and hope, and this idea of redemption was also where Elihu concluded this section.

GOD IS NOT ANGRY—HE PROTECTS

There is some risk of misinterpreting Elihu's point here as simply a gentler version of the Standard View. I found this approach articulated in several modern commentaries. In summary, this interpretation understands Elihu's speech as making these points: first, God warns, then punishes, but God always communicates in some form of divine judgment.

God, in this formulation, is the stereotypically angry deity in the sky dispensing warnings and punishments to a slave-like humanity trapped in the gaze of an unblinking omnipresence.

This very problematic view of God was what Job had complained about in his fourth speech:

> *²⁷"You fasten my feet in shackles;*
> > *you keep close watch on all my paths*
> > *by putting marks on the soles of my feet."*
>
> JOB 13:27

But this problematic understanding of God is not what Elihu was advocating for. He did describe God as issuing warnings and punishments, but not to release his anger and vengeance. Elihu went on to explain:

> *²⁹"God does all these things to a person—*
> > *twice, even three times—*
> *³⁰to turn them back from the pit,*
> > *that the light of life may shine on them."*
>
> JOB 33:29–30

Do you see the difference that Elihu was articulating? God's actions may be very similar to what the Standard View proposes—he warns and punishes—but God's purpose and heart behind these actions are very different from what the three friends were advocating.

God delivers warnings in the night "to preserve them from the pit" (33:18). The person being punished had been "draw[ing] near to the pit" (33:22). The mediator found a ransom to "spare them from going down to the pit" (33:24). The saved soul rejoiced that "God has delivered me from going down to the pit" (33:28). God does these things "to turn them back from the pit" (33:30).

How many references to the pit do we need before we see that everything God does is to save people from the pit?

Everything God does is predicated on his desire to save. The alternative to the pit, the joy that a person is saved for, is the "light of life" (33:28, 30).

GOD IS LOVE

Do you see the difference here? The Standard View is about appeasing the divine—pacifying an angry and dangerous god. This god sounds more like the storm deities and other pagan gods of the ancient Mesopotamian world than they do the God of compassion and mercy revealed in scripture and brought to its clearest fulfillment in Christ. God's different communication routes that Elihu described here are focused not on punishment but rather on the corrections of a shepherd and the loving discipline of a compassionate father, founded on one underlying goal: to save his children from the pit and bring them to the light.

In other words: God is love.

WHAT DOES THIS HAVE TO DO WITH JOB—OR ME?

Elihu's ideas are fantastic. But how did they apply to Job? Job was not on his way down to the pit when these troubles occurred. How did Elihu's ideas fit with Job's story?

As I came to this place in my own study of Job, I also found myself asking the question, Okay, how does this apply to me? While not perfect, I was not, to my knowledge, headed in any direction even remotely tilted toward the pit. Was there something in my heart, in my character, in my marriage, or in my future that would have led to spiritual disaster had my daughter's relentless medical crises not exploded into our lives? Was there a lurking danger so dark that, in addition to my daughter's medical issues, I (or my wife) also needed my wife's catalog of surprise medical issues, an assault outside the hospital late at night, occupational challenges, financial challenges, and so on?

Elihu had refocused the lens slightly. He had adjusted how God's actions should be interpreted, but he had not yet provided anything that could be explicitly applied to Job's situation—but he was not done talking yet either.

PAUSING FOR FEEDBACK

Before Elihu went on, however, he paused to see if Job had an issue with anything he had said so far.

> ^{31}*"Pay attention, Job, and listen to me;*
> *be silent, and I will speak.*
> ^{32}*If you have anything to say, answer me;*
> *speak up, for I want to vindicate you.*
> ^{33}*But if not, then listen to me;*
> *be silent, and I will teach you wisdom."*
>
> JOB 33:31–33

Elihu had set a high bar for himself, but he also repeated the invitation to the two-way dialogue he had first offered in 33:5–7. There, he had called Job to prepare himself to answer or even confront Elihu. Here, Elihu requested that Job speak up if he had anything to say. If Job had nothing to say, then he should sit back and let Elihu continue.

As part of his plan to continue, Elihu promised that what he had to offer was wisdom. The boldness of describing oneself as wise may put some modern readers off and may further contribute to the misinterpretation that Elihu was as prideful and dogmatic as the other three friends. However, it is important to recognize that Elihu's boldness does not automatically justify our dismissing him. What was he bold about?

So far, he had boldly asserted that God is a God not of punishment but of salvation. God's mission is not to punish wrongdoers but to help them avoid the pit or redeem them if they're already there. God is love—that is a message worth being bold about! That is a message worth calling wisdom.

Job had no issue with what Elihu had said so far, and so Elihu was free to continue.

REFOCUSING ON JOB'S FRIENDS

> ^{1}*Then Elihu said:*
> ^{2}*"Hear my words, you wise men;*
> *listen to me, you men of learning.*
> ^{3}*For the ear tests words*
> *as the tongue tastes food.*
> ^{4}*Let us discern for ourselves what is right;*

let us learn together what is good."

JOB 34:1–4

Elihu had started his speech addressing the friends, and then in 32:16, he had switched to solely addressing Job. Now he had readjusted his focus again and was back to addressing the friends: "you men of learning."[113]

As Elihu did so in 34:3, he quoted Job's own words from 12:11 back at the friends. The effect is subtle, but by using Job's own words to address the friends, Elihu was creating solidarity between himself and Job. He will go on from here to address the friends' criticisms of Job. He will do so from a position alongside Job and not in opposition to him.

A DIFFICULT BALANCING ACT: EMOTIONAL CANDOR VERSUS WISE RESTRAINT

This next section is difficult. It directly addresses some of the parts of Job's speeches that were the rawest and the most disturbing.

Unlike the friends, Elihu will quote Job accurately in this section, and some of the things that Job said were of genuine concern. As we looked at previously, some of what Job said walked right up to almost slandering God, and perhaps even crossed over that line. Still, we also saw, forecasting the end of the book of Job, how God's mercy allowed for the emotional context of Job's accusatory language. Grace covered Job in these things—but if no one ever mentioned what was problematic about Job's emotionally charged language, readers might overlook the fact that grace was required at all.

We mentioned this grace as we started our study of Elihu. If no one said anything about some of Job's statements, later readers could take away the message that highly emotional situations make extreme irreverence permissible and maybe even advisable. However, the problem is that if God himself were to correct some of these statements, a later reader could take away the other problematic message that God does not permit honesty in moments of deep pain. In this scenario, the model for godliness would be a plastic

---

113 The differentiation of plural versus singular audience based on the Hebrew pronouns as provided by Reyburn, 624.

artificiality. The suffering saint would seek to master a stoical silence rather than reach out in genuine candor to a loving heavenly Father.

The solution to this dilemma appears to be: let Elihu address it. He could thread the path between both extremes. His words would be wise, but to avoid the absolutist response that would inevitably result if God spoke them, they would instead be offered by Elihu, who was just a friend. He was someone who was not a threat to Job physically or spiritually (33:6–7).

Elihu handled his task well. Job did not resist anything Elihu said. God will not correct Elihu in the final chapter either when he rebukes the other three friends. Let's look at how Elihu's wisdom unfolded in this following speech, which Elihu addressed to Eliphaz, Bildad, and Zophar.

51

JOB CALLS GOD A LIAR

ELIHU CHARGED JOB next with something pretty serious. Here's the charge in Elihu's own words:

> ^{5}"*Job says, 'I am innocent,*
> *but God denies me justice.*
> ^{6}*Although I am right,*
> *I am considered a liar;*
> *although I am guiltless,*
> *his arrow inflicts an incurable wound.'"*[114]
>
> JOB 34:5–6

These are incredibly serious charges. Did Job really say these things?

---

114 Interestingly, the Hebrew does not say "his arrow." It says "my arrow." This appears to have been an interpretative problem for some modern translations, and so the Hebrew "my" has been switched to "his." The verse is apparently easier to understand if it is God's arrow that afflicts Job and not Job's own arrow. There is no need, however, to alter the Hebrew. The arrow here is clearly not literal (Job was never shot in this story), and as a metaphor, it is open to interpretation based on the context. Job's own arrow can simply mean the arrow—that is, the fate, the pain, the source of trouble, or the source of injury and death that was personal to Job—had inflicted an incurable wound. "His arrow" means God sent the arrow. "My arrow" means it was the arrow meant for Job. Either way, the verse comes out meaning the same thing. "My arrow" just happens to be the way the Hebrew text phrased it and therefore how modern translations ought to have left it.

Elihu lifted Job's first statement—that he was innocent and God had denied him justice—straight from Job's speech in chapter twenty-seven.[115]

What about the claim that others consider Job a liar? In most English translations, it is very easy to trace this claim back to the implications of the friends' speeches. Job had proclaimed his innocence while Job's three friends had sought to prove the opposite. Eliphaz's third speech in chapter twenty-two had been particularly forceful in this regard.

But here is the rub. Our translation phrases this statement passively: "I am considered a liar." On the whole, this is relatively innocuous. But the Hebrew is subtly and significantly different. A more literal translation would read, "He lies about my case." He—who? He—God. God lied about Job's case.

God lied?

Did Job call God a liar?

In 27:2, Job complained that God had denied him justice. Then, in 30:20–22, Job charged God with being the author of his troubles. Finally, in 31:35, Job cried out that he wanted his accuser to put the charges against him in writing. What had elicited these statements?

The Standard View. Bad things only happen to bad people. According to the Standard View, God's role in the world is to bless the good and curse the bad. Furthermore, others can identify who is good and bad by observing what happens to them. By the Standard View's logic, a blessed person—one who is happy and successful—must be a righteous person. A cursed person must be bad, whether or not others can readily identify the sufferer's sins. We can deduce the divine testimony about a person by simply counting the blessings or curses that unfold in the person's life. Job's troubles were God's testimony against him. This logic had founded Eliphaz, Bildad, and Zophar's confidence as they had attacked Job. As Eliphaz had sarcastically asked, "Is it for your piety that he rebukes you and brings charges against you?" (22:4). Job's trouble was so severe that Job's first three friends could only conclude that Job was evil beyond anyone's imagination. In Eliphaz's own words, Job's wickedness must be "great" and his sins "endless" (22:5). God's judgment could mean nothing else.

And so, Job wanted justice. He wanted God to stop communicating his

---

115 See 27:1–6.

charges through vague trials that were open to subjective interpretation and to instead put his charges in writing.

So did Job call God a liar? Not explicitly. Search for the word lie, and you will not find it directed at God in Job's speeches. But did Job call God a liar implicitly? Yes. Job's tragedies were God's charges against him, and the charges were false, so by the logic of the Standard View, God must have lied.[116]

ANOTHER ISSUE WITH JOB

We said in the last chapter that this section of Job is difficult. Elihu tackled some tough material. Job was a righteous person, suffering innocently, but some bad theology right at the beginning of this book had seriously distorted God's apparent role in all of Job's troubles. Job had fought through the bad theology to find a place of hope and faith with eternity and redemption to look forward to, but as he waded through the mire of the Standard View, some muck had stuck to his shoes. His conclusion accepted that God did work within the Standard View's framework, that God must have erred in Job's case, and that God must be waiting to correct the error at an unspecified future date, possibly after Job's death. Job's assumption that God had erred was the source of Elihu's anger in 32:2. Job's resolution justified him rather than God. Job would come out okay in the distant end—God's reputation would not.

Elihu was not done with Job yet. He had this yet to say:

> *⁷"Is there anyone like Job,*
> *who drinks scorn like water?*
> *⁸He keeps company with evildoers;*
> *he associates with the wicked.*
> *⁹For he says, 'There is no profit*

---

116 It is worth noting that this charge was too much even for many ancient scribes to stomach, and therefore many ancient manuscripts change "he lies about my case" to something less confrontational, such as the NIV's "I am considered a liar." In other words, this change was not made just by sensitive modern translators but by many ancient scribes as well who simply passed this change on to modern translations.

in trying to please God.'"

JOB 34:7–9

"Drinks scorn like water." In English, this sounds like Job was receiving a great deal of scorn. In Hebrew, the phrase is an idiom that means "he deals scorn out freely." Thus, a literal translation like the one above may not be the best here. A more meaningful one for a modern reader might be "Who is like Job, who pours out scorn like water?" or "Who else is like Job, who is a fountain of scorn?" The point is that, around Job, scorn was an abundant liquid.

It is in this way that Job associated with evildoers. Elihu was not charging Job with doing evil but voicing concern that Job's words had aligned him with evildoers. The specific charge is that Job stated that "there is no profit in trying to please God."

Once again, did Job actually say this? Here again, Elihu was summarizing Job's words, specifically Job's points from 9:22–24, 21:17–34, and 24:1.

By focusing on self-defense within the framework of the Standard View, Job had achieved personal hope but at the expense of God's reputation. Further, he had candidly stated that devotion to God is profitless and, therefore, one could infer, pointless.

These were Elihu's two charges.

THE MODERN PROBLEM WITH ELIHU

The mere whiff of charges against Job solidifies Elihu's marginalization in modern commentaries and his classification as just another critical friend. However, there is a key difference between Elihu's charges and the three friends' attacks. The three friends sought to find the source of Job's suffering and put the blame on Job. They intended to diagnose Job's tragedies within the cause-and-effect logic of the Standard View. They were looking for sins that predated Job's suffering and therefore explained it.

In contrast, Elihu dismissed this punishment paradigm and explained that God speaks in various ways, but regardless of his timing and method, his purpose is always the same: to save people.

Elihu's charges were not about Job's theoretical misdeeds that might have earned him these punishments.

Elihu's corrections were focused on what Job said as a result of his tragedies and as a result of buying, at least partially, into the God-versus-Job dilemma that his friends' philosophy had created. Job's error, ultimately, was a theological error facilitated by a kind of naivete in the heat of debate. The Standard View created an inevitable God-versus-Job scenario. At times, Job was able to shake off the illogic of this view and argue against it, but at other times he succumbed to the simplistic formula. When he did submit to the formula, he justified himself instead of God, and so in his candor he cast doubt on the value of serving God.

SPEAKING OF THEOLOGY

There is a tendency in some Christian circles to dismiss theology as a tiresome source of endless arguments. The history of useless debates over the centuries regarding generally irrelevant matters makes this disdain seem reasonable. But theology, spiritual philosophy, a mature understanding of the nature of God—let scholars debate the fine distinctions between these ideas, but for practical living-my-life purposes, they are one—are of great significance for every believer. They shape and color the lens through which Christians interpret real life. If an individual believer sees every storm, setback, and phantom pain as punishment from the Almighty, that worldview will significantly impact that believer's faith and life. If God is a terror, the believer will be terrified or, depending on their personality, rebellious and resentful. In neither case is trust a reasonable outcome to expect—theology matters.

Elihu's theology taught him that God is a God who intends to save people from the pit. His theology taught him that God is love. Five times in chapter thirty-three, Elihu made that point.

Elihu had an issue with Job's conflicted theology—a theology that sought to find a way beyond the Standard View and succeeded at redeeming Job but failed to go all the way. Job had not grasped that God is not the keen punisher that the friends had presented him as. Rather, God is a savior. God is a rock to cling to and not the crushing stone that the Standard View implies. God himself is the Redeemer.

Listen to Elihu's practical take on this theology:

10 "So listen to me, you men of understanding.

> *Far be it from God to do evil,*
> *for the Almighty to do wrong.*
> *^{11}He repays everyone for what they have done;*
> *he brings on them what their conduct deserves.*
> *^{12}It is unthinkable that God would do wrong,*
> *that the Almighty would pervert justice.*
> *^{13}Who appointed him over the earth?*
> *Who put him in charge of the whole world?*
> *^{14}If it were his intention*
> *and he withdrew his spirit and breath,*
> *^{15}all humanity would perish together*
> *and mankind would return to the dust."*
>
> JOB 34:10–15

This passage is still directed at "you men," that is, at minimum, the three friends. The message is clear: God does not do evil. The idea that God had committed an injustice in Job's case was inadvertently rooted in the false dilemma the friends had set up to prove the opposite. Because of the three friends' false theology, confusion now reigned. Was God wrong? Had God miscarried justice in Job's case? Had God committed evil?

The answer is no. God cannot do evil. It is unthinkable. In fact, God is so focused on caring for people that if he withdrew his attention, all living things would perish, and all living things would return to the dust. God is the God of creating, sustaining, and saving.

And Elihu, we see, was very interested in making a case for God's goodness, even amid Job's trials. Theology matters after all. But Elihu had more to say about Job's situation than refining points of theology for the three friends. He had a message for Job as well.

52

CULLING THE HERD

As Elihu continued his speech, the "you" in the next verse (34:16) switches back to singular. Elihu was continuing his argument in defense of God but had changed audiences and was now, once again, addressing Job personally.

> *¹⁶"If you have understanding, hear this;*
> *listen to what I say.*
> *¹⁷Can he who hates justice govern?*
> *Will you condemn the just and mighty One?*
> *¹⁸Is he not the One who says to kings, 'You are worthless,'*
> *and to nobles, 'You are wicked,'*
> *¹⁹who shows no partiality to princes*
> *and does not favor the rich over the poor,*
> *for they are all the work of his hands?*
> *²⁰They die in an instant, in the middle of the night;*
> *the people are shaken and they pass away;*
> *the mighty are removed without human hand."*
>
> Job 34:16–20

The observant reader will notice that verses nineteen and twenty are both unbalanced three-line verses. The Hebrew poetic rhythm is off here. "[F]or they are all the work of his hands" stands out, as does "the mighty are removed without human hand." Both of these third lines refer to God's hands, albeit engaged in different activities. The English reader might skim over this detail. However, for the careful reader of the original text, this rhythmically awkward third line in two back-to-back verses stands out. This structure highlights God's engagement in both the creation (34:19) and ongoing management (34:20) of humanity. Elihu did not depict God as an impersonal judge dealing out punishments but as a concerned Creator caring for his creation, just as a rancher culls his herd where necessary to save the remaining population.

But how did this description of God help Job? Was Elihu implying that Job needed to be removed "without human hand" for some reason? What possible reason could there be?

GOD DOESN'T NEED A COURTROOM

Elihu was not quite ready to tread on this mystery yet. He continued establishing God's role as an orderly care provider who does act justly when addressing evil, but he does so in his own time. Here's how Elihu explained it:

> ^{21}*"His eyes are on the ways of mortals;*
> *he sees their every step.*
> ^{22}*There is no deep shadow, no utter darkness,*
> *where evildoers can hide.*
> ^{23}*God has no need to examine men further,*
> *that they should come before him for judgment.*
> ^{24}*Without inquiry he shatters the mighty*
> *and sets up others in their place.*
> ^{25}*Because he takes note of their deeds,*
> *he overthrows them in the night and they are crushed.*
> ^{26}*He punishes them for their wickedness*
> *where everyone can see them,*
> ^{27}*because they turned from following him*
> *and had no regard for any of his ways.*
> ^{28}*They caused the cry of the poor to come before him,*
> *so that he heard the cry of the needy."*
>
> JOB 34:21–28

That is great. But how did that help Job? How did that relate to Job's circumstances?

One key point of contact with Job's situation is found in verses twenty-three and twenty-four: God does not need a courtroom to investigate suspects. God knows the deeds of humanity. No inquiry is required. He executes judgment overnight, and there is no dark place where evildoers can hide from the divine hand.

The connection between God's omniscient judgment and Job's situation is twofold.

First, disaster had struck Job suddenly, from multiple sides, in the kind of overwhelming fashion that Elihu described, and without inquiry or presentation of charges.

Second, Job's desire for a hearing was pointless since God does not give hearings, and they would serve no purpose from God's perspective. Hearings would satisfy only the demands of humanity, and God is not subject to humanity's demands.

This is a disaster. If Elihu had intended to provide Job with at least a partial solution to his situation, he had instead drifted into a restatement of the friends' cold-hearted judgment. But Elihu had promised that he would not answer Job with the friends' arguments (32:14). It is important to keep Elihu's words in context. This passage describing judgment without trial merely rebalances Job's implied argument that this world is chaotic and meaningless, and that the only hope for personal redemption will be in the next life. By contrast, Elihu had been at pains to articulate that God is actively engaged in the world, in this life, to save people. From creating the world to managing oppressors to serving as a heavenly overseer to those in need, God's hands have been and are still actively involved. He is a hands-on God—and not one who does evil.

GOD IS COMPLICATED

What then are we to make of Job's situation? Was Elihu drifting into describing the kind of black-and-white, cause-and-effect predictable world that the three friends were supporting? If Elihu's speech ended here in 34:28, that would appear to be the case. But Elihu was not done speaking.

> [29] *"But if he remains silent, who can condemn him?*
> *If he hides his face, who can see him?"*
>
> JOB 34:29A

Ah. This is closer to Job's situation. God does not always act in a way that people recognize as appropriate or timely. Sometimes he does not act when it appears that he should. Or at least he does not appear to act.

God is God.

God is love.

God is also complicated.

And God does not always explain himself.

A TRAVESTY OF TRANSLATION

If God's actions at times appear to be inscrutable, putting him on trial is not an option at our disposal. God is God. He is God not just of individuals but also of entire peoples. Elihu goes on in the following verse to relate this in plain language.

> *Yet he is over man and nation alike,*
> [30] *to keep the godless from ruling,*
> > *from laying snares for the people.*
> [31] *Suppose someone says to God,*
> > *'I am guilty but I will offend no more.*
> [32] *Teach me what I cannot see;*
> > *if I have done wrong, I will not do so again.'*
> [33] *Should God then reward you on your terms,*
> > *when you refuse to repent?*
> > *You must decide, not I;*
> > *so tell me what you know."*
>
> JOB 34:29B–33

The phrase "Should God then reward you on your terms, when you refuse to repent?" is misleading. It implies that Job had sinned, that God's action (or inaction) was a consequence of Job's sin, and that God had no reason to reward Job since Job refused to repent. This is a travesty of translation. It implies that Elihu's view was the Standard View and that he presumed Job was guilty. Almost every translation choice in this passage is an error.[117]

First, the sinner in this passage is not explicitly Job. Elihu began this section with "suppose someone." This is a hypothetical case here, and the translation should continue to refer to a hypothetical person rather than switch to talking to Job directly. Elihu was still just using an example to make a general point, not to attack Job himself.

Second, the terms that this hypothetical person is expecting God to abide by are Standard View terms. That distinction is not clear when the "you" in this verse appears to be targeting Job, who was not a Standard View supporter. But, again, Elihu was providing a generic example. He was asking, "Should God reward a Standard View supporter according to the rules of the Standard View?" That was Elihu's intended meaning.

Third, the phrase "refuse to repent" is not a good translation. The phrase would be better translated as "since you [or better, "since the sinner"] does not like what God does."

Taken altogether, here is how these verses should read:

> "*Suppose someone says to God,*
>   '*I am guilty but I will offend no more.*
> *Teach me what I cannot see.*
>   *If I have done wrong, I will not do so again.*'
> *Should God then reward this person on their terms,*
>   *when they do not like what God does?*
> *You must decide, not I;*
>   *so tell me what you know.*"

With this translation in mind, we can see how Elihu could simply be carrying on the theme that he started in previous verses: God is God and not subject to humanity's demands. According to the Standard View's rules, humans can manipulate God and force him to grant them their wishes like an enslaved Hollywood-style genie. According to the Standard View, humanity's words and behavior are the inputs that dictate God's programmed response.

God, in this formulation, is an unthinking, magical being without free

---

117 For technical references backing my commentary on 34:29-33, see Reyburn, 640-643.

will or autonomy, controlled by his own creation. If things are going badly for a person, it is that person's fault for not entering the correct input of righteous action that would cause the preprogrammed cosmos to spit out happiness and prosperity. In this formulation, God is just a submissive cosmic computer program. He set up the rules and is now somehow bound by them.

Elihu poured contempt on this viewpoint. This is what Elihu asked: If someone doesn't like what's happening in their life, can they then just find out what caused the glitch, fix the broken code, and get their preprogrammed God back up and running to produce predictable and comfortable outcomes? Is that how the world should work? Is this the kind of God we should serve?

As Elihu put it:

> "You must decide, not I;
> so tell me what you know."
>
> JOB 34:33B

Job had no answer for Elihu. The Standard View is attractive for its predictability, but Job was never a true believer in it. He let its logic color his case against God, but his own life was proof that the Standard View was false. Job's behavior was outstanding by God's own measure —blameless and upright—but his life had turned into a disaster zone.

PEOPLE SAYING BAD THINGS ABOUT JOB

Elihu now addressed some of the bad things people had been saying about Job.

> ³⁴"Men of understanding declare,
> wise men who hear me say to me,
> ³⁵'Job speaks without knowledge;
> his words lack insight.'
> ³⁶Oh, that Job might be tested to the utmost
> for answering like a wicked man!
> ³⁷To his sin he adds rebellion;
> scornfully he claps his hands among us

and multiplies his words against God."

JOB 34:34–37

If we start off assuming Elihu was a bad guy, this passage helps reinforce that view. Wise men had said, in Elihu's hearing, that Job's words lacked insight. Elihu quoted these men, and accurately so,[118] but then he appeared to go on and agree with them. He demanded that Job be tested, calling him a wicked and rebellious person who multiplied his words against God.

There is a problem with understanding this verse: where do we put the quotation marks? Ancient Hebrew scribes did not use quotation marks, and the original text did not include them. Where we choose to put them today is a translation problem that is inevitably influenced by interpretative biases. If you have decided that Elihu is a bad guy, then having him quote the friends and then support their views in his own words makes sense—but there is nothing in the original Hebrew text to suggest that Elihu's quotation stops at verse thirty-five.

The entire passage from verse thirty-five through thirty-seven should be taken as Elihu quoting the friends. There is nothing in Hebrew to contradict this interpretation, but there are strong reasons that support it beyond my own opinion.

First, it would be out of character for Elihu to attack Job. He had warned Job that he would challenge him, but Elihu had also insisted that he would do so gently and without using the friends' arguments. To take verses thirty-six and thirty-seven as Elihu's own opinion (as the NIV's placement of quotation marks implies) would mean that Elihu's attitude and beliefs had suddenly changed. He had gone from helping Job to assaulting him. That interpretation does not make sense.

Second, the things that Elihu said in verses thirty-six and thirty-seven were, in fact, quotes from the friends. They were not Elihu's new opinions but rather quotations of what the friends had actually said. The wish that Job would be tested can be found on Zophar's lips in 11:5–6. The charge that Job answers like a wicked person can be found, among other places, in Eliphaz's speeches in 15:4–6 and 22:4–5. The charges of rebelling, scornfully clapping his hands, and multiplying words against God summarize several

---

118 See, for example, Eliphaz's words in 15:1–3.

of the friends' speeches. The friends had the hardest time accepting the idea that a person in pain could address the Almighty God with Job's raw candor. Anything other than formulaic obedience—fortified by a measure of false confession and theatrical repentance if necessary—was rebellious and dangerous and undermined piety (15:4–6). Job's transparency and honesty with his Maker was something they did not accept.

All three verses of 35:35–37 are a quotation. These are things that "men of understanding" and "wise men who hear me"—that is, wise men that are sitting right here listening to this speech—have said (34:10, 34). These claims were not what distant, mysterious people had said. They were what Eliphaz, Bildad, and Zophar had said, men who were present as Elihu called them out on it. Elihu was talking to Job, but he was talking about what the three friends had been saying.

So Elihu was dealing with a collection of nasty things that the other three friends had said about Job. How did Elihu intend to help Job in the face of these troubles?

53

THINK BIGGER

Faced with the three friends' bad behavior, Elihu had called them out on their false statements in the previous chapter. But moving forward, Elihu will not address the three friends' verbal abuse of the suffering Job any further. And, surprisingly, he did not focus on comforting Job amid that abuse either. Instead, Elihu completely changed the topic. Look at where he took this conversation next.

> *¹Then Elihu said:*
> *²"Do you think this is just?*
>   *You say, 'I am in the right, not God.'*
> *³Yet you ask him, 'What profit is it to me,*
>   *and what do I gain by not sinning?'"*
>
> Job 35:1–3

As we examined in the last chapter, Job wanted justice—to be cleared by God. Instead, he got false charges from his friends that added to his pain.

Job's whole situation starts to beg the question, Why live righteously at all? If trouble can relentlessly pile up on someone of such good character as Job, what hope is there for any of us?

That is the question that Job's three friends feared. Job's life challenged the reliability of the Standard View. If the Standard View fails, how can we know how to live? If punishment becomes arbitrary and blessings are no longer automatic, then what are the implications for society?

Job's life and words risked undermining piety for all people (15:4).

As we saw in the last chapter, the three friends wanted judgment to come upon Job—the sooner, the better—to shut Job up. On the other hand, Job wanted justice for himself—the sooner, the better—to shut his friends up. Both the judgment and justice positions are human-centric, and Elihu's method for addressing both Job and his friends was to take them beyond mere human-scale considerations.

Here's how he tackled this challenge:

> *⁴"I would like to reply to you*
> *and to your friends with you.*
> *⁵Look up at the heavens and see;*
> *gaze at the clouds so high above you.*
> *⁶If you sin, how does that affect him?*
> *If your sins are many, what does that do to him?*
> *⁷If you are righteous, what do you give to him,*
> *or what does he receive from your hand?*
> *⁸Your wickedness only affects humans like yourself,*
> *and your righteousness only other people."*
>
> JOB 35:4–8

As Elihu dug deeper into Job's situation, he took the conversation beyond human-scale considerations.

Look at the heavens.

Change your perspective.

There.

Now.

With that perspective in view, consider this: where is the balance really? How do your actions, good or bad, affect God?

With your eyes on the clouds—we have not even gone as high as the stars yet—with your eyes on just the clouds, consider how much your good or bad acts really affect God.

With the cosmos in view, our actions seem irrelevant.

Just looking at the clouds makes the Standard View suspect.

FROM NEW MOTIVES TO A NEW CONTEXT

Elihu had introduced a new perspective on God's motives in chapter thirty-three: his motive was not to judge but love. Here, Elihu introduced a new perspective on God's context, which is not human but divine.

Elihu will return to these two ideas, putting both motive and context together, but first he stepped back and spoke about a different sort of person: the sort of person who directly defies God and does not reach out to him.

A SUDDEN DETOUR

> [9] "People cry out under a load of oppression;
> they plead for relief from the arm of the powerful."
>
> JOB 35:9

They cry out—to who?

Not to God. The next line makes that clear. Elihu was not talking about Job. He was talking about a class of people who do not reach out to God during times of trouble. He went on to explain further:

> [10] "But no one says, 'Where is God my Maker,
> who gives songs in the night,
> [11] who teaches us more than he teaches the beasts of the earth
> and makes us wiser than the birds in the sky?'"
>
> JOB 35:10–11

Elihu was talking about a class of people very different than Job. They were even different than the sinners that Job's friends discussed. These were not Standard View adherents but ungodly people with no regard for order in the universe or the existence and involvement of the Creator.

This was not just an odd detour in the middle of Elihu's discussion on God's unique motives and context. Instead, this was an integral part of his developing argument.

God exists above Standard View manipulation, and ultimately our good or bad actions do not directly harm or benefit God. But that very viewpoint might inspire someone to ask the question, What do I gain by not sinning?

And if the answer is nothing, because the Standard View is not a mathematical certainty, and if God exists in a context beyond our individual actions (i.e., he is not like a pagan idol, strengthened or weakened by our worship or lack thereof), then some people will draw the logical conclusion that calling out to God in times of distress is pointless. This is because God either does not exist or has no personal role in the real world. That implication is the very slippery slope that Job's friends feared.

So what is the outcome for these atheist or agnostic individuals? Elihu's answer is straightforward:

> ^{12}*"He does not answer when people cry out
> because of the arrogance of the wicked."*
>
> JOB 35:12

The crying people and the arrogant wicked are not two different groups. This verse reads that way to an English reader, but that's because we're used to reading English literature. Remember, Hebrew poetry rhymes ideas. The people crying out to an unanswering God in the first half of the verse are the same arrogant people in the second half of this verse. These are the arrogant people who did not reach out to God. Now, in times of trouble, they do cry out—though the verse does not specify whether they're crying to God—but regardless, God is no longer listening.

Was Elihu saying that God does not respond to the cries of the wicked? Yes. He was building on his argument from 34:33.

This does not mean that God cannot respond to the wicked or that he'll never respond to them, but Elihu's point was to reinforce the anti–Standard View message that humanity's behavior cannot program God's actions. God is not a genie.

Elihu's message was very different from the Standard View. Elihu was describing a reality where God is in the driver's seat—not people.

AN UNEXPECTED REBUKE

Elihu's next words were an unexpected rebuke:

> ^{13}*"Indeed, God does not listen to their empty plea;*

> *the Almighty pays no attention to it.*
> *¹⁴How much less, then, will he listen*
>   *when you say that you do not see him,*[119]
> *that your case is before him*
>   *and you must wait for him,*[120]
> *¹⁵and further, that his anger never punishes*
>   *and he does not take the least notice of wickedness.*[121]
> *¹⁶So Job opens his mouth with empty talk;*
>   *without knowledge he multiplies words."*
>
> JOB 35:13–16

When I first studied these verses, this sudden rebuke laid on the suffering Job took me by surprise.

These are all things Job did, in fact, say (see the footnotes for specific references). This is where a righteous man in extremis let his emotional candor push him past the boundaries of respect for the divine. God does not listen to those who do not acknowledge him. How much less should he listen to the believer who does not trust him and speaks out against him.

Eliphaz had set up this God-versus-Job framework. The friend who had come intending to comfort and console had instead led Job down a bad spiritual path. More dangerous than Satan's original assault and more insidious than his wife's blunt counsel, his friends' words had managed to slip a wedge between Job and God that had grown wider as their debate progressed. Thus, Job's greatest spiritual danger had not come from Satan but from his friends.

Job had eventually found hope in the idea of redemption beyond the grave, but Elihu was after communion with God on this side of eternity, and to get to that union, he needed to pull Job back from the path that bad counsel had set him down and show him that there was more yet to be said on God's behalf.

---

119 This line is referring to Job's words from 23:8–9.

120 This line is referring to Job's words from 13:18 and 31:35.

121 See 21:28–34 and chapter 24.

54

A COMMITMENT TO ACCURACY

ELIHU DID NOT know why bad things had happened to Job. What he did know was that these things had not happened because God was unjust, evil, absent, incapable, or otherwise not to be trusted. God may be inscrutable in the particulars, but his motives are good in the long run, and his context is beyond the merely human scale.

> *¹Elihu continued:*
> *²"Bear with me a little longer and I will show you*
> *   that there is more to be said in God's behalf.*
> *³I get my knowledge from afar;*
> *   I will ascribe justice to my Maker.*
> *⁴Be assured that my words are not false;*
> *   one who has perfect knowledge is with you."*
>
>   JOB 36:1–4

Elihu's statement that "one who has perfect knowledge is with you" can be a little off-putting for the modern reader. If we understand "perfect" as parallel (rhyming with) the first half of the verse ("not false"), it then becomes clear that Elihu did not mean that he was perfect but that his knowledge was perfect. He was going to give Job accurate information. In particular, he will speak accurately on "God's behalf," and he will "ascribe justice" to his Maker. Elihu's introduction in chapter thirty-six should not be disconcerting but reassuring as we learn where Elihu was coming from and hear his request to "bear with" him a little longer.

A CASE STUDY: UNNECESSARY SUFFERING

Elihu provided a case study next to help his listeners understand what he was saying:

> *⁵"God is mighty, but despises no one;*
> *   he is mighty, and firm in his purpose.*
> *⁶He does not keep the wicked alive*
> *   but gives the afflicted their rights.*
> *⁷He does not take his eyes off the righteous;*
> *   he enthrones them with kings*
> *   and exalts them forever.*
> *⁸But if people are bound in chains,*
> *   held fast by cords of affliction,*
> *he tells them what they have done—*
> *   that they have sinned arrogantly."*
>
> JOB 36:5–9

Remember the context here as you read through this. Who had sinned arrogantly in Elihu's speeches so far? Elihu defined these arrogant people as those who would not cry out to God their Maker. Presumably, if this person ever did cry out, it would be to their idol and not to God.

Elihu was not indirectly talking about Job here. He was still building on the theoretical case study he had started working with in chapter thirty-four, and he went on speaking about these persons:

> *¹⁰"He makes them listen to correction*
> *   and commands them to repent of their evil.*
> *¹¹If they obey and serve him,*
> *   they will spend the rest of their days in prosperity*
> *   and their years in contentment.*
> *¹²But if they do not listen,*
> *   they will perish by the sword*

> *and die without knowledge."*
>
> JOB 36:10–12

Read quickly, and this passage looks like the Standard View. So what was Elihu up to?

Sometimes God does address sin through a corrective punishment in a manner that is very Standard View compatible. Even Job had acknowledged this in chapter twenty-seven.

Here is the difference: where Job focused on punishment, Elihu focused on the potential for salvation. Now, always trying to keep his arguments balanced, Elihu also reminds us that death does await those who don't listen. However, it is a specific type of death that Elihu highlighted: death without knowledge.

We all die. Elihu reminds us that we can die understanding what is going on—or we can die in confusion, not understanding.

A SECOND CASE STUDY: UNDESERVED RESCUE

Here is Elihu's second case study to help his audience understand:

> [13] *"The godless in heart harbor resentment;*
> *even when he fetters them, they do not cry for help.*
> [14] *They die in their youth,*
> *among male prostitutes of the shrines.*
> [15] *But those who suffer he delivers in their suffering;*
> *he speaks to them in their affliction."*
>
> JOB 36:13–15

There is a careful choice of words in this passage—a detail hidden in plain sight that is easy to miss.

Previously, Elihu had discussed the punished sufferer who would not acknowledge and turn to God even in their darkest hour. These were people who God would not save. But then here, in verse fifteen, he addressed those who suffer and are delivered in their suffering—not from their suffering but in their suffering.

It is tempting to infer that the saved sufferers in verse fifteen are different than the wicked who suffer. When I studied this verse in my first few passes through Job, I wanted it to say "but those who suffer and repent he delivers from their suffering." But "and repent" is not in the verse. Nor is the idea of deliverance from suffering. The English translation of the Hebrew is quite adequate here. There is no mistake.

Did you catch that?

Elihu stated that God focuses on salvation. He admitted that punishment for sin is a part of God's repertoire, but in 36:15, he returned to God's desire to save. It is not a desire based on people's good deeds but a desire based on God's character. Some experience God's deliverance in their suffering even though they don't deserve it. Unlike the purveyors of the Standard View, Elihu had no magic formula to offer for obtaining God's grace in these situations. God remains God and not a genie that does humanity's bidding. God is love. God is also complicated—and he does not always explain himself.

Elihu's second case study here is a case study on grace.

55

LET'S GET PRACTICAL

UP UNTIL NOW, Elihu had applied his spiritual philosophy to theoretical scenarios only. Elihu had focused on God's nature and avoided formulaic prescriptions and confident judgments. However, at some point Elihu needed to take his theology and make it personally practical for Job. Now was the time for that shift. Here he went:

> [16]*"He is wooing you from the jaws of distress*
> *to a spacious place free from restriction,*
> *to the comfort of your table laden with choice food."*
>
> JOB 36:16

God works to save. He is love. He is complicated. He does not always explain himself. But he is still love. Elihu assured Job that even in Job's current situation, God was wooing Job through a dark valley, the very jaws of distress, to something good. The psalmist in Psalm 23 described something similar:

> [4]*Even though I walk*
> *through the darkest valley,*
> *I will fear no evil,*
> *for you are with me;*
> *your rod and your staff,*

they comfort me.

PSALM 23:4

Do not make the mistake of thinking that the rod and staff are instruments of punishment. On the contrary, shepherds use these tools to guide, count, rescue, and defend.

Elihu and the psalmist were describing similar circumstances. Neither the psalmist's "darkest valley" nor Elihu's "jaws of distress" comes with a clear cause. These images paint a picture of adverse life circumstances with broad brush strokes, allowing the reader to insert their own jaws of distress, their own valley of darkness, into the picture.

Neither Elihu nor the psalmist offers any formulaic remedy for these dark hours. Their only offer is an assurance that even in these circumstances, God is with us. He provides comfort. He is wooing us to a better place. The Standard View promises specifics, whereas Elihu and the psalmist both only offer generalities. The Standard View might feel better, but the view espoused by Elihu and the psalmist is actually, universally true.

Why was Job in the jaws of distress to begin with? Elihu did not know.

Why did David pass through so many valleys of the shadow of death? He was just a simple shepherd boy who sang songs and played an instrument in the fields. Why was he chosen to be king and marched through one trial after another? Some difficulties came by his own foolishness, as a careful study of 1 and 2 Samuel will show. Still, most of his trials, particularly the early ones, came unbidden and undeserved as a direct consequence of God's anointing. Why did these terrible trials happen to these people and so many other men and women before and after them?

Elihu did not know.

God is complicated. God does not always explain himself.

What Elihu did know was what the psalmist also knew—that even amid distress, God is working for good.[122]

This is fine as armchair theology, but when savagery has torn your life apart, and the pain is unendurable, armchair theology provides little comfort. The question of why rings louder with every platitude.

---

122 See Romans 8:28–39.

ANTICIPATING AND AVOIDING NEW TROUBLE

Here is one answer to the question of why:

> ^{17}*"But now you are laden with the judgment due the wicked;*
> *judgment and justice have taken hold of you."*
>
> JOB 36:17

This verse is not saying that Job was wicked but rather that the fate of the wicked had somehow landed on Job. Job would like to know why.

The friends had decided that they knew why and assaulted Job with their theory dressed up as fact. They were wrong.

Elihu did not know why these things had come upon Job, but unlike Job's three friends, Elihu was not about to hazard guesses either. He was, however, aware that the friends' assault had hurt Job's heart and that these debates had also strained Job's relationship with God.

Elihu could not answer Job's question of why, but he could warn Job about a new danger he saw coming. Job was living through a very dark hour in which the fate of the wicked seemed to have fallen on him. In this hour when cynicism and faithlessness might begin to exert their appeal, Elihu shared an important warning.

> ^{18}*"Be careful that no one entices you by riches;*
> *do not let a large bribe turn you aside.*
> ^{19}*Would your wealth or even all your mighty efforts*
> *sustain you so that you would not be in distress?*
> ^{20}*Do not long for the night,*
> *to drag people away from their homes.*
> ^{21}*Beware of turning to evil,*
> *which you seem to prefer to affliction."*
>
> JOB 36:18–21

Was Job really in danger of being tempted by money? Was someone about to offer him a bribe that threatened his integrity?

THE DANGEROUS APPEAL OF ESCAPE

As my wife and I went through our daughter's medical trials, one traumatic event seemingly followed immediately on the heels of another, not just regularly but also endlessly. Weeks turned into months that turned into years without respite, spiritual explanation, or even a medical diagnosis to provide the release found in final grief or hope or some form of closure. In the midst of this, we were immune to the temptations of money or bribery. We just wanted our daughter to live and thrive, my wife's health to normalize, and our lives to stabilize again.

But. As time went on a new weakness crept in. It was persistent. It was persuasive. It was often irrational. It was also consuming. The weakness that crept in was the desire for Escape.

An acute crisis can sharpen the mind and perhaps even the spirit. It can be clarifying like a dip in cold water. But a marathon of chronic medical problems and the grind of uncertainty and grief brought to mind Proverbs 13:12: "Hope deferred makes the heart sick." Our hearts grew sick.

I have shared already the suicidal escape thoughts that my wife and I at times felt—both my own and my wife's—the exhausted thoughts as I drove from work in White Rock to hospital in Vancouver to home in Coquitlam that first year, and the later similar darkness as my wife's postpartum depression followed our son's birth in Hamilton. But there were other escape attempts as well.

We were debt-free when Mackenzie was born. However, by the time Jackson was born a few years later, we were swamped with both credit card debt and a line of credit stretched to its limit.

No one offered us money to betray our integrity. Instead, we had tossed aside our financial integrity in favor of Escape. The evidence could be seen in our finances. We did not even go anywhere fancy or buy anything particularly exciting. Still, somehow we spent the money.

I never swore at my wife during our marriage—until after Mackenzie was born. Then I swore. The tension became too much, and my offered bribe was to insult and wound my bride. It was not a bribe of money but one of release: one second of sinful satisfaction seemed to be worth the emotional betrayal of a verbal assault. I longed "for the night to drag people away from their homes," as Elihu poetically put it. I longed for release, for the end.

Good or bad, I wanted escape.

I mentioned previously that my wife and I benefited a great deal from the services of a marriage counselor who helped us understand how we each dealt with stress and gave us exercises and tools to help us understand and aid one another. But the escape problems that I am describing now—the finances, the swearing, even a recurrence of suicidal escape thoughts—came later. We benefited from those counseling sessions and experiences of growth at the time, and yet we still chose escape at many turns. Sometimes the choice was deliberate. Sometimes the choice was unconscious. In all circumstances, it was a bribe offered in the tender of a bounced check.

Overspending did not provide escape—it just added more stress.

Swearing did not provide escape—it just created distance.

We seemed to prefer the bribe to our suffering—but the bribe was a rubber check, and the suffering persisted and was even made worse by our attempts to cash that fraudulent draft.

What did Elihu say again?

> [21] *"Beware of turning to evil,*
> *which you seem to prefer to affliction."*
>
> JOB 36:21

Elihu's words cut me deeply. I knew what he was saying. I also knew that the choice was not between righteous affliction and unrighteous peace because peace could not be found anywhere. With unrighteousness, I still suffered—just more of the suffering was self-inflicted. Affliction would be present regardless.

The offered bribes had nothing in them that brought peace. The choice was between righteousness and unrighteousness—suffering remained a constant whatever my choice. What the Escape offered was a lie that I kept trying to make true.

Why sin has any power to tempt us at all in this context is a lesson in human nature. A beautiful lie can, at times, seem preferable to the unhappy truth. And the truth is that God is love, God is complicated, and God does not always explain himself.

INSTEAD OF ESCAPE, THE (HARD) REALITY OF GOD

Elihu continued to make his case:

> *²² "God is exalted in his power.*
> *Who is a teacher like him?*
> *²³ Who has prescribed his ways for him,*
> *or said to him, 'You have done wrong'?*
> *²⁴ Remember to extol his work,*
> *which people have praised in song.*
> *²⁵ All humanity has seen it;*
> *mortals gaze on it from afar.*
> *²⁶ How great is God—beyond our understanding!*
> *The number of his years is past finding out.*
> *²⁷ He draws up the drops of water,*
> *which distill as rain to the streams;*
> *²⁸ the clouds pour down their moisture*
> *and abundant showers fall on mankind.*
> *²⁹ Who can understand how he spreads out the clouds,*
> *how he thunders from his pavilion?*
> *³⁰ See how he scatters his lightning about him,*
> *bathing the depths of the sea.*
> *³¹ This is the way he governs the nations*
> *and provides food in abundance.*
> *³² He fills his hands with lightning*
> *and commands it to strike its mark.*
> *³³ His thunder announces the coming storm;*
> *even the cattle make known its approach.*
>
> *¹ "At this my heart pounds*
> *and leaps from its place.*
> *² Listen! Listen to the roar of his voice,*
> *to the rumbling that comes from his mouth."*
>
> JOB 36:22–37:2

It is easy for the sufferer, faced with bribes large and small, to at some point question God's actions in the world. Why does he cause or allow trouble to occur?

Elihu's answer to this implied question was not a formula that lays God's actions along a predictable (and programmed) path. Instead, he reminded the questioner that God is God—no one gets to teach him or correct him. He is God.

Instead of challenging God, Elihu instructs us to extol what God has done. We are to consider that amid a crisis, we view his work only from afar (36:25)—and God's work is beyond our understanding.

People eat food. That is an immediate blessing. But God brings about that food in part with a water cycle of evaporation, precipitation, thunder, and lightning. These distant heavenly events would seem to be completely unrelated to the granular immediacy of a hungry person biting into a fruit or grinding grain, but in fact, they are intricately connected.

God understands everything. On the other hand, we might complain about today's rain, which is required for next season's meal. That is the message Elihu was relating through his poetry. We don't know what God is doing—we only see his work distantly. When we question today's rain—asking him, "What are you doing?"—God is actually providing tomorrow's food.

> *[31] "This is the way he governs the nations*
> *and provides food in abundance."*
>
> JOB 36:31

But God doesn't explain himself along the way.

We'll come back to this verse, as Elihu will use it to make a larger point later. But there is something that Elihu did next in 37:2 that is also significant.

56

LISTEN CAREFULLY

ELIHU'S NEXT VERSE starts with a word that links Elihu's speech to Job's own words earlier in the book.

> *²"Listen! Listen to the roar of his voice,*
> *to the rumbling that comes from his mouth."*
>
> JOB 37:2

This "Listen! Listen…" in Hebrew literally means "hear and hear." The phrase's immediate point is to create emphasis.

Beyond this immediate meaning, the phrase also reminded Job of his own words in previous speeches. Elihu used Job's own unique phrasing to make Job listen carefully to what Elihu was going to say next.

In chapter thirteen, Job had used this same "hear and hear" phrase:

> *¹⁷"Listen carefully to what I say;*
> *let my words ring in your ears."*
>
> JOB 13:17

What the NIV translates as "Listen carefully" in 13:17 is the same Hebrew phrase that it translates as "Listen! Listen…" in 37:2— i.e. the Hebrew for both is "hear and hear." What Job wanted his friends to hear in chapter thirteen was his defense. "Can anyone bring charges against me?" he asked in 13:19. Job had two requests of God: to stop terrifying him and to summon him to trial so Job could argue his case. He went on to accuse God of having written "down bitter things against me" (13:26). God had done no such thing, but this was a logical conclusion when locked into the Standard View's adversarial framework.

Job used this "hear and hear" phrase one other time.

> ²"*Listen carefully to my words;*
> *let this be the consolation you give me.*"
>
> JOB 21:2

Again, "listen carefully" is this same "hear and hear" phrase in Hebrew, and once again, what follows this preface is an argument. In this case, Job was not defending himself, requesting a trial, and charging God with writing down bitter things about him. Instead, Job was accusing God of letting the wicked live on (21:7), not dealing with their sin (21:9, 17–18), and generally supporting a meaningless existence for sinners and saints alike (21:23–25). Job backs these serious charges by referring to the witness of travelers (21:29) and to common human observations about how the world works in real life.

Hear and hear.

Listen carefully.

Job had used this phrase to attack the self-satisfied smugness of the Standard View.

Elihu now turned this same phrase back on Job to penetrate Job's morbid despair, pull him beyond the limited viewpoint of human perspective, and help him see things in the divine context.

GOD GETTING OUR ATTENTION

Here is what Elihu wanted Job to "hear and hear."

> ²"*Listen! Listen to the roar of his voice,*
> *to the rumbling that comes from his mouth.*
> ³*He unleashes his lightning beneath the whole heaven*
> *and sends it to the ends of the earth.*
> ⁴*After that comes the sound of his roar;*
> *he thunders with his majestic voice.*

> [5] *When his voice resounds,*
> > *he holds nothing back.*
> [6] *God's voice thunders in marvelous ways;*
> > *he does great things beyond our understanding.*
> [7] *He says to the snow, 'Fall on the earth,'*
> > *and to the rain shower, 'Be a mighty downpour.'*
> [8] *So that all men he has made may know his work,*
> > *he stops every man from his labor."*
>
> JOB 37:2–8

When the cook on a western ranch in the movies rings the big bell outside the cookshack, the farmhands know it's dinner time. If a newbie from the city does not understand the signal and has no one to interpret it for him, he might miss dinner. Likewise, the clanging and flashing lights at a railway crossing warn pedestrians and vehicles alike that a train is coming. Failing to read the signals properly does not stop the train. The signal is the signal. It is up to the public to interpret the signal accurately.

In the case of the cook's bell, a worst-case scenario might be missing dinner. In the case of the train, misinterpreting the signals could result in major injury or death.

When was the last time it rained very hard, and you interpreted the rain as God telling you and your entire city, your entire county or region, to stop your labor and notice him? When was the last time you were housebound in a blizzard or startled by a bolt of lightning—the following deep bass of bottomless thunder rolling through you—and thought, God?

Science is a fantastically useful field of study. But if we use it to inoculate ourselves to God's wonders, we have only scratched the surface of true knowledge and robbed ourselves of the awe that Elihu wanted to bring back to our attention. There is more to the wonder of thunder than just noise. There is more to lightning than just sudden light. In the context of Elihu's salvation-focused God, who seeks to save all people from the untold numbers of pits, even the thunder and lightning, rain and snow are reminders of God and his love for us. He wants the world to pause, regularly it would seem, and know his work. It is up to us to read the signs properly.

PUNISHMENT AND BLESSING IN THE SAME PACKAGE

Elihu continued:

> ^{8}"The animals take cover;
>   they remain in their dens.
> ^{9}The tempest comes out from its chamber,
>   the cold from the driving winds.
> ^{10}The breath of God produces ice,
>   and the broad waters become frozen.
> ^{11}He loads the clouds with moisture;
>   he scatters his lightning through them.
> ^{12}At his direction they swirl around
>   over the face of the whole earth
>   to do whatever he commands them.
> ^{13}He brings the clouds to punish people,
>   or to water the earth and show his love."
>
> JOB 37:8–13

Did you catch that? "He brings the clouds to punish people, or to water the earth and show his love." The same clouds and the same rain are sometimes punishment and sometimes love.

The phrase "punish people" in Hebrew can be literally translated as to "whip men." Make no mistake about it: sometimes God punishes, and he punishes hard. The word used for love here is a Hebrew word that means "constant love."[123] Also, make no mistake: when God demonstrates love, it is not a flighty, flirty, transient love. It is a constant, steadfast love. The word loyalty is sometimes used to translate that particular Hebrew word. Loyal, constant, steadfast love.

If we take this verse in light of chapter thirty-three, we could even stretch Elihu's meaning not only to encompass an either/or scenario (punishment or love), but also to reflect an and meaning: punishment and love.

Elihu had already referenced this duality of God's actions in 36:31. There, he had noted that God uses the wonders of the rain cycle to both

---

123 Reyburn, 683.

govern and provide for the nations. Here, Elihu brought the same point down to the level of individual people: he recast governance and provision more intimately as punishment and love. These are not different things. Governing nations is parallel to punishing individuals. Providing for the nations is parallel to bestowing constant, steadfast love on individuals. Elihu was describing how the same God operates, using the same tools for the same purposes at two different levels.

STAND AND CONSIDER

Elihu made this personal for Job in the following verse:

> [14] *"Listen to this, Job;*
> *stop and consider God's wonders."*
>
> JOB 37:14

The command to "stop" here in Hebrew can be translated as "stand." Stand and consider God's wonders. Get up off your seat, stand tall and alert in the light of God's actions, and do not just look but consider, think about, even study God's wonders. Give this some serious attention.

Amid deep pain, it is very easy to be overwhelmed by life's events. The falling, drowning, trampling emotions that sweep along in tandem with trauma lend themselves readily to a myopic, introspective mindset easily ensnared by a false premise, bent theology, or emotional bribe. Job was caught in such a snare.

In chapter three, Job had despaired of life. He had been in a very vulnerable state. Into this vulnerable space had jumped Eliphaz, who had charged in not with prayer but judgment. He had entered not by considering with an open mind the mystery of God and his yearning to love and save but instead by laying out a rigid framework onto which he was determined to fit Job's circumstances.

To Job's credit, he had not been completely overwhelmed by the combination of his tragedies and the misguided attention of his friends. But Job had floundered. He had felt his way toward eternity and redemption, thus overcoming his friends' bad counsel, but as his defiant final speech made clear, and though chapter thirty-one made clear that he was still committed to righteousness, he was also in a state of pain (30:15–31). It was this committed-but-still-hurting Job that Elihu called to stand and consider God's wonders. He called Job to go beyond the trap the three friends had sprung and to instead lift his eyes beyond the narrow rigidity of human viewpoints and interpretations.

LOOKING PAST THE (STORM) CLOUDS—WITH A FRIEND

Elihu continued:

> ¹⁵"*Do you know how God controls the clouds*
> *and makes his lightning flash?*
> ¹⁶*Do you know how the clouds hang poised,*
> *those wonders of him who has perfect knowledge?*
> ¹⁷*You who swelter in your clothes*
> *when the land lies hushed under the south wind,*
> ¹⁸*can you join him in spreading out the skies,*
> *hard as a mirror of cast bronze?*
> ¹⁹*Tell us what we should say to him;*
> *we cannot draw up our case because of our darkness.*"
>
> Job 37:15–19

When Job had spoken about confronting God, he had described doing it alone. When the three friends had referenced this, they too had described Job facing God alone.

When Elihu spoke about this meeting, he asked "what *we* should say to him"—he spoke about how "*we* cannot draw up *our* case because of *our* darkness" (37:19; emphasis mine). We. We. Our. Our. Job was not alone here.

Elihu had promised at the beginning of his speech that he would speak differently, and he had assured Job that Elihu was just like Job before God—they were equals (33:6). Now, as his speech wound down, he was still alongside Job as he helped Job lift his gaze, and Elihu did so not as a teacher or master looking down on the hurting Job but as a friend who was with him in this struggle.

In the very next verse, Elihu suggested that he might even want to speak on Job's behalf. Far from leaving Job alone in his pain, Elihu would have liked to mediate on his behalf, but he was concerned that the human viewpoint was too limiting and held no value before this awesome God. Bringing God down to humanity's perspective and then arguing an artificially restrictive case with him would be of no value, regardless of whether Job argued the case for himself, Elihu argued on his behalf, or they argued it together.

What did have value was lifting Job's perspective closer to God's. So in the following verses, Elihu pulled Job's gaze upward.

> [20]*"Should he be told that I want to speak?*
> *Would anyone ask to be swallowed up?*
> [21]*Now no one can look at the sun,*
> *bright as it is in the skies*
> *after the wind has swept them clean.*
> [22]*Out of the north he comes in golden splendor;*
> *God comes in awesome majesty.*
> [23]*The Almighty is beyond our reach and exalted in power;*
> *in his justice and great righteousness, he does not oppress.*
> [24]*Therefore, people revere him,*
> *for does he not have regard for all the wise in heart?"*
>
> JOB 37:20–24

ELIHU'S CONTRIBUTION

What had Elihu communicated in these six chapters?

Elihu had brought some human comfort to Job. He had been the first friend to call Job by name and come alongside him, not to parrot the Standard View but to assure Job of his co-humanity before God and to position himself as Job's co-complainant or even his mediator before God.

He had also corrected Job. However, he had not corrected him in the way the friends had by trying to diagnose the cause of Job's tragedies. Rather, Elihu had helped Job turn away from the bad direction that his friends' arguments had led him to, a misstep that had come from his tragedies but had not caused his tragedies.

Elihu had also done a substantial amount of work defending God. He showed how God punishes and loves both nations and individuals and how the tools of both correction and blessing often are the same. Beyond this reality, even in apparent judgment, God is focused on saving people from falling into a pit, and when they already have fallen, he is then focused on rescue.

But Elihu had not developed an airtight theory of God's behavior that a person could use to predict, program, or even flawlessly interpret God's actions in life. Instead, Elihu made it plain that God acts in ways that suit God's own purposes, and people are powerless to force God's hand in any direction. God's perspective is different than humanity's, and only he knows how his actions fit into his larger purpose to save.

In light of both God's salvation focus—his love for people—and his ultimate sovereignty, Elihu's final push was to raise Job's gaze beyond the immediate rainfall in his life and to help Job see the God behind the rain. God acts so that people will stop and consider his work. So Elihu called Job to stand and consider God's work.

As Elihu's speech wound down, he very artfully moved from the imagery of thunder and lightning, snow and rain to that of the sun appearing in a sky that had been swept clean. That sun is too bright for any person to gaze upon, and that sun is God coming in "golden splendor" and "awesome majesty" (37:22). That God, exalted in power, loves. He does not oppress. He has regard for the wise in heart.

Elihu could not solve Job's problems, but he had marvelously prepared the stage for God's speeches, which will come next.

Job had no rebuttal for Elihu. There was nothing to refute. Job stopped floundering now. He stood and considered.

And then God spoke.

57

PEOPLE FORMING OPINIONS IN THE DARK

> *¹Then the Lord spoke to Job out of the storm. He said:*
> *²"Who is this that obscures my plans*
> *with words without knowledge?*
> *³Brace yourself like a man;*
> *I will question you,*
> *and you shall answer me."*
>
> Job 38:1–3

The Hebrew word translated as "Lord" here is Yahweh, that most holy name that Job used only once and that the three friends and Elihu never used at all. Identifying God with his most sacred name creates an atmosphere of divine reverence that sharply contrasts with the preceding hurly-burly of debate, argument, soliloquy, and exposition. Now, Yahweh spoke.

And what did Yahweh say?

"Who is this that obscures my plans?" God had something very clear in mind when he set the events of the book of Job in motion. That clear intent had been obscured by arguments and debate built on a foundation of words without knowledge.

The three friends stood behind a rigidly held passion for the Standard View. When Job had illustrated that the Standard View was wrong in his case and in many others, as both he and travelers had observed, the three friends had rebuked him. They had pressed on, reiterating with ever more passion and assurance that the Standard View was right.

Elihu's contrasting message had not offered certainty. Elihu had left God's divine reasons within God's unsearchable hands. He had insisted that God was goodness and God was love. According to Elihu, God's tools for enacting that goodness and love are easily misinterpreted when viewed from the limited perspective of a human being.

"Who is this that obscures my plans with words without knowledge?" Who is this that muddles your human understanding of my actions by trying to explain things that you don't actually know anything about?

This passage's first verse tells us that God was talking to Job directly. In verse three, it is Job who was to brace himself "like a man." God was instructing not his friends but Job alone to ready himself like a responsible grownup. God was addressing Job.

In 9:16, Job had voiced his desire for a direct hearing with God. At that time, he had doubted that God would show up for such a hearing even if he did have a way to summon him. In 13:22–23, Job had suggested that if it was not appropriate for Job to summon God, then let God instead summon Job. In 14:14–17, Job had suggested that if this confrontation occurred beyond the grave, perhaps a good result could come from it. Job just wanted a hearing.

Early on, Job had looked for a mediator or an advocate to help with this confrontation. Later, he had settled on a Redeemer to save him from it. Whether he was the accused or accuser, Job just wanted to face God on the issue of his unjust punishment so that God might redeem Job's integrity in the face of the apparent injustice and defamation. Elihu, however, had already exposed that Job's case was based on a false dilemma. The Standard View was too simplistic—something Job already believed—making any debate on the justice or injustice of Job's tragedies a pointless exercise.

Now Job got his hearing with God. But the grounds for that hearing were not what he had originally wanted. The case we are going to hear in God's speeches is not a defense of God's actions within the Standard View—because the Standard View is not a universal truth and is a false foundation for a debate. Instead, we are going to hear God definitively proclaim his overall wisdom, power, and right. Elihu had spoken to God's intentions and heart. God will speak about his authority, knowledge, and capability.

GOD'S QUALIFICATIONS

> [4] *"Where were you when I laid the earth's foundation?*
> *Tell me, if you understand.*
> [5] *Who marked off its dimensions? Surely you know!*
> *Who stretched a measuring line across it?*
> [6] *On what were its footings set,*
> *or who laid its cornerstone—*
> [7] *when the morning stars sang together*
> *and the angels shouted for joy?"*
>
> JOB 38:4–7

The surface of God's point is clear—Job had not even been born yet when God created the world, and Job had no idea where he was when God laid the earth's foundations.

Looking at the question from God's point of view, with the advantage of a twenty-first-century knowledge of physics and geology, this is more than just an existential question. Never mind for a minute where Job was when creation happened. God also asked what the earth's foundations were set on. There are many answers to that question. Every one of the correct answers would have blown Job's third-millennium-BCE mind.

One answer could be that there are no footings—the earth is a ball, floating in space, kept in orbit around the sun by gravitational principles that twenty-first-century math can represent but are still otherwise difficult to grasp on a large scale.

Another answer could be to focus less on cosmology and more on geology. The earth's footings—the earth's crust—are set not on a solid foundation but a swirling liquid. The tectonic plates that form the earth's footings float on a sea of pressurized molten rock that forms the earth's mantle. Job's solid ground is a raft of rock on a sea of pressurized liquid fire.

At the microlevel, the answer to God's question could be that the whole world is founded upon particles called atoms, which are bundles of electrons, protons, and neutrons that subatomic forces hold together in their own orbits of energy. Most shockingly, these bundles of particles and energy that form all matter in the universe are over 99 percent empty space.

On what are the earth's footings set? At both the celestial and the subatomic level, earth's footings are set on nothing but bodies orbiting in mostly empty space. And in between those two extremes, earth's footings float on a sea of fire.

If you think that this twenty-first-century take on God's question inappropriately overlays modern sensibilities onto an ancient question, consider this: God described himself as being the one who "marked off [the earth's] dimensions," "stretched a measuring line across it," established its "footings," and "laid its cornerstone" (38:4–6). In other words, God was describing himself as creation's architect, surveyor, engineer, and contractor. Mentioning the foundations of the earth was not just a poetic illustration. God was making a practical, physical point to his audience here. God knows all that was involved in every stage of the earth's formation. The angels were present to witness this work (38:7). Job was not present and had no clue about the details.

God could have stopped talking there. Briefly revealing what the earth's foundations actually are would have exposed to Job (and, by extension, his friends) that they really knew nothing about even the most elementary things. To question God's plans is for an infant to question a Nobel Prize-winning mathematician's calculations. It is even more absurd because the infant might grow into a Nobel Prize winner him- or herself—but the human will never become God.

But God did not go all Discovery Channel on Job. He asked the questions. He did not provide the answers. The fact that Job did not know the answers was enough. Yahweh does not explain himself. Yahweh was there. Yahweh did it. The angels witnessed it. Job had no knowledge of it.

God continued his speech.

> [8] *"Who shut the sea behind doors*
>   *when it burst forth from the womb,*
> [9] *when I made the clouds its garment*
>   *and wrapped it in thick darkness,*
> [10] *when I fixed limits for it*

> *and set its doors and bars in place,*
> *¹¹when I said, 'This far you may come and no farther;*
> *here is where your proud waves halt'?"*
>
> JOB 38:8–11

The reference here is, of course, to events recorded in Genesis:

> *⁹And God said, "Let the water under the sky be gathered to one place, and let dry ground appear." And it was so."*
>
> GENESIS 1:9

FORESHADOWING MONSTERS

This verse is doing more than just referencing how God formed the seas and dry land. The seas in Job's day were an uncharted mystery. They were vast bodies of water that whipped up storms of overwhelming force. Even in times of calm, the tides advanced and retreated upon the land in a way that was unstoppable, predictable, but, in Job's day, unexplained. It behaved like a monster.

Comparing the ocean to a monster is not interpretative overreach. In the ancient Mesopotamian mythologies that permeated the culture, the sea was a symbol of chaos personified. The sea was more than water. It was a source of power and the home of dark forces.

This passage foreshadows the much more direct monster imagery to come, but for now, the reference is oblique, and the message is that this matchless force, symbolic of chaos, finds its match with God.

God shut the sea behind doors. God decided where its boundaries would be and how far the tides would advance, and he dressed its expanse with clouds, which further adds to its danger and mystery. The ocean's waves have fatal power and are proud, but they halt where God tells them to halt.

For now, let's move on from monsters and talk about light.

58

GOD OF THE MORNING

AFTER FORESHADOWING THE topic of monsters, God moved back to more common human experiences, such as each day's dawn.

> *¹²"Have you ever given orders to the morning,*
> *or shown the dawn its place*
> *¹³that it might take the earth by the edges*
> *and shake the wicked out of it?*
> *¹⁴The earth takes shape like clay under a seal;*
> *its features stand out like those of a garment.*
> *¹⁵The wicked are denied their light,*
> *and their upraised arm is broken."*
>
> JOB 38:12–15

The sun was an object of worship throughout Mesopotamian culture. The Egyptians had their sun god, as did the Sumerians, the Hittites, and many others. More specific to Job's context, the Sabeans and Chaldeans, who had raided Job's farm, worshipped the sun.

But God did not mention the sun. The sun is just a tool. God gives orders to the morning, and while humanity recognizes the sun as the actor that creates morning, God revealed that it is the morning itself he gives orders to. The sun is just a secondary tool that gets the job done. The sun is nothing special in this context. The sun is the servant. The sun is the object that does what it's told, not even taking its orders directly from Yahweh but taking them secondhand via the morning. God is the boss, and the sun—worshipped by the surrounding pagan nations—does not even get to talk to the boss. God had exposed his multifaceted involvement in forming the earth's foundations—he was their architect, surveyor, engineer, and contractor—and had revealed his power over the otherwise all-powerful oceans. Now he stripped the sun god of its power. The sun itself did not even warrant a specific mention.

What about the purpose of the sun, worshipped as it was by those in the surrounding regions? God informed Job that its purpose is to expose the wicked. There is clearly irony here. The wicked worshipped the sun, but their natural light was darkness. Recall how Job had pointed this out previously in chapter twenty-four.

> *¹⁶"In the dark, thieves break into houses,*
> *but by day they shut themselves in;*
> *they want nothing to do with the light.*
> *¹⁷For all of them, midnight is their morning,*
> *they make friends with the terrors of darkness."*
>
> JOB 24:16–17

The wicked preferred the light of darkness because it cloaked their deeds. But they worshipped the sun even though the sun, as the servant of the morning, exposed them. It did not just expose them but broke their "upraised arm." This poetic word choice paints a dramatic picture of violence halted. The morning strips the wicked of their cover and does so under God's orders.

THE GATES OF DEATH

What about death? Now that we've dragged the wicked and their evil deeds into this speech, what about the ultimate end of human beings? God talked about that next.

> *¹⁶"Have you journeyed to the springs of the sea*
> *or walked in the recesses of the deep?*
> *¹⁷Have the gates of death been shown to you?*
> *Have you seen the gates of the deepest darkness?*

> ^{18}*Have you comprehended the vast expanses of the earth?*
> *Tell me, if you know all this."*
>
> Job 38:16–18

On an emotional level, Job had plumbed the depths that God was referring to. With the sea as a cultural symbol of monstrous chaos, Job had walked these recesses on a poetic and emotional level. His farm had been destroyed. Hundreds of people who worked for him had been murdered. All his children had been killed. Widows, orphans, and sudden poverty surrounded him. He had friends who had sought to blame him. He had gone from social pillar to social pariah. And his skin crawled with an itching, painful disease that even robbed him of sleep. He had, metaphorically and emotionally, seen the very gates of death.

But had Job actually seen these mythical gates? Actually seen them? No. Metaphor and poetry are one thing. But no, Job had not actually seen the actual gates of death.

Did Job comprehend the vast expanse of the earth? No. Of course not. But just in case Job, gripped by emotion and conviction, was tempted to take poetic image in hand and protest his experience and defend his level of comprehension, God went on to illustrate very specifically what he was asking. God was not asking about poetic metaphors.

SPECIFICS, NOT JUST METAPHORS

Imagine hearing the very voice of God speaking to you from a storm, asking you the following questions:

> ^{19}*"What is the way to the abode of light?*
> *And where does darkness reside?*
> ^{20}*Can you take them to their places?*
> *Do you know the paths to their dwellings?*
> ^{21}*Surely you know, for you were already born!*
> *You have lived so many years!*
> ^{22}*Have you entered the storehouses of the snow*
> *or seen the storehouses of the hail,*
> ^{23}*which I reserve for times of trouble,*

> *for days of war and battle?*
> *²⁴What is the way to the place where the lightning is dispersed,*
> > *or the place where the east winds are scattered over the earth?*
> *²⁵Who cuts a channel for the torrents of rain,*
> > *and a path for the thunderstorm,*
> *²⁶to water a land where no one lives,*
> > *an uninhabited desert,*
> *²⁷to satisfy a desolate wasteland*
> > *and make it sprout with grass?*
> *²⁸Does the rain have a father?*
> > *Who fathers the drops of dew?*
> *²⁹From whose womb comes the ice?*
> > *Who gives birth to the frost from the heavens*
> *³⁰when the waters become hard as stone,*
> > *when the surface of the deep is frozen?*
> *³¹Can you bind the chains of the Pleiades?*
> > *Can you loosen Orion's belt?*
> *³²Can you bring forth the constellations in their seasons*
> > *or lead out the Bear with its cubs?*
> *³³Do you know the laws of the heavens?*
> > *Can you set up God's dominion over the earth?*
> *³⁴Can you raise your voice to the clouds*
> > *and cover yourself with a flood of water?*
> *³⁵Do you send the lightning bolts on their way?*
> > *Do they report to you, 'Here we are'?*
> *³⁶Who gives the ibis wisdom*
> > *or gives the rooster understanding?*
> *³⁷Who has the wisdom to count the clouds?*
> > *Who can tip over the water jars of the heavens*
> *³⁸when the dust becomes hard*
> > *and the clods of earth stick together?"*
>
> JOB 38:19–38

Job had no detailed knowledge of these things. He had experienced rain and snow, seen the stars, and observed lightning, but he had not been to the place where these things have their start. He did not know the laws of the heavens. He might attempt to count the clouds—a slippery task at best—but there is only one answer to the question of who endowed humanity with the wisdom and understanding even to attempt this. God is the answer to all of the who questions in these verses.

These verses range across many topics of physics. The source of light; the complexity of weather phenomena; the physics of rain, snow, and ice; the wheeling pattern of stars in the sky; and the physics of lightning bolts—God laid out all these questions for Job to expand upon his first question in verse eighteen: "Have you comprehended the vast expanses of the earth?" That question, followed up by this survey of physical phenomena, illustrates how specifically God wanted Job to reconsider how much he truly knew.

THIS IS NOT THE VAGUENESS OF HUMAN PHILOSOPHY AND FUZZY MYSTICISM

Something about our human religious nature makes us want to grandly state and forcefully pronounce how the human condition specifically works, based on vague generalities and incomplete understanding. From the poverty of human knowledge, a wellspring of opinion and assertion readily flows. In the face of mystery, unfounded certainty overruns humility.

This is a very human flaw: pride. From this kind of pride, Job's friends had launched a vigorous defense of the Standard View, and it is this Standard View framework, constructed from sketchy inputs at best, from which Job had struggled to break free. He did so partially, but his charges against God remained rooted in the very viewpoint he sought to free himself from. He wanted to bring God into a courtroom confrontation, and God had shown up—but God also changed the rules of the meeting. This was not a conflict where Job would defend his case and God would exonerate him or at least explain the cause of Job's apparent punishment. Instead, this was a confrontation where God would reveal how groundless it is for any person to challenge God's wisdom and actions in the world. People just do not know very much. God had started with physics. Now he is going to move on to zoology.

59

CONCLUDING GOD'S FIRST SPEECH

THE CASE OF CARNIVORES

IN THE NEXT verses, God will shift his focus from physics to zoology with a brief discussion of carnivores such as lions and ravens.

> *^{39}"Do you hunt prey for the lioness*
> *and satisfy the hunger of the lions*
> *^{40}when they crouch in their dens*
> *or lie in wait in a thicket?*
> *^{41}Who provides food for the raven*
> *when its young cry out to God*
> *and wander about for lack of food?"*
>
> JOB 38:39–41

As in the physics discussion, these verses similarly examine both Job's knowledge and ability: what Job knew and what he could do. Who provided for lions and ravens? Did Job know? Did Job do it?

But carnivores could be considered the high bar. A mere human might complain that studying and engaging with these sorts of creatures could put a person on the menu, particularly in the case of lions. So let's discuss other equally wild animals who, in contrast, pose no danger to people: let's discuss wild herbivores. Let's make the task even less threatening and discuss wild herbivores in moments of vulnerability: giving birth.

That's what God talked about next.

SWITCHING TO HERBIVORES

> *¹"Do you know when the mountain goats give birth?*
> *Do you watch when the doe bears her fawn?*
> *²Do you count the months till they bear?*
> *Do you know the time they give birth?*
> *³They crouch down and bring forth their young;*
> *their labor pains are ended.*
> *⁴Their young thrive and grow strong in the wilds;*
> *they leave and do not return."*
>
> JOB 39:1–4

Job did not know these activities, but he had seen their product: wild mountain goats thriving in the wild. Humanity's knowledge or involvement was not required. People know little and do nothing, even in the case of wild herbivores.

A DOWNGRADE FURTHER TO DOMESTIC ANIMALS

So how about formerly tamed animals who have become wild? Perhaps this is a more realistic place where humans might know something. After all, Job sought to confront God, so to be bold enough to challenge God, he must be operating from a strong understanding of "the vast expanses of the earth" (38:18) and "the laws of the heavens" (38:33). Wild carnivores and herbivores had escaped Job's sphere of knowledge and influence, so let's discuss domesticated donkeys. Job himself probably had donkeys escape and become wild. Surely these creatures, formerly farm animals, fall within his authoritative dominion.

And so, God continued his speech.

> *⁵"Who let the wild donkey go free?*
> *Who untied its ropes?*

> *⁶I gave it the wasteland as its home,*
> *the salt flats as its habitat.*
> *⁷It laughs at the commotion in the town;*
> *it does not hear a driver's shout.*
> *⁸It ranges the hills for its pasture*
> *and searches for any green thing."*
>
> JOB 39:5–8

Job may have once owned escaped donkeys, but he no longer provided for or controlled them. These donkeys laugh at their former captor. The wild donkeys do not hear the shout of their former driver. They are free. God provides for them. They find sustenance in a place where people would die: the wastelands, the salt flats. In a place where people would perish in a day, the escaped donkeys make their home.

What about potential new sources of domesticated animals? Forget the wild donkey. How about a sturdier source of animal labor? Can humanity tame a more productive beast than the donkey? That was God's next question.

> *⁹"Will the wild ox consent to serve you?*
> *Will it stay by your manger at night?*
> *¹⁰Can you hold it to the furrow with a harness?*
> *Will it till the valleys behind you?*
> *¹¹Will you rely on it for its great strength?*
> *Will you leave your heavy work to it?*
> *¹²Can you trust it to haul in your grain*
> *and bring it to your threshing floor?"*
>
> JOB 39:9–12

Humanity might watch the power of the wild ox with envy, but we cannot harness that power. To this day, there are fantastic mammals of considerable power in parts of Africa and elsewhere that would serve the needs of developing nations marvelously—but these beasts remain untamable even for us today. I live in Canada—we don't farm moose. Understanding genetics and breeding strategies does not help. Domestication techniques and tools that have worked across the world on various animals fail on many of these large animals. The African buffalo is another good example. Neither the African buffalo nor the moose can be coerced into pulling a plow. The zebra would make a powerfully muscled domestic breed, but they will not be domesticated. All attempts fall short. The ibex will not consent to help humans with manual labor, and the rhino would sooner kill than contemplate submission. There is muscle there, but it is not muscle that farmers can access.

These examples—the escaped donkey, the untamable wild ox—are here to show Job how limited people are. People know very little. People only manage to do what God has enabled them to do. Some animals can be tamed, but where God has made them untamable, so they remain. The lion and raven provide for themselves. Mountain goats do not need people's help, or even their awareness, to thrive in high, rocky places.

But what about apparently stupid creatures? Surely people can take some sort of pride over creatures that appear foolish and pathetic. God's following example seems almost comedic.

SILLY CREATURES

> [13] *"The wings of the ostrich flap joyfully,*
> *but they cannot compare*
> *with the wings and feathers of the stork."*
>
> JOB 39:13

This verse is setting up two things here. First, this verse that introduces the ostrich appears to focus on physical appearance: the ostrich looks joyful as it flaps its flightless wings, but its beauty is no match for the stork's graceful elegance in flight. This image at least partially serves to highlight the ostrich's physical ridiculousness. The ostrich's wings cannot fly and seem to serve no other function either. But another subtext is at play: many cultures characterize the ostrich as a careless parent. On the other hand, the stork embodies the opposite—so much so that in modern Western culture today, we tell fanciful stories about storks delivering human babies and feature stork illustrations in much baby-announcement paraphernalia. This introductory verse makes fun of the ostrich's comical appearance by comparing it to the stork, but the verse's real focus is on the creatures' contrasting parenting styles, as God went on to describe next as he told Job more about the ostrich.

> [14] *"She lays her eggs on the ground*
> *and lets them warm in the sand,*
> [15] *unmindful that a foot may crush them,*
> *that some wild animal may trample them.*
> [16] *She treats her young harshly, as if they were not hers;*
> *she cares not that her labor was in vain,*
> [17] *for God did not endow her with wisdom*
> *or give her a share of good sense."*
>
> Job 39:14–17

So here we now have the heart of God's ostrich and stork imagery. This is not the terror of the predatory lion, the unreachable mystery of the flying raven and the distant mountain goat, the frustration of the rebellious escaped donkey, or the stubbornness of the wild ox. Instead, this is the inept parenthood of an ungainly flightless bird. This is a creature, finally, that people might be tempted to scorn and smugly claim to have a seat of dominance over. But what did God say about the ostrich next?

> [18] *"Yet when she spreads her feathers to run,*
> *she laughs at horse and rider."*
>
> Job 39:18

Even the ostrich makes a mockery of humanity's knowledge and power.

CONSIDERING HORSES

This horse and rider reference brings to mind one area of creation where people can surely take some pride. The horse is a domesticated creature that evokes images of power, beauty, and awe. A plow horse is useful. A warhorse is terrifying. Even into the beginning of the twentieth century, horses were the fast attack weapon of choice both for well-equipped armies and for the literal heavily armored cavalry. Even today, we measure the output of our engines in units of horsepower. The sleek muscle car of my teenage dreams came with a 425 HP engine. There were 425 horses under the hood. Surely the horse is a creature that even ancient civilizations could take some pride in. So God asked about horses.

> [19] "Do you give the horse its strength
> or clothe its neck with a flowing mane?"
>
> JOB 39:19

Let's stop right there a moment. Can people really take any pride in the horse? Did we make the horse strong? No. Of course not. But God took the question one step further—did we give the horse a handle to hold on to? How far would we have gotten with horses by Job's day without a mane?

Moose make terrible riding animals—and they don't have manes. Deer cannot be tamed for riding—and they don't have manes either. The horse is perfect. God gave the horse its strength, its ability to be domesticated—and a handle.

I have had the pleasure of riding bareback. It is not easy. The back of a horse moves. You do not notice it the same way when you have a saddle. The ribs, the shoulders, the spine—they move. The bones move in independent directions. And horses sweat, so they get slippery too. That mane is all you've got, and the first people to tame and ride horses did not invent the bit, bridle, and saddle before figuring out how to ride bareback on the intricately mobile back of a galloping horse. From this simple, practical point, God went on to remind Job of the power and splendor of this creature.

> [20] "Do you make it leap like a locust,
> striking terror with its proud snorting?
> [21] It paws fiercely, rejoicing in its strength,
> and charges into the fray.
> [22] It laughs at fear, afraid of nothing;
> it does not shy away from the sword.
> [23] The quiver rattles against its side,
> along with the flashing spear and lance.
> [24] In frenzied excitement it eats up the ground;
> it cannot stand still when the trumpet sounds.

> ^{25}*At the blast of the trumpet it snorts, 'Aha!'*
>   *It catches the scent of battle from afar,*
>   *the shout of commanders and the battle cry.*
> ^{26}*Does the hawk take flight by your wisdom*
>   *and spread his wings toward the south?*
> ^{27}*Does the eagle soar at your command*
>   *and build his nest on high?*
> ^{28}*It dwells on a cliff and stays there at night;*
>   *a rocky crag is its stronghold.*
> ^{29}*From there it looks for food;*
>   *its eyes detect it from afar.*
> ^{30}*Its young ones feast on blood,*
>   *and where the slain are, there it is."*
>
> JOB 39:20–30

From horses, God had moved back to carnivores and birds, and thus this zoological survey has come full circle. First, God explored physics: the formation of the earth and its foundations, the boundaries of the sea, the movement of celestial bodies, the patterns of weather, and the laws of the heavens.

Then there was the zoological survey: carnivores, birds, wild herbivores, escaped domestic herbivores, untamable herbivores, the foolish-looking ostrich that still mocks us, the majestic horse, and then back to birds and carnivores.

WAS GOD BEING A BULLY?

There is a sizable population of critical commentaries that take exception with God's speech so far. Such critics characterize the speech as piling excessive contempt onto Job. They describe God as a bully who pummeled the suffering Job with point after point that only served to expose Job's ignorance and impotence. This viewpoint is further reinforced by how the following verses are typically translated.

> ^{1}*The Lord said to Job:*
> ^{2}*"Will the one who contends with the Almighty correct him?*

Concluding God's First Speech

> *Let him who accuses God answer him!"*
>
> JOB 40:1–2

This translation sings as a put-down. It sounds like God was saying, "Who are you to tell me what to do?" There is an element of that in the original, but the tone is different. Strictly speaking, a more literal translation of the word "correct" would be "yield."

> *Will the one who contends with the Almighty yield to him?*

But even a more strictly literal translation fails to capture the feeling that is in the original Hebrew poetry. This translation would better match the original verse's tone:

> *Will the one who contends with the Almighty yield to him or answer him?*
> *Since you accused God, you should answer God.*[124]

These alternate translations do not necessarily make God's words more palatable, but they do alter the tone. God was not shutting the conversation down but rather insisting on opening the conversation up. Will you yield to me, or will you answer me? Either option is open to you. You should choose to answer.

God did not want Job to shut up. God wanted Job to answer. He was not bullying Job; he was engaging with him.

How, in these circumstances, should Job respond? God had physics and the natural world all taken care of. He understands the weather and biology, astronomy and geology. Neither carnivore nor herbivore is a mystery to him. The wisdom and understanding that people do have is a gift from God. The animals that people have managed to usefully tame were given their usefulness and ability to be tamed from God himself. He knows all. He does all. He has the natural world wrapped up from a place of both knowledge and ability. There are no mysteries for the Creator. The natural world is his.

---

124 Translation options provided here based on Reyburn, 736-737.

BUT JOB WAS NOT DEALING WITH PHYSICS OR ZOOLOGY

The natural world did not challenge Job. The natural world seems to follow natural laws. The sun rises according to a predictable pattern. The carnivore always eats meat. The ostrich might seem stupid, but it also seems to know what it's doing after all and even laughs at people, even those on powerful warhorses. The donkey is happy being free and does just fine for itself, even in the wasteland. The natural world does just fine without people and is fairly predictable and orderly on its own.

The problem is that this was not the world that was giving Job trouble. On the contrary, predictable order is the exact opposite of what Job had been enduring. Chaos, excruciating and undeserved tragedies, and the apparent punishment of the righteous rather than the wicked were the violent, unnatural world that Job inhabited.

God had established his dominion over the normal world. Job's crisis, though, was abnormal.

Will Job yield? Or will Job answer?

60
JOB'S PASSIVE-AGGRESSIVE RESPONSE

³Then Job answered the Lord:
⁴"I am unworthy—how can I reply to you?
I put my hand over my mouth.
⁵I spoke once, but I have no answer—
twice, but I will say no more."

JOB 40:3–5

ONCE AGAIN, THE translation here supports the impression that God was bullying Job with Job immediately surrendering abjectly before the divine assault. But there is a crucial word in Hebrew that somehow got left out of our translation. Job's reply starts with the keyword if.

If I am unworthy—how can I reply to you?

If. If I am unworthy. If we accept as truth that I don't know anything, and if we accept that I have somehow been wicked and therefore deserve these tragedies, that the morning sun has risen and broken my upraised arm justly (38:15), then how can I reply? If.[125]

---

[125] The omission of this keyword *if* is consistent across all of the eight English translations I consulted. Some of these translations do, however, insert the word *behold* at the beginning, which is also a valid translation of this missing Hebrew word. The Hebrew word in question can mean either *behold* or *if*. The undertone

Job did not, however, believe that he was unworthy. Job did not believe that he deserved these troubles. Job was not dealing with natural situations. Job was dealing with the unnatural, and he had questions about God's handling of the unnatural events that had swamped his life.

The Standard View framework had created a God-versus-Job dilemma—either Job was secretly wicked or God was unjust.

Elihu had already tackled this false dilemma in his own way. He had shown Job the various ways God can act in the world and how we can interpret trouble in our lives. Even more pointedly, Elihu had sought to show that God, above all and regardless of appearances, is good, loves his children, and works through all situations for their good.

God is love. God is complicated. God doesn't always explain himself. But God is still love.

Whether Elihu's message failed to penetrate fully or God's overview of the natural world had lifted Job's cause-and-effect thinking back to the fore—whatever the cause—Job's response is borderline sarcastic. If I'm unworthy, how can I respond to you? I'll tell you what—I'll just shut up now.

Job was unhappy. Job was dissatisfied. Job may have yielded to God, but it was a sullen kind of yielding—and while yielding, he had also answered God back. If.

God can read between the lines. God knew what that if meant. God had a person before him who had not truly yielded or answered.

Theoretically, God could accept Job's response at face value and ignore the subtlety of the response, and we would be free then to just jump to the contents of chapter forty-two. God, however, was not willing to leave Job in his state of

---

of passive resistance in the poetry, however, remains even if we prefer the *behold* translation. "Behold, I am unworthy" does not in any way acknowledge God's greatness (as we will instead see in Job's second response in chapter forty-two), and it does not show that Job had accepted God's actions in the world. The *behold* translation just emphasizes his agreement to be quiet. The poetry of a *behold* statement is still Job-focused and upset, not God-focused and reconciled. The verse still conveys the "fine—I'll shut up now" posture. The other valid translation, *if*, displays Job's resistance to the Divine message even more clearly. He was agreeing to shut up. But God did not want him to shut up; God wanted him to answer. And Job was not answering; Job was shutting up even though he was clearly unhappy and not yet fully reconciled with God. For a reference regarding that missing *if*, see Janzen, 242-243.

false submission and sullenness. He told Job in 38:3 to "[b]race yourself like a man; I will question you, and you shall answer me." God expected more than sullen false submission. He expected Job to speak candidly and completely—to express his true heart—to engage with God truly. Yield or answer—either option was open. But a token nod in the direction of neither—where Job functionally told God to "interpret me as you see fit"—was not acceptable, and so before moving on, God restated his charge to Job in 40:7.

But before we look at 40:7, we have 40:6 to contend with.

SPEAKING FROM DARKNESS

⁶Then the Lord spoke to Job out of the storm…

JOB 40:6

We did not address this before, but in 38:1, God "spoke to Job out of the storm." Now in chapter forty, he continued to speak from the storm. What kind of storm? Wind? Rain? Snow? Thunder and lightning? Hail? Inevitably, whatever the storm, it would have been dark.

Elihu had described God's arrival as something that would come in golden splendor, linking it to the dawning of the sun sweeping clear the skies. It was a picture of awesome majesty, glory, and brightness—a new day. And yet, when God did arrive, he spoke in darkness, from a storm.

Elihu had described Job as someone "who swelter[ed] in [his own] clothes when the land lies hushed under the south wind," unable to assist God in his work of "spreading out the skies" (38:17–18). Elihu had also described God as someone who "brings clouds to punish people, or to water his earth and show his love" (37:13). God was the actor here. Job was the observer and just one of the many who experienced God's actions.

What was the basis for God speaking from the gloom, noise, and discomfort of a storm when Job longed for the clarity of blue skies and the peace that Elihu had foreshadowed in the final words of his speech?

When Elijah suffered, God came explicitly not in the storm but in "a gentle whisper" (1 Kings 19:11–12). Why did God subject the distressed Job to more distress? Why did the God of the rain—which could be both a blessing and a curse—come to Job in a storm?

NOT MEETING THE NEED

At the beginning of this book, I described how I started studying Job with a sense of seriousness and even anxiety. I hung my faith in God on the book of Job and its meaning or lack thereof. Either it would meet the needs of a suffering soul, or it was useless. My view of the whole of scripture was put on trial by this one part.

This was perhaps not a wise or humble approach to serious scripture study, but it was engaged. Like Jacob with the angel, I would not let go without a blessing.[126]

Job did not respond positively to God's first speech, and my own reaction was not dissimilar. I recognized that God was not quite the bully that a first reading (and numerous commentaries) implied. Still, I failed to see how God's catalog of impressive physics and zoological accomplishments could meet Job's need. Judging from Job's response, it did not. And it did not meet mine either.

MAKE IT STOP

We moved to Oakville, Ontario, when Mackenzie was four years old. When she started kindergarten, we finally had to acknowledge that she would not walk and introduced a wheelchair into her life. Until then, we had held out hope that she would get stronger. However, when she turned five, she still could not walk. She still ate through a tube attached to the little "gas cap" on her stomach. She threw up nearly every night.

Imagine a child with the stomach flu and the gift of projectile vomiting maintaining that stomach flu for five years straight. It is a small thing, the flu, manageable in a dosage that lasts less than a week, but after five years, we were exhausted, and so were the burned-out washing machine and the stink in our

---

126 See Genesis 32:22–32. The writer of Genesis identifies Jacob's opponent as a man. Jacob identified him as God. However, scripture later identifies Moses as the only person to see God face-to-face, suggesting that the identity Jacob ascribed to his opponent (but which his opponent did not acknowledge) was not accurate. Clearly Jacob's opponent was more than just a local shepherd. I take the view that Jacob's opponent was an angel, albeit one that obviously held back in his wrestling match with a mere mortal. Whether the opponent was a man, angel, or God, the point remains that Jacob *engaged* and would not willingly give up the contest without a blessing.

car. We bought a new washing machine, which we could ill afford to do. We scrubbed the upholstery in the car. But there was no place to buy a new us.

Jackson during this time was Mr. Enthusiasm. He started walking on his first birthday, but he had been a stair and furniture climber for six months already before that. He wanted to do things. He wanted to go places. His parents wanted peace, sanity, a day without vomiting, just one full night's sleep.

Our lives were not Job's life, but I empathized a great deal with what I interpreted to be Job's passive, resistant response to God's first speech. My thoughts were, You can do all this, but you can't make my daughter walk. Or you won't. Never mind walking, how about just getting her to stop vomiting every single day of our lives? Five years of projectile vomiting is too much. Make it stop. Make her sleep at night.

CALM BEFORE THE STORM

God spoke to Job out of a storm.

Perhaps Job would not have heard anything else.

We lived in a storm—work stress, marital strain, medical crises, sleep deprivation, needles, tests, false diagnoses. We either needed God to speak to us from a storm, or we needed peace—an oasis of time in which to collect ourselves. One or the other.

God came to Job in a storm.

He gave us a moment of calm before a new storm and spoke in that calm.

I was offered the opportunity to preach in our new church shortly after moving to Oakville. The minister made the offer. The only thing I was interested in exploring at the time was Job. I had been at it for several years already. I offered to preach Job, but I warned that I could not do it in one sermon. How about a series? Once every six weeks or so.

It was kind of a bizarre request for a new member afforded the honor of one sermon to counter with asking for a series and even more unusual for the minister and elders to agree to it. And so began a three-and-a-half-year preaching journey. Once every six weeks quickly became once a month. On Sunday mornings, once a month, I took the church slowly through the book of Job. We left no stone unturned. No chapter was skipped. We had never done anything like it before as a congregation, but for three and a half years, verse by verse, that is what we did.

The series was an act of faith. I had studied the book to the end numerous times. Even before starting the series, I felt like I was on solid ground, at least until chapter forty. Once we got into God's speeches, I felt less secure. My life was still a storm. I still did not yet see how God helped with what he said.

Contrary to many commentaries' viewpoint, Elihu offered some value. There was a human, humane, and balancing perspective there. But God's speeches from the storm still left me uncertain. God knew a lot and could do a lot, but the end of God's speech did not resolve for me God's role in chaos; in the uncertain; in the unfair, unreasonable, and unsearchable; in pain and even despair. Like Job, I took the point that I should just shut up before this powerful deity. I got no comfort from the first divine speech's message that God knew what he was doing in the unusual, in the out-of-the-ordinary, in the broken situations.

God made the universe orderly.

But where was he when it fell apart?

STARTING ON FAITH

We went ahead and started that sermon series. The church did not know that my own faith in how the book of Job ended was still shaky. I kept that nugget to myself. I pressed on in faith. It would be over three years before I got to chapter forty. I had time. I had more study to do. In the worst-case scenario, if I eventually had nothing of value to share, I would either have to offer up a sermon of platitudes—regurgitated secondhand fluff—or else I would have to acknowledge that ultimately this book of Job had failed to help a believer—me—when I had needed it most.

The book of Job appeared to promise something of meaning. Would it deliver? I had already read a dozen critical essays on Job that implied that in the end, it was a big disappointment. But then, many of these same essays and commentaries had also criticized Elihu inappropriately. So I had hope that there was specific, personally applicable meaning to be found in God's speeches as well.

We, the local church and I, would find out together.

61

A REBUKE AND COMMAND TO ENGAGE

Before God dove into the heart of his second speech to Job, he challenged Job to engage. Passive resistance or false compliance were not acceptable. Job was to brace himself like a man and engage. Here's how God put it:

> *⁷"Brace yourself like a man;*
> *I will question you,*
> *and you shall answer me.*
> *⁸Would you discredit my justice?*
> *Would you condemn me to justify yourself?"*
>
> Job 40:7–8

This was the heart of Elihu's concern with Job, as we noted in previous chapters. Job and his friends were playing a zero-sum game: either Job was guilty and God was justified, or Job was innocent and God was wrong. There had to be a loser here.

After charging Job to brace himself like a man and engage, God here spoke out against the zero-sum game Job and his friends had played and, more particularly, against Job's role within that debate where he had focused on his own defense rather than anything else. But really, how could a person in pain do anything but try to recover his sense of security in the face of everything he had already endured? Does God not understand that in addition to Job's physical and emotional pain, an even deeper spiritual and existential crisis had overwhelmed Job's relationship with his Creator?

It seems like God didn't acknowledge this but instead pressed on, escalating his challenge into a sarcasm-tinged rebuke. Here is what God said next:

> [9] "Do you have an arm like God's,
>   and can your voice thunder like his?[127]
> [10] Then adorn yourself with glory and splendor,
>   and clothe yourself in honor and majesty.
> [11] Unleash the fury of your wrath,
>   look at all who are proud and bring them low,
> [12] look at all who are proud and humble them,
>   crush the wicked where they stand.
> [13] Bury them all in the dust together;
>   shroud their faces in the grave.
> [14] Then I myself will admit to you
>   that your own right hand can save you."
>
> JOB 40:9–14

God appears to be relentless here. In chapters thirty-eight and thirty-nine, God had surveyed physics and zoology and had demonstrated that God knows, did, and does far more than humanity can even begin to imagine, design, create, or maintain. Within the context of the zero-sum justice debate between Job and his friends, the implication of God's speeches—an implication beyond the specifics of physics and biology—was that God alone also had the power to define and enforce justice. Only God spoke with a voice of thunder. Only God could bring the proud down.

In chapters thirty-eight and thirty-nine, God had spoken in poetic images, and then here in 40:9–14, God more precisely applied these images to Job's situation. In keeping with Elihu's thesis, and even going a step beyond Elihu, the message of chapters thirty-eight and thirty-nine is this: God alone can provide salvation.

Elihu had taught that this is what God wants to do—God intends to save. But God was making it very clear here that the task to save is also one only God can complete—the very thing that people cannot do. Job could not save himself—no one can save themself. But God can save.

Job's situation so far had been hell—was hell, emotionally speaking.

---

[127] This verse is subtly referencing Elihu's description of God's awesome power. See 37:4.

God let Job know that God has both the knowledge and the power to save Job from this hell.

Job could not save himself. The zero-sum contest between Job and God was not on. God was Job's only hope. Regardless of how much a worldly philosophy or tradition of religious logic might tie up a person in knots, when that analysis leads to a people-versus-God debate, the analysis is fatally flawed. God was Job's only hope.

A rebuke had occurred here. It is poetic. It is literary. But it is clear. Before giving this rebuke, God had reissued his challenge for Job to engage. It was not just a challenge but a command. God said, "You shall answer me" (38:3).

I can imagine Job, hearing God speak to him out of a storm in a voice like thunder, blinking in surprise and perhaps fear. This was not an impersonal survey of physics and biology anymore. This was God planting a rebuke like a two-by-four in the middle of Job's forehead.

I sat up as I read this. I had been a fan of the prophets, particularly Jeremiah, from my early twenties. God's language here is Jeremiah-like. It is a rebuke laced with divine sarcasm and a bit of anger. There is a command, a challenge, and an implied threat. God is not someone you want to be in a contest against.

I can imagine Job gasping. All the trials and agonies until this point collapse when the physical world is stripped away and a person is solo before God, getting it straight from the heavenly Father.

The mouth might gasp. The heart might race. The spine may cause a soul to sit up straight. A person might sit down, grip the arms of their chair, even tremble. A rebuke, thundered in the voice of God from a storm, might leave a soul wondering, Is there no hope anywhere here for comfort?

Is there nothing for the overpowered and deeply suffering soul to cling to, to find hope in, to find some warmth and divine love in?

Is God this unrelentingly fierce forever?

Do we have to wait for thousands of years until Christ comes and weeps at Lazarus's tomb, until Jesus has compassion on widows and bereaved parents and the sick, handicapped, and suffering—do we have to wait for the cross before we get some light of hope and kindness from our Creator?

62

THE MONSTER COMES

Something started happening in my daughter's body as I began preparing my sermon on Job chapters forty and forty-one. She was a month shy of her eighth birthday. After I had written the sermon but before I preached it, something big happened.

It started on a Monday night in January 2009. The kids were tucked into bed upstairs.

My wife was on the main floor in the kitchen, checking email, and I was upstairs taking a shower. My wife heard a low moaning sound, and at first, she thought it was the plumbing making strange sounds while I had my shower. She heard it again and went to the foot of the stairs to get a better idea of where the sound was coming from, but it had stopped. She went back to the kitchen. Again the low moaning sound appeared. And then a third time. Each time, she went to the foot of the stairs, and the sound stopped.

I came downstairs a short while later, and Carolyn asked if I had heard the strange moaning sound. I hadn't heard anything and dismissed it—Mackenzie probably could not sleep and had made up some new sound to entertain herself. So we sat down in the family room to watch a movie.

Jackson was his usual silent, four-year-old, out-like-a-light self, but Mackenzie was probably still awake. The earlier noises had unsettled Carolyn, and so before the movie started, she decided to go upstairs to check on Mackenzie.

The phrase "the calm before the storm" could describe the months leading up to that night. We'd had a nice Christmas and quality time with friends.

Work was finally going well again. It was the sort of period that any healthy family could expect to enjoy.

It was the calm before the storm. Or a God-given hiatus—a sabbatical from stress to recharge before the next leg in the journey. We had grown almost complacent about Mackenzie's health. At least she was stable. Likewise, Carolyn's depression and mysterious blackouts and seizures had not vanished, but they had become manageable. Some of the anti-romantic impacts of the medication were reduced with a new prescription. Jackson was nearly five now and past some of that early-toddler high-maintenance stage. Finally, after almost eight years, we had found a new version of normal we could live with.

Carolyn went upstairs to check on Mackenzie. I was absentmindedly watching commercials and waiting for my wife to come back downstairs with a status-quo report when I suddenly heard her shouting my name.

When you have lived through eight years of medical crises, a few months of calm and complacency do not dull the reflexes. I sprinted up the stairs.

Mackenzie's body was twisted into a rigid arc, lips pulled back into a terrible Joker grimace, and saliva foamed at her mouth. Her eyes rolled around wildly, and her arms and legs clenched and released in uncontrolled spasms. We called to her. I picked her up, and she was a stiff board, oblivious to both gravity and daddy's hug.

Our efficient selves kicked in. The communication protocol and roles we had developed over the previous eight years came into full swing—we had developed a role-clarity practice in our home at great emotional cost. My wife raced to our bedroom to call 911 while I disconnected Mackenzie's feeding apparatus from her stomach and took her into our room to try to calm her on a larger bed where I would not risk dropping her. I cleaned her face, talked to her, caressed her hair, tried to reach her. Carolyn raced downstairs to the computer to print out copies of Mackenzie's medications and dosages, health card number, and case doctors' names.

Mackenzie had never seized before. She went from a child with many medical problems but never seizures to suddenly having a full grand mal seizure. We learned the new, proper terminology later: it was a tonic-clonic seizure. We also learned later that they usually last seconds or a couple of minutes. Anything more than a minute or two risked brain damage.

Mackenzie's first seizure had probably gone on for twenty minutes or more before my wife went up to check on her. It would go on for nearly six hours.

The ambulance arrived at the same time as the fire truck with its paramedics. They filled our front foyer with people, a gurney, medical bags. They administered valium on the spot to no effect. Our daughter's breathing was desperate. Her little, usually weak body could not be bent to conform even to the slope of the gurney. The paramedics were unable to control the seizure and raced her out to the ambulance.

I grabbed my cell phone and raced to our car to follow, leaving my wife in a state of shock to look after our still sleeping son and clean up the floor littered with wet boot prints, emptied syringes, and discarded medical packaging. I followed the siren and flashing lights across town, mindless of red lights and traffic, slightly deranged. I could barely see through the tears in my eyes. I had seen Mackenzie through many things, but I had never seen that Joker grimace, the foam at the mouth, and the set, bug-eyed, absent expression.

At home, Carolyn collapsed, recovered, then called one of her friends, who called another. Then she called her mom to come and stay over with Jackson so she could come to the hospital. While Carolyn was packing a bag for Mackenzie, our friend Hazel arrived, noting that an emergency vehicle was still outside. Perhaps someone was still writing up a report.

As soon as Carolyn's mom arrived, Carolyn and Hazel left for the hospital. Pulling out of the driveway, they realized that the emergency vehicle still parked outside was empty. The motor was still running. The vehicle had been abandoned as all personnel had left with our daughter.

It was around nine o'clock when we rushed across town to the old Oakville Trafalgar hospital. The seizure lasted nearly six hours, despite the valium the paramedics had administered in our house and then again in the ambulance, despite the anti-seizure drugs administered in the hospital. When they put her under a general anesthetic, the seizure kept pushing its way through. She threw up with clenched teeth, inhaled, and then stopped breathing. The emergency-room staff forced her seizure-clenched jaws open to clear her lungs and put her on a breathing machine. I stayed, talked to her, held her fist, tried to calm her. Even though the medical team had the breathing machine to support their efforts, they had trouble keeping Mackenzie's oxygen levels up. Her blood pressure kept dropping. Her heart would start racing and then suddenly slow down, too slow, heartbreakingly slow. And she kept seizing as the anesthesia weakened. For nearly six hours, this went on until they got enough drugs into her to stop, or at least conceal, the seizure activity for good. At around half past two in the morning, the Pediatric Critical Response Team transferred her to the ICU at McMaster Children's Hospital in Hamilton, a forty-minute drive away. This was Monday night and Tuesday morning. They did blood work, an EEG, a CT scan. Nothing. No explanation.

We'd had no explanation for her health problems for the nearly eight years of her life, so why change now?

She woke up for about five minutes on Tuesday night, recognized us, touched our hands, then went back to sleep. She had been unconscious for over twenty-four hours, and now she slept again.

On Wednesday, she was considered stable as far as her vital signs were concerned. She still had not woken up, but her heart rate and breathing were both stable, and so she was transferred out of the ICU to a regular children's ward at McMaster. She did not wake up at all on Wednesday.

Finally, on Thursday night, she woke up again. She had been asleep for over three days. She woke up, talked, played in her bed, gave hugs, and held our hands. She had never been able to say the words "I love you," but she seemed to be communicating that in every way that she did know how. I left the room at one point, and when I came back, I found my wife curled up on the tiny child's bed with Mackenzie, the two of them very quiet together and peaceful again.

BREAK TIME IS OVER

By this point, I had been preaching through the book of Job on Sundays for over three years. I started preaching one sermon every six weeks, and then we quickly moved toward a monthly schedule. Until this point, we had been blessed with nearly six years without an actual full-blown medical crisis. We'd had our challenges. Learning she would not walk and making a wheelchair a part of our home were big emotional challenges. I would never walk my daughter down the aisle. I would never see her run and jump with friends. She had developed a vocabulary but not a big or eloquent one, and so learning that she would probably never speak or communicate as clearly as we would like was hard. When she was a baby, I told people that I did not care if she ever made it to the Olympics; I just wanted to have a good conversation with my daughter. Understanding that this too would be denied to us was hard. Adapting to the G-tube and feeding pump was as emotional as it was medical.

These were just some of the various hurts to handle. The ongoing, year-after-year sleep deprivation and seemingly endless vomiting brought their own stress, but we had been spared a full-blown medical crisis for several years. She hadn't had an ambulance-requiring emergency since she was two years old. No sirens or emergency rooms or ICUs, blood, needles, orders shouted by urgent professionals in white. None of that. A blessed respite.

During that whole period, I had kept studying Job. For three years, I had been preaching it.

Mackenzie came home by the end of the week. That was January 2009. In February, she turned eight. On Mother's Day, she seized again. Another rush to the hospital, but this time we identified the strange noise immediately and had our own supply of the antiseizure drugs to administer ourselves. By the time the ambulance arrived, she was trembling but quiet. She came home around one in the morning, and I was out the door by six o'clock for work. I had an interview that morning for my first senior manager job and had to manufacture calm on three hours of sleep and an internal swirl of fear and distraction. The craziness of her early years seemed to be returning.

Mackenzie continued to have small seizures. They began to increase in frequency to the point where they were occurring several times a week. Each time we caught them quickly, but she seemed to be losing the ability to resist them herself. They happened more often. Every seizure was dangerous, and in clusters, they signaled an accelerating problem, but no one could explain why they were occurring. Two occurred on the same day.

Finally, in June, we were scheduled for an MRI at McMaster Children's Hospital. It was a Monday morning. Another Monday. That first visit to a breastfeeding clinic in Vancouver had been on a Monday—the one that was supposed to end in a Stanley Park picnic and instead turned into visiting three hospitals in one day and staying for ten days before we went home again. I've become leery about Mondays.

I took this Monday morning off work to attend the appointment and planned to be back at work in the afternoon. An MRI requires the patient to be perfectly still, and for Mackenzie, that required a general anesthetic. The nurse came and took Mackenzie away to prep her for the anesthesia, and we remained in the waiting area until they were ready for us. We could hear Mackenzie around the corner.

"Something is wrong," Carolyn said. "I know that sound."

The nurse came out a few minutes later and said, "She's not cooperating, so it's taking longer than expected."

"Not cooperating?" My wife turned to me. "I know that sound she makes. Something is wrong. She's having a seizure."

Sure enough, when the doctor finally came out, he told us that Mackenzie had seized. The standard drug had not worked. They tried another. It did not work. They had a full anesthesia team at her bedside prepping for the MRI in one of the premier children's hospitals in all of Canada, and they could not get her to stop seizing. She went downhill fast. From a cocktail of antiseizure drugs to eventually a general anesthetic, she wound up back in a coma and on a lung machine.

The doctor informed us that the MRI did not go ahead, that Mackenzie had seized very badly, and that she was in the process of being transferred immediately to the Pediatric Critical Care Unit on the other side of the hospital. ICU for kids. We were not going home. When we got to her room, she was unconscious. A large clear plastic tube was forcing her mouth open and traveling down her throat, where it forced oxygen-rich air in and out of her lungs. She had an IV line and a tiny blood pressure cuff. She had heart monitor suction cups and wires sprouting from her naked chest. She was supposed to come home with us now. It was just a quick morning appointment—a simple test. She was laughing this morning and giving hugs.

Later in the week, they tried to remove the breathing machine. I was keen to get it out. She was unconscious but still fought the machine and gagged on it even in her sleep. I strongly encouraged the doctors to free her from the contraption and let her rest. The decision was made. They removed the tube, and she stopped breathing altogether. Her throat collapsed, her oxygen levels sank, and her heartbeat went wildly irregular. I watched, horrified, jammed in the corner of the room behind the specialist doctors and nurses as they held her convulsing body down, stabbed her with adrenaline injections, squeezed the breathing equipment back down her throat, and reattached IV lines and electrical leads.

It was my fault, of course. At least, that was what I told myself. I was the one who wanted her off the machine.

Eventually, Mackenzie stabilized. She was in a coma for a week. While she was in the coma, the medical team finally got to do that MRI.

My wife and I took turns sleeping in the hospital so that one of us was always with Mackenzie. I missed my son's fifth birthday party, during which he managed to contract chicken pox because apparently, we needed more to focus on at once. One morning, I left the Pediatric Critical Care Unit, showered and shaved, put on a suit, and took the train into Toronto for the second interview for that senior manager role. I deserved an Oscar for best lead in a male role for the simple act of staying calm and professional through that grueling interview. Afterward, I took the train straight back to Hamilton, still in my suit, to find my wife surrounded by doctors explaining things in that Latin code so beloved by medical professionals.

There was something wrong with Mackenzie's brain, but it was inconclusive. It was, however, suggestive. The doctors ordered more tests.

They transferred Mackenzie from the critical care unit to a regular ward eight days later, where she finally woke up. She came home eventually.

AFTER EIGHT YEARS, A DIAGNOSIS

I got the new job. It was a long-awaited promotion. I was set to start on a Monday in September.

On the Friday beforehand, Carolyn had a results appointment in Hamilton to attend. As it was my last day on the old job, and as over the past eight and a half years test results had always been inconclusive, there did not seem to be any point in me attending. So I spent the last Friday getting ready to start my new job and tidying up the old. When you live with an ongoing medical crisis, you must negotiate daily what needs to take priority: maintaining your emotional wellbeing or keeping the mortgage paid and groceries on the table. The decision to choose work and let my wife handle the appointment seemed appropriate at the time.

Carolyn called me at work that afternoon. We had a diagnosis. After over eight and a half years, we had a diagnosis. After countless appointments over eight and a half years, the one I missed was the one I should have attended.

Mackenzie had a cytochrome c oxidase deficiency (COX deficiency). It was terminal. It was not curable. Most kids did not make it past age three or four. For kids who lived longer, the onset of seizure activity at around eight years old was normal. It marked the beginning of the end. The body from here broke down slowly but relentlessly.

Starting seizures at eight years old was the first thing Mackenzie ever did in her life on schedule. We might have another two years with her. Maybe five. Some lived into their teens, and some lived longer, but living into adulthood was rare and was usually accompanied by losing most skills and abilities. Survival, when it did occur, cost nearly everything.

The diagnosis fit. The not eating, the vomiting, the weakness and inability to walk, the seizures before her eighth birthday—it all fit. Other things fit as well. She had been slowly losing her vocabulary for over a year. This was a subtle development. It was the kind of thing that was easy to ignore or put down as her being lazy. So when she did sign language for music instead of just saying it or began to mispronounce things, it was easy not to credit it as serious. But as her vocabulary shrunk from about eighty words to half a dozen, we could not pretend it wasn't happening any longer. Now it was a symptom. And the symptom fit the diagnosis.

How much time did we have? No one knew. She did not have the well-known versions of the COX deficiency—the ones that took kids at two or three or four. She had one of the types that were much more poorly understood. Two years more? Five? The teen years were usually the final straw, so she would not outlive those years for sure. This deficiency usually could not handle the growth stresses of puberty, so puberty was a death sentence.

We got the news on a Friday. I started my new job on Monday, leading a new team in a technology area of the bank, having never worked a technology job before. That first day on the job, I felt like a white-hot blade had sliced my soul cleanly down the middle, but only underneath the skin where no one could see. I had a leadership job to perform with responsibility for three technology teams, and I'd never worked in technology before, and I had that new job to do with a father's heart that cried on the train station platform in the early morning darkness and came unglued in the evening.

WHERE DOES JOB FIT INTO THIS?

Why have we reviewed this long personal story amid our study of the book of Job?

This personal detail is very relevant to our study. Let me explain.

I started this study because of Mackenzie. By the time her first seizure occurred, I was three years into preaching through the book. By the time we got her diagnosis, I was done preaching the series. The preaching series had lasted three and a half years, and my personal study had started another five years before that. All this effort was motivated by a faith shaken, and after eight and a half years, it begs the question: did it help?

Did I learn anything from the book of Job that helped?

In January of 2009, when the first seizure occurred, I had only preached up to chapter thirty-nine of the book of Job. I had written the sermon for chapters forty and forty-one, but I had not preached it yet.

And so, the question: was there anything that I had preached up to chapter thirty-nine of Job's book that helped when the first seizure happened, or that helped as the subsequent seizures and further crises unfolded, or that helped when we finally received a horrible diagnosis?

The honest answer is no.

Nothing that I had preached up until that night in January helped in the crisis. Nothing.

Chasing the ambulance that first Monday night, trying to make it to the hospital at the same time as my daughter, standing at the head of her gurney in the emergency room while they inserted three different IV lines, while she seized uncontrollably, while they vacuumed out her throat and lungs and inserted a breathing tube and hooked her up to a ventilator, oxygen saturation monitor, respiratory monitor, heart rate monitor, her clothes cut from her nearly eight-year-old body for the sake of speed and efficiency—nothing in thirty-nine chapters of Job helped. There were more doctors and nurses working on her little body than there was space for them around her, and I finally had to stand back and watch from several feet away to make room for people who had more training and could do more for her, and nothing that I had preached so far in thirty-nine chapters of Job helped to calm me. Thirty-nine chapters and nothing helped. Nothing Job's friends said helped; Job's example was meaningless to me; Elihu's points were academically interesting, but they did nothing to touch my heart; and even God's first speech did not help. It did not help Job, and it did not help me.

It was all useless material.

Thirty-nine chapters did not help.

But chapters forty and forty-one helped.

God have mercy, chapters forty and forty-one helped.

THEN GOD SPOKE

I had already written several versions of the sermon on these chapters before that Monday-night ambulance. All the way to the hospital, following the ambulance, running red lights, chasing the flashing lights, trying to make sure I was going to be there when my daughter got there, crying so hard I could hardly see—the whole way I kept repeating the title to the sermon and remembering the points. And it helped. It helped so much it made me cry harder. I cried from fear. I cried for my daughter. But I also cried from gratitude. I cried from hope. I kept repeating the title of the sermon.

You will figure the title out for yourself soon.

But let me just say that after thirty-one chapters of Job and his three friends trying to figure life out, they got nowhere. Then Elihu spoke in chapters thirty-two to thirty-six, and he had some good stuff to say, but he did not fix things. Job could not argue with Elihu. Elihu was the only friend God did not get angry with. He had good things to say. But Elihu did not fix anything.

Then God spoke.

God's first speech established the background. It was foundational. Elihu had laid the groundwork of God's motives—to save and love—and he had offered the qualifiers that God was complicated, that he did not always explain himself, and that he operated in a context beyond the mere human gaze.

God himself had then laid the groundwork for the scope of his influence: he created and maintains all—even the foundations of the earth, the laws of physics, the order of zoology, and the wonder of the heavens. But these two background speeches did not resolve Job's pain. He said as much himself in his first response to God.

God's response was stern. He was not rebuking Job's hurt. Instead, God was verbally taking Job by the chin and making him look God in the eye. God responded by calling for Job's undivided attention. God commanded Job, for the second time, to engage. To focus. To hear. And to respond.

The following two chapters are the record of God's next words to Job.

And God have mercy, it was what I had been looking for from the beginning of my study on Job. Behind the ambulance, in the emergency room, in the critical care units, through the beeping of monitors and Darth Vader breathing of the mechanical lungs and the eventual diagnosis of a terminal, uncurable condition for my only little girl—what God had to say next helped. It did not just help. It made me cry for good reasons.

We need to take God's second speech very slowly. It matters. It matters a great deal.

63

INTRODUCING GOD'S FIRST MONSTER

> *15 "Look at Behemoth,*
>   *which I made along with you*
>   *and which feeds on grass like an ox."*
>
> JOB 40:15

IT WILL HELP to get one thing straight right from the beginning. For the rest of this chapter, we will be hearing God discuss the behemoth, and in chapter forty-one, we'll learn about the leviathan. These two creatures are so thoroughly misrepresented in most commentaries that it borders on a conspiracy to obscure God's point. Such commentaries describe the behemoth as a land-based herbivore. The leviathan is apparently both terrestrial and aquatic and, one would assume (although it's not explicitly stated), a carnivore. Much ink has been spilled trying to identify these two creatures in modern zoological terms. The behemoth is variously billed as either an elephant or a hippopotamus. Although its description sounds more like something from the Jurassic period or a dragon from mythology, the leviathan often gets called a crocodile. As we will see, attempts at zoological classification appear to miss God's point.

Until now, God had talked about the wonder and mysteries of mundane physics, geology, and ordinary zoology. He had depicted the world as orderly and positioned himself as the only one with full knowledge of and power over this orderly world. But Job had not been dealing with an orderly world. Job had been dealing with a world in disorder.

After his tour of physics and zoology, God had rebuked Job for his either/or, zero-sum, Standard View approach for interpreting the disorder Job was experiencing, and he made it clear that God, and only God, could save Job from this chaos.

What came next was not repetition, and it was not personal revelation either. God was not circling around for yet another zoology tour. God had done that already. He was not revealing the order behind Job's personal chaos either. What God was about to do through his discussion of the behemoth and the leviathan was to speak of an unmatchable power that humanity cannot control—of a horror-filled chaos that only God can master.

Job was dealing with a monstrous turn of events and the aftermath of these horrors. Now, through the behemoth and the leviathan, God addressed monsters. God addressed monsters, and he addressed humanity's inability to have any effect on these monsters. Then he addressed his own authority and power over even the monsters.

> [15] "Look at Behemoth,
> which I made along with you
> and which feeds on grass like an ox."
>
> JOB 40:15

In Hebrew, behemoth is just the normal Hebrew word for animal or beast.[128] You could use it to describe cattle. A farmer might go out and milk his behemoth, and it would raise no eyebrows. However, in the Hebrew of this verse, the word is plural: the verse literally translates as "Look at the behemoths." The plural here is notable for a grammatical irregularity: the following verses refer to this creature in the singular. One interpretation of this oddity is that using a plural form for a singular creature is a poetic device that serves to portray a dimension of exceptionality or greatness. That is, it was a large beast. Perhaps that's why the NIV chose to capitalize their use of the word.

Think of this interpretation as a writer looking at a single creature and saying, "Look at the creatures." There is only one. But it is a big one—so big in fact that the viewer labels it as more than one.

---

128 Reyburn, 745.

The behemoth was a big land animal. The hippo and elephant are not bad mental images, but do not get hung up on actually identifying the beast. Power is the point, not zoological classification in an era before zoos or other means to examine these sorts of creatures up close in a nonthreatening setting. In the wild, in an era before steel and gunpowder, the behemoth was a biological tank, and its grass-eater status was small comfort to the person who might stumble on one in the field. Maybe the rhinoceros would be a better mental image for us to carry as we follow the rest of God's discussion of this creature.

> *16 "What strength it has in its loins,*
> *what power in the muscles of its belly!*
> *17 Its tail sways like a cedar;[129]*
> *The sinews of its thighs are close-knit.*
> *18 Its bones are tubes of bronze,*
> *its limbs like rods of iron.*
> *19 It ranks first among the works of God,*
> *yet its Maker can approach it with his sword."*
>
> JOB 40:16–19

This great beast "ranks first among the works of God." What does that

---

[129] The exact meaning of the Hebrew word that the NIV translates as "tail" here is uncertain. Clearly there is nothing on the rhino or hippo that sways like a cedar. The elephant-supporters interpret the word as "trunk" and claim zoological classification victory. But elephant trunks don't sway like cedars either. They loop around every which way with seemingly infinite flexibility. But remember what we learned about Hebrew poetry: the first and second line should be parallel to each other. Their meaning should rhyme. What body part does verse sixteen discuss? Both the first and second line speak of loins and muscles in the belly. They rhyme. What about verse eighteen? Bones and limbs. Again the ideas rhyme. So how should we understand verse seventeen? An unknown word describing a body part that sways in the first line, and the second line speaks of sinews of the creature's thighs. The unknown word should be parallel in meaning to thighs—or the sinews of the thighs. Or legs. Definitely not tail or trunk. Perhaps it is the legs that sway like a cedar. That image actually isn't a bad description of an elephant's gait. "Its leg sways like a cedar, the sinews of its thighs are close-knit." If by chance this is an elephant under discussion, then presumably it's the upsized African elephant and not the more diminutive Indian version.

mean? Did God make it first? Was it the boss? The king of the region? The top prize creation?

Given that the preceding verses emphasize the behemoth's strength, its bones like bronze, and other significant features, perhaps the first line of verse nineteen is conveying that this creature is at the top of the power hierarchy. This interpretation would certainly fit with the second line of verse nineteen: the second line would rhyme with and expand upon the first line not by repeating the same idea but by contrasting against it. Yet. The first line says one thing, and the second line provides a contrasting point: the beast ranks first, yet its Maker can approach it. This is another very typical poetic use of parallelism in Hebrew poetry and one the reader was likely familiar with from the book of Proverbs, where examples of the construction "the fool does this, but the wise does that" abound. The great beast "ranks first among the works of God, yet its Maker can approach it with his sword."

As great as this behemoth is, God can deal with it. Why approach it with a sword? Our English translation suggests that God can deal with the behemoth, but only if he has a sword for protection. This is an unfortunate inference, as it suggests that God without a sword might have some difficulty with the behemoth. The Hebrew phrase says that God can approach the behemoth with his sword, but the implied meaning in Hebrew is not that God needs the sword but rather that he uses the sword to signal his intent when he approaches. You use a sword to defeat something or someone. The meaning for the original reader was "yet his Maker can defeat him." If it said God could approach the behemoth with a paintbrush, the verse would mean that God could get close enough to paint a picture of it. Instead, the verse says that God can approach with a sword. God can defeat the behemoth. The behemoth ranks first among the works of God, but it does not rank next to God. The behemoth is a monster in size and power, impervious to the assaults of humankind (as we will see in verse twenty-four), but God masters even this monster.

What else did God say about this creature?

> [20] "The hills bring it their produce,
> and all the wild animals play nearby.

> *²¹ Under the lotus plant it lies,*¹³⁰
> > *hidden among the reeds in the marsh.*
> *²² The lotuses conceal it in their shadow;*
> > *the poplars by the stream surround it.*
> *²³ A raging river does not alarm it;*
> > *it is secure, though the Jordan should surge against its mouth.*
> *²⁴ Can anyone capture it by the eyes,*
> > *or trap it and pierce its nose?"*
>
> JOB 40:20–24

"Can anyone capture it by the eyes?" Who captures something by the eyes? You do not go hunting and seize something by grabbing it by the eyeballs. It sounds ridiculous, and it is ridiculous, and it is not what the Hebrew says. The Hebrew says "Can anyone take him with his eyes?"¹³¹ In other words, can you capture the behemoth by eye power? Since there is no point in talking about trapping this powerful and massive creature by brute force, can you mystically stare down the beast to capture it? No, of course not, and that is the point.

"Or trap it and pierce its nose?" This sounds less ridiculous. People pierce the snouts of pigs so they do not tunnel their way out of pens. Maybe

---

130 There is something odd about the parallelism in verses twenty-one and twenty-two, which perhaps accounts for a mistranslation by the NIV and other modern translations. The "lotus plant" and "lotuses" in these verses are not the flowering water lily that the English word suggests. This focus on aquatic plants perhaps accounts for the popularity of the theory that the behemoth is a hippo despite its lack of a tail, trunk, or legs that could be described as "sway[ing] like a cedar" (40:17). The plant the original Hebrew references is actually not an aquatic organism at all but a thorny tree. The unusual parallelism here, however, is that the first line of verse twenty-one speaks of the behemoth lying under this thorny tree (a reasonable image in a hot climate), but then the second line describes the beast as hidden in the reeds in the marsh. This verse here is presumably drawing a parallel between the various places where the behemoth hangs out to escape the heat. But then verse twenty-two uses the same parallel structure: the first line describes a resting place beneath dry-land foliage and the second beneath aquatic plants. This switch of locations perhaps accounts for the NIV's preference to keep the scene in the water for all lines of these two verses. So the NIV translators replaced "thorny tree" with "lotus."

131 Reyburn, 749.

somebody would pierce the behemoth's nose to control it, but once again, that is not what the Hebrew says. The Hebrew says "or pierce its nose with a snare." [132] This is not a trap-and-then-pierce scenario. The verse describes piercing the beast with a thin rope in an attempt to control it. The snare here is not the modern woven wire or a nearly invisible synthetic line. This is an ancient plant-fiber snare. Even if you trapped the behemoth, held it down, and kept it very still, you are still not going to pierce any part of him with a piece of rope. A rope is not a piercing tool. And the behemoth is not yet trapped. It is a wildly massive creature with legs (or some other body part) that sway like a cedar, the first among God's works. The image is one of impossibility. Since you cannot capture it by eye power, it sure would be nice to use a snare to pierce its nose somehow and presumably gain some control over it. But how would you trap it and keep it still so you could pierce its nose in the first place?

You cannot trap a behemoth by eye power. You cannot pierce its nose with a rope. There is no point in even trying to wrestle it into submission by brute strength. You are useless against the behemoth. It has body parts that sway like a cedar, it is unalarmed by the raging of a river against its mouth as it wades in a treacherous current, it has bones like bronze—it is a behemoth.

But God can deal with the behemoth.

---

132 See RSV and Reyburn, 749.

64

GOD'S SECOND MONSTER

WE HAVE COVERED physics, geology, astronomy, and general biology.

Now we've covered a monster.

It was a vegetarian monster, but a monster nonetheless. A creature that people are helpless to control.

But Job's situation was even beyond being illustrated by an unmatchable force that is otherwise fairly benign. People cannot conquer the behemoth, but the behemoth does not really bother humanity in return either. All the wild animals play nearby this beast (40:20). It appears to be a gentle giant. Try to capture it, and you might be in trouble, but leave it alone, and it is a monster that will not bother you.

In Job's case, however, a monster had entered his life that was not benign. It was a predatory, fire-breathing, building-collapsing beast that had killed hundreds of workers, wiped out the house where Job's children dined and left all ten of them dead, and destroyed his family, community, livelihood, income, health, and even his spiritual confidence. Job had to face not an avoidable behemoth but a monster that hunts. How could Job hope to deal with this horror?

God talked about this kind of creature next.

> [1]*"Can you pull in Leviathan with a fishhook,*
> *or tie down its tongue with a rope?*
> [2]*Can you put a cord through its nose*

> *or pierce its jaw with a hook?"*
>
> Job 41:1–2

A pattern will form in this discussion of the leviathan. God will depict humanity's inability to deal with this creature almost like a cubist artist, exploring every possible angle in an awkwardly isolated fashion.

These first two verses propose this question: can humankind control this creature by force? Killing it is not the goal. Mastering the leviathan is the goal. Fishhooks hurt, but they capture a creature alive. By tying its tongue down, you prove your mastery and force the creature to submit to you. A cord through the nose is a crude bridle fed through some sensitive tissues. The hook through the jaw is more brutal yet—think of a fisherman's gaff: a large meat hook attached to a beefy handle for hauling large fish, squid, or other aquatic creatures out of a net or fishing line that had already pulled them from the depths.

Can people do any of this to the leviathan? These are rhetorical questions, of course. The answer is no.

So what is the leviathan? Saltwater crocodiles seem to offer the closest reference point. Still, even more so than the behemoth, the leviathan resists specific zoological identification, as we will see in the coming verses. The leviathan is something far more fierce than a crocodile. God went on to describe this beast in greater detail next.

> *³"Will it keep begging you for mercy?*
> *Will it speak to you with gentle words?*
> *⁴Will it make an agreement with you*
> *for you to take it as your slave for life?*
> *⁵Can you make a pet of it like a bird*
> *or put it on a leash for the young women in your house?"*
>
> Job 41:3–5

After establishing that people are unable to subdue this beast by force, God went on to ask a series of even more preposterous questions. God was challenging humanity to think beyond simply subduing the leviathan and consider the more heroic challenge of taming it—making the leviathan a plaything for the young. Young women even. The distinction might seem sexist to our modern society, but the writers made it with obvious poetic effect within a literary context from more than three thousand years ago. Turning this carnivorous monster into a pet that is now leashed and speaks with gentle words would be really conquering the monster.

But Job would be happy with just destroying the monster. So let's talk about that.

> *⁶"Will traders barter for it?*
> *Will they divide it up among the merchants?"*
>
> JOB 41:6

To divide up a leviathan among the merchants, you have to kill it first. Job would be very happy for this monster in his life to be dead. Of course, people cannot capture the leviathan by force and certainly cannot go the extra heroic step of taming it, but can we at least kill it?

God addressed that very question in the following verses.

> *⁷"Can you fill its hide with harpoons*
> *or its head with fishing spears?*
> *⁸If you lay a hand on it,*
> *you will remember the struggle and never do it again!*
> *⁹Any hope of subduing it is false;*
> *the mere sight of it is overpowering."*
>
> JOB 41:7–9

No. People cannot even succeed in killing the leviathan. Therefore, any hope of conquering this monster is false—but false what? False hope. Any fight between the human and the leviathan is hopeless. This is truly a monster.

God got personal next.

> *¹⁰"No one is fierce enough to rouse it.*
> *Who then is able to stand against me?*
> *¹¹Who has a claim against me that I must pay?*

Even the Monsters

Everything under heaven belongs to me."

JOB 41:10–11

"Everything… belongs to me." Even the leviathan. Even the monsters. There is more to these verses. We'll come back to them, but let's move on for the moment and let God continue to describe the leviathan.

¹²"I will not fail to speak of Leviathan's limbs,
  its strength and its graceful form.
¹³Who can strip off its outer coat?
  Who can penetrate its double coat of armor?
¹⁴Who dares open the doors of its mouth,
  ringed about with fearsome teeth?
¹⁵Its back has rows of shields
  tightly sealed together;
¹⁶each is so close to the next
  that no air can pass between.
¹⁷They are joined fast to one another;
  they cling together and cannot be parted."

JOB 41:12–17

There is still a crocodilian quality here to this description, but the following verses clarify that this monster is no natural reptile.

¹⁸"Its snorting throws out flashes of light;
  its eyes are like the rays of dawn."

JOB 41:18

I have seen crocodiles up close and from a distance, in water and on land. I have never seen one snort out flashes of light, and their eyes are more like black holes that absorb light than a source of dawn-like rays. One might argue that crocodilian eyes glow when a light is shone on them at night, but that is not a quality unique to reptiles. Most animals' eyes glow when spotlighted in the dark. And no one had spotlights in Job's day.

This demonic description does not end with glowing eyes. Instead, God continued this monstrous description.

> *^{19}"Flames stream from its mouth;*
> *sparks of fire shoot out.*
> *^{20}Smoke pours from its nostrils*
> *as from a boiling pot over burning reeds.*
> *^{21}Its breath sets coals ablaze,*
> *and flames dart from its mouth."*
>
> JOB 41:19–21

Which came first: God's description of the leviathan in Job or humanity's mythology of the dragon? The fire-breathing reptilian monster described here has moved well beyond anything crocodilian or even something once living and long extinct. This is a dragon. Pure myth. Pure horror. A monster, an early form of the myth, an aquatic as well as a terrestrial beast. One that, as we will see in coming verses, had no wings but was otherwise very similar to our modern concept of a dragon—and this was God's chosen image for the unnatural horrors that had brought themselves upon Job.

The leviathan is God's (41:11). Humanity has no hope against God's monster. But it is still God's. Therefore, God can deal with the leviathan. People can only wilt before it, as God stated next.

> *^{22}"Strength resides in its neck;*
> *dismay goes before it."*
>
> JOB 41:22

The leviathan does not permit false bravado. Your monster may be different from mine, but its impact is the same: "the mere sight of it is overpowering" (41:9); "dismay goes before it" (41:22). The brave are made weak—the strong tremble. The strongest, wisest, richest, and bravest are brought to dismay before the leviathan.

But be wary of overapplying this powerful image to problems you might encounter: if you are not overwhelmed by the challenge in front of you, it is not a leviathan-grade monster in your life. Let me repeat that: if you are not overwhelmed by the challenge in front of you, it is not a leviathan-grade monster in your life. The leviathan is an image for the challenge that seems to be too much to bear. Through the image of the leviathan, God was not describing Job's exact circumstances but rather the effect those circumstances had on Job. As Job himself had said:

> ²⁵*"What I feared has come upon me;*
> *what I dreaded has happened to me."*
>
> JOB 3:25

Earlier in that same first speech, Job himself had referenced the leviathan (3:8), calling on those who were dangerous enough to rouse this monster to curse the day of Job's birth. It is Job's own chosen monster that God was using in this chapter.

God was not done describing his monster. He went on.

> ²³*"The folds of its flesh are tightly joined;*
> *they are firm and immovable.*
> ²⁴*Its chest is hard as rock,*
> *hard as a lower millstone.*
> ²⁵*When it rises up, the mighty are terrified;*
> *they retreat before its thrashing."*
>
> JOB 41:23–25

Just taking the translation as we have it, the point is clear: the leviathan is unconquerable. It is armor-plated in an era before armor-plating. Even the mighty are terrified.

There is, however, an additional layer of meaning to unpack here. The word *mighty* in Hebrew is the plural of the Hebrew word *el*. At the risk of oversimplifying, *el* is the Hebrew equivalent of how we use the word *god* with a small *g*. In English, we use the word *god* with a lowercase *g* to mean a deity from a non-Christian religion with a multi-god pantheon, whereas we use the word *God* with an uppercase *G* to refer to Yahweh, the singular all-powerful deity of Christianity and other religions. Likewise, the Hebrew word *el* could be used in many ways.

A clearer English translation of verse twenty-five would be:

> *When it rises up, the gods are terrified,*
> > *they retreat before its thrashing.*

God is not terrified. Yahweh is not terrified. But the gods are. Are there other gods? No, of course not. Dragons don't exist either, but the purpose of this line is to create an emotional and poetic image of an unstoppable, horrific monster with a chest like a rock that terrifies even junior celestial powers (that is, small-g gods). The leviathan is mythological, and so is the reach of its impact.

God had more to say about this monster.

> ²⁶*"The sword that reaches it has no effect,*
> > *nor does the spear or the dart or the javelin.*
> ²⁷*Iron it treats like straw*
> > *and bronze like rotten wood.*
> ²⁸*Arrows do not make it flee;*
> > *slingstones are like chaff to it.*
> ²⁹*A club seems to it but a piece of straw;*
> > *it laughs at the rattling of the lance.*
> ³⁰*Its undersides are jagged potsherds,*[133]
> > *leaving a trail in the mud like a threshing sledge.*
> ³¹*It makes the depths churn like a boiling caldron*
> > *and stirs up the sea like pot of ointment.*
> ³²*It leaves a glistening wake behind it;*
> > *one would think the deep had white hair.*
> ³³*Nothing on earth is its equal—*
> > *a creature without fear.*
> ³⁴*It looks down on all that are haughty;*
> > *it is king over all that are proud."*
>
> JOB 41:26–34

---

[133] Potsherds are broken pottery. The idea is that the passage of the leviathan tears up the ground. For a modern equivalent, think of the passage of a bulldozer shredding the ground as it passes.

The leviathan traces a route through the lives of individual people on land to disappear into the sea. It leaves the realm of humanity, tears up the seashore, makes the sea boil, and then disappears, leaving only a glistening wake behind to mark its passage.

The leviathan is horror. The leviathan is impersonal horror. Unfazed by humanity's assaults, indifferent to the lives and hearts and hopes it destroys, it appears, wreaks havoc with its teeth and fiery breath, and then drifts off. It leaves behind an aftermath of chaos and a trail of bubbles and foam in deep water as it vanishes into an inaccessible underwater realm where it cannot be pursued. The sea boils at its passage. Chaos boils. We have encountered sea imagery before in our study of Job: the sea as a symbol of chaos.

In 38:8–11, the sea was the mysterious, monstrous force that God shut behind doors. God prescribed its limits. The sea was not eliminated but contained. The sea was deadly and unknown, described as chaos personified, but it was also boxed in. God made its boundaries.

Here at the end of chapter forty-one, the sea reappears as the inaccessible realm that the leviathan returns to once it is done terrorizing the abode of humankind. The sea is God's. Chaos is God's. The monster that comes from chaos and spreads hopelessness and dismay is also God's (41:11). God put bounds on the sea, but he lets the leviathan slip those bounds and enter the world of humanity with devastating effect.

As God said:

> [33] *"Nothing on earth is its equal—*
> *a creature without fear."*
>
> JOB 41:33

A more literal translation of this verse's second line is "it is made to be fearless."[134] It is a creature without fear because God made it to be without fear. Fearlessness is part of its design.

We should not be shocked at this. From the opening chapters, God had never shirked responsibility for his role in the trouble, the monster, that had come into Job's life. Remember how this book started:

---

134 Reyburn, 768.

> ³*Then the Lord said to Satan, "Have you considered my servant Job? There is no one on earth like him; he is blameless and upright, a man who fears God and shuns evil. And he still maintains his integrity, though you incited me against him to ruin him without any reason."*
>
> JOB 2:3

Three verses later, God had set the exact limits that Satan's testing of Job could reach. Nothing was permitted or occurred beyond the boundaries that God set. But within those boundaries, the enemy had free rein.

God can deal with the enemy. God can deal with the behemoth. God can deal with the leviathan. The leviathan slips into the sea and eludes humanity's inspection, but even the sea is subject to God's authority. He sets its bounds. He determines its limits. Nothing is outside of God's sovereign control. Nothing.

Everything is subject to God.

Even the monsters.

And that is where God's speech abruptly ended.

65

WANTING TO KNOW THINGS

JOB WANTED REASONS. Job wanted justice along the clean lines of the Standard View. Job wanted clarity.

The clarity that Job received was that God is sovereign, that God is humanity's only hope, and that opposing God is misinformed and short-sighted behavior.

In Job's first speech, he confessed that the monster he faced was so severe that he longed for his life to be retroactively terminated at birth, and as a result, he called on "those who are ready to rouse Leviathan" to curse the day of his birth (3:8). God responded to this call by telling Job that no such person exists:

> ^{10}No one is fierce enough to rouse it.
> Who then is able to stand against me?
> ^{11}Who has a claim against me that I must pay?
> Everything under heaven belongs to me.
>
> JOB 41:10–11

The only hope that exists is God himself, which is a hope that we do not control. Everything under heaven is God's. We have no grounds for making a claim against God. The Standard View does not provide leverage with which to force God's hand. Everything belongs to him. Nothing belongs to us.

In light of this, Elihu's description of God's motives when he uses his power—his motives to save and to show his love—stands out that much more dramatically. God's love is not the love of one under obligation to people. God's love is a love given to a people who have no claim against him, who have nothing to offer him, who are entirely dependent upon him, and who pose no threat to him. And we are also constantly in danger of being swamped by monsters against whom we are also powerless.

God loves. God loves for no reason and no personal gain. If the leviathan creeps from the sea and cuts a swath through the lives of people, it is something that does not escape God's notice. It does not occur without his awareness. It does, however, take place within set boundaries that are predetermined by God.

God states that even the acts of the leviathan fit within his larger plan to love and save us (Romans 8:28–39), but he also makes it clear that he is under no obligation to get our buy-in to that plan or even to articulate how that plan will unfold or how the current monster fits within the larger design. As God himself said:

> *"Who then is able to stand against me?*
> *11 Who has a claim against me that I must pay?*
> *Everything under heaven belongs to me."*
>
> JOB 41:10B–11

Thank God that his motives are love and not hurt. I have wished many times, however, that God's methods were more transparent. I want to know. I want to know what God is doing and how he is doing it. I want to know what God is doing and how he plans to do it so that I can judge the suitability of the plan.

I want a seat on the board.

But that is not how God works. He does not run a corporation, nor does he manage a democracy.

My desire for knowledge and control is an ancient desire. The original temptation of humanity was this exact desire stirred by the enemy in the Garden of Eden. Remember what Genesis chapter three says:

Even the Monsters

> *⁴"You will not certainly die," the serpent said to the woman. ⁵"For God knows that when you eat from it your eyes will be opened, and you will be like God, knowing good and evil."*
>
> GENESIS 3:4–5

The first sin, the Fall of Humanity, was founded on this desire to be like God.[135] To know. And once knowing, then perhaps to judge.

Even the angels are affected by this desire to know more than they are granted. In his first letter, Peter described the work of the ancient prophets preparing the way for Christ and his salvation, and Peter states that for those Old Testament servants of God:

> *¹²It was revealed to them that they were not serving themselves but you, when they spoke of the things that have now been told to you by those who have preached the gospel to you by the Holy Spirit sent from heaven. Even angels long to look into these things.*
>
> 1 PETER 1:12

Even angels long to look into these things.

The Apostles talking face-to-face with the risen Christ had a similar desire. Their burning concern was to know when God planned to restore the kingdom to Israel. Jesus's response was simple: "It is not for you to know the times or dates the Father has set by his own authority" (Acts 1:7).

It is not for you to know.

It was not for Job to know why. Elihu had articulated God's underlying motive: to love and save. God had articulated the boundaries of horror: everything is his. Everything is under God's control. Everything. Even the monsters.

Even the monsters.

---

[135] Genesis 3:6 describes this temptation as the "[desire] for gaining wisdom."

66

NOT KNOWING

Before we get into the final chapter of the book of Job, I think it is important that, having punctured the Standard View, we avoid the trap of creating a replacement. Let's call the thing we want to avoid creating the Neo-Standard View. Much bad theology has been born over the centuries by well-meaning efforts to correct previous errors.

The Standard View promised programmable predictability to the cosmos: know what makes God tick, and you can get him to sing and dance at will. The implication for Job was that, since things had gone horribly wrong for him, he was obviously guilty of some horrible crime and therefore needed to put things straight with God. I hope by now that you see how wrong that view of reality was in Job's particular case.

There is the risk with this new teaching, what I'm calling the Neo-Standard View, that God now only provides insight into what he is up to on a strictly need-to-know basis—and apparently, God usually underestimates how much people need to know. God, in this new view, is an information hog. God is no longer programmable, but this pendulum swing risks making him seem unapproachable and unreasonable as well.

The Standard View could not box God in, and he cannot be pigeonholed in other ways either. God does what he does out of love, to save. Sometimes the process includes a scarcity of information. But sometimes, it includes a surprising amount of transparency. A few examples beyond Job's story might help.

Joseph is an example of one who faced his own monster: he was betrayed by his brothers, sold to a group of traveling merchants as a slave, traded in

Egypt's slave market, and further treated cruelly by his owner's wife. He eventually fell to the status of slave-prisoner in an Egyptian dungeon, and all this happened under God's sovereign awareness and control. Genesis 45:4–8, however, shows that Joseph was granted great clarity later in life as to what God was up to the whole time. It took over two decades for Joseph to traverse the confusion of Genesis thirty-seven to reach the clarity of Genesis forty-five. Still, Joseph did obtain clarity within his own lifetime.

The book of Esther provides another example of a captive soul who received clarity later. In Esther's case, insight into her leviathan's purpose came at the apex of her trial (Esther 4:14). It was an insight that gave her the courage to go on.

An even more transparent case was that of the Apostle Paul. Before the leviathan entered his life, God told him about the suffering he would endure (Acts 9:15–16). God also provided Paul with a vision of the value of his suffering and the joy that awaited him at the end of it (2 Corinthians 12). He maintained the joy and hope of that vision even into the imprisoned end of his life (2 Timothy 4:6–8), despite trials that even included the loneliness of friends deserting him (2 Timothy 4:9–10).

We would all probably like to be Paul and know the degree, purpose, and worth of our pain upfront. Failing that, many of us would settle for being Esther and accept our insights mid-trial to help strengthen our courage for the remainder of the battle.

Failing both of these options, many of us may expect that we will, at the very least, be given Joseph's end-of-life clarity. And maybe we will. If you are reading this, you are still alive. God may yet grant you a private viewing of his purpose in your life on this side of heaven.

But for many of us, the story of Job is our lot. Or many others' in scripture. Even many of the prophets appear not to have fully understood components of their own prophecies.[136]

---

[136] Jeremiah is a great example of this sort of prophet. His book is laced with a record of his own doubt, anger, and unhappiness, and his ministry, from a human point of view, was an apparent failure. Sent by God to turn people from sin and prevent the Babylonian captivity, he suffered through four decades of reluctant prophesying, he apparently failed in his mission since the nation did not respond and did eventually go into a Babylonian captivity, and he wound up concluding his ministry as a kidnapped victim packed away to Egypt—the very place he had prophesied that God's people should not go. It was not until decades after his death

Like Job or many of the prophets, our role is to trust God. Our role is to put our confidence in him and in him alone.[137]
To trust him—with even the monsters.

---

that his writings were respected and the people responded.

For centuries prior to Jeremiah's ministry, Israel had been an idolatry-addicted nation that had never been able to shake their devotion to idols. During the captivity, in part due to Jeremiah's ministry, the next generation of Jews finally purged this idol lust from their system. Post-Babylon, idolatry was never again a problem in Israel. Jesus dealt with many things when he came, but he never had to address idol worship. The nation was healed of that disease. Jeremiah's suffering was part of a plan that changed the course of an entire nation, saved thousands, even millions of souls, and paved the way for the coming Messiah. But none of this would have been clear to Jeremiah in his lifetime, and his personal outbursts, spotted throughout the book of Jeremiah, illustrate this clearly. Other prophets similarly struggled with trials and missions they did not fully understand.

137 This was God's specific instruction through Jeremiah in Jeremiah 17:5–8. Trust was not to be in man (or by extension, the sort of insight and clarity that people take confidence from), but in God alone.

67

JOB'S CHANGE OF HEART

IMAGINE BEING JOB. Not the suffering part of his reality, which perhaps we have already explored sufficiently, but instead, the awestruck part of his reality. He had just engaged with God in conversation. The first installment of that conversation did not go well. The Divine Creator spoke of normal and predictable reality, and Job's response was as unimpressed as he dared to express. He committed to be silent but offered no agreement. God rejected Job's offer of silence. The Almighty Yahweh repeated his command that Job brace himself like a man and face his Creator (40:7). And then God spoke of monsters.

In this second phase of their conversation, God spoke with Job about matters that did touch on Job's personal situation. What had been said before, going back even as far as Elihu's speeches, was the necessary background that led up to what Job needed to hear. God loved Job, and God's intention was always to save, and God was in control of even the monsters.

Job needed to hear and to know that the reality of mythological horror come to life was a state that God also had within his power. These horrors were grounded by the assurance that God's purpose in all things, even his sovereignty over monsters, was ultimately about the salvation of individuals. God may not be fully transparent with his immediate actions and decisions. He definitely cannot be controlled by human cause-and-effect formulas, nor does he answer to our demands for clarity and explicit justification for particular events. But he loves people, and nothing escapes his notice or effective will. And he works to save—even when it does not look like that from a limited, human point of view.

Job responded to God's speech on behemoths and leviathans next.

> ^{1}*Then Job replied to the Lord:*
> ^{2}*"I know that you can do all things;*
> *no purpose of yours can be thwarted.*
> ^{3}*You asked 'Who is this that obscures my plans without knowledge?'*
> *Surely I spoke of things I did not understand,*
> *things too wonderful for me to know.*
> ^{4}*You said, 'Listen now and I will speak;*
> *I will question you,*
> *and you shall answer me.'*
> ^{5}*My ears had heard of you*
> *but now my eyes have seen you.*
> ^{6}*Therefore I despise myself*
> *and repent in dust and ashes."*
>
> JOB 42:1–6

The beginning of Job's response makes perfect sense. Job had come to understand God beyond the Standard View's creature-centric justice and punishment-oriented mentality. He had come into the presence of God himself—and not just the God of physics and biology but also the God of monsters. He grasped now that not only are there things too wonderful for him to know, but that these unknowable things are known and controlled by God.

But the second half of Job's speech comes across as slightly odd. "I despise myself" sounds like some kind of self-hate. Repenting "in dust and ashes" sounds like the actions of someone who has committed great sins. Was the sullenness of Job's first response creeping back in? What was going on here?

Translation choices are at issue here. First of all, the Hebrew original does not literally say "I despise myself." It simply says "I despise."[138] I despise— what? The text does not directly say.

---

138 Reyburn, 772.

To understand what Job despised, we examine the line's context within the rest of Job's response and apply our understanding of parallelism in Hebrew. "I despise" is the first line of a two-line verse. The second line's meaning should rhyme with it. The second line should help us understand the first.

> *Therefore, I despise*
> *and repent in dust and ashes.*

But in the second line, we encounter another translation issue. The original Hebrew text does not literally say "and repent in dust and ashes." It says "repent concerning dust and ashes."[139] Job was not doing the dust and ashes thing again. Job was stopping the dust and ashes routine.

Let's read that verse again, but with a more literal translation this time:

> *Therefore, I despise*
> *and repent concerning dust and ashes.*

Does the second line support this idea that Job despised himself? It does not. The second line is about Job's former grief-stricken horror at the trials that had come upon him. Remember the beginning of this book:

> *⁸Then Job took a piece of broken pottery and scraped himself with it as he sat among the ashes.*
>
> JOB 2:8

> *¹²When [Eliphaz, Bildad, and Zophar] saw him from a distance, they could hardly recognize him; they began to weep aloud, and they tore their robes and sprinkled dust on their heads. ¹³Then they sat on the ground with him...*
>
> JOB 2:12–13A

They sat on the ground with him—and Job sat among ashes.

Dust and ashes were expressions of deep grief and mourning. In that society, this dust-and-ashes mourning sometimes symbolized mourning in

---

139 Janzen, 254-259.

repentance. More typically, however, it represented the mourning of loss—it was how people responded to funerals, news of tragedies, and other great events of grief and trial. Job was clearly mourning the huge number of deaths that had occurred as well as the other tragedies that had come so suddenly upon him, his family, and his community.

Here in chapter forty-two, though, Job did not repent in dust and ashes. Instead, he was repenting concerning dust and ashes. That deepest phase of mourning had passed. The losses still hurt, but the hopeless and suicidal depression that had swamped him in chapter three and beyond was now banished with this phrase.

Jesus wept at Lazarus's tomb,[140] but he did not tear his robes and pile on dust and ashes. Lazarus's situation was an occasion for grief, but it was not an occasion for the hopeless despair that dust and ashes symbolized. After he was done weeping, Jesus raised Lazarus from the dead. No need for despair. Grief, sure. Despair, no.

Job had previously had despair in abundance. He did not despair any longer. Dust and ashes were no longer appropriate.

Death is a monster. Through this book, Job had gone from imagining something beyond death to developing a faith in the afterlife. Death itself is still a monster, but not an unconquerable one. God is the master of all things, even the monsters.

Job likely still felt a deep loss. Perhaps he wept in private moments, but he no longer felt the hopeless despair of chapters two and three and beyond. He had repented concerning dust and ashes.

The word repent is a very religiously loaded word for us today, but it just means to change your mind. Job had changed his mind about this deep, distraught mourning.

Job had turned away from dust and ashes. That kind of despair was no longer required.

Now that we have mined that second line for all it's worth, what does it tell us about the first line?

> *Therefore I despise*
>   *and repent concerning dust and ashes.*

---

140 See John 11:35.

Despise what? The Hebrew poetry leaves us to fill in the blanks.

Did Job despise dust and ashes? That is the obvious interpretation.

Did Job despise the thinking that had led to dust and ashes to begin with? That is also a possible and appropriate interpretation.

Whatever it was that Job explicitly despised, it was not himself. The only thing that Job was trying to communicate about himself was that his worldview had changed. God had asked why people without knowledge were obscuring God's actions, and Job now acknowledged that he (and, by extension, his friends) really did not know much about what they were talking about. And what they did think they knew led to unnecessary spiritual and emotional pain.

Job had now tossed the whole basket of ideas and opinions overboard and had sided with God—the God of even the monsters. The Standard View and its attendant entanglements are for the rubbish heap.

But the story does not end here. Not yet.

68

DEFINITE INFORMATION

Eliphaz, Bildad, and Zophar were guilty of the serious crime of having distorted Job's faith from the beginning. They posited God as an imperial and remote judge consumed with issues of crime and punishment. Elihu's salvation-focused God was not in their view at all. Their attacks on Job were more than just assaults on the integrity and emotional stability of a friend. Their attacks were also slurs against the very nature of God.

God had a few things to say to these three friends next.

> *⁷After the Lord had said these things to Job, he said to Eliphaz the Temanite, "I am angry with you and your two friends, because you have not spoken the truth about me, as my servant Job has."*
>
> Job 42:7

Once again, the text identifies God by his most holy name: Yahweh.

Elihu had been angry with these three men in chapter thirty-two. Now Yahweh addressed them with similar anger. God was speaking directly to Eliphaz—perhaps because he was the eldest of the three or because he had spoken first and set the opening tone—but God's message was addressed to all three. The "you" in this verse is plural in Hebrew

God stated that the three friends had spoken wrongly but that Job had spoken the truth. What truth had Job spoken of? Was it his confession of ignorance and wonder in the preceding half-dozen verses? Was it his willingness to speak of God's unpredictability amid real-life circumstances? His candid complaints? His refusal to compromise his integrity to make the Standard View fit? His acceptance of the spirit's Contrary View?

The English phrasing leaves the charge somewhat vague. The Hebrew, however, is not vague. The Hebrew phrasing makes it clear that God was upset with Eliphaz, Bildad, and Zophar because they had not spoken "what is correct and consistent with the facts."[141] Saul used the same phrase in 1 Samuel 23:23 when he was looking for David and sent out spies to report back to him "with definite information." Using the 1 Samuel translation of this phrase as a guide, the three friends had failed to speak about God "with definite information."

MAKING THINGS RIGHT

Job had definite information: God was not predictable or programmable in the manner that the Standard View implied. In a truly blunt sense, there is an aspect of God that can sometimes even seem—from a limited, human point of view—horrible.

There is a deep irony in what came of Eliphaz, Bildad, and Zophar's efforts. To make God seem nicer than the circumstances warranted, they had lied about God. Like a self-appointed public relations team, they had tried to spin Job's tragedies in a way that would keep God looking good—and instead, they just made him look bad. They meant to help Job—and instead, they hurt him. Rather than surrendering their attempts to master the evident mysteries, they had insisted on parsing every uncertainty. They had allowed no unanswered questions. In the absence of definite information, they had relied on religious philosophy to fill in the blanks. They had spoken forcefully and wrongly about things they did not know, and for this God was angry with them.

What follows is God's prescription to address that anger.

> [8]*"So now take seven bulls and seven rams and go to my servant Job and sacrifice a burnt offering for yourselves. My servant Job will pray for you, and I will accept his prayer and not deal with*

---

141 Reyburn, 774.

> *you according to your folly. You have not spoken the truth about me, as my servant Job has." ⁹So Eliphaz the Temanite, Bildad the Shuhite and Zophar the Naamathite did what the Lord told them; and the Lord accepted Job's prayer.*
>
> Job 42:8–9

In verse seven, God spoke of "my servant Job." In verse eight, we again see "my servant Job" not once but three more times. "My servant Job." The three friends were the object of God's anger. Job was God's servant. God's well-regarded one. God stated it four times in two verses for emphasis, just in case we missed it the first three times.

In verse seven, God charged the three friends with not saying accurate things. They had not spoken according to the facts. They had not spoken with definite information. And again, in verse eight, God repeated this charge. Both expressions of this charge are mated with the contrasting clause "as my servant Job has."

God praised Job. The three friends, however, were in trouble.

Elihu, of course, was not in trouble. Nor was he commended. He was not relevant to the right-versus-wrong tension between Job and the three friends. He had served as part of the transition from humanistic philosophical debate and interpersonal tension to divine revelation. He had set the stage by asserting that above all, God is a God of salvation. That had been Elihu's message, and now having played his part, he was offstage.

However, the crime that the three friends were responsible for is heinous, and they were not yet offstage. They had insulted the character and nature of Yahweh such that he had stepped into human reality in person to set things straight. They had added to Satan's attacks on the innocent Job by increasing his suffering.

However, the God of love and salvation is not the eager punisher that the friends had implied, and this aspect of his character held true even in the case of Eliphaz and company. As a result, even for these three friends, God provided a way for their salvation (42:7–8).

Interestingly, the friends had to offer an expensive sacrifice—seven bulls and seven rams—but God did not say that he would accept this sacrifice. They were to make the sacrifice—and by its very nature, it would be a public affair—but their sacrifice would not buy them God's favor. It was required but not, apparently, effective. Sacrifices were not a new formula for manipulating God.

Following the sacrifice, the text says that Job would pray for his friends, and God would "accept Job's face," as the Hebrew phrase literally says. Job's prayer would be accepted. The friends would make the sacrifice, but Job's prayer, Job's relationship with God, would be the effective force here.

Job had longed for a mediator—instead, he found direct access to God without one and became the mediator for his friends.

There is something else of note here in how these concluding events occurred. God not only brought forgiveness to the three friends but also brought healing to their relationship with Job. It was not enough to rebuke them. It was not enough to provide them with an escape from judgment "according to [their] folly" (42:7). God, the God of love and salvation, also made sure to structure that forgiveness in a form that took down the wall of emotional hurt between Job and his friends. They had been "miserable comforters" to Job in his distress (16:2), and it would be easy for Job to maintain that bitterness even through his vindication, perhaps even more so because of his vindication.

Instead, God structured the friends' forgiveness such that Job needed to provide his friends the good and effective comfort they had not given him. The friends would be publicly humbled by both their sacrifice of valuable livestock and by having to rely on Job's prayer on their behalf. Job's bitterness and sullied reputation were purged by serving as the conduit for his friends' forgiveness. Job, remember, was still in poverty, still consumed by his illness, and still mourning the loss of ten children and hundreds in his labor force, but in this crippled and still physically tortured state, he was to pray for his friends. And, of course, he did.

Job was a good person. The greatest among the peoples of the east. A blameless and upright person even after everything he had been through. His character here shone through like clean steel polished to a mirror finish.

Here is what happened next.

> *[10]After Job had prayed for his friends, the Lord restored his fortunes and gave him twice as much as he had before. [11]All his brothers and sisters and everyone who had known him before*

> *came and ate with him in his house. They comforted and consoled him over all the trouble the Lord had brought on him, and each one gave him a piece of silver and a gold ring.*
>
> JOB 42:10–11

Even the prose sections of Job contain poetically rewarding parallelism. Moreover, the book's larger structure rings with this resonant parallelism, as the prose conclusion of Job nicely dovetails with its prose beginning.

At the beginning of Job, God had referred to "my servant Job" two times (1:8; 2:3). At the end of the book, God doubled this, referring to "my servant Job" four times (42:7–8). At the beginning of the book, Job's wife had offered him grievous advice, and Job had called her out on it—likewise, at the end, God called out Job's friends for their foolish advice. In the beginning, Job had interceded for his children with sacrifices. In the end, there was another series of sacrifices, and again Job served as intercessor. There had been a feast at the beginning, which had ended in tragedy. And there was another feast at the end, which ended in blessing. Friends had come to comfort Job at the beginning—and they failed. Friends and family came at the end again to bring comfort—and they succeeded.

It is noteworthy as well that this second group of friends and family gave Job practical comfort: they shared food, they ate in his house with him (not sitting in ashes in the yard), and they gave him material items that would help with his financial crisis. Perhaps the shift was partly because Job himself had changed—he no longer let himself wallow in ashes—but beyond this, it is also clear that these friends came to do, not to pontificate.

Crucially, to understand the book of Job's ending, we must note how these friends came to comfort and console him "over all the trouble that the LORD had brought on him." They had no philosophical drive to try to blame Job for the trouble he had endured. God had brought the trouble. The friends did not question why. It had happened, and the why was between God and Job. This new batch of friends and family came to help, not to interpret or judge. The only definite information they had was that Job was in need—so they met the need.

OUR ROLE: TO HELP OTHERS

There is a lesson here for every soul confronted with a friend or family member in trouble: in the absence of definite information, your role is to help where the need presents itself.

Did you get that?

In the absence of definite information, your role is to help where the need presents itself.

God took care of the monsters.

Job's friends and family took care of dinner and immediate financial matters.

69

NEW BLESSINGS

God was not yet done with interfering in Job's life, but his next interventions were blessings. Here's how the text puts it:

> *¹²The Lord blessed the latter part of Job's life more than the former part. He had fourteen thousand sheep, six thousand camels, a thousand yoke of oxen and a thousand donkeys.*
> *¹³And he also had seven sons and three daughters.*
> *¹⁴The first daughter he named Jemimah, the second Keziah and the third Keren-Happuch.*
> *¹⁵Nowhere in all the land were there found women as beautiful as Job's daughters, and their father granted them an inheritance along with their brothers.*
> *¹⁶After this, Job lived a hundred and forty years; he saw his children and their children to the fourth generation. ¹⁷And so Job died, an old man and full of years.*
>
> Job 42:12–17

This is a beautiful ending to the book of Job. However, as with so many events within the book, there is more going on here than appears on the surface. In 42:10, the text reads that God "restored his fortunes and gave him twice as much as he had before." This restoration came in sheep, camels, oxen, and donkeys. One presumes that this increase in livestock also came with an increase in the land he controlled since grazing livestock need land to graze and working animals need fields to plow and harvest.

But what about the children? He had seven sons and three daughters before. So why didn't he wind up with fourteen sons and six daughters? This many children would be material for an intrusively voyeuristic reality TV show at the beginning of the twenty-first century, but in Job's day, your children were your wealth. That was your retirement plan. Children provided your pension in addition to love and belonging. Fourteen sons and six daughters would have been joy and wealth overflowing in Job's day. So why were the children not doubled as well?

Ah, but they were.

At the beginning of Job, the theology of an afterlife was either immature or, more likely, nonexistent. By the end, it had become clear that death was just another monster that God has within his power. Job's vision of a tree resprouting and streams reappearing was not fantasy or misguided faith but reality. Job truly would see his Maker again beyond the grave—and his children as well. He would not only be reunited with his new generation of ten children—and his grandchildren and great-grandchildren and so on—but he would also be reunited with his original ten. He would stand again before his Maker with fourteen sons and six daughters.

A CLOSER LOOK AT THE DAUGHTERS

What about those daughters? At the beginning, the text did not name Job's sons nor his daughters. The text also does not name his sons at the end of the book. So why is it that the text suddenly finds cause to name the second group of daughters? Not only does the text spell out their names, but it also makes special note of their inheritance status alongside their brothers. It was not the custom for daughters to receive a piece of their father's inheritance in Job's day. So what point is the text making here?

When I first presented to the church the last sermon on the book of Job, I did not know the answer. We had not yet received our daughter's diagnosis and were still in the middle of that traumatic six months of seizures, bookended front and back by extended periods of life support in the ICU. I knew that the text was communicating something important about Job's daughters, but my search through commentaries and translation aides came up empty. In the sermon on this passage, I mentioned that there was something significant here but that I had failed to find a satisfactory explanation as to what that something was. I left it to the church to discover the meaning on their own and closed out the series on Job.

Since then, I have had the opportunity to work through all the text of Job again as I have translated my sermon notes into book form, and along the way, the puzzle of Job's daughters has become clearer.

One thing that became clear was that the exact meaning of the daughters' names was not meaningful—at least not to a twenty-first-century student. The names likely do mean something. However, the challenge came when almost all the commentaries I bought ascribed different meanings to the names and different interpretations to their own choice. If a name means "beautiful," that can be interpreted a certain way, but if another scholar thinks the name means "dove," that can be interpreted differently. And if "plenty" is the understood meaning—you get the idea. We are no longer working with definite information when we try to parse the meaning of Job's daughter's names.

But we are working with definite information when we note that they were named. That was unlike the children at the beginning and unlike even the sons at the end. The daughters were definitely set apart. They were beautiful daughters. That, too, is definite information. And they had an inheritance along with their brothers. This last point is also clear, and it is also very unusual within the cultural context of the day. Daughters did not get an inheritance. A daughter's inheritance was typically that of her husband's family. She might bring a dowry into a marriage, but in Job's era, she did not keep an inheritance for herself.

A modern reader might wonder what difference this makes. In short, a dowry is bound to a marriage, and an inheritance is not. By giving his daughters financial independence, Job also gave them the free choice to choose whether they wanted to get married or not. Leaping into our own era, that is also the social significance of allowing women to own land, have their own jobs, and be in control of their bank accounts—it gives them the freedom to choose their relationships and control their lives without being forced into marriage and their husband's will by financial constraints and manipulation.

So why were Job's daughters provided with this unusual (for the era) gift? This seems to be different even from Job's plan for his first three daughters.

Is it that having lost daughters, Job now valued his new daughters even more and therefore accorded them the distinction of an inheritance as a measure of his joy and love for them? Possibly. But as much as Job is a personal book, it is also a sophisticated literary work with deep theological significance woven into its design.

One of Job's key discoveries during the book was the need for a mediator between God and his creations. At the end of the book of Job, Job himself got to serve in that mediator role for his friends. His other key discovery was the idea of confidence in life beyond death—the end is not the end. Each person has the possibility of inheritance with God beyond the grave, and at the end of his story, Job ensured that not only will his sons have an inheritance, but his daughters will as well. Just like the inheritance God provides for his children.

Perhaps beyond the practical benefits of an inheritance in this life, the point is to show that our ultimate inheritance with God is a blessing for both men and women. If this is his point, illustrated through a physical, this-world inheritance for both his sons and daughters, then the point is subtle. The singling out of his daughters by stating their names, extolling their beauty, and noting their granted inheritance is not subtle. The scripture has a point.

God "blessed the latter part of Job's life more than the former part" (42:12), and over half of the following paragraph that articulates this blessing is focused on Job's daughters. Perhaps my interpretation is inaccurate, and the point is much simpler: in a society that undervalued girls and women—the effects of which we still see today throughout the world—the ending of the book of Job makes a point of correcting that wrong. These comments may seem off topic to some since the value of women has not been a subject of the book at all so far, and it might be easy to dismiss this interpretation as shameless twenty-first-century sociology intruding into the reading of an ancient text. Still, Job's daughters need some explanation. If their prominent position in this passage is not an allusion to their equal inheritance in heaven, it must be some comment on Job's renewed sense of their value and worth in this life. Or maybe the point is that both interpretations are valid.

A QUESTION OF LINEAGE

It is interesting to note that there is one other famous biblical figure who scripture explicitly mentions as having seen his children's children to the fourth generation, and that is Joseph.[142]

And there was someone else that the Bible describes as having died as "an old man and full of years": Joseph's great-grandfather Abraham (Gen. 25:8).

The odds seem high that the events in the book of Job occurred sometime within the Abraham-to-Joseph timeframe. If so, then Abraham's line, and Job's, reflect separate lines of people devoted to God. So what happened to Job's line?

Scripture leaves many things unstated. Abraham's line became Israel. Job does not appear to have descended from Abraham, as he is not in Abraham's family tree as either an ancestor or a descendant. The text does not even identify him as Jewish but rather as one of the "people of the East" (1:3). Yet he worshipped God. Scripture does not explain where his family line went.

Job is not the only mysterious figure in scripture. Abraham and Job were not the only Yahweh worshippers in their day. Genesis chapter fourteen identifies someone called Melchizedek, king of Salem, a "priest of God Most High" (Gen. 14:18), who blessed Abraham and to whom Abraham offered a priestly tithe. Where did Melchizedek come from? How was there a priesthood before Moses recorded the books of Exodus, Leviticus, and Deuteronomy? Not only does the scripture consider this to be a legitimate Yahweh priesthood in Abraham's time, but Jesus himself is referred to as a priest "in the order of Melchizedek" (Heb. 6:20), and scripture expounds upon the comparisons between Jesus and Melchizedek further in Hebrews chapters seven and eight. Scripture describes Melchizedek as someone "without father or mother, without genealogy, without beginning of days or end of life, resembling the Son of God, [who] remains a priest forever" (Heb. 7:3).

There is a mystery here. It is a mystery beyond this book's scope, as are many others left exposed and then unexplained in scripture.

What happened to Job's line? What exact point is the scripture communicating by calling out Job's daughters so uniquely? And why, at the end of all this, did these trials come upon Job?

---

142 See Genesis 50:22–23.

Did God stage all this so that we could learn from Job's example and the friends' mistakes? Was this all a setup to provide God with an opportunity to teach future generations? Was this not really about Job at all but rather about God shaping events in Job's life to expose and deal with the sinfulness in Job's friends? Is the explanation something else?

One thing seems clear: Job's trials were not about proving Satan wrong. The enemy was the catalyst that set this book's events in motion—but even that is not completely true. God brought the topic of Job up to begin with. Satan was only as much of a catalyst as God allowed him to be. God was doing something. The enemy was just the tool. Satan does not even appear again in the book after the opening few verses of chapter two. God was doing something here, not Satan. And throughout the entire book, through Elihu's good speeches, through Job's discoveries, even through God's own speeches, God never says why he allowed these things to happen.

If we imagine for a minute that God was a mere human—more particularly, someone who puts things into executive summary bullet points—we might summarize his message as follows:

- I am God;
- I do what I do to save people;
- I am complicated;
- I don't always explain myself;
- but I control everything;
- even the monsters.

What God did not explicitly say but implied is this:

- So trust me.

When God says, even by implication, "trust me," he does not mean "shut up." The book of Hebrews compares Jesus to Melchizedek and also describes him as one who "offered up prayers and petitions with fervent cries and tears to the one who could save him from death, and he was heard because of his reverent submission" (Heb. 5:7). The success of Jesus's prayers was a consequence of his submission.

God says, "Trust me." God also says, "Talk to me." God says, "Brace yourself like a grownup and answer me."

ALTERNATIVE RESPONSES

There are many responses other than trusting God that we might gravitate toward when faced with monsters in our lives. Spineless acquiescence is one response. Such religious submission simply papers over bitterness with false servility. Job's reply to God's first speech seems to be such a response.

Another pseudo-religious but false response is to take refuge in religious philosophies that try to make God something humanity can manipulate or control. This was the approach of Job's three friends. They found a pseudo-religious framework that avoided the mystery of Job's case by laying guilt where it did not belong. They invented reasons for Job's culpability with no definite information. They held firmly to a flawed ideology rather than let themselves out into the dark of uncertainty that required trust without explanation. Their focus was on easing their own psychological tension. Unfortunately, their attempt to comfort themselves made them blind to the inadequacy of their philosophy and even less aware of the evil effect their arguments had upon Job. I am sure many of us have observed people like this. They are sometimes the stubborn, worst expression of what passes for Christianity. Job's observation about these people in 12:5 is nicely succinct: "Those who are at ease have contempt for misfortune as the fate of those whose feet are slipping."

One response that the book of Job does not directly personify is that of atheism: ascribing ultimate power to meaninglessness and chaos. Though the book did not directly personify this despair, it nevertheless covered this erroneous path in an overlapping fashion, as every character in the book takes on pieces of such despair. The pieces, taken together, create a patchwork whole. Job dabbled with this view but then pulled back from it. Job's three friends reacted to it and clung to the Standard View as a bulwark against the terror of unguided unpredictability. Finally, Elihu touched on it and dismissed it by insisting on God's saving purpose as the underlying purpose of every event. God made it clear that chaos, even the home of chaos, is within his control. There is no such thing as unguided unpredictability. God has control of even the monsters.

God is complicated.

God doesn't always explain himself.

But his purpose is still ultimately fulfilled. There is meaning.

Meaningless chaos is not a risk.

The last potential response to tragedy and trial that I will touch on here is Job's. What did Job do? He was a good person. Blameless. Upright. God praised him at both the beginning and end of this book. What was Job's praiseworthy response?

When Job was overwhelmed, he expressed it.

When his friends' responses hurt Job, he did not shut them out but engaged with them more fiercely.

When Job drifted into depression he turned from his friends, not into himself but toward God. His friends had become "miserable comforters" (16:2), and there is only so much miserable comfort that a soul can handle, but isolation was not Job's alternative. Prayer was.

In turning to God, he expressed his need for a mediator and his desire for something beyond this life, and in those prayers, he eventually found his way from need and desire to faith and hope and redemption. With that faith and hope, Job began engaging with his friends once more. He did not let his depression lead him into isolation but used it as a goad to concentrate more deeply on his prayer life and thought life, which ultimately led him to the opposite of isolation. Toward the end of his speeches, Job moved beyond his pain, and he counseled and warned his friends.[143] He rebuked his friends, taught them, stayed engaged with them, and eventually served as their mediator. But don't forget: this came later. Job had a long journey before he got to that kind of productive engagement.

The reward for all this effort was not just God's favor and the ultimate restoration of Job's prosperity but something deeper: God rewarded Job with faith and hope in a future beyond this life. This was a gift that, in the end, was far larger than the doubling of livestock, lands, or family.

---

143 For example, recall Job 19:28–29; 21:29–34; and 26:1–14.

70

HAPPILY EVER AFTER?

It would be a mistake to assume that everything in Job's life after chapter forty-two was easy. "They lived happily ever after" is not how the book ends. Job did live a long life beyond chapter forty-two. He eventually died when he was old and full of years, and God blessed him richly, but that does not mean life was stress-free.

There were ten new children to birth and raise—diaper stages all over again in a world before disposable diapers, scheduled municipal garbage pickups, or even running water. Hundreds of widows did not just miraculously find new husbands and swing back into community life. Children needed new fathers, and some probably never got them—that became their monster to deal with. Perhaps some of the women were not even looking for new husbands but were instead consumed with the process of giving birth to children they had been pregnant with when they had lost their husbands. Perhaps some of the women were in their later years, not just mourning their husbands but also mourning their grown sons who would have been their security in old age. Job had hundreds of new farmhands to hire and train. Those thousands of animals restored to Job had to be sourced, bought, delivered. Organic growth occurred as those animals gave birth, and the wild animals that had undoubtedly been attracted to and flourished on the carcasses of Job's previous disaster had to be beaten back, hunted, and guarded against. Market contracts had to be renegotiated. Supply chains had to be reestablished. The entire business had to be rebuilt. The community had to be rebuilt. Job's family had to be raised all over again.

Life was not a cakewalk after chapter forty-two, but God's blessings were evident. Amid all the undoubtedly tumultuous life experience that followed chapter forty-two, I am certain that four things remained constant for Job:

- He knew that, regardless of what drama might be evident on life's surface, God loved him.
- He knew that this life isn't all there is. Eternity is real.
- He knew that redemption was a reality—his place in that eternity was guaranteed.
- And on the way to that eternity, Yahweh had all the details of his temporary and fragile life sorted out and under his control.

Even the parts with monsters.

EPILOGUE

As I write this epilogue for the second edition, we are in the midst of our second COVID-19 spring. After a year in an evolving pandemic lockdown, I can't help but be reminded of Job 37:2–8 and wonder how it applies to this strange season.

Mackenzie's story started just before 9/11 and continues into our second COVID-19 summer. Those are unusual bookends to a story that is not yet over. As I write this, she is just over twenty years old.

My plan is to release this second edition on her twenty-first birthday, February 10, 2022.

That I can have that plan makes her a miracle. Ninety percent of kids who have her primary diagnosis don't live past age three. Ninety-nine percent don't live past the teen years. This edition, God willing, will celebrate her miraculous twenty-first birthday.

We received a second diagnosis for Mackenzie shortly after the first. It was a condition so rare that there are only a hundred cases in the worldwide medical literature, and no other known child has had these two conditions together. The new diagnosis forecast heart disease and more seizures, among other things, starting in her late teens—assuming the first diagnosis even let her live that long. By the time she turned thirteen, it was clear that she would probably not last the year.

Then a third diagnosis showed up. It was a genetic disorder never found in humans before and only known in lampreys. Lampreys? The impact of this abnormality in humans was unknown, but seizures and other neurological damage were expected. We didn't even really absorb that third diagnosis. We were already too far into the unbelievable to make any sense of it. Seriously… lampreys?

What is it like to be the only girl on the planet with her combination of rare conditions? What is it like for a parent to care for such a beautiful but fragile wonder?

I wish I could describe a life filled with Paul's ahead-of-time insights, or Joseph's late understanding of what it all meant, or even Job's perpetual mystery but a turnaround in earthly circumstances. Unfortunately, at this stage of our lives, I think our family is looking at something more like Jeremiah's scenario: we're not ever going to get relief from the pressure, and we'll find out in heaven what it all meant. For now, we endure.

When Mackenzie turned twelve years old, four years after I had finished preaching the sermons this book is based on, I woke up one night to a gurgling sound. I ran into her room to find one wall covered in blood like a scene from a horror movie. She was seizing, had bitten her tongue, and was drowning. The ambulance, local hospital's emergency room, escalating drugs, medically induced coma, medical transport to the children's hospital, a week in ICU—it was a story we had lived before.

She had a six-month run of escalating seizures, sometimes five or six in a day, and hospitalizations became routine again. One hospital made a mistake and overdosed her on antiseizure drugs and almost ended her life by inadvertently shutting down her breathing. Her throat had started to collapse before they could get a ventilator in place. It took her a week to wake up from that mistake.

She was misdiagnosed with pneumonia a year or so later. She was slowly suffocating on useless antibiotics before doctors discovered that granulomas were growing in her throat and closing off her airway—likely the result of damage caused by getting that breathing apparatus into her the summer before. We spent New Year's Eve in the hospital that year as she recovered from emergency surgery to open up her airway. Six months later, she had the surgery again when the granulomas grew back.

Mackenzie said her last word a few months after she turned thirteen. She can no longer talk intelligibly anymore. She can gesture, hug, and cry or clap her hands together to get attention, but both verbal and sign language are now gone.

She used to get around with a wheeled walker. When we took her to the local mall, she thought it was the best thing in the world. She would start running, sprinting as fast as she could through the crowds, running by everyone and risking crashing into people who were remarkably understanding as she squealed with delight and the freedom of being able just to run—to be a kid and run.

She doesn't run anymore. A degenerative condition degenerates. She doesn't walk anymore either. The wheelchair is her home now. Speechless and unable to walk, her world shrinks little by little, year by year.

We moved into a new phase of puberty-related problems. Her heavy periods could last for four or five weeks at a time, and somehow the hormones played havoc with the seizures as well. We climbed the scale of aggressive seizure activity to where ten or fifteen seizures a day is normal now. We don't even call an ambulance. You can't call an ambulance a dozen times a day, every day. Forty-five seizures in one day has been her record so far. You can do the math on a twenty-four-hour day and realize that she's barely recovering from one when the next starts. But then she'll have a two-day break with maybe only a couple of seizures a day. Then the storm starts again. We think it is related to hormonal cycles, but then I can't get the spreadsheets to agree with the perceived pattern and neither can the army of neurologists, endocrinologists, and others who track her case.

Mackenzie is maxed out on antiseizure drugs for her age and size, and she's maxed out on palliative care supports as well. We get over forty hours of in-home nursing support a week between the Canadian medical system, supplemental support through my work healthcare plan, and out-of-pocket spending. This is wonderful because she cannot be left alone at all now—and only mom and dad or trained medical staff (registered nurses or higher) are permitted to handle some of the emergency medications we have to give her regularly. So for forty hours a week, I go to work, and my wife manages the household, doctor's appointments, and so on. For the remaining 128 hours a week, we're on our own. Which means we don't sleep. If I had to pick the one thing that is the hardest to endure in this marathon, it would be a tie between the regular, daily adrenaline spikes when Mackenzie goes into a tonic-clonic seizure and the ongoing grind of sleep deprivation. Seizures don't stop just because it's sleeping time. So if we get three hours of uninterrupted sleep without a crisis, it is a night to celebrate.

Friends surprised us when Mackenzie was eight years old by organizing a fundraiser to build an elevator in our home. Mackenzie was getting too big for Carolyn to carry up and down the stairs in our home safely. Hazel and Megan took the lead. Patty, Audrey, Ros, and many others, dozens of others, formed the committee and made it happen. We did not ask them to. It did not even occur to us as an idea. The price tag we were facing was close to $30,000. Our friends raised half.

My friend Geoff built a website to support their efforts, and they collected many donations online before the fundraising event even occurred. The amount raised roughly paid for permits, the architect's drawings, the engineer's approval and supplementary drawings, and the actual installation—but we still had to buy the equipment. Almost a year later, a homeowner on the other side of Toronto found Mackenzie's fundraising website the last week before the website address expired and was set to be taken down. They had equipment like what we needed in their home, left by the previous owner. It was not equipment they needed. They contacted Hazel through the website, gave us the equipment, and recommended a contractor.

The equipment was almost exactly what we needed. The door was positioned in a way that was not quite right—but we could make it work. For $15,000 in free equipment, we could make it work.

We got a quote from the recommended contractor. When he came to our house and saw the space, he mentioned that he had the equipment with the exact door configuration that we needed in storage, and he was willing to make a straight trade. The donated equipment went to him. The equipment we needed came from him to us. We paid nothing for the trade.

And so Mackenzie got her elevator. Both my wife and child are safe moving between floors. I took our son on his first camping trip the next summer without fear that the girls would have an accident on the stairs while we were out of town. We still use it more than a decade later. What a blessing it has been.

Beyond the blessings and the kindness of friends and the long-term hope Carolyn and I have, it is the short-term unknowns that strike closest to our hearts, especially given our personalities. I work in a bank. She worked in a law firm before Mackenzie entered our lives. We had deliberately designed our lives to cater to our personalities, which thrive on control, predictability, and being on top of things.

Now, we're on top of almost nothing. Monsters pop up unexpectedly daily, and they're often different from the ones we've seen before. Vomiting, stomach surgery, medical equipment accidents and malfunctions, misdiagnoses, overdoses, blood on the wall, throat surgeries, insomnia, infections, and endless, endless, endless runaway seizures—we can predict nothing. We cannot predict what will happen five minutes from now. We cannot even go out for dinner together without spending hundreds of dollars on a private nurse and then having to leave the restaurant before we've finished eating because an ambulance has been called at home.

In these past twenty years, we've also called ambulances too many times for my wife as well for her still-undiagnosed blackouts and seizures. The best explanation the medical establishment has come up with is that her episodes result from a stress reaction in her brain. The non-medical way it gets explained to us is that her psyche informs the world that it has had enough and blows the circuit breaker. She can hear and see during these attacks, but she's locked in and cannot move or speak. Her basic reflexes don't even work. She's not faking it, as many an emergency-room reflex test has demonstrated. Her brain shuts her down. The stress is too much. It lets her see and hear, and that is all.

I'd like to think I'm built of tougher stuff, but the reality is that I'm not. Many, many times, I've been forced to my knees in tears and prayer. I've cried out that it's enough now. I've tried to figure out how to juggle a career; care for a child that sits on death's doorstep but never crosses over, a child who still wants to hug and play despite the loss of mobility and language; and being a good father to my healthy son and husband to my wife, and I don't know how to do that, how to plan for that. All this stress was compounded by my wife's and my own personal health issues. When I wound up with a lump in my throat a few years ago, and it turned into a cancer diagnosis and throat surgery, I'm ashamed to say that there was a small part of me that saw the whole affair as an escape hatch—my ticket off this drama train. I did not sign up for this—I was ready for the exit.

But I'm still here. God's not done with me yet.

Carolyn and I take separate vacations now that Mackenzie cannot be left without one of us or medical professionals to care for her. I'll take Jackson camping or go deeper into the woods with just some of the guys. Carolyn will get away with some of her girlfriends, or in a non-COVID-19 season, take Jackson to visit relatives down south. We used to get Mackenzie into a respite hospital now and again, and my wife and I could escape for a weekend to sleep without medical equipment alarms going off in the night. We would stay up or sleep in or go out without worrying about limited windows between medication times and gathering up syringes and supplies for the next procedure. We would treasure every one of those getaways, whether they were alone, with friends, with Jackson, or as a couple.

After turning nineteen, Mackenzie aged out of most of those programs. We still hope for an adult version to be developed in the future.

But here is the thing: the respite hospitals may never be a thing for us again, and Carolyn's or my own health may continue to be challenged, and one day one of us may be looking after both daughter and spouse—that would be a new evolution of our monster. Whatever happens, what seems guaranteed is that unpredictable new flavors of crises are coming. As far as I can tell, that's just how life works—those who don't know it yet are simply too young or have been otherwise insulated from real life so far. So far, however, is not forever—after all, every one of us suffers from a degenerative, terminal condition. Most of us simply take a long time for that to become apparent. For our family, Mackenzie has made the truth about life's fragility brutally obvious right from the beginning. At ten days old, she let me know she might not be around long and forced us to pay close attention early and do something about it.

So we do something about it.

We make sure to love what we've got, and we mourn what we've lost, and we make no apologies for either.

We make sure that life is not only medical drama, even though for us, medical drama has been a dozen-times-a-day affair for over two decades now. Carolyn sews. I write. We both work on a garden of indoor and outdoor plants. We're trapped at home—not just during COVID—and so we make our home as livable as we can. COVID has just made the rest of the world live as we normally do. The rest of the world will go back to normal. We won't. Neither will others dealing with their own monsters, seen or unseen, publicly revealed or privately endured.

I cannot engage in deep discussions with my daughter like I wanted to when she was a baby and I talked to her, even while she was still in the womb. But I still have one-sided conversations with her, and she listens. I can't go for adventurous hikes in the mountains with her or take her to the backcountry places I go with Jackson, but we invested in a three-wheel adult-sized stroller with inflatable tires that lets me take her on the local jogging trails. She loves the outdoors, and those are fun trips together. Sometimes, she waves her hands around in the air on those walks and laughs like she's conducting the universe and having fun doing it. Sometimes she has a seizure on those walks, which blows the mood, but I bring the emergency meds with me, and if we have to, we deal with syringes and anticonvulsive drugs on a trail. She can have a dozen or more of these attacks a day. One of them will be her last. So if she's going to go violently, eventually, I guess in the fresh air, under the trees, is as good a place to go as any.

Whatever happens, four fundamental things won't change:

- Whatever drama might be evident on life's surface, God loves my family and me.
- This life isn't all there is. Eternity is real.
- Redemption is a reality. My family's home in that eternity is secure.
- And on the way to that eternity, Yahweh has all the details of our temporary and fragile lives sorted out and under his control.

All the details. All of them.
Even the monsters.

ACKNOWLEDGMENTS

(First Edition)

People who help are a treasure. Living the events that gave rise to this book required the help of countless people: friends, family, medical professionals, community workers, and so on. The original sermon series the book is based on was likewise aided by the abundant encouragement provided by those who listened and gave feedback. I could not even begin to list their names and, in some cases, did not even know their names. Thank you to all of you.

This book's actual writing involved a smaller group of people willing and able to devote time to reading the first manuscript and providing their honest feedback and evaluation. Thank you to all of my first readers who took it upon themselves to digest that first draft and provide me with the necessary criticism and encouragement. They are Henry Oberholster, Geoff Campbell, Roman Kobko, Tim Smith, Ron and Sharon Potter, and my wife, Carolyn Potter. A heartfelt thank you to all of you.

Following a few rewrites, this project stalled once I'd encountered a translation copyright issue (see the following appendix). A special thank you to Geoff Campbell for badgering me for almost two years to solve the impasse. It was he who suggested that I crowdsource my own translation of Job. While I did not act on that specific solution, his persistence and passion did push me to find a resolution. Without that push, this book might still be just a large stack of paper in the bottom of my office cabinet. Thank you, Geoff.

I would like to thank Caleb Lightening, a friend who came into my life with no experience of the history that this book addresses. With completely fresh eyes, Caleb tackled the final draft from an unsentimental perspective. I owe a great debt to Caleb for identifying the many simple but distracting mistakes evident in what I thought was my final draft. Thank you!

Last, I want to acknowledge my beautiful little girl, Mackenzie. She is the catalyst that set all the life events in motion that resulted in this book. She has no idea. She smiles, plays, and hugs. Then medical trauma swamps her. Yet, when she recovers, even if she is diminished in the aftermath, she is still herself. I love her. We all love her. She changed everything.

ACKNOWLEDGMENTS

(Second Edition)

I ORIGINALLY SELF-PUBLISHED this book with limited distribution in 2015. After its publication, a childhood passion for fiction was reawakened within me. When I was ten years old, I had declared that I would be a novelist one day, but beyond a few bad manuscripts that will forever remain in a storage box and several decades' worth of intense research for a historical fiction series that I never actually started writing, I had not achieved my dream.

After Even the Monsters went on sale, the passion to be a novelist became too much to push off any longer, and I began toiling away on a new project: a series of historical fiction novels set in the period 135 BCE to 135 CE.

In the spring of 2021, I published the first of these novels, Keziah's Song, through Paper Stone Press, working with the wonderful editor Amelia Wiens and proofreader Robin Larin as well as all the other folks involved in cover design, typesetting, narration, sound engineering for the audiobook version, and other publishing disciplines that I had no idea existed when I first self-published Even the Monsters.

After the successful launch of Keziah's Song, Blind Man's Labyrinth followed in the fall of 2021, with Bitter for Sweet planned for spring 2022. However, before Keziah's Song was even launched, my wife started asking questions. She had seen the value of professional cover design and typesetting, professional editing, and proofreading with my novels—attention that Even the Monsters had not benefited from. She had also joined the recent trend of becoming an audiobook fan.

"Why not republish Even the Monsters through Paper Stone Press?" she asked.

The answer to that was easy. Paper Stone Press was not a nonfiction publisher. I had grown comfortable working with Amelia, for example, on editing. Her focus was on literary, historical, and fantasy fiction—not memoirs or biblical commentaries or really nonfiction of any kind.

But my wife kept asking—and I kept putting her off. And Mackenzie had lots of seizures in the middle of these various conversations, so it's not as if these were relaxed and casual coffee chats when we had nothing else to distract us.

I participate in a fantastic fiction writers' group on a biweekly basis. During a conversation with this group, Frederick Faller, formerly a teacher at a church in Boston (now retired and living in Maine), provided me with some exceptional encouragement and feedback regarding the first edition of Even the Monsters. He pointed out a few of the book's self-published editorial flaws, but the bulk of his message was one of great encouragement and an insistence that people needed to hear what this book had to say, even with the book's flaws. I dare say he sold a few copies on the strength of his endorsement alone.

I had done nothing to promote sales for Even the Monsters when it first launched. I knew nothing then about book promotion. It was a personal passion project, but hearing from Fred and a few other folks and working with Paper Stone Press had enabled me to see its publication flaws more clearly. The book had more potential that warranted more care and attention than I had initially been able to give.

While I was managing the cover design for Blind Man's Labyrinth and taking part in the marketing work for Keziah's Song, I finally concluded that Even the Monsters deserved a second edition that was to Paper Stone Press standards. Then it should be given a proper marketing push. Geoff's original passion for the work was right. My wife was right. Fred was right. Once I made the decision, everything else fell neatly into place. Even my fiction editor and proofreader were on board.

And so once again, a thank you is owed to others who made this happen: Geoff, my wife, Fred, Matt Levy, Ed and Sarah Chappelle, Sam Madeiros, and the many others who have contacted me over the years telling me how much Even the Monsters meant to them. I hope that this new Paper Stone Press edition reaches an even wider audience and touches more hearts of those who need it the most.

God has more than just trouble in his grasp. He has good things too. Not just monsters.

For more information, please visit www.darylpotter.com.

If you found this book helpful, please consider taking a minute to leave a review wherever you purchase books. Reviews help other readers find my work, and it would mean a great deal to me if you took a moment to tell other readers about your experience.

APPENDIX

An Explanation Regarding Biblical Quotations and Copyright Rules

This book is partly a memoir and partly a critical commentary. It aims to make the entire contents of the book of Job both clear and meaningful for a soul going through a period of personal suffering and for someone looking to help a loved one going through a difficult time.

I preferred to include within these pages a reproduction of the entire book of Job. The idea was that the reader would have easy access to each section of Job as I referenced it. Most commentaries do not typically reproduce the book they comment upon but rather expect the reader to have a Bible handy to refer to. I did not write this book for the academic reader but rather for readers like me, readers who are searching for accessible and personal insight. People might read this book on a train or plane or bus, during a break at the beginning or end of the day, or in any other context in which having a second book (or app) open for reference may not be convenient.

I also preferred to comment on everything in Job. I wanted to expose the entire book and discover all its applications, not just the highlights. I believe that God inspired the whole text, and therefore the whole text is useful, not just the outline. And a soul undergoing a deep existential trial needs access to everything useful.

While I had used multiple translations (and a translator's handbook) in my research, I chose the New International Version (NIV) as the text to reproduce in my first draft.

Upon completing the first draft, I began to explore publication options. In the process, I discovered that to reproduce an entire book of the Bible in English would violate copyright law. The various English translations have their respective copyright owners, and the rules are quite clear and firm.

I attempted to gain the necessary permission from the owner of the NIV copyright and failed. Finally, in exasperation, I proposed a million dollars for the permission to use the NIV text of Job in my book, and that offer too was rejected. That was just as well since I didn't have a million dollars.

There are 1,070 verses in Job. Unfortunately, the NIV would only permit the reproduction of 500 verses. So I began to assemble a list of other potential English translations and their associated copyright details to find a more accommodating copyright standard I could work with. To my dismay, I discovered that 500 verses was an industry standard. Almost every translation I considered had the same 500-verse restriction. The King James Version and similarly old translations are in the public domain and free to use without permissions or fees, but as my goal was clarity, simplicity, and accessibility, these older styles of English did not suit my purpose.

At one point, I considered reproducing the book of Job using three different translations, perhaps using the NIV for Job's dialogue, the New American Standard Bible for his friends' dialogue, and some other version for God's dialogue. However, this strategy fell apart once I actually began counting verses by actor and discovered that Job's dialogue alone amounted to 513 verses. Job's own quotations would singlehandedly violate the NIV copyright rules and that of nearly every other English translation. Job's words would have to be in two different translations for that plan to work.

I considered not including the biblical text after all (I now understood why most commentaries do not reproduce the Bible's text), but my own preference and the feedback from my first readers both counseled against this idea. It was just helpful to have the verses right there amid the commentary.

One innovative friend suggested I craft my own translation or crowdsource a translation. I appreciated the idea but did not pursue it. The memoir portion of this book is already sufficiently subjective and personal. If the Bible itself becomes my personal translation, the commentary on that scripture—and the entire project—might start to appear unreliable. So no, I needed authoritative, published translations to work with, even if that meant Job had to speak in three different translations or something similarly awkward.

Fortunately, I eventually discovered the English Standard Version (ESV), published by Crossway, a publishing ministry of Good News Publishers. This translation did not merely cut and paste the industry-standard 500 verses as their reproduction limit but rather offered a more generous 1,000-verse cap. Of course, this was still 70 verses short of the whole book of Job, but at least I could offer a copy of my book without having Job's own dialogue be in multiple translations.

And this is the reason why Even the Monsters now has the entire book of Job embedded within its pages in two translations: ESV and NIV.

The quotations are organized as follows:

Unless otherwise noted, all biblical quotations in chapters 1–48 of this book (which cover chapters 1–31 of the text of Job) are from the ESV translation of the Bible and are subject to the following copyright notice:

Scripture quotations are from The Holy Bible, English Standard Version® (ESV®), copyright © 2001 by Crossway, a publishing ministry of Good News Publishers. Used by permission. All rights reserved.

All material from chapter 49 onward (which equates to the examination of chapters 32–42 of the book of Job) is from the NIV translation of the Bible (except where noted otherwise) and is subject to the following copyright notice:

Scripture taken from The Holy Bible, New International Version®, copyright © 1973, 1978, 1984, 2011 Biblica. Used by permission of Zondervan. All rights reserved.

Most readers will likely not notice this translation shift some three-fourths of the way through this book, as the ESV and NIV translations are remarkably similar in style and language. This legal accommodation allows the reader to access the entire text of Job and my analysis of it in the same book.

I wish you, the reader, God's blessing as you absorb the important messages within the book of Job, and I hope that my personal story and commentary will aid your spiritual journey through whatever period of personal difficulty or darkness that may have drawn you to these pages.

Daryl Potter
Monday, May 25, 2015
Oakville, Ontario